Compositing Visual Effects in After Effects

Create vibrant visual effects with Adobe After Effects. Gain the tips, tricks, and applied knowledge you need to carry out essential visual effects tasks and bring your digital compositing to the next level.

In *Compositing Visual Effects in After Effects*, industry veteran Lee Lanier covers all the common After Effects techniques any serious visual effects artist needs to know, combining the latest, professionally vetted studio practices and workflows with mini- and multi-chapter projects and hands-on lessons.

Engaging, full-color tutorials cover:

- Color space management
- Color channel manipulation
- Chroma keying
- Rotoscoping and masking
- Matchmoving and motion tracking
- Working in the After Effects 3D environment
- Recompiling 3D render passes
- Color grading

The companion website (www.focalpress.com/cw/lanier) features video image sequences, 3D renders, matte paintings, and other tutorial materials, allowing you to immediately apply the techniques taught in the book.

Lee Lanier has worked in the motion picture industry since 1989, having spent hundreds of hours on live-action sets and thousands of hours working with high-end animation and compositing software. He's created visual effects for Walt Disney Studios and served as a senior animator in the modeling and lighting departments at PDI/DreamWorks on *Antz* and *Shrek*. In addition to having taught at the Academy of Art University and Gnomon School of Visual Effects, Lee has written seven books on visual effects and digital compositing, has recorded tutorials for lynda.com and The Foundry, and is a member of the Visual Effects Society.

Compositing Visual Effects in After Effects

Essential Techniques

Lee Lanier

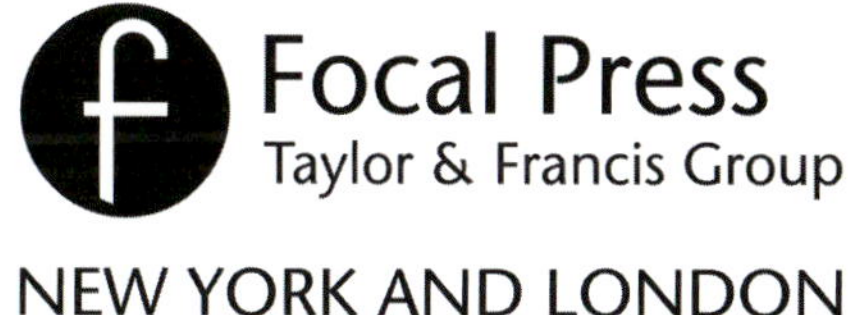
Focal Press
Taylor & Francis Group
NEW YORK AND LONDON

First published 2016
by Focal Press
70 Blanchard Road, Suite 402, Burlington, MA 01803
and by Focal Press
2 Park Square, Milton Park, Abingdon, Oxon OX14 4RN

Focal Press is an imprint of the Taylor & Francis Group, an informa business

Library of Congress Cataloging in Publication Data
Lanier, Lee, 1966-
Compositing visual effects in After effects : essential techniques / Lee Lanier.
pages cm
1. Cinematography—Special effects—Data processing. 2. Computer animation.
3. Photomontage. 4. Adobe After Effects. I. Title.
TR858.L358 2016
777'.9—dc23
2015024211

ISBN: [9781138803282] (pbk)
ISBN: [9781315753775] (ebk)

Typeset in Myriad Pro
by diacriTech

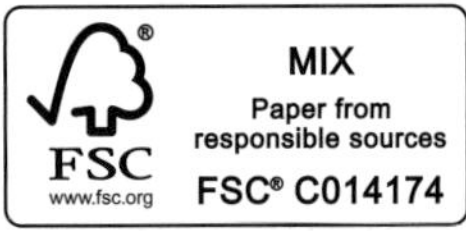

Printed and bound in the United States of America by Sheridan Books, Inc. (a Sheridan Group Company).

Contents

Introduction

Visual effects compositing is rarely boring and is often surprising. Every shot you are tasked to work with will undoubtedly contain new challenges. With time and practice, you'll develop your own tricks and workflows to create professional results—and that is what this book is about. I've worked as a professional animator and VFX compositor for almost 20 years, spending thousands of hours working in Adobe After Effects and similar compositing programs. The VFX compositing wisdom I've gained through mistakes, successes, and long hours is contained in this book. I have no intention to cover every After Effects effect, plug-in, parameter, option, and so on. Instead, I've included the most critical information on the most useful components of the program, along with tips and tricks for utilizing them. To strengthen this knowledge, I've included a number of short "mini-tutorials" that allow you to master VFX tasks quickly. In addition, each chapter includes a longer tutorial that steps you through more challenging compositing tasks.

You, the Reader

Compositing Visual Effects in After Effects is aimed at beginning compositors who have a basic working knowledge of After Effects who would like to expand their knowledge of visual effects compositing techniques. This book is also suitable for those professional compositors who wish to transition from other areas of compositing, such as motion graphics, to visual effects work. In addition, this book will prove useful for any digital artist wishing to transition from other compositing programs, such as The Foundry Nuke. Basic interface information is also included at the end of this introduction to help a new user get up to speed quickly.

Topics Covered

Compositing Visual Effects in After Effects covers critical visual effects theory and technique, including:

- Color space management
- Color channel manipulation
- Chroma keying
- Rotoscoping and masking
- Matchmoving and motion tracking
- Working in the After Effects 3D environment
- Recompiling 3D render passes
- Color grading

In addition to the coverage of After Effects built-in tools and effects, this book covers plug-ins commonly used in the visual effects industry. These include:

- RE:Vision Effects Twixtor and ReelSmart Motion Blur
- Red Giant Primatte
- Red Giant Trapcode Particular
- The Foundry CameraTracker
- Neat Video Reduce Noise

The book also explores bundled third-party party programs that are designed to work directly with After Effects. These include Imagineer Systems Mocha AE and Maxon Cinema 4D Lite.

Required Software

This book was written with Adobe After Effects CC 2013 and After Effects CC 2014. In addition, the files were tested with beta copies of After Effects CC 2015. Any significant differences between CC 2013, CC 2014, and CC 2015 are noted in the text. The majority of tutorial files are saved in the Adobe After Effects CC 2013 .aep format. A few files are saved in the CC 2014 and the CC 2015 formats as they require more recent effects. After Effects CC comes bundled with Mocha AE and Cinema 4D Lite. The non-bundled plug-ins discussed in this book are not mandatory for successful learning; however, they are useful and are available for trial download from their respective software websites (listed in each chapter).

Screen Snapshots

The book's screen snapshots are taken with After Effects CC 2013 and CC 2014 running on 64-bit Windows 7 and 8 systems. A minor difference between CC 2013/2014 and CC 2015 is the color scheme of the program interface (Figure I.1). Nevertheless, this has little impact on the program as the menu options and basic workflow are unaffected. Any exceptions to this rule are noted in the book.

System Requirements

After Effects will run poorly unless your computer's hardware and operating system software meets the minimum criteria. The criteria is carefully spelled out at the following web page: helpx.adobe.com/x-productkb/policy-pricing/system-requirements-effects.html

Downloading the Tutorial Files

Example tutorial files are provided for this book and may be downloaded from www.focalpress.com/cw/lanier. These include several gigabytes of After Effects project files, video image sequences and QuickTime movies, Maya and

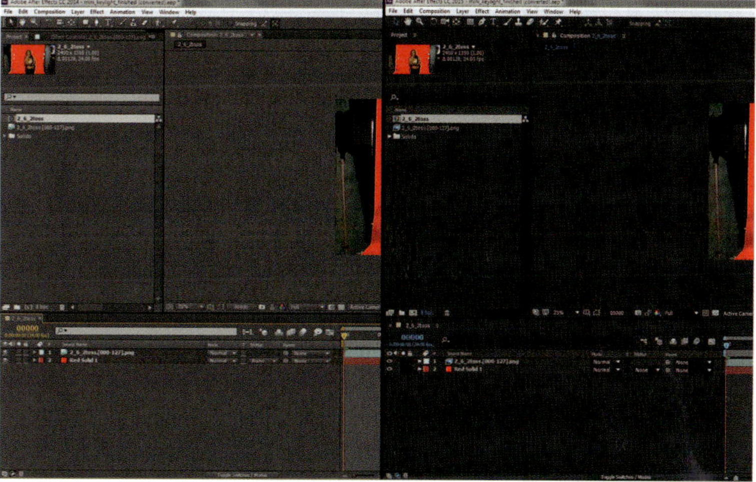

FIG 1 Left: After Effects CC 2014 on a Windows system; Right: After Effects CC 2015 (release 13.5).

Cinema 4D rendered image sequences, camera files, static artwork, and matte paintings. The files are organized in the following directory structure:

ProjectFiles\aeFiles\Chapter*n*\	After Effects .aep project files
ProjectFiles\Plates*Category*\ *PlateName*\	Video image sequences (.png and .dng) and QuickTime movies (.mov)
ProjectFiles\Renders*RenderName*\	Maya and Cinema 4D 3D renders (.png and .exr)
ProjectFiles\Data\	Maya and Cinema 4D geometry and camera files (.ma, .c4d, and .rpf), plus Adobe Illustrator .ai files
ProjectFiles\Art\	Static images and matte paintings (.tif, .jpg and .png)

About the Source Files

Many of the video image sequences in this book are culled from a music video, the copyright of which is held by BeezleBug Bit, LLC. The reader may use these image sequences for educational purposes but may not redistribute the sequences in any fashion. Commercial use of the sequences is not granted. A few additional movies and sequences are used under a Creative Commons Public Domain License and were sourced from the Prelinger Archive at www.archive.org. Additional information on Prelinger material is included with each chapter. Several texture bitmaps included with the project files are also used under a Creative Common license—a text copy of the license is included in the \ProjectFiles\Art\ directory.

Using the Tutorial Files with Windows and Mac Systems

I recommend that you copy the project files, with their current directory structure, directly to your root directory (C: on a Windows systems or / on a Mac system). In general, After Effects is very robust when it comes to locating required project files. However, if the program is unable to locate a file and a piece of footage (this is indicated by a colorbars substitute), you can update the file or footage by RMB-clicking the file/footage name in the Project panel and choosing Replace Footage > File.

Naming Conventions

Compositing Visual Effects in After Effects uses common conventions when describing mouse operation. A few examples follow:

click	Left mouse button click
double-click	Rapidly click left mouse button twice
MMB-drag	Drag while pressing middle mouse button
RMB-click	Right mouse button click
Shift+LMB	Left mouse click while holding Shift key

The Ctrl key on a Windows system and the Cmd key on a Mac PC serve the same function. Hence, a call to press either key is written as Ctrl/Cmd. The Alt key on a Windows system and the Opt key on a Mac PC serve the same function. Hence, a call to press either key is written as Alt/Opt.

Updates

For updates associated with this book, please visit www.focalpress.com/cw/lanier.

Contacting the Author

Feedback is always welcome. You can contact me at comp@beezlebugbit.com or find me on popular social media networks.

Interface Overview

For the new user, it's important to be familiar with the interface components listed in Figure I.2. As mentioned earlier in this introduction, color changes between CC 2014 and CC 2015 do not affect the component naming or basic functionality.

The following frames and panels are marked with letters:

- A: The project frame, which contains the Project panel and Effect Controls panel. Each panel is indicated with a named tab at the top left of the panel.

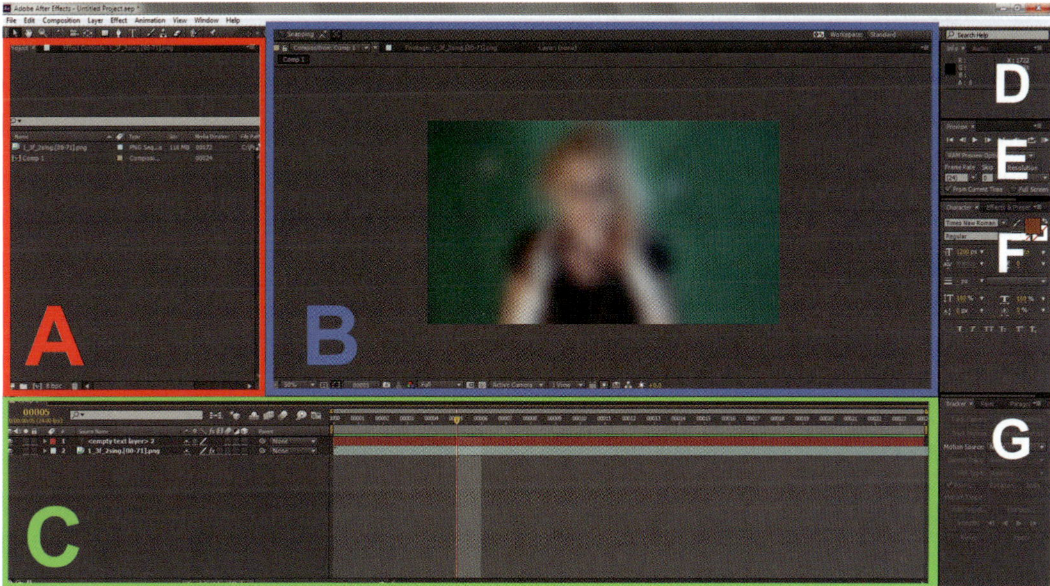

FIG 2 After Effects CC 2014 interface.

- B: Viewer frame, which holds the Composition, Footage, and Layer view panels.
- C: Timeline frame, with the layer outline on the left and timeline on the right. You can LMB-drag the time indicator (time slider) back and forth.
- D: Info panel
- E: Preview panel with playback controls
- F: Multipurpose frame that carries the Effects & Presets panel, plus the Character panel when the Text tool is used
- G: Multipurpose frame that carries the Tracker panel. In addition, this holds the Paragraph panel for the Text tool and the Paint panel for the Paint, Erase, and Clone Stamp tools.

After Effects and Visual Effects Terminology

When referring to components of After Effects, I've used terminology established by the After Effects help files and support documents. When discussing visual effects techniques, I've used words and phrases commonly used in the visual effects industry. Note that many terms were originally developed to describe techniques applied to motion picture film. For example, here are a few words and phrases used throughout this book:

- **Live-action:** Film of actors in a real-world location. *Live-action* does not refer to documentary or news-gathering footage of real events, nor does it include animation.

- **Footage:** Motion picture film shot for a particular scene or at a particular location. You can also use this term to refer to digital video.
- **Shot:** A single camera set-up of a multi-shot scene. For example, a shot may be a close-up of an actress or a wide-angle of a street. With film or video, a *scene* is a series of shots captured at one location that represents a particular period of time.
- **Plate:** A shot intended for visual effects work. For example, a plate may be a shot of a city street that requires the addition of an explosion or an animated robot. A plate may be static or may contain movement. Plates often include green screen and may be shot at an extra-high resolution (such as 70mm with motion picture film or 4K with digital video).

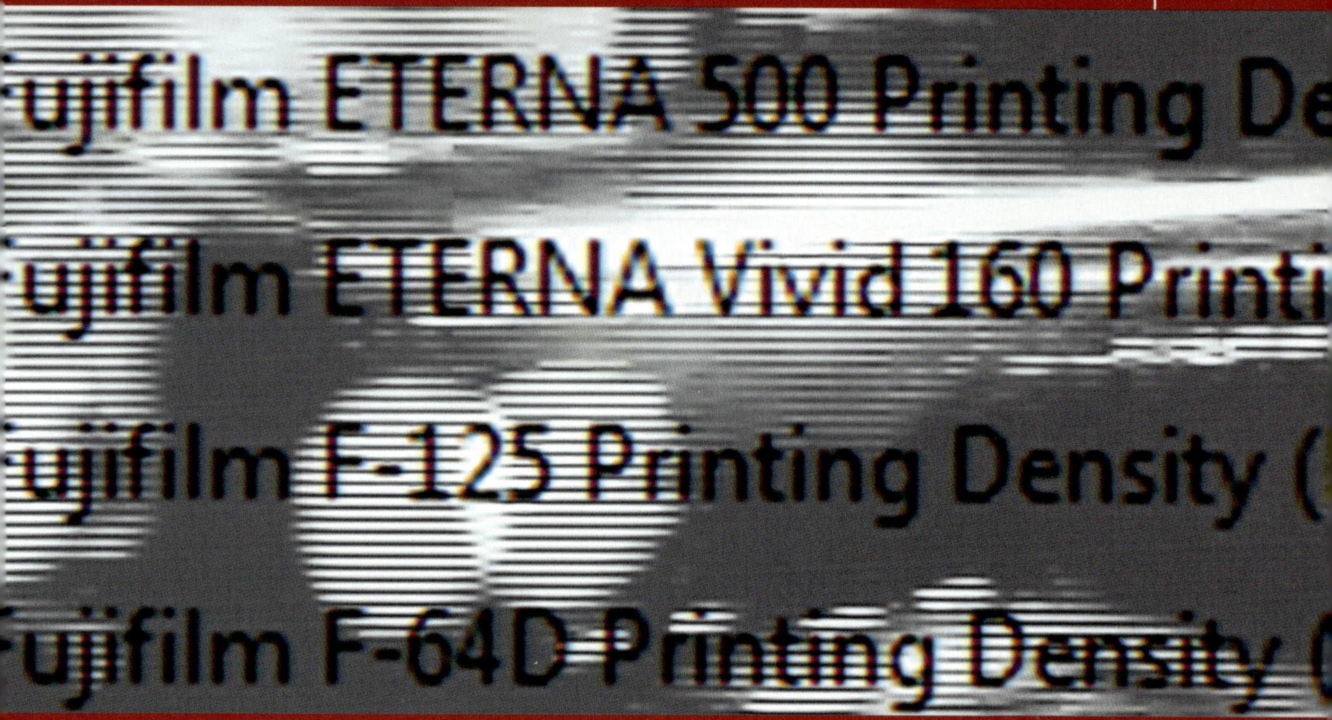

CHAPTER 1

Selecting Color Spaces, Resolutions, and Frame Rates

When compositing for visual effects, it's wise to consider color space. The color space you choose determines the number of potential colors you can work with and the overall accuracy of effect applications and transformations. By the same token, each composition you create shares two basic qualities: resolution and frame rate. Due to the wide variety of common resolutions and frame rates, decisions must be made to select appropriate resolutions and rates for the project. To complicate matters, the footage you import may carry multiple frame rates. You can also manipulate frame rates for stylistic purposes, creating "time warps" that speed up or slow down footage.

This chapter includes the following critical information:

- Selection of bit-depths and working color spaces
- Converting between color spaces on import and at render time
- Choosing and converting between different frame rates and resolutions

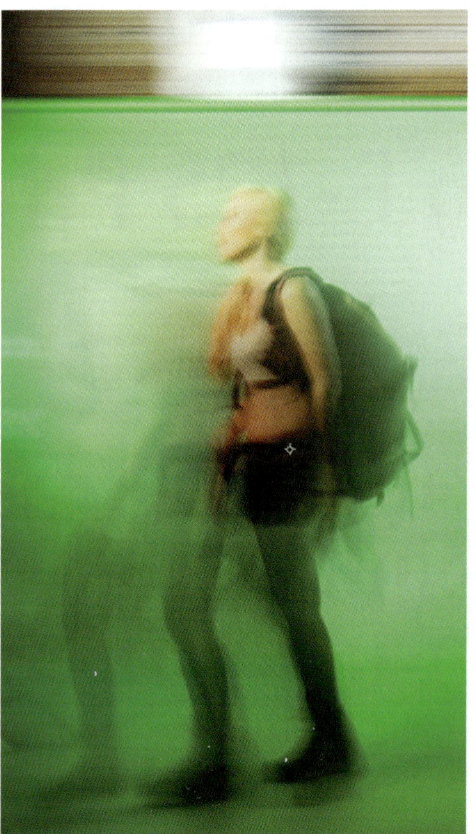

FIG 1.1 Footage is time warped with the CC Wide Time effect, creating a ghost trail. This project is saved as *wide_time.aep* in the *\ProjectFiles\aeFiles\Chapter1* tutorial directory.

Choosing Bit-Depths and Color Spaces

A *bit-depth* determines the number of colors available to a single channel of a pixel. A *channel*, within a digital image, carries the values of a single component of a color model. A *color model* is a mathematical description of a color through specialized sets of numbers. Digital art, animation, and video use the RGB color model, where red, green, and blue channels are added to produce an image on a monitor (Figure 1.2). RGB is additive, whereby equal amounts of red, green, and blue produce white. The absence of these colors produces black. *Color space* represents all the colors a device can produce using a specific color model.

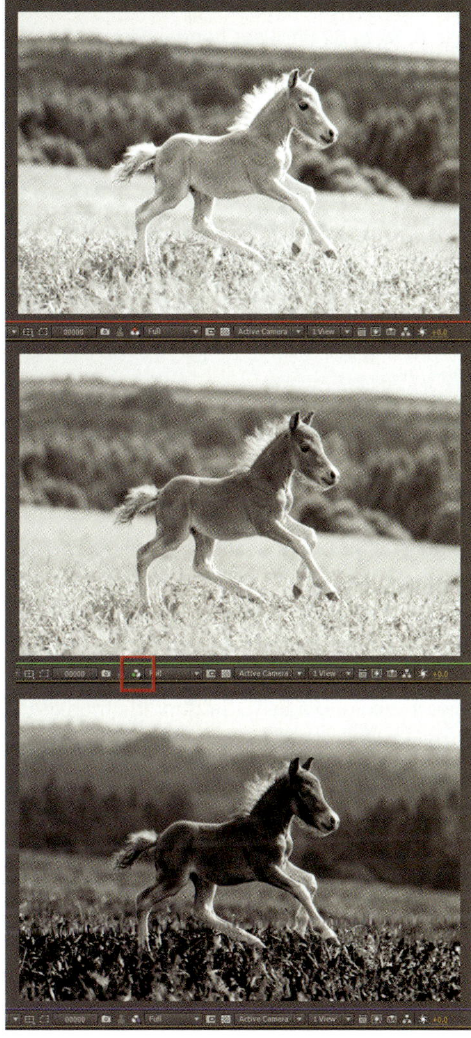

FIG 1.2 From top to bottom: The red, green, and blue channels of an image. Each channel stores intensity values for its associated color, hence each channel appears as grayscale. You can view channels in After Effects by changing the Show Channel menu button in the Composition, Layer, or Footage view panel. The menu is surrounded by a red box in this figure. *Horse photo © DragoNika/Dollar Photo Club.*

An Overview of Common Bit-Depths

After Effects can read a wide range of bit-depths. In addition, the program offers three specific bit-depths in which you can work. That is, all the calculations within the project are carried out at the bit-depth accuracy that you choose. The three bit-depths are 8-bit, 16-bit, and 32-bit. The number in each bit-depth signifies the number of potential colors (also referred to as tonal steps) available to each of the RGB channels. For example, 8-bit carries 2^8 colors per channel. To find the total color capacity of a bit-depth, multiply the channels together. Thus 8-bit RGB offers 256 × 256 × 256, or 16,777,216 colors. Note that After Effects "16-bit" color space actually uses 15 bits per channel; nevertheless, this produces trillions of colors when the channels are multiplied togther.

You can set the bit-depth by choosing File > Project Settings and changing the Depth menu to 8, 16, or 32 Bits Per Channel (Figure 1.3). Note that the 32-bit setting uses a floating-point architecture, which is discussed in the next section.

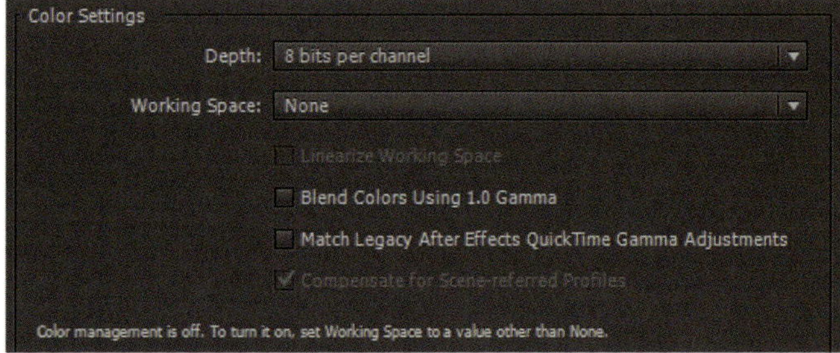

FIG 1.3 The Color Settings section of the Project Settings window in its default state.

When choosing a bit-depth, you can follow these general rules:

- Choose the highest bit-depth that allows you work comfortably. The higher the bit-depth, the greater the mathematical accuracy, but the longer the render times.
- Aggressive effects, such as heavy blurs, require a high bit-depth to avoid color banding (also known as *posterization*). Color banding appears as abrupt changes in a color gradient that should otherwise appear smooth. For example, color banding is sometimes visible in a clear sky. If you are using effects to drastically alter an image, use a 16- or 32-bit depth.
- Test your compositions at different depths. You can change the Depth menu at any time. If a lower bit-depth is sufficient to produce an acceptable quality, consider working at that depth.

Note that most computer monitors operate at an 8-bit depth. Thus, higher bit-depth quality is not necessarily *visible* on your monitor. This holds true for higher-quality 10-bit monitors. Nevertheless, you should strive to produce a quality image for the targeted output format. Output formats may range from HDTV (high-definition television) broadcast video to something suitable for web streaming. Note that the majority of image formats available to After Effects for rendering are 8-bit. Several formats, such as OpenEXR and TIFF, support 16- and 32-bit variants. The Raw format supports additional high bit-depth variations. For more information on the Raw format, see the "Importing Raw Files" section later in this chapter. For information on working with OpenEXR files, see Chapter 7.

Integer versus Floating-Point

8-bit and 16-bit color spaces in After Effects use integer values. That is, the color values use whole numbers and do not carry decimal places. Hence, a red channel value might be 10, 73, or 121. In contrast, the After Effects 32-bit color space utilizes a floating-point architecture. This allows the color values to be stored with decimal-place accuracy. Thus, a value might be 10.27542 instead of 10. Although you're unable to work directly with the decimal place values, their existence ensures greater accuracy when transforming layers, adjusting effects, or changing blending operations. In addition, the 32-bit floating-point space supports *superwhite* values—that is, values beyond the standard 0 to 1.0 color range. This allows you to work with the large color ranges found within high-dynamic range (HDR) images.

Working with Color Management

One difficult aspect of digital image manipulation is the proper and consistent display of those images. No two monitors display digital images in the same way. Variations in engineering and manufacturing standards cause monitors to vary significantly. In addition, monitors "drift" during their life. That is, regular use of a monitor causes it to display colors differently as it ages. Hence, what may look good on your monitor may appear very different on a client's monitor. The problem is compounded by a wide variety of non-monitor devices, including digital projection systems, television sets, computer tablets, smartphones, and so on.

The process of color management attempts to minimize these problems by using standards by which monitors and other devices can be made to match. A variety of standards are crafted by the ICC (International Color Consortium) and manufacturers (such as software and hardware makers). The standards are presented as color profiles. The profiles contain data defining the color model, color ranges (lowest and highest supported color values per channel, also known as a *gamut*), black and white points (color coordinates that define what is "black" and "white"), and mathematical mechanisms for converting the profile to different color spaces. (Each profile creates a unique color space that can produce a particular range of colors.)

Calibrating Monitors

Color profiles are supported by common operating systems, software, and firmware. When you apply a color profile to a monitor, it affects the way in which colors are interpreted by the monitor. The process of applying the profile is known as *monitor calibration*. This may be as simple as choosing an ICC profile provided by an operating system. For example, with Windows 7 and 8, you can select a profile through the Color Management tool.

It's also possible to create a custom profile with monitor calibration software and/or hardware. Software-based calibration generally requires the user to choose a white point by selecting a color temperature that makes maximum RGB values appear the most neutral (without a color cast). *Color temperature* is the temperature a theoretical body reaches to create a specific hue of light.

Color temperature is measured in K, or kelvin units. Various display devices support specific color temperatures, whereby their screen is biased toward a specific hue. For example, 6500 K appears slightly bluish while 5400 K appears slightly reddish. This ability helps white pixels appear "white" in different viewing environments where the native light has its own color temperature. In addition, the software generally requests the selection of a specific gamma. *Gamma*, when discussing color management, is a nonlinear operation that converts pixel values to screen luminosity. Gamma curves, expressed as a function value such as 1.8, are applied to compensate for human vision, which is more sensitive to differences in dark tones as compared to differences in bright tones, and are a legacy holdover from early CRT monitors, which used a nonlinear voltage-to-screen intensity relationship. Calibration software that utilizes a colorimeter (a device that measures the wavelength of visible light from a screen) is often more accurate. In either situation, creating a custom profile is desirable as it takes into account the peculiarities of an individual monitor.

Using a Working Space in After Effects

You can choose to work within a specific color space provided by a specific color profile within After Effects. This color space is referred to as a "working space." A working space may be advantageous if you are preparing to export the images to a predetermined output, such as broadcast HDTV. To select a working space, choose File > Project Settings and change the Working Space menu to one of the provided color profiles (see Figure 1.3 earlier in this chapter).

If the working space does not match the color space of imported footage, the color values are converted between spaces. Because each color space has a unique set of colors it supports, the conversion between spaces may lead to the loss of information or the distortion of color values. For example, converting between an sRGB IEC61966-2.1 profile (commonly used for digital images) to a HDTV (Rec. 709) 16-235 profile (a variant of HDTV) causes the values below 16 on a 255 (8-bit) scale to be clipped to 0-black. Although some color space conversions may lead to subtle or imperceptible changes, it's important to be aware of potential color shifts.

When you import footage, After Effects detects embedded color profiles. If you are using a working color space, the program converts the footage color space to the working color space. To adjust this operation, RMB-click over the footage name in the Project panel and choose Interpret Footage > Main. In the Interpret Footage window, switch to the Color Management tab (Figure 1.4).

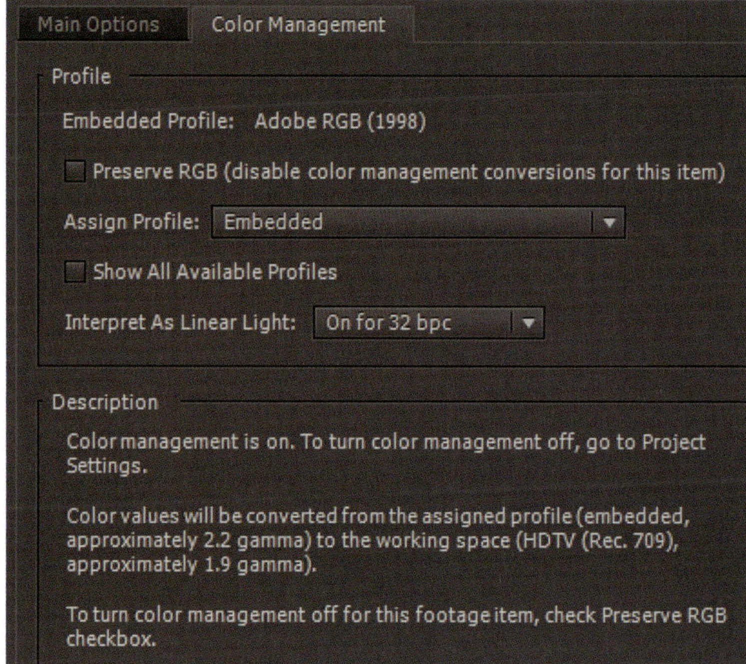

FIG 1.4 The Color Management tab of the Interpret Footage window. You can access this tab when a working color space is selected through the Project Settings window. The working space is set to HDTV (Rec. 709). The embedded profile of the imported footage is recognized as Adobe RGB (1998). Note that the Description area describes the color space conversion that is applied.

When an embedded profile is detected, the Embedded Profile property lists the profile and the Assign Profile menu is set to Embedded. If no profile is carried by the footage, Embedded Profile is set to None and the Assign Profile menu is set to a default profile (such as sRGB IEC61966-2.1). You are free to change the Assign Profile menu to a different profile to employ a different profile interpretation. For example, an image sequence generally lacks an embedded profile; hence, you can change the Assign Profile menu to a video-specific or a camera-specific profile. (Software installed in support of hardware, such as a digital camera, often adds its own set of ICC profiles to the system.)

Here are descriptions of a few common profiles:

sRGB IEC61966-2.1 Commonly used for home and business computing. Developed by Microsoft and HP in 1996. It's the default working space for Adobe Photoshop.

SDTV The standard for pre-digital standard-definition television.

HDTV (Rec.709) The standard broadcast HDTV.

Adobe RGB (1998) and Wide Gamut RGB Two profiles developed by Apple that carry a wider gamut (range of colors) than what is available to sRGB.

ProPhoto RGB Developed by Kodak, this profile carries an extra-wide gamut specifically designed for digital cinema work. For accurate color space conversions with wide-gamut color spaces, set the project depth to 16-bit.

To skip the color space conversion and use the imported footage values as is, select the Preserve RGB check box. Avoiding the conversion may prevent color loss or distortion; however, the footage may appear significantly different and may require additional color adjustment through color effects.

In addition, when you use a working space, you have the option to export renders with a different color space. To do this, open the Output Module Settings window (click the Output Module link in the Render Queue tab after queuing a render) and switch to the Color Management tab. With this tab, you have the same set of options presented when interpreting footage. Selecting Preserve RGB causes the renderer to output the color values as defined by the working space and prevents the conversion to a different color space. To activate the conversion, deselect the Preserve RGB button and choose a color profile from the Output Profile menu. Note that the ability to carry a color profile is dependent on the output file format. Nevertheless, the resulting color values of the rendered images are affected by the Preserve RGB and Output Profile settings.

Working in Linearized Color Space

When using a working color space, you have the option to linearize the project. Linearization prevents the working space color profile from applying a gamma correction (the gamma value is set to 1.0). This may be useful if edge artifacts, such as fringes and halos, appear in the composition. These artifacts are often associated with layer blending that involves high-contrast or saturated colors or when heavy motion blur is added to an animated layer. To activate Linearization, select the Linearize Working Space check box in the Project Settings window.

Note that the linearized workspace appears low-contrast and washed out. By default, when you render the footage, the values stay linearized. However, you can turn off the output linearization and return to a non-1.0 gamma by changing the Convert To Linear Light menu to Off. This menu appears below the Output Profile menu in the Color Management tab of the Output Module Settings window. The gamma curve applied as part of the conversion is established by the color profile selected by the Output Profile menu. For example, HDTV (Rec. 709) uses a gamma of approximately 1.9.

It's recommended that you only linearize the working space when operating in 16- or 32-bit color space.

Previewing and Converting Different Color Spaces

If you are not using a working space, image values are sent straight to the system monitor *without* being converted by the color profile provided by the operating system. In this case, the RGB values are preserved, but the image may look incorrect. If you are using a working space, the RGB values are converted by the system color profile. As such, the image appears appropriate for the monitor; however, the RGB values are altered. You can deactivate the color space conversion by the system color profile by toggling off View > Use Display Color Management (Shift + number pad /). This may be useful for checking the look of a composition on a non-color-managed device (e.g. a web browser on a tablet or smartphone).

You can also force After Effects to simulate the output on a device that does not exist on your system. To do so, choose View > Simulate Output > *output*. For example, if you want to preview your work as if it was transferred to motion picture film and projected in a theater, select View > Simulate Output > Universal Camera Film To Kodak 2383. (Use Display Color Management must be left on for this to work.)

Note that a look-up table (LUT) is an array designed to convert one color space to another. For example, you can use a LUT to convert a PAL/SECAM color space to an HDTV (Rec. 709) color space. Aside from using the color management methods described in previous sections, you can use Effect > Utility > Apply Color LUT. When you choose this tool, the program asks you to load a supported LUT text file. Such files are often exported from dedicated color grading software, such as Blackmagic Design DaVinci Resolve. Common LUT formats include .3dl, .cube, and .csp.

Linear versus Logarithmic

After Effects carries out its calculations in linear color space. The majority of file formats use linear color space. In contrast, Cineon and DPX files use logarithmic color space. With an 8-bit linear format, changes in brightness (changes in pixel intensity) occur in regular steps. For example, the intensity change from a value of 10 to 20 is equivalent to an intensity change from a value of 200 to 210. Although this is satisfactory for general digital image manipulation, it does not replicate human vision or the light sensitivity of motion picture film stock. Human vision is logarithmic in that it is more sensitive to changes of intensity in dark regions as compared to changes in bright regions. Motion picture film stock, due to its photochemical makeup, reacts logarithmically with more sensitivity towards variations in low light as compared to equivalent changes in bright light. As a mathematical term, the *logarithm* of a number is the exponent to which another fixed value, the *base*, must be raised to produce that number. For example, $\log_{10}(10) = 1$, $\log_{10}(100) = 2$, and $\log_{10}(1000) = 3$. With this series, 10 is the base and 1/2/3 is the logarithm. Note that the logarithm progresses in regular increments (1 to 2 to 3), yet the results progress exponentially (10 to 100 to 1000). Ultimately, logarithmic color spaces better match human vision and are more ideal for capturing motion picture film stock through film scanning. (The Cineon and DPX file formats were developed for film scanning.) Note that linear color space should not be confused with linearized color space. As previously discussed, linearization applies a 1.0 gamma.

When importing a Cineon or DPX image or image sequence, it's best to choose the color profile that best matches the film stock used to shoot the footage. To see the full list of available color profiles, select the Show All Available Profiles check box of the Color Management tab of the Interpret Footage window. After Effects provides a number of profiles that match Kodak and FujiFilm motion picture film stocks as well as profiles that match projection environments (Figure 1.5). Note that these are grouped near a cluster of color profiles designed for commonly used, high-end digital motion picture cameras, such as those made by Panavision, Arriflex, and Viper.

FIG 1.5 Section of color profiles designed for motion picture film stock, high-end digital cameras, and projection environments.

Fujifilm ETERNA 250 Printing Density (by Adobe)
Fujifilm ETERNA 250D Printing Density (by Adobe)
Fujifilm ETERNA 400 Printing Density (by Adobe)
Fujifilm ETERNA 500 Printing Density (by Adobe)
Fujifilm ETERNA Vivid 160 Printing Density (by Ado
Fujifilm F-125 Printing Density (by Adobe)
Fujifilm F-64D Printing Density (by Adobe)
Fujifilm REALA 500D Printing Density (by Adobe)
Kodak 5205/7205 Printing Density (by Adobe)
Kodak 5218/7218 Printing Density (by Adobe)
Kodak 5229/7229 Printing Density (by Adobe)
Universal Camera Film Printing Density

ARRIFLEX D-20 Daylight Log (by Adobe)
ARRIFLEX D-20 Tungsten Log (by Adobe)
Dalsa Origin Tungsten Lin (by Adobe)
Panavision Genesis Tungsten Log (by Adobe)
Viper FilmStream Daylight Log (by Adobe)
Viper FilmStream Tungsten Log (by Adobe)

Fujifilm 3510 (RDI) Theater Preview (by Adobe)
Fujifilm 3513DI (RDI) Theater Preview (by Adobe)
Fujifilm 3521XD (RDI) Theater Preview (by Adobe)
Kodak 2383 Theater Preview 2 (by Adobe)
Kodak 2393 Theater Preview 2 (by Adobe)

As an alternative to selecting a film-specific profile, you can apply the Effect > Utility > Cineon Converter tool to the footage after it's placed on a layer. The effect allows you to make a logarithmic to linear conversion and apply a new black point, white point, and gamma curve.

Importing Raw Files

Camera Raw files, whether they are still images or image sequences, require a unique workflow in After Effects. The Raw format captures image data from a digital camera sensor and adds minimal processing along the way. As such, Raw images are not immediately available for use, but must be processed first. Raw files are often captured at higher bit-depths, including 10-, 12-, 14-, and 16-bit.

If you import a Raw file into After Effects, it first opens a Camera Raw window. The window provides a long array of options used to interpret the values stored in the file. These range from color adjustments to sharpening tools to noise reduction (Figure 1.6). It's not necessary to adjust every option. Alternatively, adjust only the sliders that improve the quality of the preview image. (You can apply some functions, like sharpening and noise reduction, as effects after the footage is placed in a composition.)

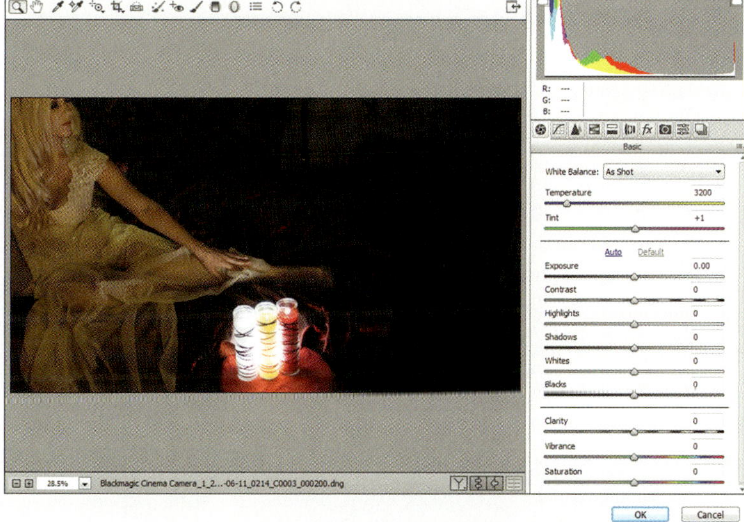

FIG 1.6 The Camera Raw window with default settings.

One goal of the Raw interpretation is to make the footage look acceptable or aesthetic within the color space you intend to work in (such as a working space) or as a rendered output (such as an image sequence or movie file). Hence, you have the option to "push" high values down into a lower bit-depth area. The Camera Raw window provides a histogram (at the top-right) so you can visualize this process. A histogram represents the distribution of values by drawing a series of lines. The left side of the histogram represents the dark parts of the image. The right side of the histogram represents the bright areas of the image. Any given line represents the number of pixels that carry a specific value (or small range of values if the histogram is simplified). For example, there might be 100 pixels in an image that carry a value of 75 on a 1.0 to 4,096 12-bit scale.

You can "push" the color distribution by using any of the color sliders in the Camera Raw window. For example, lowering the Exposure value pushes the distribution to the left. Lowering the Highlights value does the same but biases the highest values so they move more rapidly. For a practical demonstration, see the following tutorial.

Importing Raw files mini-tutorial

The goal of this tutorial is to set up a color space in After Effects that is appropriate for the following scenario:

- The shot you are working with is given to you as a 12-bit Raw image sequence.
- The desired output is a QuickTime movie destined for web streaming.

You can follow these steps:

1. Create a new project. Choose File > Import > File. Navigate to the *\ProjectFiles\Plates\RAWFootage\3-1-4hand* directory. Select the first image of the Raw image sequence. (With this sequence, the first frame is numbered 200.) With the Camera Raw Sequence check box selected, click the Import button.
2. The Camera Raw window opens and displays the first frame of the sequence. Note that the candles in the shot appear overexposed while the remainder of the shot appears dim. Lower the Highlights slider to –60. This moves the high values to the left of the histogram, leaving the candles with a better exposure. Essentially, the high values are lowered so that they are visible in the 8-bit color space of a common monitor. The mid-tones and low-tones are also biased to the left side of the histogram. Change the Exposure to +1.0 to re-brighten the entire image. Lower the Saturation slider to –20 to remove some of the heavy yellow tint created by the stage lights (Figure 1.7).

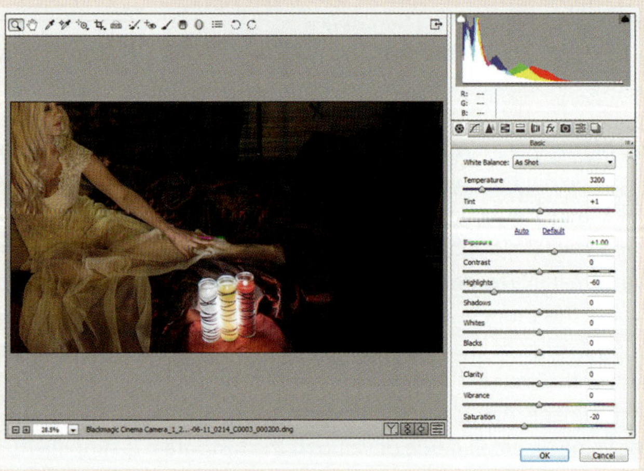

FIG 1.7 The adjustment of the Highlights, Exposure, and Saturation sliders improves the overall look of the footage and prevents excessive overexposure of the candles. Note the subtle difference in the histogram distribution as compared to Figure 1.6 in the previous section.

3. Switch to the Detail tab (the third tab to the left with the triangle symbol). Reduce the Amount slider to 0. This turns off additional sharpening during the import process. If the footage needs to be sharpened, it's better to apply a sharpening filter inside a composition. Click the OK button to import the footage.
4. Although you adjusted the footage through the Camera Raw window so it looks good on an 8-bit monitor, the footage remains 12-bit. To ensure that the compositional calculations are at the highest quality for 12-bit, switch the project to 16-bit. To do so, choose File > Project Settings and change the Depth menu to 16 Bits Per Channel.
5. In the Project Settings window, change the Working Space menu to sRGB IEC61966-2.1. sRGB is suitable for a movie designed to stream through web browsers on consumer PCs and tablets. Click the OK button to close the Project Settings window.
6. RMB-click over the footage name in the Project panel and choose Interpret Footage > Main. In the Interpret Footage window, switch to the Color Management tab. Note that Camera Raw is listed as the recognized embedded profile. As such, you cannot select a different color profile through the Assign Profile menu, nor do you have the option to select Preserve RGB. The Camera Raw window replaces the functionality of this tab. Close the Interpret Footage window.
7. Create a test composition by LMB-dragging the footage from the Project panel to the empty timeline. A new composition, named after the footage, is created and is automatically given a resolution and duration that matches the footage. (The frame rate is a default value; see the "Selecting Resolutions and Frame Rates" section for more information.)
8. Add the composition to the render queue by selecting the composition in the Project panel and choosing Composition > Add to Render Queue. In the Render Queue tab, click the word *Lossless* beside Output Module. In the Output Module Settings window, switch to the Color Management tab (Figure 1.8). Note that the Output Profile is set to Working Space—sRGB IEC61966-2.1. This means that the color values produced in the sRGB working space are maintained and rendered out. You have the option to change the Output Profile to a different color profile and thus force the program to convert the sRGB color space to a new color space as it renders out the composition.

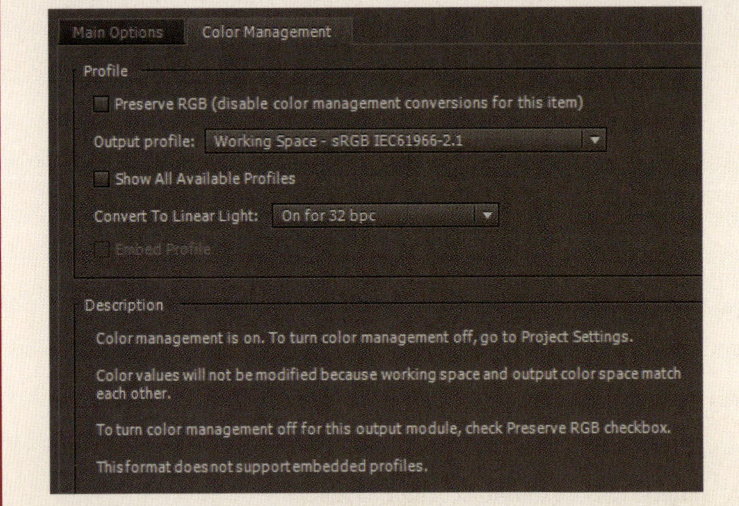

FIG 1.8 The Color Management tab of the Output Module Settings window.

The color management is finished for this tutorial. A project file is saved as *mini_raw.aep* in the *\ProjectFiles\aeFiles\Chapter1* directory. Note that it's not necessary to use the View > Simulate Output option unless you'd like to preview the composition on a device you do not possess. For example, you can choose View > Simulate Output > HDTV (Rec. 709) to see what the shot would look like if displayed on an HDTV television.

Selecting Resolutions and Frame Rates

Every composition you work with has three universal properties: resolution, frame rate, and duration. While duration is simply the length of the composition as measured in timecode or frames, resolution dictates the frame size in pixels in the X (horizontal width) and Y (vertical height) directions. Frame rate, on the other hand, determines the number of frames played back per second when the playback is in real time.

There are two ways you can display time in After Effects: timecode and frames. You can make this selection in the Time Display Style section of the Project Settings window. (The majority of project files that accompany this book use the Frames setting.) When working with video footage, timecode is generally desirable. When working on individual visual effects shots that use image sequences, frames are generally desirable.

Overview of Resolutions

You can create a composition at any resolution that you desire. Enter px (pixel) values into the Width (X) and Height (Y) fields in the Basic tab of the Composition Settings window. The window appears when you choose either Composition > New Composition or, if an existing composition is selected, Composition > Composition Settings. Note that the Width and Height are linked by default (Figure 1.9). If you change the Width value, the Height value automatically changes to keep the previous aspect ratio. An *aspect ratio* is the relationship of the frame width to frame height, or X:Y. For example, the HDTV aspect ratio of 16:9 indicates that the width is 1.78 times greater than the height (16 divided by 9 equals 1.78). You can break this relationship and enter your own Width and Height values by deselecting the Lock Aspect Ratio check box. A nonstandard resolution may be useful for assembling tiled matte paintings or specialized particle simulations with After Effects. (For information on matte paintings, see Chapter 5; for particle demonstrations, see Chapter 6.)

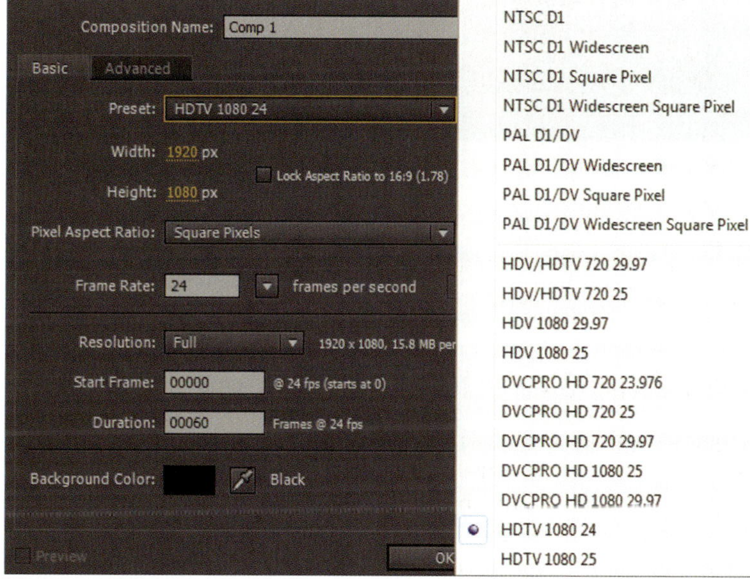

FIG 1.9 The Composition Settings window with the resolution set to 1080 HDTV and a partial list of available resolution presets revealed.

In general, visual effects composites require standard resolutions that are common to the film and television industries. After Effects provides a number of these standards as presets through the Preset menu in the Composition Settings window. Each composition in a project can carry its own unique resolution, frame rate, and duration.

A Note on Nonsquare Pixels

In general, visual effects composites make use of square pixels. That said, some pre-digital and early-digital video formats use nonsquare pixels. Hence, the Composition Settings window provides a Pixel Aspect Ratio menu. Usually, a particular pixel aspect ratio (also known as PAR) is tied to a particular format. For example, DVCPRO HD 1080 uses a PAR of 1.5, which means that each captured pixel is stretched 1.5 times in the horizontal direction to create an image on a display that appears correct (Figure 1.10). The Pixel Aspect Ratio menu contains six presets for video formats and one for motion picture film. The Anamorphic format is designed for anamorphic motion picture film, where the image was captured on film with a special "squeeze" lens then re-stretched by a companion lens in a theater to create an extra-wide result.

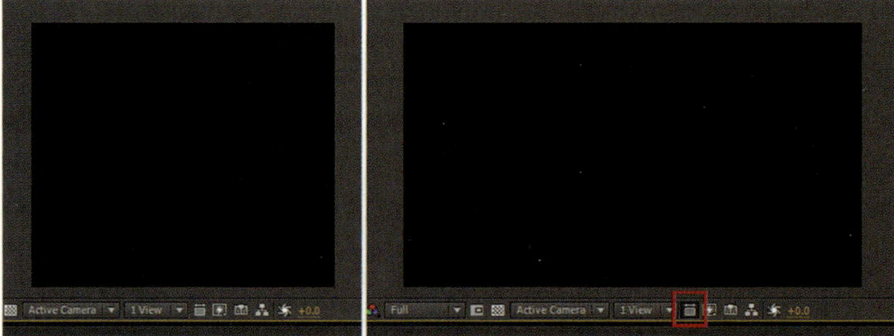

FIG 1.10 Left: An empty DVCPRO HD 1080 composition displayed with no stretching. Right: Same composition with the Toggle Pixel Aspect Ratio Correction button activated (the button is shown with a red box in this figure). Toggle Pixel Aspect Ratio Correction stretches the image into its intended display aspect ratio.

If a PAR is greater than 1.0, the image is stretched for final display. If a PAR is less than 1.0, the image is squeezed for final display. These manipulations always occur in the horizontal, or X direction. If you work with a nonsquare PAR, you have the option to display the composition (and the footage therein) in its native, captured format or with the intended final squeeze/stretch. If the Toggle Pixel Aspect Ratio Correction button is toggled on in the Composition view panel, the squeezed/stretched version is displayed. If the button is toggled off, the native version is displayed.

Choosing a Frame Rate

As with resolutions, there are common frame rates. The most common rates are 24, 25, and 30 frames per second (fps). 24 fps is the standard fps for pre-digital motion picture film. 30 fps (a rounded off 29.97 fps, which itself is simplified) originated as the frame rate for NTSC standard-definition television (SDTV). 25 fps is the PAL and SECAM standard for SDTV. (NTSC was used in North America and Japan while PAL and SECAM standards were used throughout the remainder of the world.) The advent of digital video and the HDTV standard has supplanted SDTV, but has not eradicated the legacy frame rates. In fact, HDTV supports 24, 25, and 30 fps, both in progressive and interlaced variations (see the "Interlaced versus Progressive" section).

When you import footage into After Effects, the program interprets the frame rate. If the footage is a self-contained movie (QuickTime, AVI, and so on), the frame rate is read from the file. If the footage is an image sequence, After Effects applies a default frame rate interpretation. Image sequences do not carry frame rate information. The frame rate applied by the program is set by the Frames Per Second field (Edit > Preferences > Import). The interpreted frame rate appears beside the footage thumbnail in the Project panel when the footage is selected (Figure 1.11).

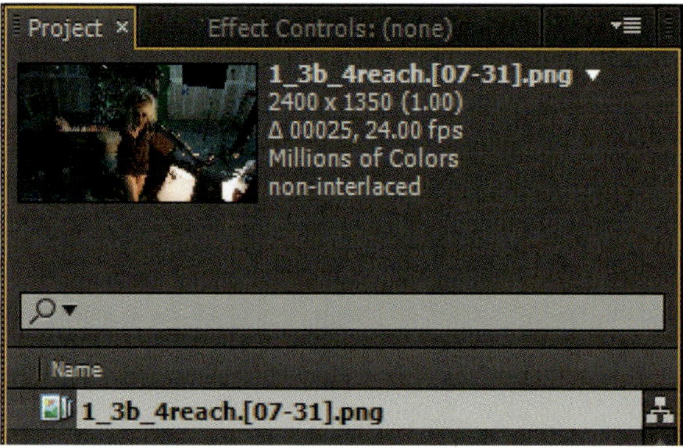

FIG 1.11 A Project panel footage thumbnail reveals the interpreted frame rate of an image sequence, as well as the footage resolution, pixel aspect ratio (square pixels are expressed as *1.0*), duration, and bit-depth (expressed as a rough value, like *Millions of Colors*).

You can alter the frame rate of imported footage at any time. To do so, RMB-click on the footage name in the Project panel and choose Interpret Footage > Main. In the Interpret Footage window, click the Assume This Frame Rate radio button, enter an fps value in the accompanying field, and click the window's OK button.

In general, the composition's frame rate should match the frame rate of the footage. However, you have the option to use multiple pieces of footage with multiple frame rates in a single composition. In that situation, you should choose a composition frame rate that matches your desired output. For example, if the project is intended for HDTV that broadcasts at 24 fps, then set the composition to 24 fps. Combining disparate frame rates in a composition leads to frame dropping or frame duplication. This is discussed in the section "Speeding Up and Slowing Down Footage" later in this chapter.

Interlaced versus Progressive

There are two variations of digital video frame rates: progressive and interlaced. Progressive rates use "whole" frames and are equivalent to image sequences where each frame is a complete still image. In contrast, interlaced rates use a series of interlaced "half" frames, known as *fields*. Interlaced field rates sometimes include decimal numbers. For example, 59.94 fields per second is the interlaced version of 29.97 fps. Other times, whole numbers are used. 50 fields per second is the interlaced version of 25 fps. Interlacing stems from the technological limitations of SDTV and is a legacy system.

In general, it's desirable to work with progressive frames as part of a visual effects project. Interlacing presents difficulties for such operations as green screen removal and motion tracking due to the incomplete nature of each field. Should you be forced to work with interlaced footage, it's possible to convert the footage to a progressive image sequence. The following mini-tutorial steps you through this process.

Interlaced to progressive mini-tutorial

The following steps allow you to convert interlaced video into a progressive image sequence. Progressive frames are superior for visual effects compositing as they offer whole frames instead of half-frames.

1. Create a new project. Use File > Import > File to import the *Interlaced.mov* file from the *\ProjectFiles\Plates\Interlacing* tutorial directory. After Effects recognizes the interlacing and indicates this by adding the phrase *Separating (Lower)* beside the footage thumbnail. *Lower* indicates which half-frame (known as a *field*) is given priority for a frame (one field is drawn first and the remaining field is drawn second). The lower field is composed of every other even-numbered scanline starting at the image top whereas the upper field is composed of every other odd-numbered scanline starting from the top.
2. You can change the field interpretation through the Interpret Footage window (RMB-click over the footage name and choose Interpret Footage > Main). You can switch the field priority by changing the Separate Fields menu between Lower Field First and Upper Field First. If this menu is set to Off, the program combines the fields. Turning the menu to Off is the first method of deinterlacing. However, the resulting quality is often poor with strongly visible interlacing lines (Figure 1.12). For this tutorial, leave the menu set to Lower Field First.

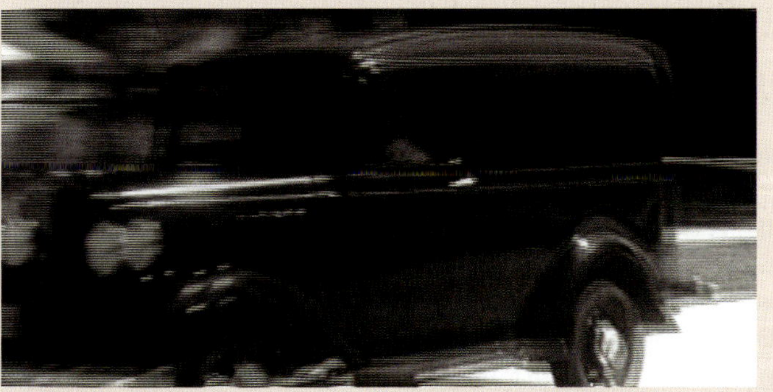

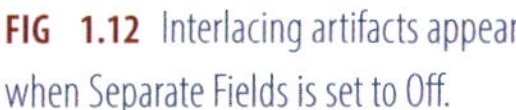

FIG 1.12 Interlacing artifacts appear when Separate Fields is set to Off.

3. LMB-drag the movie from the Project panel to the empty timeline. A new composition is created with the footage name. The resolution, frame rate, and duration are matched to the movie. Note that the timeline does not reveal individual fields. In fact, compositions are always progressive. As such, the fields are combined to show you frames within the Composition view (Figure 1.13). Nevertheless, the resulting quality of the frames is significantly better than setting the Separate Fields menu to Off. Note that you can view the fields in the Footage view (double-click the footage name in the Project panel to open it in the Footage view). You can step through individual fields in this view by pressing the Page Up or Page Down keys. Page Up moves backwards in time while Page Down does the opposite. Each time you press Page Up or Page Down twice, you step through one whole frame and two fields. The view of each field is completed by repeating scanlines for that field. Each field varies slightly from its counterpart field—this is most noticeable along high-contrast edges.

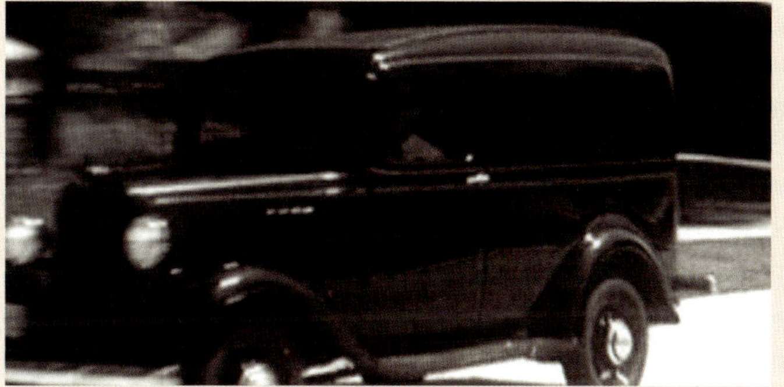

FIG 1.13 The footage is deinterlaced when Separate Fields is set to Lower Field First. This clip is taken from "Facts on Friction," an industrial film from the Prelinger Archives, made available via a Creative Commons Public Domain license. For more information, visit www.archive.org/details/prelinger.

4. You can sharpen the edges of the combined fields, which tend to become soft, by returning the Interpret Footage window and selecting the Preserve Edges check box. Alternatively, you can apply a sharpening effect, such as Effect > Blur & Sharpen > Sharpen. You must return to the Composition view to see the sharpening on the combined fields.

You can now work with the footage as progressive frames. You can also choose to render out the composition as an image sequence that you can then use for a different project or composition. Each frame you see in the Composition view becomes a frame of the sequence. To render an image sequence, choose a still image format, such as TIFF, PNG, Targa, and so on. This project is saved as *deinterlaced.aep* in the *\ProjectFiles\aeFiles\Chapter1* tutorial directory. In addition, a converted image sequence is saved as *\ProjectFiles\Plates\Interlacing\Deinterlaced\Deinterlaced.###.png*.

Speeding Up and Slowing Down Footage

Although motion picture or video footage is captured with a specific frame rate, you are free to apply your own frame rate interpretation for a stylized result. You can apply this creative interpretation to an individual piece of footage or to an entire composition with all its contents. There are several methods for achieving this inside After Effects, including the intentional mismatching of frame rates and the addition of time effects.

Mismatching Frame Rates

If the frame rate of a piece of footage within a composition doesn't match the composition frame rate, one of two things happens: frames are dropped or frames are duplicated. You can follow these general rules:

- If the composition frame rate is greater than the footage frame rate, the footage frames are duplicated.
- If the composition frame rate is less than the footage frame rate, frames from the footage are skipped ("dropped").

For example, if 12 fps footage exists in a 24 fps composition, the footage frames are doubled. That is, each frame is displayed twice. Footage with a lower frame rate than the composition is essentially shown in slow motion. If 48 fps footage exists in a 24 fps composition, every other frame is dropped. Footage with a higher frame rate than the composition is essentially shown sped up. Thus, mismatching frame rates is a basic way to "time warp" footage, whereby the footage is artificially sped up or slowed down.

If one composition is nested within a second composition, the same rule applies if the frame rates do not match. The slowing down or speeding up is applied to the nested composition layer. For more information on nesting, see Chapter 4.

Frame Blending

Whenever there is a frame rate mismatch and frames are duplicated for a piece of footage, you have the option to apply frame blending. Frame blending synthesizes new in-between frames from surrounding frames as an alternative to simply repeating frames as is. Frame blending often appears much smoother than duplication. In fact, the blending can often disguise the fact that time warping is occurring.

You can activate frame blending for any layer. However, you can only see its effect on a layer that carries the footage with mismatched frame rate. To activate frame blending, select the layer in the layer outline and choose Layer > Frame Blending > Frame Mix or Layer > Frame Blending > Pixel Motion. The Frame Mix method simply combines two surrounding frames through partial opacities to create a new in-between frame. Although Frame Mix is superior to no frame blending (Layer > Frame Blending > Off), the blending method may be visible with moving objects and/or a moving camera.

In contrast, the Pixel Motion method uses an advanced motion estimation algorithm to track feature movement over time. Pixel Motion is able to create in-between frames with moving objects in correct in-between locations along their motion paths. Pixel Motion often creates new frames that are indistinguishable to those captured with the original camera. Nevertheless, motion estimation techniques can fail in certain circumstances. These circumstances include:

- Object occlusion—moving objects occlude each other or the background
- Objects crossing the frame edge

As an alternative to Layer > Frame Blending > Pixel Motion, you can apply the Timewarp motion estimation effect. Timewarp generally offers better quality. The RE:Vision Effects Twixtor effect plug-in also offers superior results. These effects are discussed in the next three sections.

Note that Pixel Motion significantly increases render times. You can also activate frame blending by clicking the Frame Blending button beside the layer name in the layer outline (Figure 1.14). If you don't see the button, click the Toggle Switches/Modes button at the bottom of the layer outline. A single click produces a backslash (After Effects CC 2014) or a small pair of film frames (CC 2015), which puts frame blending into the Frame Mix mode. Two clicks produce a forward slash (CC 2014) or a right-facing arrow (CC 2015), which puts frame blending in the Pixel Motion mode. Note the frame blending is only functional for the composition if the large Enables Frame Blending button is activated.

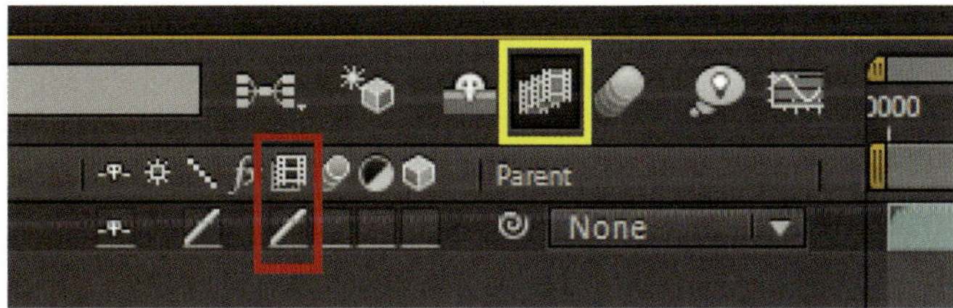

FIG 1.14 The Frame Blending button for a layer is indicated with a red square. Frame blending is set to Pixel Motion, as is indicated by a forward slash in After Effects CC 2014. The Enables Frame Blending button for the composition is indicated with a yellow square.

Time Warping with Timewarp

The Timewarp effect (Effect > Time > Timewarp) offers an alternative to the frame blending available through the Layer > Frame Blending menu. Its main advantage is a long list of properties that you can adjust. The following tutorial steps you through its use.

Slow-motion mini-tutorial

The following steps will slow down footage so it runs twice as long and half as fast using the Timewarp effect.

1. Create a new project. Use File > Import > File to import the *1_3a_3hand.##.png* image sequence from the *\ProjectFiles\Plates*

TimeWarping\1_3a_3hand tutorial directory. Make sure the footage frame rate is 24 fps. If it's not, RMB-click over the footage name in the Project panel and choose Interpret Footage > Main. In the Interpret Footage window, select the Assume This Frame Rate radio button, enter 24 into the corresponding field, and click the window's OK button.

2. LMB-drag the footage from the Project panel into the empty timeline. A new composition is named after the footage and carries the correct resolution, frame rate, and duration. The image sequence features a close-up of a hand moving along the edge of a chair. Play back the timeline using the RAM preview button. Note the general speed of the hand. (After Effects CC 2015 integrates the RAM preview button functionality into the standard playback buttons.)
3. With the footage layer selected, choose Effect > Time > Timewarp. Go to the effect in the Effect Controls panel. Note that the Method menu is set to Pixel Motion, much like the standard frame blending. You can switch this menu to Frame Mix or Whole frames if need be. By default, the Speed property is set to 50. This slows the footage down by 50 percent. The slowed footage is played within the original 16 frames and the end frames are discarded. Set Speed to 200 percent. Speed values over 100 percent speed up the footage. Play back to view the speed change. With this setting, every other frame is discarded and the last frame is repeated to fill the 16-frame duration of the timeline.
4. Set Speed to 25 percent to slow the footage to an even greater degree. Play back the timeline. At this point, the motion estimation is creating some warping where the fingers cross over the chair arm. To see this, zoom the view to 200 percent and play back. Depending on the footage you are adjusting, the warping may be subtle, with some pixels inappropriately sliding (Figure 1.15), or more extreme, where large "rips" tear parts of the image apart.

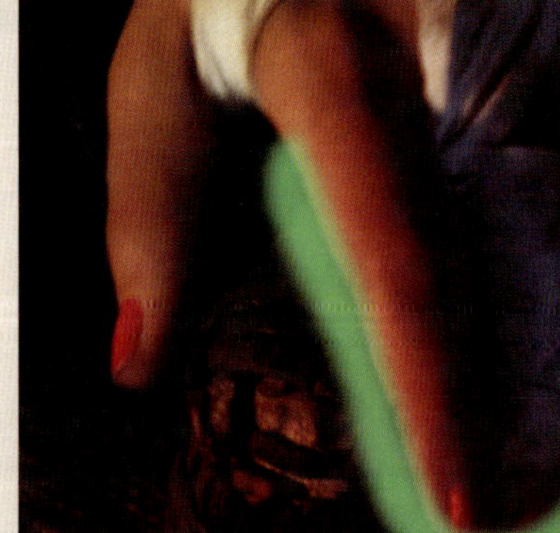

FIG 1.15 The area that suffers from pixel sliding is indicated with a green overlay (this is not visible in After Effects but is included here for reference). The sliding is caused by less than ideal Timewarp settings.

5. Raise the Vector Detail to 100. This increases the number of motion vectors used to track features within the footage. If Vector Detail is set to 100, there is one motion vector per pixel. The greater the number of vectors, the slower the calculation. Play back the timeline. The warping is decreased but still exists. Experiment with different Vector Detail values.
6. Set Vector Detail to 50 and raise Error Threshold to 10. Error Threshold sets the accuracy for pixel matching between frames. The higher the Error Threshold, the more the effect relies on Frame Mix–style blending to fill in localized detail (essentially, it ignores some of the motion vector results). You can further increase the warp quality by changing the Filtering menu from Normal to Extreme. Play back the timeline. The warping is reduced to an acceptable level (Figure 1.16).

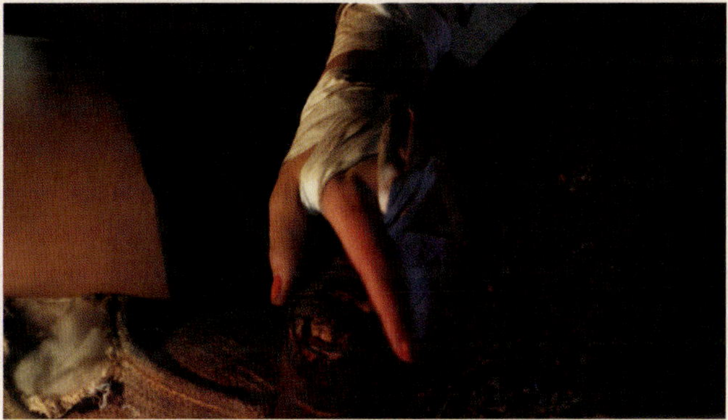

FIG 1.16 A smooth result created by setting the Timewarp effect's Vector Detail to 50 and Error Threshold to 10. The footage is slowed down by 75 percent.

Each time you apply Timewarp to a different piece of footage, it may require different settings. Note that no combination of settings may produce perfect results; however, the Timewarp effect does provide a more advanced solution than standard frame blending options. Other effect options available are grouped into the Smoothing section, which controls the resulting sharpness, Weighting, which biases the motion estimation against particular color channels, and Motion Blur, which adds an artificial motion blur to features successfully tracked with motion vectors. A finished version of this tutorial is saved as *mini_timewarp.aep* in the *\ProjectFiles\aeFiles\Chapter1* tutorial directory.

Time Warping with RE:Vision Effects Twixtor

The Twixtor plug-in, available via www.revisionfx.com, is a powerful time warping effect. Here is a quick introduction to its application:

1. With the layer you wish to warp selected, choose RE:Vision Plug-Ins > Twixtor. Go to the Twixtor effect in the Effect Controls panel (Figure 1.17).
2. Change the Frame Rate field so that it matches the composition frame rate (which should match the original frame rate of the footage).

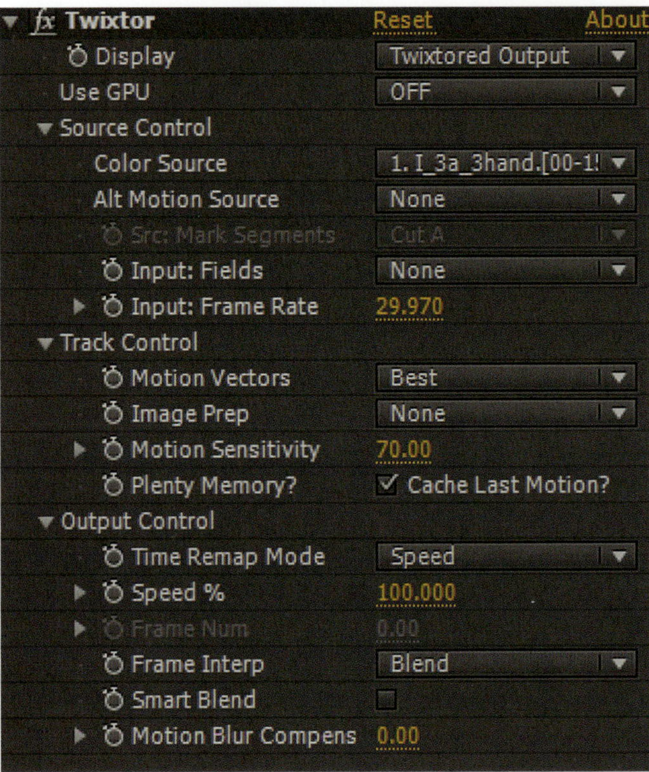

FIG 1.17 Twixtor properties with default settings.

3. Set Speed% to the desired time warp rate. Values below 100 percent slow the footage down. Values above 100 percent speed the footage up. Play back. Look for pixel sliding or edge tearing where objects cross over each other or where objects exit the frame.
4. If sliding or tearing exists, experiment with Motion Sensitivity values. If there is no improvement, return to the default value of 70. Higher values generally produce smoother results.
5. If sliding or tearing persists, try changing the Frame Interp menu. With the default method, Blend, surrounding frames are warped towards each other using the motion estimation vectors and then blended together to create a new, in-between frame. The Motion Weighted Blend method works in a similar fashion, but weights the blend based on object motion. In contrast, the Nearest method warps the earlier frame toward the later frame to create a new in-between frame.
6. Optionally, you can choose to forgo motion estimation by changing the Motion Vectors menu to No Motion Vectors. If the Frame Interp menu is set to Blend, the effect then functions in a manner similar to the After Effects Frame Mix mode.

RE:Vision Effects also provides two additional variations of the effect: Twixtor Pro and Twixtor Pro, Vectors In. The Pro versions add the ability to define masks that separate foreground from background elements (this helps to avoid tearing). In addition, the Pro versions provide a means to set tracking points to aid the effect in the identification of motion within the frame. The Vectors In variation allows you to import motion vectors from another program, such as 3D software.

Time Stretching

You can change the frame rate of a layer by applying the Time Stretch option. This prevents the need to change the frame rate through the Interpret Footage window, which may not be desirable if a particular piece of footage is used in several different locations within the project.

To slow down or speed up a layer, choose Layer > Time > Time Stretch. In the Time Stretch window, enter a value into the Stretch Factor field and click the window's OK button. Values over 100 percent stretch the footage (thereby slowing it down). Values under 100 percent shrink the footage (thereby speeding it up). The layer's duration bar, located in the timeline, shortens or lengthens in reaction to the Stretch Factor value. You can return to the Time Stretch window multiple times to select different factors. You can also activate frame blending (see the prior section).

The Layer > Time menu also provides the Time-Reverse Layer option, which inverts the frame order of the layer, and Freeze Frame, which "freezes" the current frame and repeats it across the timeline. Freeze Frame inserts a Time Remap effect with a pre-animated curve. Time Remap is described in the next section.

Time Remapping

The Time Remap effect offers a powerful means to speed up and slow down footage by providing a time curve that you can alter. To apply the effect, select a layer and choose Layer > Time > Enable Time Remapping. The effect appears below the layer name in the layer outline. To access the time curve, click the *Time Remap* name or click the Include This Property In The Graph Editor Set button, and click the Graph Editor button at the top of the layer outline.

By default, the time curve runs in a straight line from the first frame to the last in a diagonal fashion (Figure 1.18). Two keyframes store the targeted frame values. The first keyframe stores the first frame's time value. That is, if the first frame of the composition is frame 1, the keyframe stores 1.0 as a value. The last frame stores the last frame's time value. If the last frame of the composition is 60, the keyframe stores 60. This default curve means there is no time warp. The curve provides new frame values to the footage, but no warp will result unless the curve is reshaped.

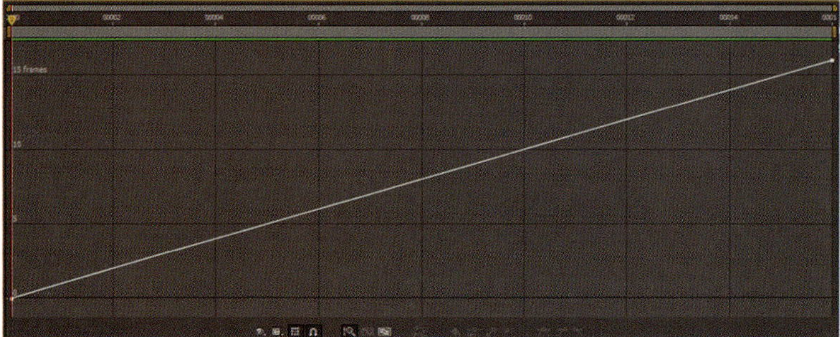

FIG 1.18 The default Time Remap effect curve with a 16-frame composition.

If you'd like to slow down the footage towards the end of the timeline, bow the right side of the curve upwards. The flatter the curve, the slower the footage is in that area of the timeline. The steeper the curve, the faster the footage is in that area. If the curve becomes flat, frames are repeated as a freeze frame—this is the same result as the Freeze Frame option (see the prior section). For a working demonstration of this, see the following tutorial.

You can activate frame blending for a layer that uses the Time Remap effect (see the prior two sections). You can remove the time warp by deleting the Time Remap effect. To do so, click the *Time Remap* name below the layer name and press the Delete key.

Speed change mini-tutorial

With the following steps, you can slow down and speed up footage all within a single layer and single timeline. This utilizes the Time Remap effect.

1. Create a new project. Use File > Import > File to import the *1_3a_3hand.##.png* image sequence from the *\ProjectFiles\Plates\TimeWarping\1_3a_3hand* tutorial directory. Make sure the footage frame rate is 24 fps. If it's not, RMB-click over the footage name in the Project panel and choose Interpret Footage > Main. In the Interpret Footage window, select the Assume This Frame Rate radio button, enter 24 into the corresponding field, and click the window's OK button.
2. LMB-drag the footage from the Project panel into the empty timeline. A new composition is named after the footage and carries the correct resolution, frame rate, and duration. The image sequence features a close-up of a hand moving along the edge of a chair. Play back. Note the general speed of the hand.
3. With the footage layer selected, choose Layer > Time > Enable Time Remapping. A Time Remap effect is added to the layer. Click on the *Time Remap* effect name in the layer outline and click the Graph Editor button. The time curve appears in the Graph Editor and runs in a

straight line from the first to the last frame of the timeline. To create a time warp, where the speed of the footage changes (that is, the frame rate varies), you can change the time curve shape.

4. RMB-click over the top of the first, leftmost keyframe and choose Keyframe Interpolation from the menu. The Keyframe Interpolation window opens. Change the Temporal Interpolation menu to Bezier and click OK. A Bezier tangent handle is added to the keyframe. LMB-drag the tangent handle (the yellow dot at the end of the yellow line) so that the curve bows downwards at the start and is essentially flat for the first two frames (Figure 1.19). This creates a brief freeze frame, a slow start, and a gradual speed up to the prior frame rate. Play back the timeline to see this change.

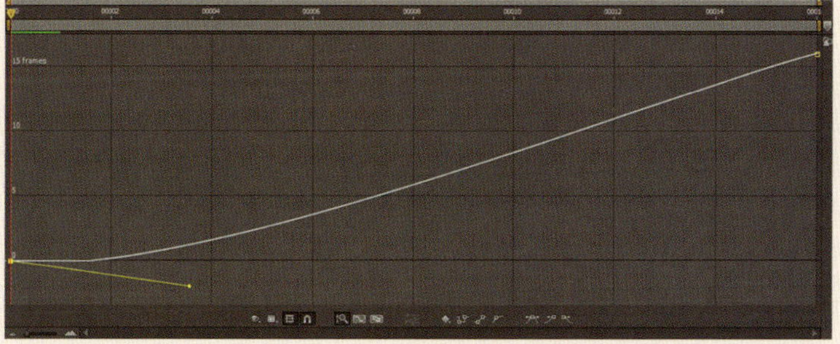

FIG 1.19 A brief freeze frame and a slow speedup are created by converting the first keyframe to a Bezier and moving the tangent handle.

5. When shaping the curve, keep the following in mind:
   - If the curve is absolutely flat, the first frame in the flat area is repeated.
   - If the curve slope is shallow, the footage is slowed down in that area.
   - If the curve slope is steep, the footage is sped up in that area.

With this in mind, convert the last keyframe to a Bezier tangent and move the tangent handle so that the footage slows back down at the end (Figure 1.20). You can pull the handle to the lengthen it and therefore have more influence on the curve shape. Play back the timeline.

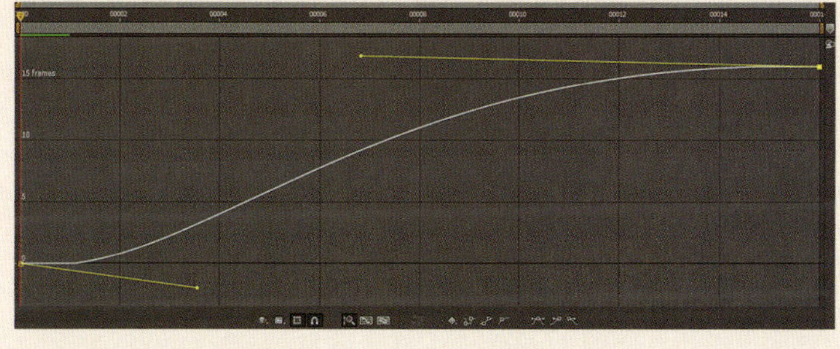

FIG 1.20 The final altered curve. A slowdown is added to the end by shaping the curve with a second tangent handle.

You can activate frame blending to blend the new slow-motion frames together. In fact, if the curve is changed to vary the speed throughout the duration, there is less likelihood that the Pixel Motion blending method will create artifacts where objects cross each other.

Optionally, you can insert additional keyframes into the curve and move those keyframes. To insert a new keyframe, Crtl/Cmd + LMB on the selected curve. To move a keyframe, LMB-drag it. Keep in mind that the left-to-right direction of the Graph Editor is time in frames while the down-to-up direction represents the curve value. In this case, the curve value is the new frame number that creates the time warp. With the example seen in Figure 1.20, frame 8 of the timeline uses frame 11 from the footage. You can determine this by placing the mouse over the curve at frame 8 and reading the curve value from the pop-up box. The timeline rounds off the curve value to come up with a new frame number. If frame blending is activated, new frames are blended by examining the exact curve values and weighting the blend toward the closest preexisting frames. A completed version of this project is saved as *mini_remapping .aep* in the *\ProjectFiles\aeFiles\Chapter1* tutorial directory.

Altering the Frame Rate with Time Effects

After Effects provides several effects that warp footage with a creative result. A few of these are briefly described here.

Echo

This effect layers multiple frames together to create a ghost-like trail. You can set the number of echoed frames through the property with the same name. You can choose the blending mode with which the frames are combined through the Echo Operator menu.

CC Wide Time

This effect also creates a ghost trail but does not overexpose the frames (see Figure 1.1 at the start of this chapter). You can choose the number of echoed frames forward and backward with the Forward Steps and Backwards Steps properties.

Time Displacement

This effect warps an image by offsetting pixels in time. The offset is based on the RGB values of a second layer. This offers a means to make one image move through the other as if there is television broadcast interference. You select the second layer through the Time Displacement Layer menu.

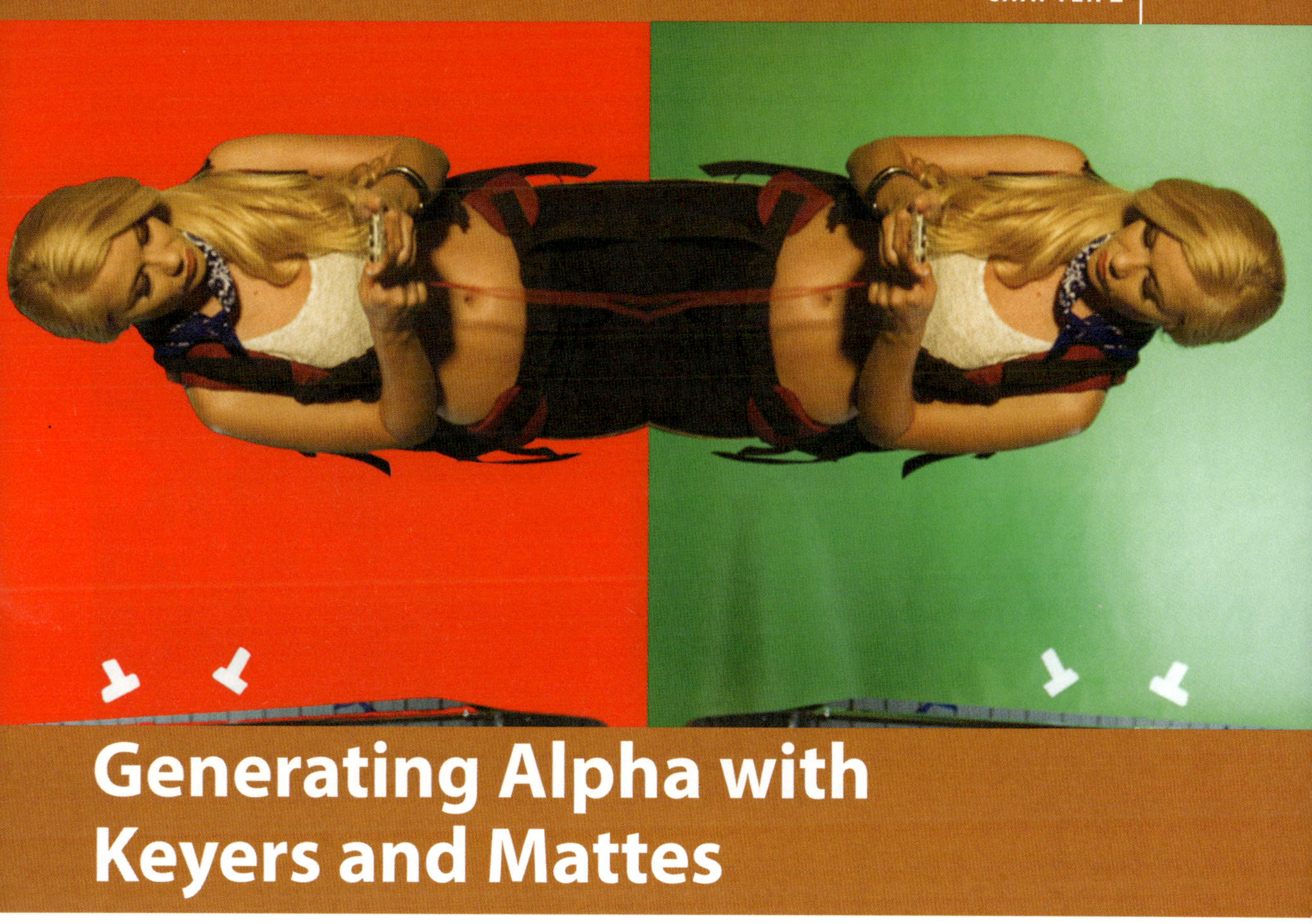

CHAPTER 2

Generating Alpha with Keyers and Mattes

Alpha channels, which provide transparency information for After Effects layers, are an important part of the compositing process. Although source files may carry their own alpha channels, as may be the case with 3D renders and Photoshop artwork, other source files may lack alpha completely. For example, video footage, whether it arrives in the form of a self-contained movie or as an image sequence, carries no transparency information. This becomes problematic if a nonalpha layer needs only partially occluded lower layers.

As a solution, you can create alpha information in After Effects by borrowing values from other channels, such as red, green, or blue. This practice is most commonly applied through chroma key tools. Chroma keyers target specific colors, such as the green in a green screen (Figure 2.1). You can also generate alpha information by creating custom alpha mattes. A matte may take the form of a rotoscope shape or manipulated values from a specific channel, such as luma.

This chapter includes the following critical information:

- Application of common keyers
- Improvement of alpha matte edges
- Creating custom luma mattes and activating Track Matte

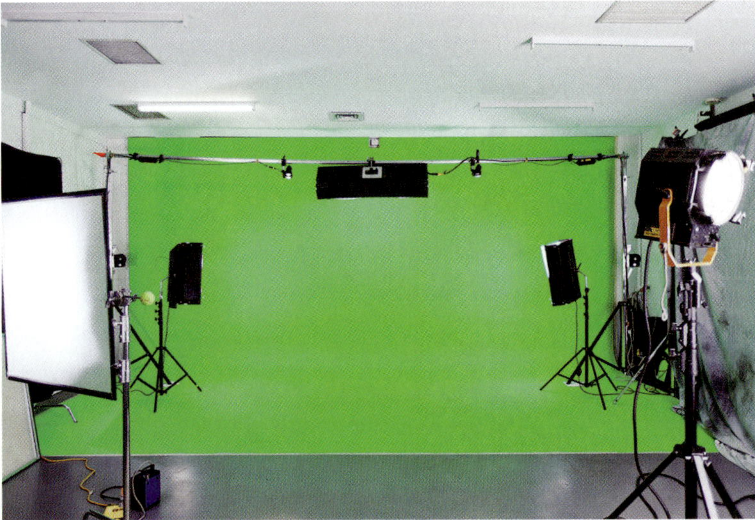

FIG 2.1 A green screen setup on a stage. *Photo © Steve Lovegrove / Dollar Photo Club.*

Generating Alpha with Chroma Key Techniques

Chroma key is a compositing process that layers multiple pieces of footage by targeting and removing a specific color. The technique was first developed during the early stages of motion picture production, at which time the visual effects were created through optical printing techniques. The process has survived to this day and remains in common use for live television broadcast, studio photography and videography, and postproduction visual effects work. Early chroma key relied on the color blue and blue screen backdrops. Green screen has since become more widely used due the technical traits of digital video (see Figure 2.1). As a technique, chroma key can target any color. Hence, you can apply the approaches discussed in this chapter to a red backdrop, an orange sunset sky, and so on. Nevertheless, for the ease of discussion, I will refer to *green screen* as a general term for a chroma key backdrop. Chroma key tools are generally referred to as *keyers* whereby you *key* a shot or piece of footage. When discussing keying, the green screen is referred to as the *background*, while the non–green screen area (the part that is to be saved) is referred to as the *foreground*. In terms of color theory, *chroma* refers to the colorfulness of a color relative to what is perceived as white. *Colorfulness* is the degree of difference between a color and gray. *Saturation* is the intensity (brightness) of a particular color.

After Effects provides several different keyers, each with its own set of unique advantages and disadvantages. Although there is not sufficient space to cover every option of every keyer, we'll cover the most critical and most useful keyer components. The keyers are located in the Effect > Keying menu.

Using Keylight

The Foundry's Keylight is the most advanced keyer that is provided with After Effects. Assuming that the green screen is properly set up, you can follow these basic steps to quickly key out the green:

1. Apply the Keylight effects to the layer that carries the green screen footage (Effect > Keying > Keylight 1.2). Go to the effect in the Effect Controls panel (Figure 2.2).

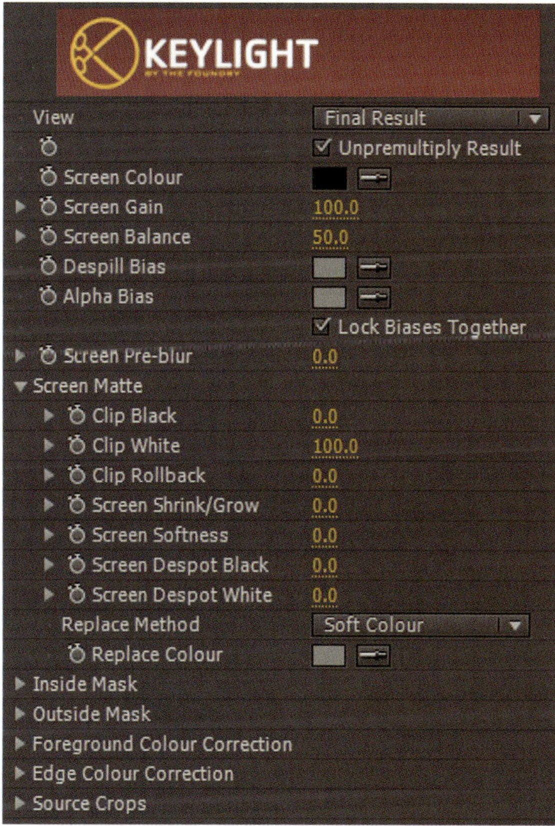

FIG 2.2 The Keylight 1.2 effect with default values with the Screen Matte section expanded.

2. Using the Screen Colour eyedropper, select a background color in the Composition view panel. For example, select the green of the green screen. Select a mid-tone color if the green screen is unevenly lit.
3. Switch the effect's View menu to Combined Matte (Figure 2.3). The alpha matte is displayed in the Composition view. The goal is to make the white areas (the opaque part of the alpha) as white as possible and the black areas (the transparent part of the alpha) as black as possible.

FIG 2.3 The Combined Matte view of a green screen before adjustment.

4. Expand the Screen Matte section. Raise the Clip Black value until any gray left in the green screen area disappears. Be careful not to erode into any alpha edges you want to maintain, such as those around a person's hair. Any pixel value lower than the Clip Black value is given a 0 value (100 percent transparent). Lower the Clip White value until the gray areas within the opaque white disappear (Figure 2.4). Again, be careful not to erode any desired edge. Any pixel value higher than the Clip White value

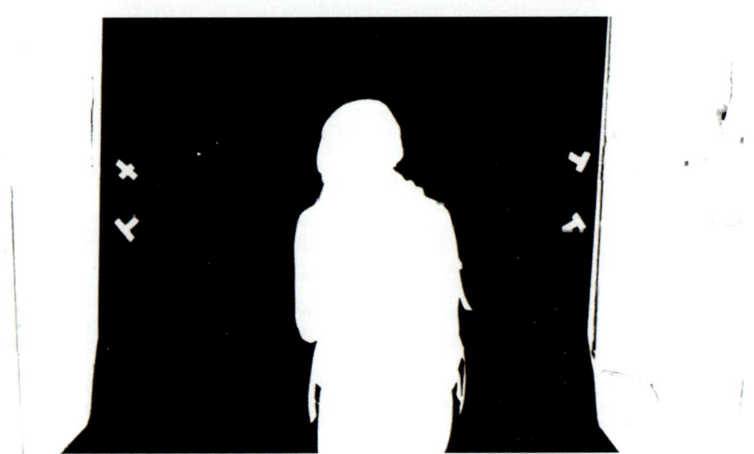

FIG 2.4 Clip Black and Clip White are adjusted so that the whites are more white and the blacks are more black.

is given a maximum value in the current color space (e.g. 255 in 8-bit space, equating to 100 percent opaqueness).

5. After the adjustments in step 4 are satisfactory, return the View menu to Final Result. You can continue to adjust Keylight settings in the Final Result view. To determine how well the green screen removal is working, temporarily place a brightly colored Solid layer below the green screen layer. You can create a Solid by choosing Layer > New > Solid.

These few steps work in many green screen situations. However, green screen setups often suffer from imperfect conditions and thus make the process more difficult. For a review of potential problems and possible solutions using Keylight, see the next two sections.

Keylight mini-tutorial

Using the recommendations in the prior section, "Using Keylight," remove the green screen in the shot illustrated by Figure 2.5. The shot is saved as *mini_greenscreen.aep* in the *\ProjectFiles\aeFiles\Chapter2* directory.

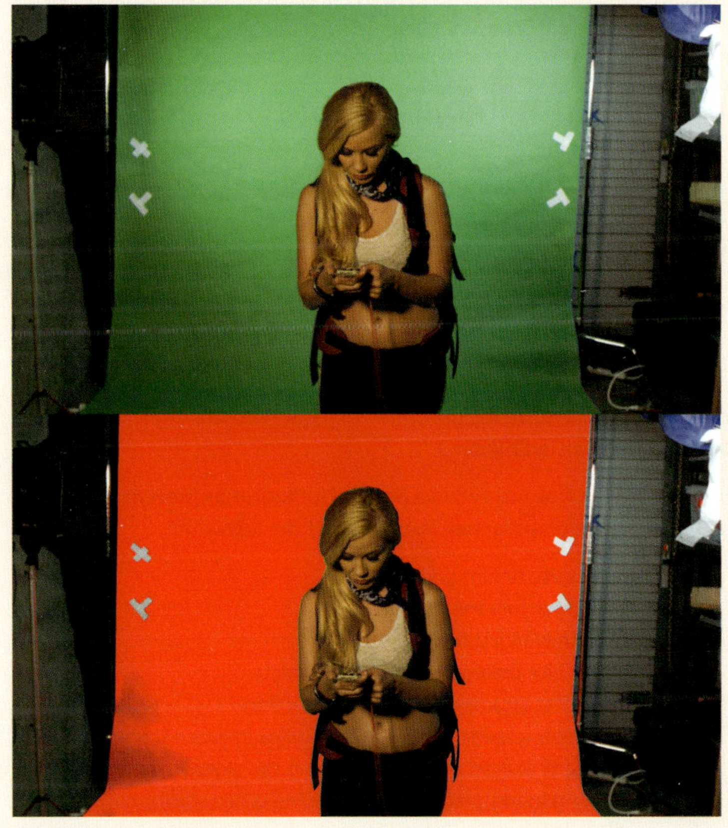

FIG 2.5 Top: Raw plate. Bottom: Plate with Keylight keyer applied. A red solid sits at a lower layer in order to gauge the success of the keyer.

Note that the motion tracking marks at the edge of the set must be removed by creating a *garbage mask* (a hand-drawn matte that removes unwanted elements). Garbage masks and their counterparts, holdout masks, are demonstrated in the next chapter. In addition, a slight noise may remain along the bottom left and bottom right of the green screen. Leaving this noise may be necessary to maintain a slightly soft edge around the actress and to prevent excess erosion of the matte edge. You can remove the noise with a garbage mask so long as the noise does not appear directly behind the actress.

A finished version of this shot, with an adjusted Keylight effect, is saved as *mini_keylight_finished.aep*. The finished version uses the following settings:

- Screen Colour = Mid-tone green (73, 154, 87 in 0-255 RGB)
- Clip Black = 30
- Clip White = 83
- Replace Method = Source

Note that the Replace Method property is discussed in the section "Working with Spill in Keylight" later in this chapter.

Working with Imperfect Green Screen

A visual effects compositor rarely receives footage with a perfect green screen setup. The most common problem is the presence of undesirable and unkeyable objects. These may include:

- Film, video, or stage equipment, including lights, flags, stands, and rigging
- The edge of the set or location where the green screen stops short
- Crew members operating practical effects, puppets, and the like

In this situation, you can rotoscope or otherwise create a garbage mask or holdout mask to remove the unwanted objects. Rotoscoping and masks are addressed in detail in Chapter 3.

Some artifacts or features within a piece of footage may prevent keyers from creating a clean alpha channel. These include the following:

- Heavy video noise or film grain
- Shadows falling across the green screen
- Significantly uneven lighting
- Heavy motion blur created by moving subjects
- Green screen that appears as part of a reflection
- Wrinkles in green screen fabric or irregularities in green screen paint
- Heavy green spill caused by subjects sitting too close to the green screen
- Motion tracking marks placed directly on the green screen backdrop
- Very small or thin detail in front of the green screen (e.g. hair, wires, threads, or fur)

As an example, Figure 2.6 features a green screen setup that suffers from shadows, wrinkles, tracking marks, and very fine hair. This green screen is the subject of the tutorial at the end of this chapter.

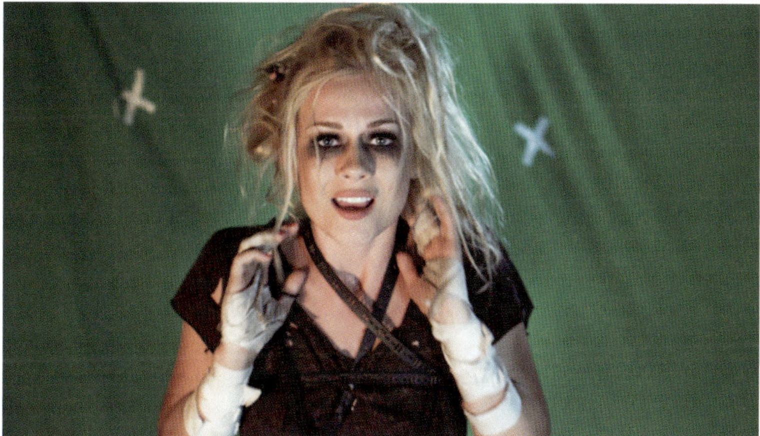

FIG 2.6 A challenging green screen.

Working with one or more of these artifacts may require the adjustment of additional keyer options, the creation of custom mattes, rotoscoping or masking, or the breakdown of the green screen footage into multiple layers. Custom mattes are discussed later in this chapter. The breakdown of footage is explored in Chapter 3.

Applying Additional Keylight Properties

The Keylight effect provides a number of properties that you can adjust when tackling difficult green screen footage. These are detailed in this section. (See Figure 2.2 earlier in this chapter for the location of properties.)

Screen Pre-Blur

Screen Pre-Blur averages the pixel values before attempting to key the Screen Colour. This may create a more successful result if the footage has heavy noise or grain. The property also has the effect of simplifying the alpha matte edge. See Chapter 9 for a more detailed look at noise and grain.

Screen Gain and Screen Balance

Screen Gain determines the aggressiveness with which the background color, as defined by Screen Colour, is removed from the resulting matte. The higher the value, the more aggressive the removal. It may not be necessary to change this property from its default value of 100. Adjusting Clip Black and Clip White often produces better results. Nevertheless, the adjustment of Screen Gain may aid in the removal of fine noise in the alpha. Screen Balance, on the other hand, interprets the saturation of the targeted Screen Colour by comparing the strongest color component (such as green) to the remaining two components (such as red and blue). Shifting the property toward 100 causes the saturation to be compared to the least intense of the remaining components. A value shifted toward 0 causes the saturation to be compared to the most intense of the remaining components. The default of 50 causes both remaining components to be equally weighted. It may not be necessary to change this property from its default value of 50. Changes to the Screen Balance value generally produce subtle variations in the matte.

Clip Rollback, Screen Shrink/Grow, and Screen Softness

These properties erode or expand the alpha matte (see Figure 2.7). That is, they either erode into the opaque area or expand the opaque area. Clip Rollback restores information to the alpha edge that may have been lost through the adjustment of other properties. This may be useful for restoring a slight edge transparency and softness that was otherwise lost. Note that high Clip Rollback values may introduce banding along semitransparent edges.

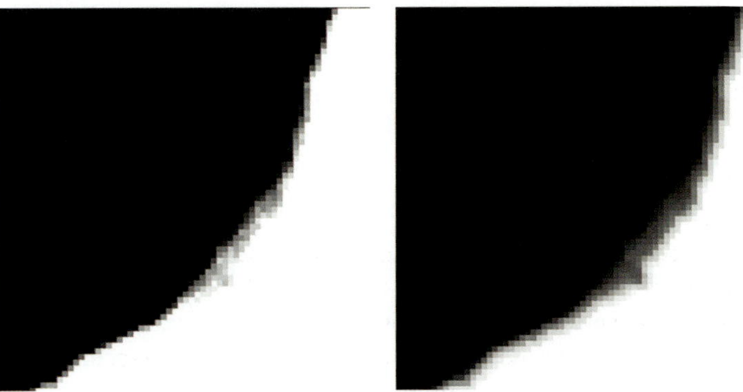

FIG 2.7 Left: Close-up of alpha matte edge. Gray pixels are semitransparent. Right: Same edge with Clip Rollback set to 1.0. The area of semitransparency is expanded, thereby softening the edge.

Screen Shrink/Grow fulfills its name by eroding or expanding while roughly maintaining the current degree of semitransparency along the alpha edge. Small negative values may be useful for eroding away unwanted dark lines that appear along the edge in the RGB channels. (The lines may result from the Replace Method property, which is discussed in the "Suppressing Spill" section later in this chapter.)

Screen Despot Black and Screen Despot White

The Despot properties simplify the resulting matte. This aids in the removal of noisy spots that other properties are unable to remove. Use caution when adjusting these, however, as high values will overly smooth alpha edges.

This may result in unrealistic edges. For example, dips or holes may cut into a person's hands, hair, or neck. Screen Despot Black attacks isolated spots of black within the white, opaque areas. Screen Despot White does the opposite.

Using the Primatte Plug-In

There are a number of third-party plug-ins you can use to key green screen footage. In particular, Primatte Keyer, released by Red Giant Software, has enjoyed a long history of success. Primatte's main advantage is its semiautomated, interactive workflow. The following mini-tutorial steps you through the Primatte keying process. You can download a trial version of Primatte Keyer at www.redgiant.com/products/all/primatte-keyer/.

Primatte mini-tutorial

The following steps represent the general approach you can take with any green screen footage. For practice, apply these steps to the *mini_greenscreen.aep* project saved in the *\ProjectFiles\aeFiles\Chapter2* directory.

1. Select the green screen layer and choose Effect > Primatte > Primatte Keyer. Go to the effect in the Effect Controls panel.
2. Click the Auto Compute button in the Keying section (Figure 2.8). Primatte automatically detects the background color and removes/reduces it. Alpha transparency automatically appears.
3. Change the View menu to Matte. If there is gray noise in the background area of the alpha, click the Select BG button and LMB-drag your mouse in the Composition view over the gray pixels. The drag path is indicated by a series of white dots. Primatte automatically targets the selected pixels and readjusts the alpha values. You can LMB-drag as many times as you like. You can also select a rectangular block of pixels by switching the Sampling Style menu to Rectangle.
4. If there is gray noise in the foreground area of the alpha, click the Clean FG button and LMB-drag your mouse over those pixels. Feel free to go back and forth between the Select BG tool and Select FG tool. Should you need to start from scratch, you can click the word *Reset* at the top of the Primatte effect.
5. After the alpha is sufficiently clean with white whites and black blacks, change the View menu to Comp. Zoom into the Viewer and examine the alpha edges and any green spill that may be present. To reduce green spill, click the Spill Sponge button, and LMB-drag your mouse of the spill area. The spill is instantly reduced. Make short selections with your mouse, else there is a danger of pulling too much background color out of the entire foreground. You can press Ctrl/Cmd + Z to undo

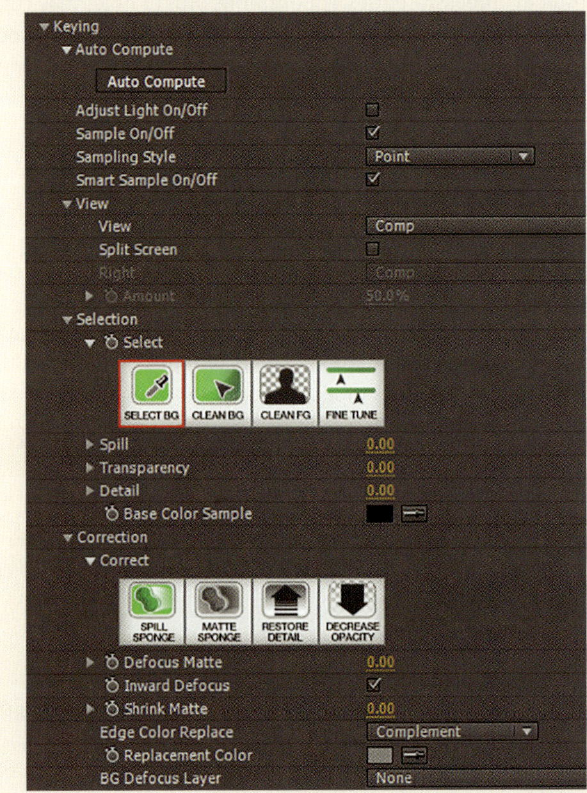

FIG 2.8 The Primatte Keyer Keying section in its default state.

the previous mouse sample. Feel free to place a new solid layer below the green screen layer to check the quality of the alpha matte.

6. If any edge becomes too eroded or overly semitransparent, you can restore foreground pixel opacity by clicking the Matte Sponge button and LMB-dragging over the edge area. Use this option carefully, as it may add noise back into the previously transparent background. Feel free to switch the Sampling Style menu between Rectangle and Point to help make sampling more efficient.
7. If an edge is too hard and lacks appropriate semitransparency and softness, click the Restore Detail button and LMB-drag of the edge area. Use this option carefully, as it may add noise back into the previously opaque foreground. You can jump back to any of the buttons at any time.
8. To soften the matte edge slightly, raise the Defocus Matte value. To erode into the matte, raise the Shrink Matte value. You can fine-tune various components of the matte by expanding the Refinement subsection and choosing the Spill, Matte, or Detail buttons, each of which has a + (plus) and – (minus) variation (Figure 2.9). With these buttons, you can restore or remove the spill, foreground, or background values.

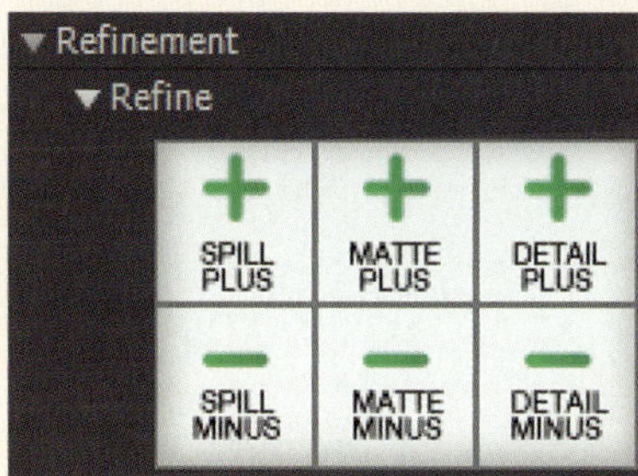

FIG 2.9 The expanded Refinement subsection.

9. Much like Keylight, Primatte automatically removes and reduces the background color in the foreground area. By default, it replaces the background color with a complimentary color (on the opposite side of the RGB color wheel), as set by the Edge Color Replace menu. You can change the menu to Color, whereby the color set by Replacement Col property is added. You can change the menu to BG Defocus, which uses a blurred version of the layer listed by the BG Defocus Layer menu. You can set BG Defocus Layer to the green screen layer and thus have it add back original pixel values.

A finished version of this tutorial, with an adjusted Primatte effect, is saved as *mini_primatte_finished.aep*.

Using Difference Keyers

Difference keyers note differences between corresponding pixels across two layers or note differences in color distribution across one layer. These effects include Difference Matte and Color Difference Key.

Difference Matte

The Difference Matte effect compares a source layer (the layer that has the effect applied to it) and a difference layer. Any corresponding pixel that does not match between the two layers is assigned opaque alpha. Any corresponding pixel that matches is assigned transparent alpha. For this effect to be successful, a clean plate should be provided. A *clean plate* is a version of the shot that lacks the foreground objects. For example, if the shot features an actor, the clean plate version leaves the actor out of the frame. A successful clean plate requires a locked-off camera (or a motion control camera that can precisely repeat the camera move each time). As an example, in Figure 2.10, an actress is separated from the background with a Difference Matte and a static clean plate. Although a solid matte is produced, the effect has difficulty interpreting RGB edge values—particularly when heavy film grain or video noise is present. Hence, green is trapped along the edges of the actress, requiring matte erosion that must be provided by another effect. (The erosion is demonstrated in the "Refining with Simple Choker and Matte Choker" section later in this chapter.)

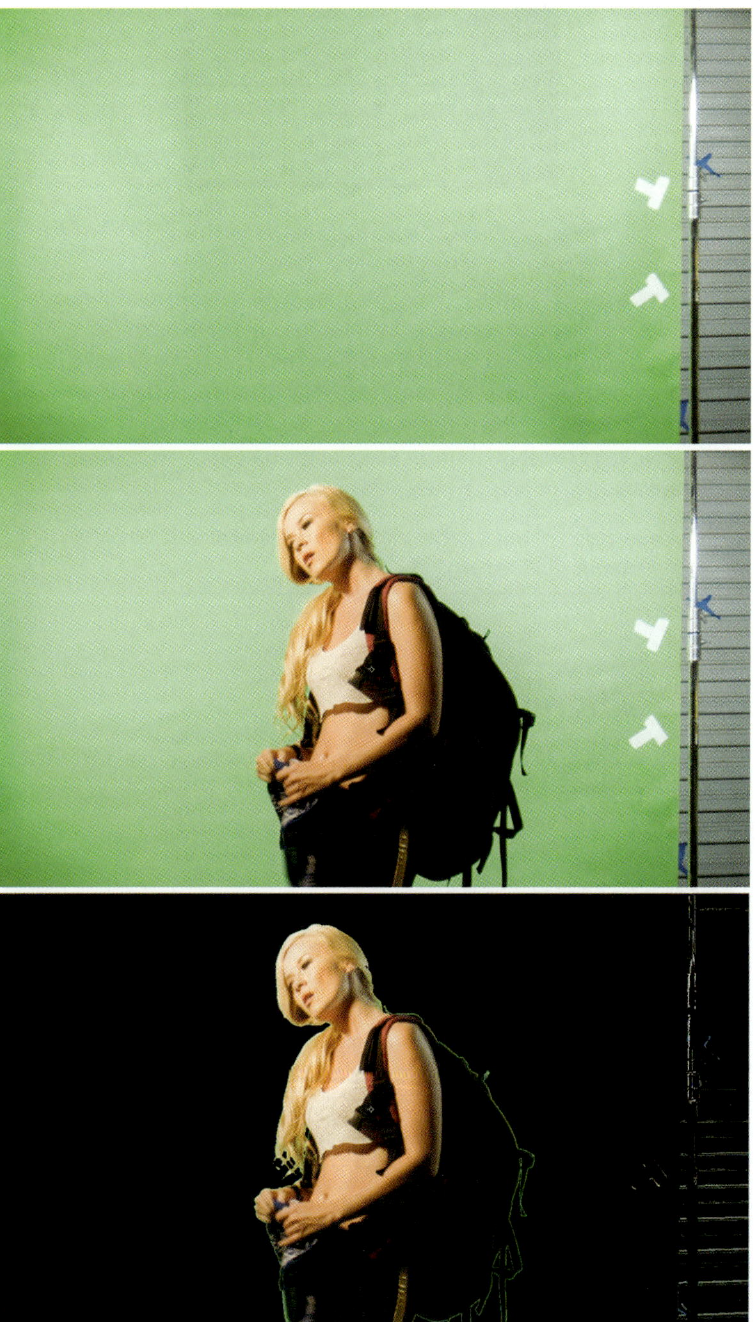

FIG 2.10 Top: Clean plate. Middle: Plate with actress. Bottom: Resulting key. This project is saved as *difference_matte.aep* in the *\ProjectFiles\aeFiles\Chapter2* directory.

To apply the effect, include the clean plate as part of the composition. You can hide the clean plate or place it below the lowest opaque layer. The clean plate can be a single frame. As for adjusting the effect settings, change the Difference Layer menu to the clean plate layer. Adjust the Matching Tolerance to make the pixel matching more or less accurate. If heavy grain or noise is present, consider raising the Blur Before Difference to soften the footage. You can also soften the matte by raising Matching Softness.

Color Difference Key

The Color Difference Key effect is unusual in that it creates two separate mattes and combines them into a final alpha matte. One matte, called Matte Partial B, is derived by targeting the background color. The second matte, called Matte Partial A, is derived by targeting a second, nonbackground color. Although the Color Difference Key is not as intuitive as Keylight or Primatte, it can produce clean alpha channels with difficult, semitransparent foregrounds, such as those with smoke or thin cloth. For an application of the effect, see the following mini-tutorial.

Color difference key mini-tutorial

The following steps represent the general approach you can take with the Color Difference Key effect. For practice, apply these steps to the *mini_smoke.aep* project saved in the *\ProjectFiles\aeFiles\Chapter2* directory.

1. Select the green screen layer and choose Effect > Keying > Color Difference Key. Go to the effect in the Effect Controls panel.
2. Using the Key Color eyedropper, select the green background color. Matte Partial A and Matte Partial B are created. You can view a thumbnail of the mattes by clicking the A and B buttons at the top right of the effect section (the thumbnail appears in the top right box). You can view a thumbnail of the final, combined matte by clicking the α button (Figure 2.11). Change the View menu to Matte Corrected to display the combined matte in the Composition view.
3. Click the middle, Black eyedropper button and LMB-click a gray area of the background in the Composition view. You can reapply the Black eyedropper and resample multiple times to update the matte. When the background area is relatively free of gray pixels, click the bottom White eyedropper button. LMB-click a gray area of the foreground in the Composition view. You can reapply the White eyedropper and resample multiple times. You can go back and forth between the Black and White eyedroppers.
4. To fine-tune the result, you can adjust the various sliders. The sliders are broken into In White, In Black, Out White, Out Black, and Gamma sets for Partial A and Partial B mattes, plus the final output matte,

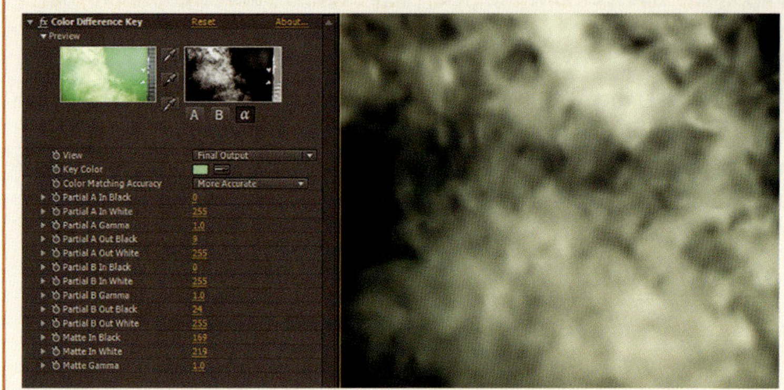

FIG 2.11 An adjusted Color Difference Key separates smoke from a green background.

labeled *Matte*. The In sliders determine what values are used by the effect. Values below the In Black values are ignored. Values above the In White values are ignored. The Out sliders determine the maximum range of values output by the effect. For example, if Partial A Out White is set to 175, no values above 175 are output for Matte Partial A. Ultimately, the best way to produce a quality matte is to experiment with all the sliders. When you are satisfied with the matte, return the View menu to Final Output. You can improve the quality of the effect by changing the Color Matching Accuracy menu to More Accurate.

Note that the Color Difference Key has the tendency to create posterization (color banding) when the project is set to 8-bit. Thus, it's recommended that you set the project to 16-bit by choosing File > Project Settings and changing the Depth menu in the Project Settings window to 16 Bits Per Channel. For more information on color spaces, see Chapter 1. A finished version of this tutorial, with an adjusted Color Difference Key effect, is saved as *mini_difference_finished.aep*.

Using Range Keyers

Range keyers convert color ranges to transparency information. These effects include Color Range and Linear Color Key.

Color Range

The Color Range effect creates transparency by targeting a range of colors in RGB, YUV, or Lab color space. The effect provides a means to generate a luma (luminance) matte through the L (lightness) channel of Lab color space or the Y (luma) channel of YUV color space. (The a and b channels of Lab and U and V channels of YUV encode the color components.) The Color Range effect includes interactive eyedroppers to refine the matte. For an application of the effect, see the following mini-tutorial.

Color range mini-tutorial

The following steps represent the general the general workflow required by the Color Range effect. For practice, apply these steps to the *mini_green screen.aep* project saved in the *\ProjectFiles\aeFiles\Chapter2* directory.

1. Apply the Color Range effect (Effect > Keying > Color Range) to the green screen layer. Select the background color with the Color Key eyedropper (the top eyedropper button). The alpha matte is updated with transparency. A thumbnail of the matte appears beside the eyedropper buttons (Figure 2.12).

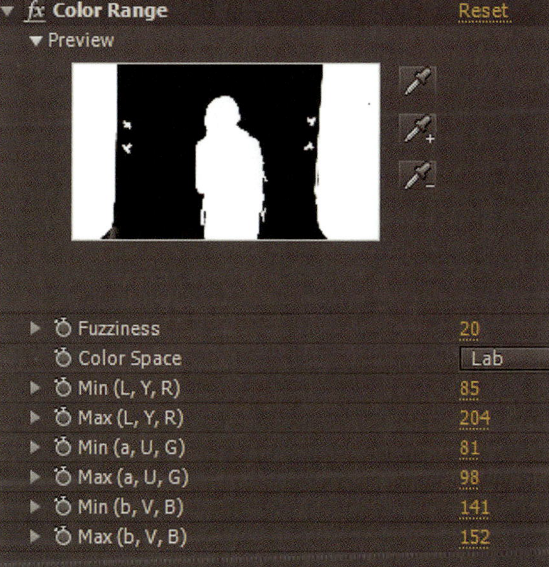

FIG 2.12 The adjusted Color Range effect. The thumbnail of the resulting alpha matte appears beside the eyedropper buttons.

2. Using the + eyedropper, sample additional areas to which you wish to add transparency. For example, click darker areas of the green screen. You can click in the matte thumbnail or click within the Composition view panel. You can apply the eyedropper multiple times.
3. Optionally, use the – eyedropper to sample areas to which you wish to return opaqueness. Fine-tune the results by adjusting the Min and Max sliders. The sliders are divided into first, second, and third channels. If you are working in Lab, the first two sliders set the range for the L channel, the middle two sliders set the range for the a channel, and the final two sliders set the range for the b channel.

A finished version of this project is saved as *mini_range_finished.aep* in the *\ProjectFiles\aeFiles\Chapter2* directory. For more information on luma mattes, see the "Creating a Custom Luma Matte" later in this chapter.

Linear Color Key

The Linear Color Key effect utilizes a range of colors to create transparency. The targeted background color is established by the Key Color swatch. The size of the color range is established by the Matching Tolerance property. If the Matching Tolerance is 0 percent, only the exact color set by Key Color is keyed. The larger the percentage, the wider the range of similar colors is keyed. The effect also provides Color Key, +, and – eyedroppers for interactive adjustment of the resulting matte. As a working example, in Figure 2.13, Linear Color Key is used to quickly remove a blue sky.

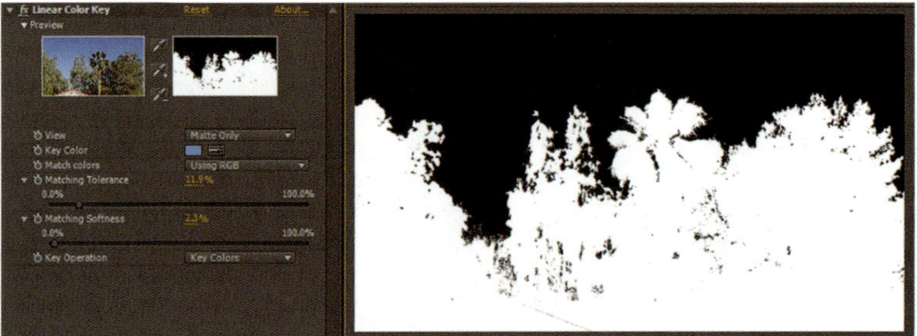

FIG 2.13 The Linear Color Key effect is used to remove a blue sky. This project is saved as *linear_color.aep* in the *\ProjectFiles\aeFiles\Chapter2* directory.

In general, the Linear Color Key effect is best suited for footage that contains little spill or has background with colors that are distinct from the foreground. In addition, the effect may be useful for targeting a secondary color ignored by a primary keyer, such as Keylight. For example, you can use the Linear Color Key effect to remove motion-tracking tape marks placed on a green screen.

Suppressing Spill

Spill is the unwanted appearance of the chroma key color within a foreground subject that needs to remain opaque. Green spill is common with green screen when the person sits or stands too close to the green screen backdrop. Spill often appears in hair (particularly light-colored hair), within skin tone, and within clothing.

Working with Spill in Keylight

The Keylight effect provides an integrated method for removing or diminishing spill. When the effect targets the background color as defined by the Screen Colour, it turns the corresponding alpha pixels transparent or semitransparent. At the same time, it reduces the presence of the background color within RGB. The color is not completely removed; that is, the green channel is not left with 0 values. However, the balance between red, green, and blue is shifted towards red and blue. You can control the type of shift by changing the Replace Method menu, in the Screen Matte section, to Source, Hard Colour, or Soft Colour (Figure 2.14). The Source option reintroduces the original RGB pixel values. If there is a heavy amount of spill in the footage, the spill reappears. If the spill is light, the Source option often creates good results. The Soft Colour option introduces a solid color, as defined by the Replace Colour swatch. Soft Colour attempts to retain the same luminance (brightness) of the original pixels. Hard Colour, in contrast, adds the Replace Colour color, but does not try to match the luminance.

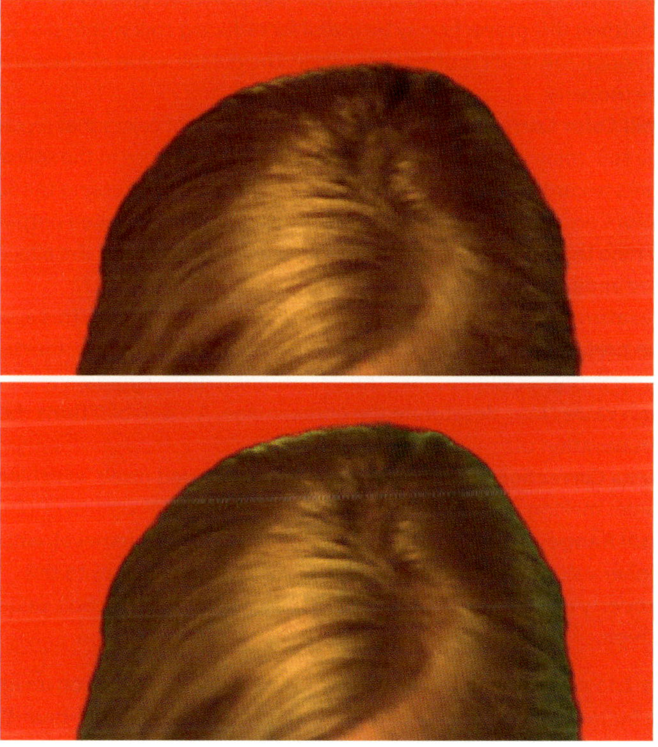

FIG 2.14 Top: Replace Method set to Soft Colour. Replace Colour is set to default gray. This results in hair that is slightly darker and redder. Bottom: Replace Method is set to Source. The hair becomes light and retains a yellow-green balance. However, green spill is more visible along the top and right hair edge. This project is saved as *mini_keylight_finished.aep* in the \ *ProjectFiles\aeFiles\Chapter2* directory. Note that the saturation in this figure is exaggerated so that the color variations are visible in print.

Applying Spill Effects

Aside from properties carried by keying effects, After Effects supplies standalone spill suppression effects. These include Spill Suppressor and Advanced Spill Suppressor.

The Spill Suppressor effect targets the spill color through the Color To Suppress color swatch. You can set the swatch to the same color used by the keyer or select a color from the keyed layer in the Composition view panel via the eyedropper. The degree of suppression is controlled through the Suppression property. Spill Suppressor is located in the Effect > Keying menu in After Effects CC 2013.

After Effects CC 2014 and CC 2015 replace Spill Suppressor with the Advanced Spill Suppressor effect. If you set the effect's Method menu to Standard, it detects the dominant background color and removes or reduces its presence. If you set the menu to Ultra, you have access to the following properties:

Key Color allows you select your own spill color.

Tolerance filters the background color out of the foreground areas. Adjusting this property may be useful for reducing spill within skin tone, although the result is often very subtle. The default value of 50 disables the property.

Spill Color Correction determines the saturation of colors that replace the spill color. If green spill is removed, the color balance in the spill areas shifts toward red and blue (producing purple). Thus, increasing the Spill Color Correction value produces a greater degree of saturated purple. Setting the value to 0 essentially turns the property off and the affected area appears gray.

Desaturate desaturates resulting colors within the image. This aids in the prevention of intense colors appearing in areas that are affected by spill. Higher values make the desaturation more aggressive. Very high values may desaturate the entire image. A value of 0 turns the desaturation off.

Luma Correction sets the intensity of spill-corrected pixels, with higher values making the spill areas brighter.

Spill Range sets the aggressiveness of the spill color removal, with higher values removing a greater degree of spill. Changes to this property are most noticeable when the Spill Color Correction value is high.

Figure 2.15 compares different spill removal approaches. The top image of the figure shows the original green screen plate. The second-from-the-top image shows the result of the Keylight effect with the Replace Method menu set to None; with this setting, the spill is not replaced and appears as blue-green trapped within the hair. The third-from-the-top image applies the Advanced Spill Suppressor with Spill Color Correction set to 100, thus inserting purple into the spill area. The bottom image also uses the Advanced Spill Suppressor effect with Desaturate set to 48, Spill Range set to 22, Spill Color Correction set to 5, and Luma Correction set to 17, leaving the hair closer to its original blonde coloration. This project is saved as *spill_suppressor.aep* in the *\ProjectFiles\aeFiles\Chapter2* directory. Note that the saturation in this figure is exaggerated so that the color variations are visible in print.

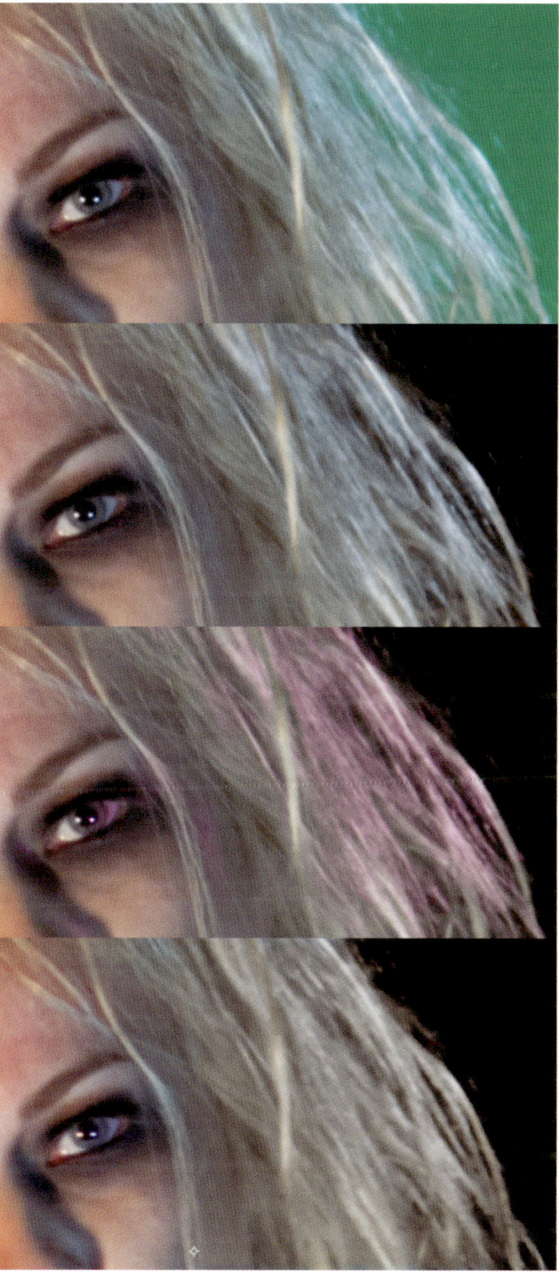

FIG 2.15 A series of spill suppression steps.

Altering Alpha with Mattes

Although chroma key tools are commonly used for visual effects compositing, there are many situations that the tools can't address. For example, the footage might not contain green screen or an otherwise solid-colored backdrop. As such, it may be necessary to generate alpha mattes through other means. After Effects provides the Track Matte function and several channel effects for this reason.

Activating Track Matte

If a composition has at least two layers, lower layers are given a Track Matte option menu. The menu appears under the TrkMat column. (If this is not visible, click the Toggle Switches/Modes button at the bottom of the layer outline.) Track Matte provides a means to borrow alpha information from the layer directly above the layer where Track Matte is activated. The layer above can remain hidden (which is usually desirable so it doesn't occlude the Track Matte result).

If the Track Matte menu is set to Alpha Matte, the alpha information is transferred as is. If the menu is set to Alpha Inverted Matte, the alpha values are inverted and transferred. As an example, in Figures 2.16 and 2.17, the sides of the set are removed by setting the green screen layer's Track Matte menu to Alpha Matte. The alpha is taken from the layer above, which is a scaled and positioned solid. The empty area surrounding the solid layer is considered transparent. Note that this Track Matte technique works in conjunction with a keyer, which removes the green screen.

You can also use Track Matte to generate a luma matte. A luma matte converts RGB brightness values to alpha values. (As a term, *luma* represents gamma-adjusted pixel brightness in digital video systems.) If the Track Matte menu is set to Luma Matte, a grayscale version of the layer directly above is transferred to the alpha channel of the layer where Track Matte is activated. The values are inverted if the menu is set to Luma Inverted Matte.

Creating a Custom Luma Matte

You can create your own luma matte by moving values between channels. As discussed in Chapter 1, a channel carries pixel brightness values, whether that channel is a color channel or an alpha channel.

The Set Matte effect (Effect > Channel > Set Matte) allows you to transfer non-alpha-channel values from any layer within the composition to the alpha channel of the layer that carries the effect. To make this transfer, change the Take Matte From Layer to the layer that has the desired channel information. Change the Use For Matte menu to the channel you wish to use. As an example, in Figure 2.18, the red channel of a fireworks layer is transferred

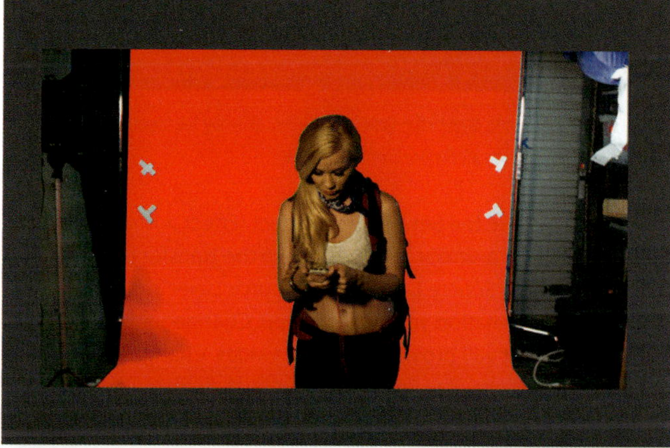

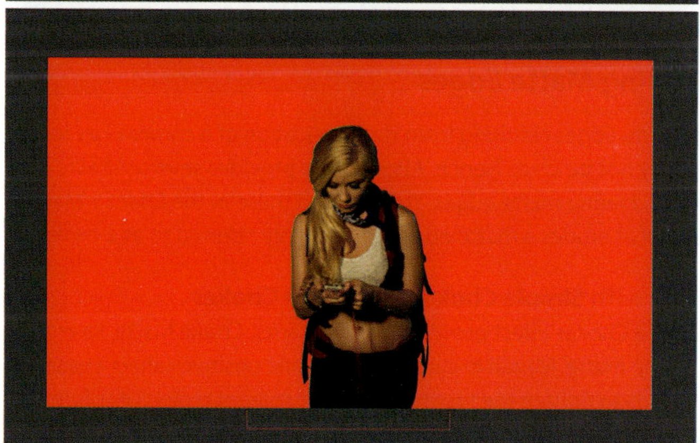

FIG 2.16 Top: A scaled solid sits on a top layer. Middle: A keyed green screen sits on the middle layer and a red solid sits on the lowest layer. Bottom: The middle layer Track Matte menu is set to Alpha Matte, which causes it to take alpha information from the top solid and thereby cut off the set edges. This project is saved as *track_matte.aep* in the *\ProjectFiles\aeFiles\Chapter2* directory.

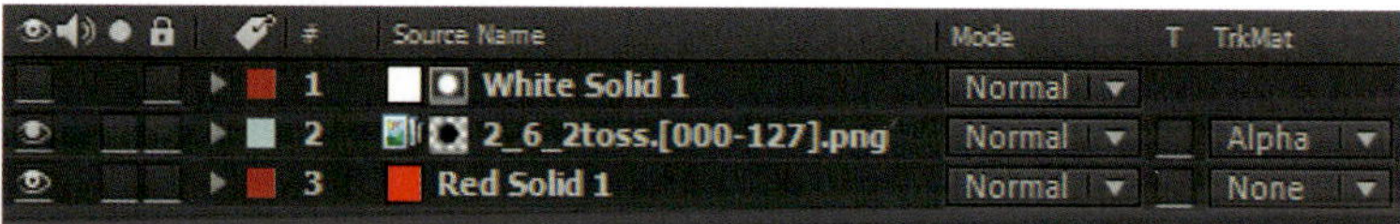

FIG 2.17 The three layers used for the Track Matte operation. The top solid is ultimately hidden by turning off the Video eye icon.

to the same fireworks layer as alpha information. Thus, the fireworks cut themselves out so they may be placed over a lower layer, which feature a city with an otherwise empty sky.

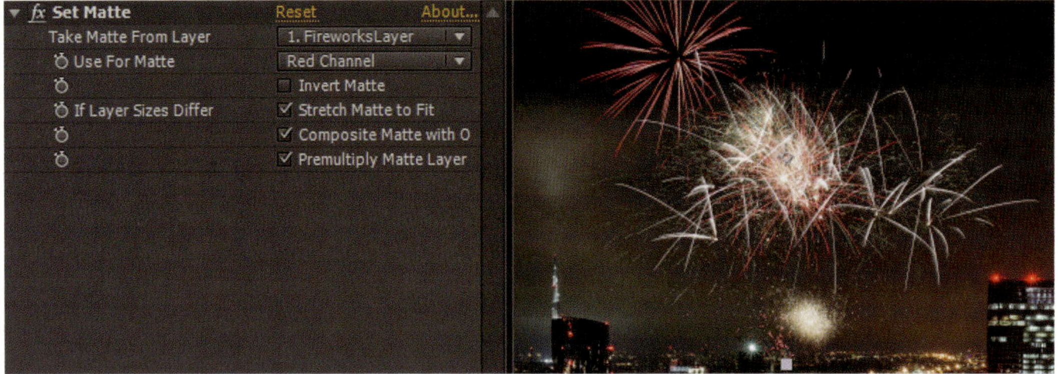

FIG 2.18 The Set Matte effect transfers the red channel values of a fireworks layer to the same layer's alpha, allowing the fireworks to appear on top of a city layer. *Fireworks photo © James Pintar/Dollar Photo Club. City photo © Simone Simone/Dollar Photo Club.*

In addition, you can use the Set Channels effect (Effect > Channel > Set Channels) to generate a similar result. To make the transfer between channels, set the Source Layer 1, Source Layer 2, and Source Layer 3 menus to the layer that has the RGB information you wish to keep. Change the Source Layer 4 menu to the layer that will provide the luma values. Change the Set Alpha To Source 4's menu to Alpha. The Set Channels effect also provides a means to transfer values between color channels to create stylistic results; for example, you can change the Set *Color* To Source *Number* menus to mismatching colors.

Improving Matte Edges

Alpha matte edges resulting from the application of a chroma key tool or luma matte may not be ideal. Hence, After Effects provides several effects designed to alter and refine matte edges. You can find these in the Effect > Matte menu. Any tool that erodes a matte edge is commonly referred to as a *choker*.

Refining with Simple Choker and Matte Choker

The Simple Choker effect provides a single slider, Choke Matte, to erode or expand the matte. Negative values erode while positive values expand. The effect tends to tighten the tapered, semitransparent region of soft matte edge.

The Matte Choker effect provides two "chokers" within one tool. Each choker is provided with three controls: Geometric Softness, Choke, and Gray Level Softness. Geometric Softness specifies the maximum pixel width of the semitransparent edge taper, as created by the effect. Choke sets the size of the matte erosion (positive values) or matte expansion (negative values).

Gray Level Softness sets the edge softness, with a value of 0 percent creating a hard edge with no semitransparent pixels and 100 percent creating the maximum softness available based on the other two settings. Note that it is not necessary to use both chokers—choker 2 is off by default as the Choke 2 property is set to 0. As a demonstration, in Figure 2.19 a keyed alpha edge is improved with the Matte Choker effect.

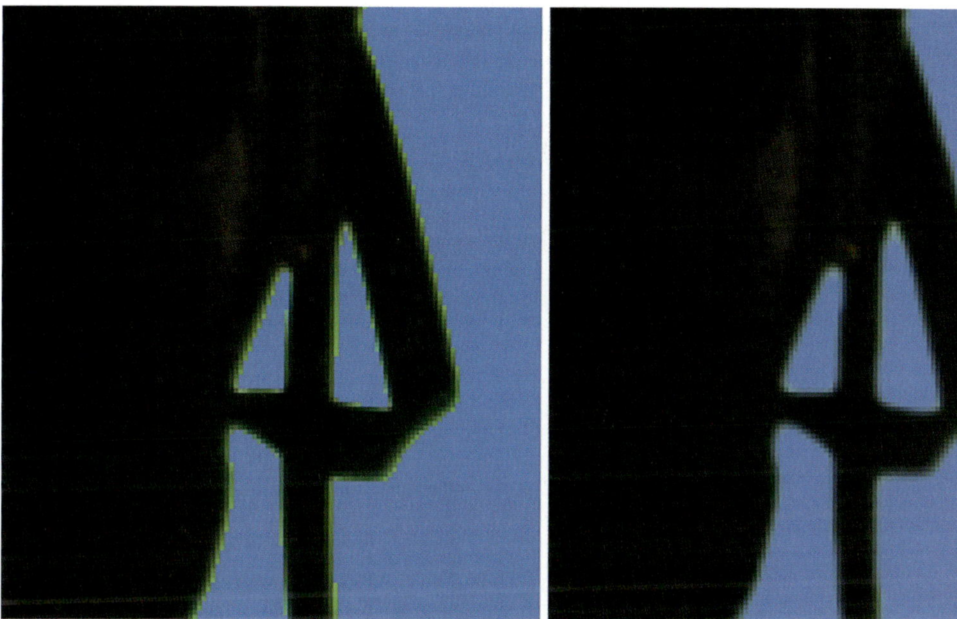

FIG 2.19 Left: Close-up of a keyed green screen that carries a hard edge with green spill. Right: The Matte Choker effect refines the edge through erosion and softening. This project is saved as *matte_choker.aep* in the *\ProjectFiles\aeFiles\Chapter2* directory.

Using Refine Soft Matte

The Refine Soft Matte effect offers a significant improvement over the older Simple Choker and Matte Choker effects. In particular, the effect is able to maintain subtle edge semitransparency around small details such as loose hairs. In addition, the effect maintains proper motion blur on fast-moving objects, something that standard keyers are unable to fully address. The improvement is achieved by tapering the edge transparency while remaining sensitive to small foreground detail that should otherwise remain more opaque.

You can alter the size of the semitransparent edge by adjusting the Additional Edge Radius value. You can visualize this edge area by selecting the View Edge Region check box. The region is colored yellow. Higher Additional Edge Radius values have the tendency to fill in otherwise desirable holes, so a default value of 0 often creates the best quality. You can further fine-tune the result by adjusting the Smooth, Feather, Contrast, and Shift Edge sliders, which control their namesakes.

As mentioned, the effect is able to maintain semitransparency created by motion blur trails (Figure 2.20). You can artificially increase the softness of these trails by selecting the More Motion Blur check box. Much like other keyers, Refine Soft Matte attempts to remove or reduce the detected background color. This is controlled by the Decontaminate Edge Colors check box. You can adjust the aggressiveness of the background color reduction by adjusting the Decontamination Amount slider.

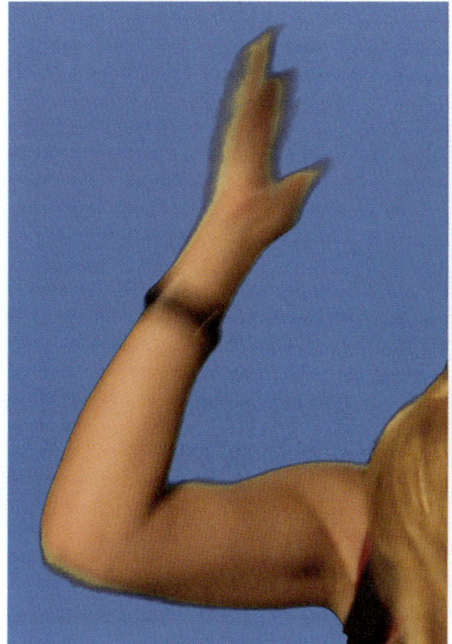

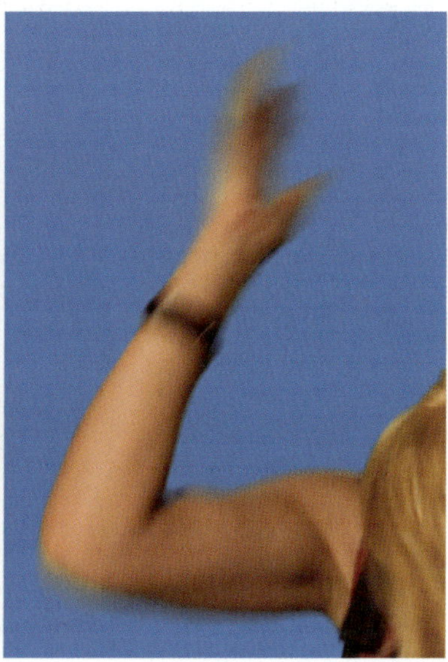

FIG 2.20 Left: A plate with a large amount of motion blur is keyed with Keylight, producing dark edges in the blur areas. Right: The Refine Soft Matte effect is applied with More Motion Blur selected, eroding the dark lines while maintaining semitransparent motion blur streaks. The blue background is added as a solid on a lower layer. This project is saved as *refine_soft_matte.aep* in the *\ProjectFiles\aeFiles\Chapter2* directory.

Note that Refine Soft Matte is particularly sensitive to the image fed to it. For example, a noisy key can cause the effect to perform poorly. In addition, unpremultiplied pixels can create harsh edges. The premultiplication process multiplies alpha values by RGB values for the sake of mathematical efficiency. Unpremultiplication does the opposite. By default, Keylight unpremultiplies its output. Hence, to create clean alpha with Keylight and Refine Soft Matte effects, deselect Keylight's Unpremultiply Result check box. Refine Soft Matte is also prone to jittering over time. Hence, the effect includes the Chatter Reduction and Reduce Chatter properties. These properties are explored further in the tutorial at the end of this chapter.

Despite the similarity in names and properties, the underlying algorithms used by the Refine Soft Matte and Refine Hard Matte effects vary. The most significant difference is that Refine Hard Matte lacks the ability to examine foreground edge detail or expand the semitransparent matte edge. As such, Refine Hard Matte does not carry the Calculate Edge Details, Additional Edge

Radius, View Edge Region, and More Motion Blur properties. Of the two effects, Refine Soft Matte generally produces superior results.

Chapter Tutorial: Keying a Difficult Green Screen, Part 1

As discussed in this chapter, green screen plates are rarely perfect. Limitations of time and money may cause the plate to carry such imperfections as uneven lighting, shadows, wrinkles, and visible tracking marks. For this tutorial, we'll work with a green screen plate that has all those problems (see Figure 2.6 earlier in this chapter). By the end, we'll produce a clean key.

1. Start with a new project in After Effects. Choose File > Import > File. Browse to the *\ProjectFiles\Plates\Greenscreen\1_3f_2sing* directory. Select the first frame of the PNG image sequence. Make sure that PNG Sequence remains selected near the bottom right of the Import File window. Click the Import button.
2. The image sequence is brought into the Project panel as a single unit. With the sequence selected, check the thumbnail at the top of the Project panel. The desired frame rate is 24 fps. If a different frame rate is listed, RMB-click over the sequence and choose Interpret Footage > Main. In the Interpret Footage window, change the Assume This Frame Rate field to 24 and click the OK button to close the window.
3. LMB-drag the footage into the empty timeline. A new composition is automatically created that carries the same resolution, frame rate, and duration as the image sequence. This sequence is 1920x1080 with a duration of 72 frames. To rename the composition, RMB-click the composition in the Project panel and choose Rename. You can type a new name over the old one and press the Enter key to finalize it.
4. With the new layer selected, choose Effect > Keying > Keylight 1.2. Go to the Effect Controls panel. (If the panel is missing, choose Window > Effect Controls.) Using the Screen Colour eyedropper, select the green of the green screen in the Composition view panel. Select a mid-tone. For example, with the eyedropper active, click a green area near the left arm of the actress. The alpha matte is automatically generated.
5. Although the matte appears fairly clean, there is noise created by the wrinkles in the green screen fabric, shadows, and uneven lighting. To see this, change Keylight's View menu to Combined Matte (Figure 2.21).
6. Expand Keylight's Screen Matte section. Slowly raise Clip Black and note the results. With a value of 33, Clip Black removes the noise from the background area. However, the fine hair is slightly eroded. Slowly lower the Clip White value and note the result. At a value of 72, Clip White returns opaqueness to the majority of the foreground (the actress). The hair is slightly restored. If you lower the Clip White slider further, any remaining black and gray pixels disappear in the foreground; however, the hair becomes hard-edged.

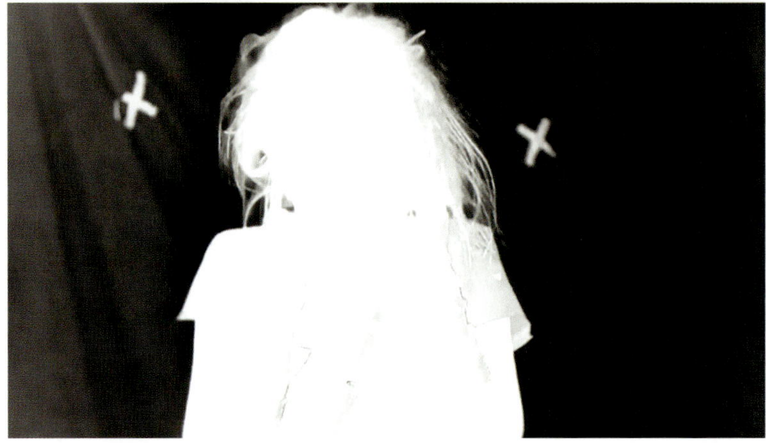

FIG 2.21 The initial key with the Keylight effect.

7. Return the View menu to Final Result. Skip across the timeline to look at several frames. Zoom into the edges and examine them. The edge along the hair remains rough. Some hairs are broken into multiple parts. In addition, the hair along the edges is somewhat gray and colorless. The gray is inserted by the Replace Method menu, which is set to Soft Colour by default. Change the Replace Method menu to Source, which adds back the original pixel values. Green spill reappears (Figure 2.22). Change the Replace Method menu to None. This deactivates the color replacement and significantly affects the alpha edge. The fine hairs reappear. Return the View menu to Combined Matte. Note that the restored area is mostly semitransparent. To see how this affects the layer, return View to Final Result and place a new solid at the bottom of the layer outline. You can create a new solid by choosing Layer > New > Solid. For example, if an orange solid is placed below the green screen layer, the outer fine hairs appear bright and glowy (Figure 2.23).

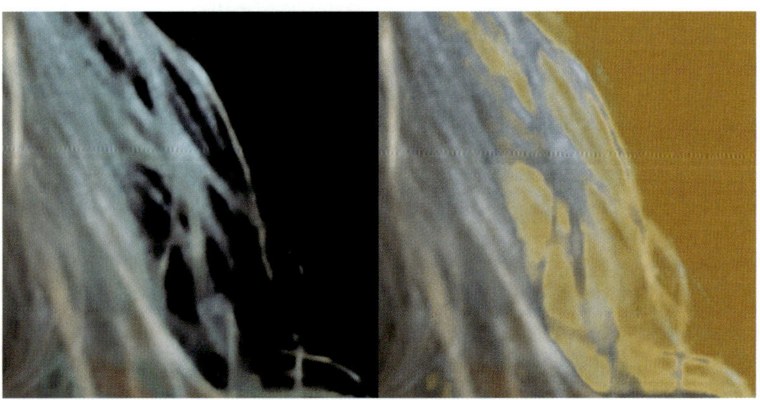

FIG 2.22 Left: Replace Method is set to Source, which reintroduces the green spill. Right: Replace Method is set to None, which creates bright outer hairs when the layer is placed over a second layer, such as an orange solid.

8. Return Replace Method to Source. We'll remove the green spill through the use of Refine Soft Matte. In anticipation of this, deselect the Unpremultiply Result check box (below the View menu). The hair edge temporarily gains a dark line. Choose Effect > Matte > Refine Soft Matte. The hair edge becomes softer. However, some areas of the hair remain blurry. Reduce the Additional Edge Radius to 0.5 to remove the blurred areas but retain some of the finer hairs.
9. The spill removal function of Refine Soft Matte causes the hair edge to become more blue-green. Return to Keylight and change the Replace Method menu to Soft Colour. Change the Replace Colour swatch to dark red (RGB values 22, 13, 7). You can use the Replace Colour eyedropper to sample a dark area of the hair. The spill area shifts slightly toward red, thus reducing the amount of blue-green (Figure 2.23).

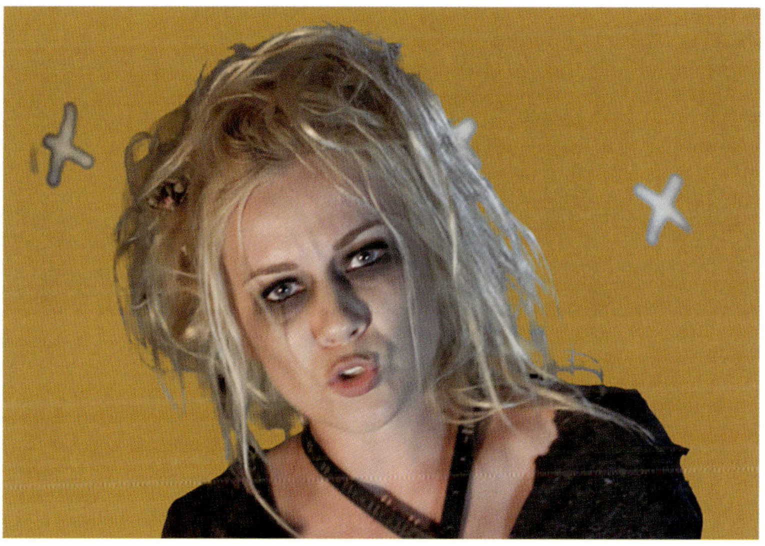

FIG 2.23 The spill area of the hair is shifted from the blue-green produced by Refine Soft Matte toward a more neutral, slightly reddish color by changing Keylight's Replace Method to Soft Colour and Replace Colour to dark red.

10. To judge the quality of the key over time, play back the timeline. The Refine Soft Matte effect causes some areas of the hair to jitter and bubble. To reduce these artifacts, deselect Calculate Edge Details. This prevents the effect from reconstructing small edge detail. Although this causes the loss of some fine hairs, the resulting key stays more consistent. Reduce the Decontamination Amount to 50 percent. This reduces the aggressiveness of the spill removal along the edges, making the colors more consistent over time. Change the Chatter Reduction menu to More Detailed and Reduce Chatter to 100 percent. These properties specifically target inconsistent edge interpretation over time. Play back the timeline again. The hair is more stable.

11. The steps thus far have failed to address the tracking tape marks and the edge of the set that appears on screen left. In addition, Refine Soft Matte effect creates a gray smudged area at the top left (Figure 2.24). Rotoscoping offers means to solve these problems. In addition, rotoscoping can provide a way to refine any edge quality that we are not completely satisfied with. Hence, we'll return to this tutorial in Chapter 3. The project, at this juncture, is saved as *tutorial_2_1.aep* in the *\ProjectFiles\aeFiles\Chapter2* directory.

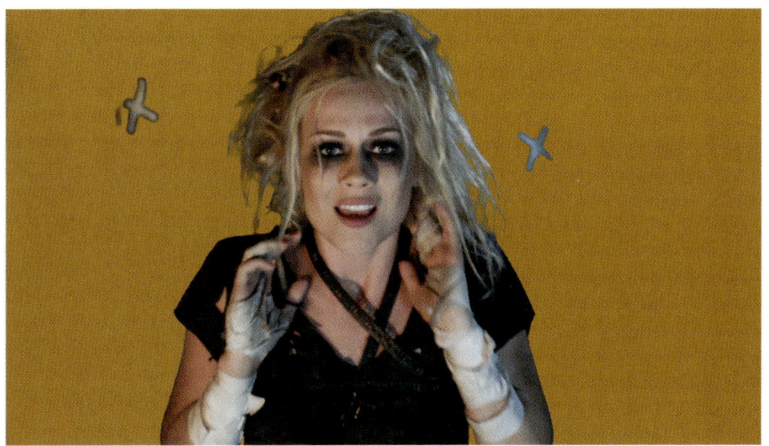

FIG 2.24 The key at the end of Part 1, as seen on frame 6.

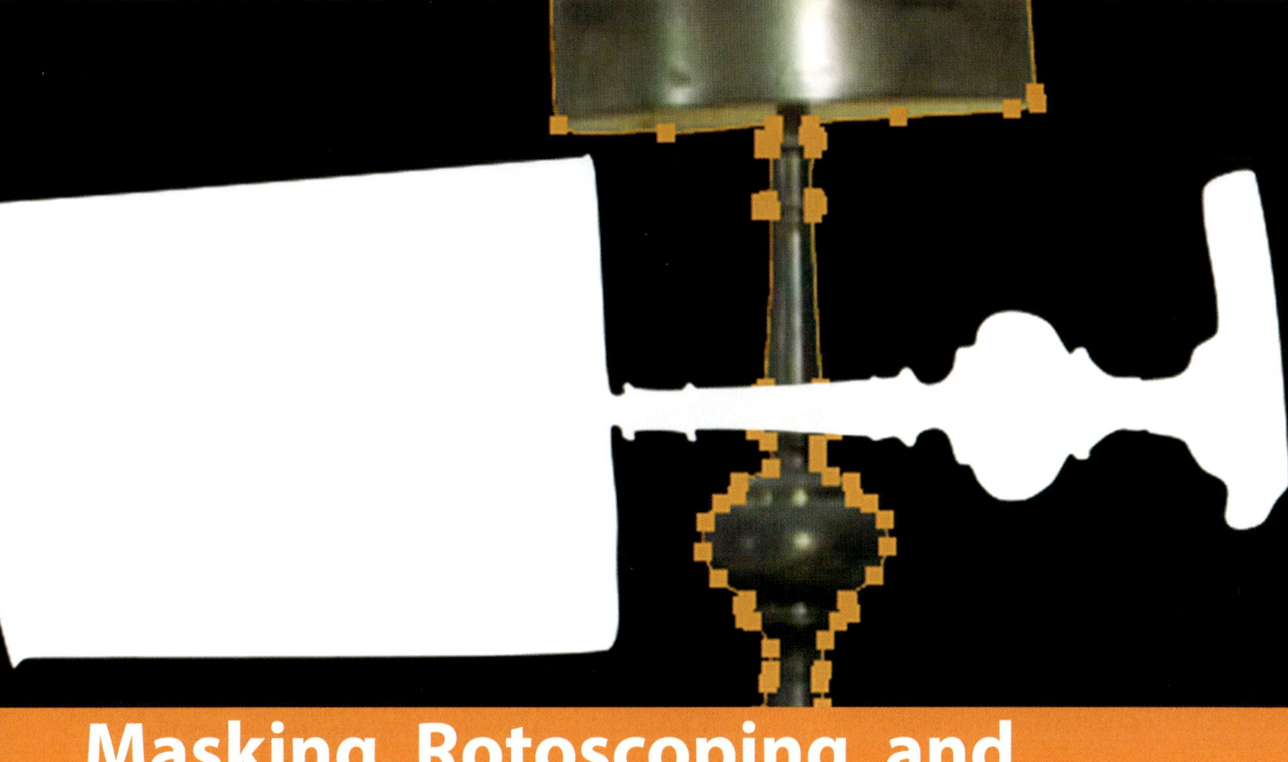

Masking, Rotoscoping, and Basic Keyframing

In Chapter 2, we discussed the creation of alpha transparency through the application of chroma key tools and custom mattes that shifted information between channels. Although these techniques are useful in many visual effects situations, there are other approaches that are commonly used. These include masking and rotoscoping. *Masking* is the process by which you draw or import a spline shape to define an alpha matte (Figure 3.1). Rotoscoping simply adds animation to the mask so that it changes shape over time. In addition to masks, you can animate properties in After Effects—these include transform properties and effect properties. The program provides a robust Graph Editor for fine-tuning the resulting keyframes and animation curves.

This chapter includes the following critical information:

- Creation and manipulation of masks with the Pen tool
- Application of Roto Brush and importation of masks
- Basic keyframing techniques on the timeline and in the Graph Editor

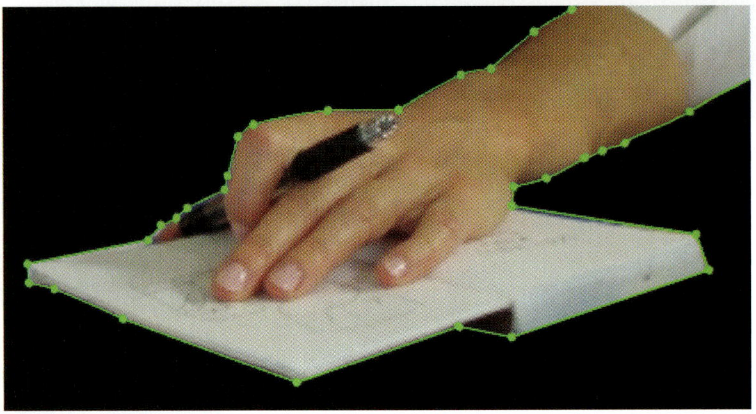

FIG 3.1 A drawn mask, colored green, separates a hand and book from the original background.

Creating Masks

Masks come in two main forms: masks that retain a part of the scene and masks that remove part of the scene. Masks that retain are often referred to as *holdout masks*. Masks that remove are often referred to as *garbage masks* (as they remove unwanted "garbage" from the frame). Note that the words *mask* and *matte* are often interchanged. For the purposes of this book, I'll refer to a *mask* as a drawn or painted shape that creates the alpha *matte*.

After Effects offers several methods for drawing masks. These include the Pen tool and its variants, as well as the Roto Brush tool.

Using the Pen Tool

You can draw a custom mask with the Pen tool, which is available via the main toolbar at the top left of the After Effects program window. The Pen tool creates a series of vertices that form a spline shape. If the shape is closed, the area within the shape is assigned 100 percent opaque alpha while areas outside the shape receive 100 percent transparent alpha values. (In terms of color vales on an 8-bit scale, transparent pixels become 0-black and opaque pixels become 255-white.)

You can follow these basic steps for the Pen tool's application:

1. Select the layer you wish to mask. Click the Pen Tool button (Figure 3.2). In the Composition view, LMB-click to place a spline vertex. Continue to LMB-click to add additional vertices to form the spline shape. Note that the spans between vertices are linear by default.

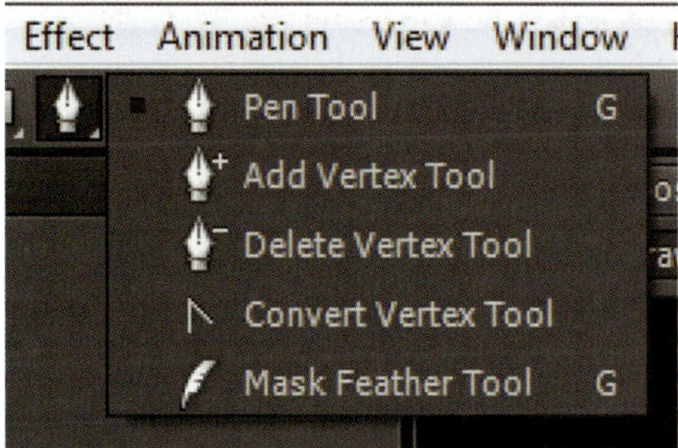

FIG 3.2 The Pen tool and its variants.

2. When you're ready to close the shape, place your mouse over the first vertex that you drew. A small "close" circle is added to the mouse icon. LMB-click the first vertex. The spline is closed and the mask is finished. The alpha values are automatically updated for the layer (Figure 3.3). Lower layers show through the transparent outer area. If there are no lower layers, the transparent area is filled in with empty black.

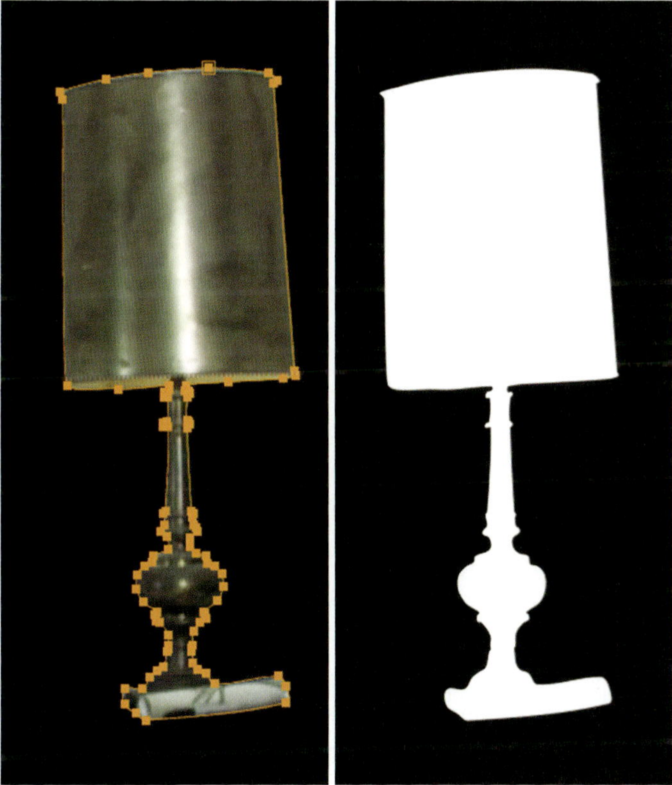

FIG 3.3 A drawn mask surrounds a lamp. The resulting alpha channel is shown on the right.

3. Access the layer properties by clicking the small expansion arrow beside the layer name in the layer outline. Expand the Masks section. The new mask is listed as *Mask 1*. Expand the Mask 1 section. The mask properties, including Mask Path, Mask Feather, Mask Opacity, and Mask Expansion are listed (Figure 3.4). By default, the mask is static. However, you can animate these properties over time to create rotoscoping (this is discussed later in this chapter).

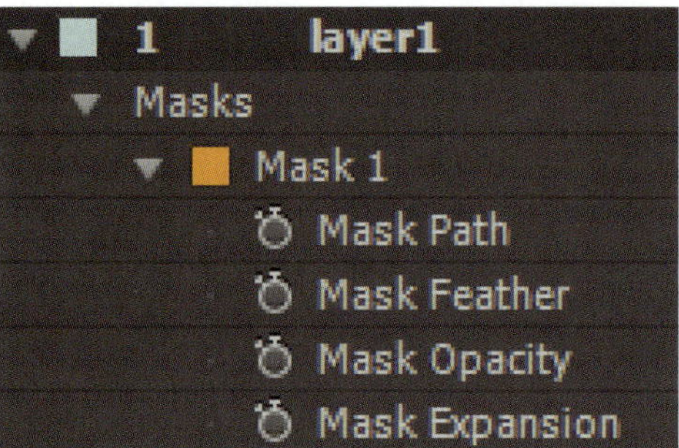

FIG 3.4 Mask properties in the layer outline.

4. To soften the mask edge, increase the Mask Feather. There are two values, X direction and Y direction, which are linked by default. To reduce the opacity of the masked shape, whereby the opaque alpha area becomes semitransparent, reduce the Mask Opacity value. To "grow" the mask, so the opaque border pushes outwards, raise the Mask Expansion value. To shrink the mask, enter negative values into the Mask Expansion field.

Altering Existing Masks

You can manipulate a mask at any point. To do so, you can apply any combination of techniques listed here:

- To move a vertex, switch to the Selection tool (the leftmost tool in the program's main toolbar), LMB-click the vertex in the Composition or Layer view, and LMB-drag. You can select multiple vertices by Shift-LMB-clicking them one at a time.
- You can also LMB-drag a selection marquee over multiple vertices after selecting the mask. To select a mask, click on the mask name in the layer outline or click on a mask segment (the line between vertices) in the Composition or Layer view.
- To deselect vertices, LMB-click off the mask in an empty area of the view panel.
- You can delete a vertex and thus alter the spline shape by selecting it and pressing the Delete key.
- You can transform a mask as a single unit by double-clicking on a mask segment. In this case, a transform box appears and all the mask's

vertices are selected (Figure 3.5). To move the entire mask, LMB-drag the transform box by placing the mouse in the interior of the box. To scale the mask, LMB-drag the box handles (the small, hollow squares). To rotate the mask, LMB-drag outside the box edge (the mouse turns into a double-headed arrow). To escape the transform box, double-click in an empty area outside the box.

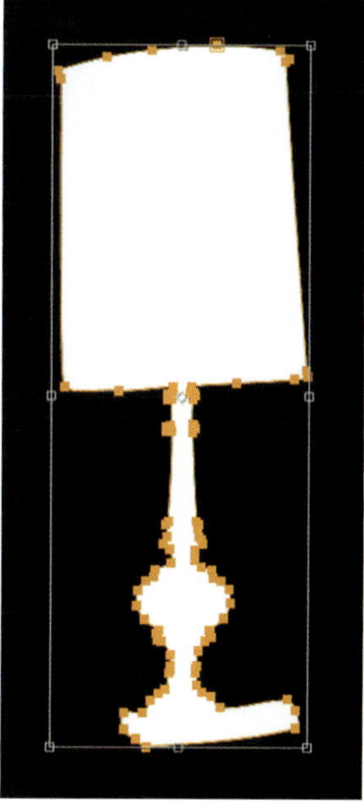

FIG 3.5 A mask transform box.

In addition, masks provide the following functionality:

- The vertex positions and overall mask shape are stored by the Mask Path property. You can keyframe Mask Path and thereby shift the mask shape over time. This is explored in the "Rotoscoping" section later in this chapter.
- If you start drawing a mask while no layer is selected, the mask is applied to a new shape layer. Hence, the mask cuts out a solid-colored shape. See the "Importing Bitmap and Vector Masks" section later in this chapter for more information on shape layers.
- If you wish to delete a mask, select a mask and press the Delete key.
- You can copy and paste a mask between layers. For example, select a mask, press Ctrl/Cmd+C, LMB-click the name of a different layer, and press Ctrl/Cmd+V.
- You can temporarily hide the mask segments and vertices in the view panel by clicking the Toggle Mask And Shape Path Visibility button. This may be useful when judging the impact of a mask or examining the quality of the resulting matte edge.
- You can close an unclosed mask by selecting the mask and choosing Layer > Mask And Shape Path > Closed. If you are drawing a mask, you can finish the spline before it's closed by switching to a different tool, such as the Selection tool.
- A layer can hold multiple masks with each one numerically named Mask *n*. You can rename a mask by RMB-clicking the mask name and choosing Rename. You can choose your own color for each mask by clicking the color box beside the mask name.
- You can create a mask with a predefined primitive shape by using the mask shape button set found on the main toolbar (to the immediate left of the Pen Tool button). You have the option to create a rectangle, rounded rectangle, ellipse, five-sided polygon, or star. Choose one of these tools and LMB-drag in the Composition view; when you release the mouse button, the mask size and rotation is fixed.

Combining Masks to Make Complex Shapes

When masking a complex shape, it's often easier to combine multiple masks. For example, you can draw one mask for a person's head, a second mask for a person's torso, and a third mask for a person's legs. In Figure 3.6, three masks are combined to separate an actress from the background.

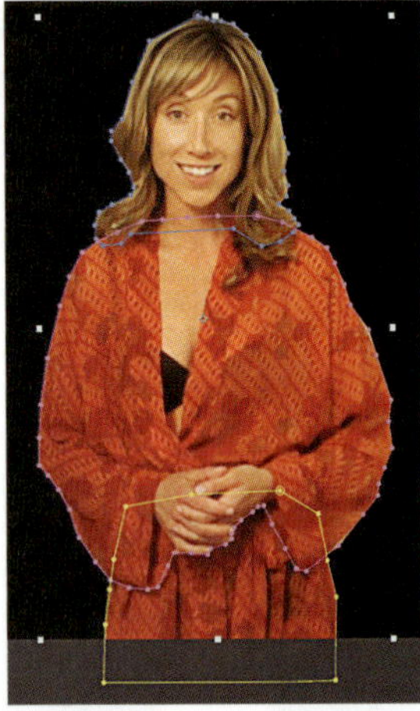

FIG 3.6 Three masks are combined to separate an actress from the background.

The larger, hollow vertex on a mask represents the mask origin (where the mask was started and closed). The white squares at the mask edges represent the bounding box of the cut out layer. Note that there is no penalty for extending a closed mask outside the edge of the frame. This ability is particularly useful when you need to animate a mask over time.

By default, all masks on a single layer are added together. That is, all the opaque areas are added together and maintained. You also have the option to select a unique mathematical blending mode for each mask. As soon as two or more masks exist on a layer, a blending mode menu appears beside each mask's name. The use of the blending mode menu is required for cutting holes into masks. For example, in Figure 3.7, two masks separate the head of an actress. However, in order to maintain a hole in the hair, a second mask is added with the Subtract blending mode.

The mask order, as they are stacked in the Masks section of the layer outline, affects the way in which masks are combined. With the Figure 3.7 setup, the large mask, Mask 1, is at the top of the Masks section. It's set to Add. The small mask, Mask 2, is at the bottom of the Masks section. It's set to Subtract.

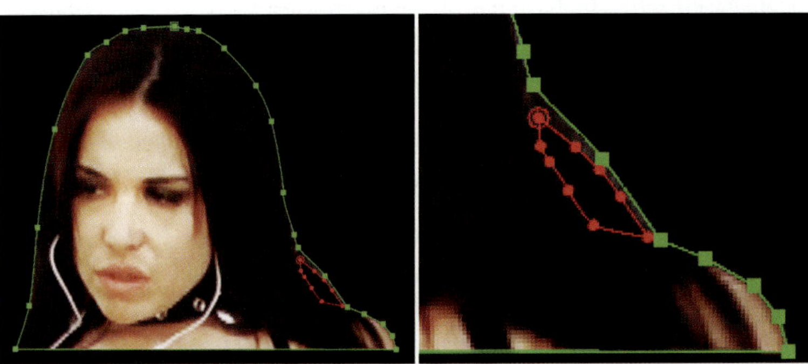

FIG 3.7 A second, smaller mask cuts a hole in the first mask when its blending mode is set to Subtract.

If you were to reverse the order and place Mask 2 on top, the masks fail to cut out the actress. Nevertheless, you are free to change the mask order by LMB-dragging the mask names up or down in the Masks section.

Aside from Add, Subtract, and None, which turns a mask off, the following blending modes are available:

Intersect keeps the overlapping section between the mask that is set to Intersect and all other masks. To make the intersection function, place the mask that is set to Intersect at the bottom of the Masks section.
Difference gives you a result that is opposite of Intersect, whereby mask areas that *do not* overlap the mask that is set to Difference are kept.
Lighten uses the highest Mask Opacity value in overlapping areas for the mask that is set to Lighten.

Darken uses the lowest Mask Opacity value in overlapping areas for the mask that is set to Darken.

Each mask also carries an Inverted check box. If this is selected, the mask is inverted and what was opaque becomes transparent and vice versa. Note that the None blending mode is useful while drawing or adjusting multiple masks in order to see the entire unmasked frame.

Adjusting a Mask with Pen Variants

The Pen tool is accompanied by additional tools for manipulating masks. These are available by LMB-clicking and holding the Pen Tool button (see Figure 3.2 earlier in this chapter). Descriptions of each follow:

Add Vertex Tool

This tool allows you insert a new vertex where you LMB-click on a mask segment. (You can also add new vertices on a preexisting mask by LMB-clicking with the Pen tool.)

Delete Vertex Tool

Delete Vertex removes the vertex that you LMB-click. It's recommended that you add or delete vertices on a mask before animating the mask.

Convert Vertex Tool

This tool converts a vertex from a linear tangent to a smooth tangent or vice versa. A smooth tangent provides a tangent handle on either side of the vertex (Figure 3.8). You can LMB-drag the tangent ends to adjust the resulting curve segments. You can also lengthen or shorten the tangent handles to affect the shape. Shorter tangent handles create tighter bends while longer tangent handles create more gradual bends. While the default linear segments may be more appropriate for masking mechanical or architectural elements, smooth tangents allow you to follow organic forms more closely. You can create smooth tangents as you draw a mask if you LMB-click and drag before releasing the

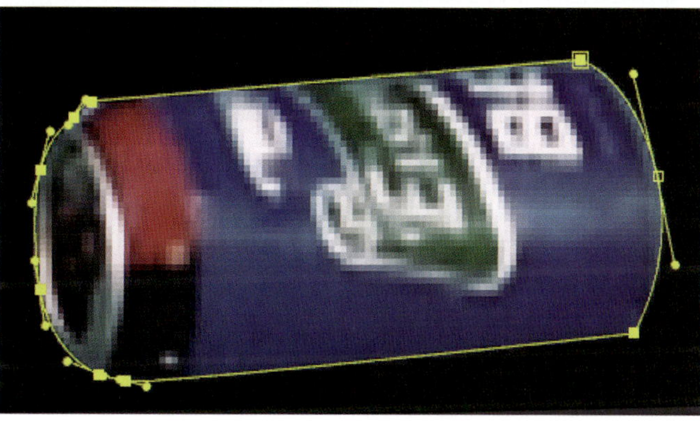

FIG 3.8 Close-up of a masked can. A combination of linear and smooth vertices is used. Note the varying length of the smooth tangent handles.

mouse button. As you drag, the tangent handle is formed in the direction of the mouse. (Adobe refers to the tangent handles as *direction lines*.)

Mask Feather Tool

By default, the transition from 100 percent opaque alpha pixels to 100 percent transparent pixels occurs over one pixel. You can "feather" the alpha matte edge, however, by applying the Mask Feather tool. When you LMB-click a mask segment with the tool, a feather point is created and a feather region surrounds the entire mask. You can LMB-drag the feather point closer or farther from the mask path to increase or decrease the feather region. The farther the feather point is from the mask, the more gradual the taper is from opaqueness to transparency (Figure 3.9). Such a taper is often useful for masking objects that carry motion blur or otherwise have a soft edge. You can vary a feather around a mask by inserting multiple feather points. You can place each feather point at a unique location and give each one a unique distance from the mask. You can adjust the "tension" of the feather—the way in which the feather segments run between feather points—by selecting a feather point with the Mask Feather tool and Alt/Opt-LMB-dragging left or right over the point. The action will make the feather segments "tighter" or "looser" to the points. You can delete a feather point by selecting it and

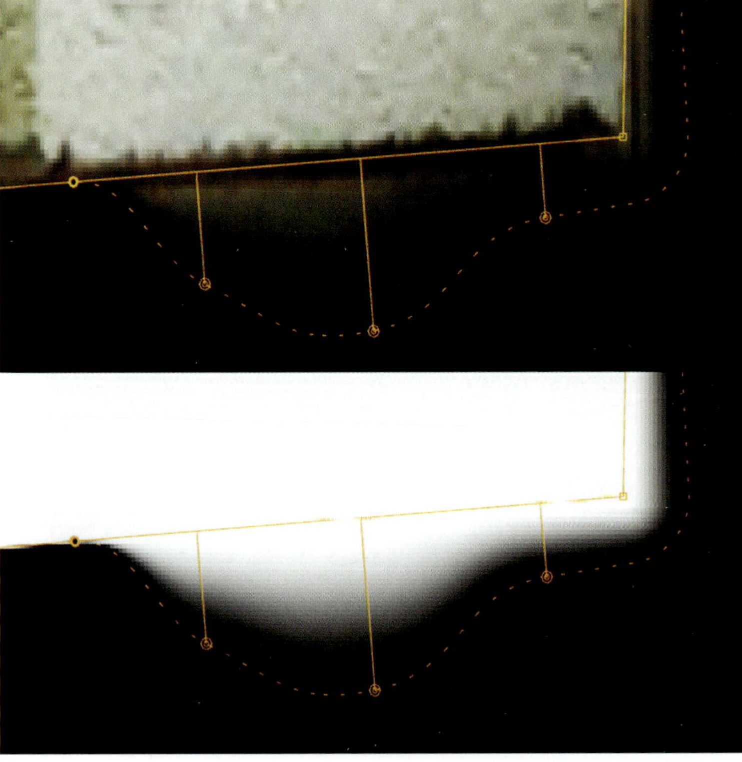

FIG 3.9 Top: A mask with four feather points placed at different distances from the mask path. Bottom: The resulting alpha channel. Note that the feather continues around the entire mask unless stopped by feather points placed directly on a mask segment (as is the case with the leftmost feather point).

pressing the Delete key. If the feather points become hidden, click on a vertex with the Mask Feather tool.

Switching to RotoBezier

After Effects provides an alternative method of controlling mask tangents via the RotoBezier option. If a significant amount of mask manipulation is necessary, whether a mask shape is intricate with a large number of vertices or the mask must constantly change shape through rotoscoping, RotoBezier may offer a time-saving method of manipulation.

To use RotoBezier, you must convert the mask. To do so, select the mask in the layer outline and choose Layer > Mask And Shape Path > RotoBezier. When the mask is converted to RotoBezier, you can interactively adjust the vertex tangents in the following ways:

- To make the segments surrounding a vertex more linear, switch to the Convert Vertex tool and LMB-drag over the top of the vertex toward the left in the Composition or Layer view.
- To make the segments surrounding a vertex smoother, switch to the Convert Vertex tool and LMB-drag over the top of the vertex toward the right in the Composition or Layer view.

To disable RotoBezier, choose Layer > Mask And Shape Path > RotoBezier so that the option becomes deselected. When using RotoBezier, the tangent handles are hidden and are not directly accessible. You can use RotoBezier with the Mask Feather tool.

Rotoscoping

Rotoscoping is the process by which you animate a mask over time to follow a moving object. Before the advent of digital compositing, rotoscoping was created by drawing and painting masks on paper in preparation for motion picture optical printing. Rotoscoping allows you to separate an object from a background so that a new background may be inserted below it. Rotoscoping is also useful for creating a garbage mask that is intended to remove an unwanted, moving object.

In After Effects, the primary method of rotoscoping is through the keyframe animation to masks created with the Pen tool. However, you can also automate the process by using the Roto Brush. In the realm of digital animation, a *keyframe* or *key* is a stored value for a property at a particular frame on the timeline. A series of keyframes form an animation curve. Positions on the curve that do not carry keyframes provide interpolated, "inbetween" values for the property. A property may be a mask shape, a transform such as Scale, or an effect slider.

As an alternative to manually keyframing a mask, you can motion track the feature isolated by a mask over time. For a demonstration, see Chapter 4.

Keyframing a Mask

When a mask is animated, you don't have access to the animation curves for each vertex. Instead, the entire mask shape is given a single curve stored by the Mask Path property. To keyframe a mask, you can follow these basic steps:

1. Move the timeline to the frame where you'd like to place the first keyframe. Click the Time icon beside the Mask Path property below the mask name. A keyframe is laid on the timeline. This stores all the vertex and tangent positions of the mask.
2. Move the timeline to a different frame. Alter the shape of the mask (see the section "Altering Existing Masks" earlier in this chapter). As soon as you alter the shape, a new keyframe is automatically laid down. Optionally, you can disable the mask by setting its blending mode menu to None; this allows you to see the entire unmasked frame.
3. Continue to move to different frames and alter the mask shape. Any frame that does not carry a keyframe generates an inbetween mask shape by interpolating between mask shapes defined by nearby keyframes.

You can edit existing keyframes. For more information, see the "Editing Keyframes on the Timeline" section later in the chapter. To determine where keyframes should be placed, see the guidelines in the next section.

Rotoscoping Approaches

There are several different approaches you can take when rotoscoping. The approach you take is largely dependent on the type of footage you are working with and the style with which you feel the most comfortable. Nevertheless, here are some general guidelines you can follow:

Straight Ahead

If the object you are rotoscoping is moving slowly or moving in a predictable fashion, you can keyframe in a straight ahead manner. *Straight ahead* is a traditional animation technique whereby keys are set from the beginning to the end of the timeline without concern for the type of motion the footage may contain at a later point. For example, you would set a keyframe at frame 1, then 10, then 20, and so on until the end. The more predictable the motion and the less the object silhouette changes, the fewer keyframes you need to successfully follow the object.

Key Poses

If the object you are rotoscoping moves in an erratic manner or the object's silhouette constantly changes, you can apply the key poses technique. In traditional animation, *key poses* are the most critical positions of the animated object or character. For example, if a character is walking, critical key poses occur where each foot touches the ground and where each foot is raised to pass the other. By studying the footage in After Effects, you can identify the most critical positions and add keyframes to those frames. Such positions often represent the largest silhouette shape changes. For example, if you are rotoscoping a baseball pitcher throwing a ball, the largest silhouette changes occur as the pitcher winds up, as he pulls his arm back to throw, and as his arm extends forward to release the ball. These changes are often referred to as *extremes*, where an appendage (an arm, leg, hand, foot, and so on) is at its most extreme position.

Bisecting

You can refine the straight ahead or key poses rotoscoping techniques by bisecting. Bisecting requires the insertion of new keyframes between old keyframes. For example, if you have keyframes at 1, 10, and 20, you would add new keyframes at 5 and 15. You can also bisect at the start of the animation process. For example, if the timeline is 200 frames long, you would add keyframes in the following pattern: 1, 200, 100, 50, 150, 25, 75, 125, and 175 (Figure 3.10). Each new keyframe is placed halfway between each pair of old keyframes. Bisecting in such a regular fashion is suitable for objects with slow-moving or predictable motion.

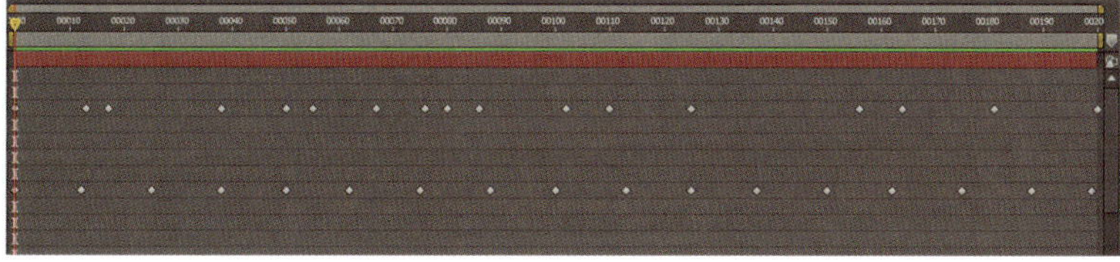

FIG 3.10 A 200-frame timeline with two animated masks. The top mask uses the key poses technique to follow erratic object motion. The lower mask uses the bisecting technique where keyframes are placed at bisected intervals.

Inbetweens

Regardless of the rotocoping approach you take, you generally need to add inbetween keyframes to take into account nonlinear variations in the object motion. These are placed wherever the mask is not accurately following. For example, an automobile may make a subtle change in speed, an actress may turn her head slightly, or an actor's hair may form different shapes due to wind. In traditional animation, inbetween keyframes are less important poses that fall between the keys, but are nevertheless needed to create continuous, smooth motion.

Rotoscoping with Roto Brush

Drawing and manipulating masks, a very common task with visual effects work, can be extremely time-consuming. Hence, After Effects supplies the Roto Brush tool to make the process semi-automated. Roto Brush allows you to interactively define foreground and background elements. With this information, the tool detects the foreground edge and forms a closed mask with opaque alpha in its center. After the foreground is defined, Roto Brush continues to update the mask shape as the timeline moves forward. Roto Brush lives on a layer as an effect and is bundled with the Refine Edge effect so that you can adjust the resulting alpha matte. See the following tutorial for a practical application of Roto Brush. Refine Matte is discussed after the tutorial. Refine Matte shares the same properties as the standalone Refine Soft Matte effect, which is demonstrated in Chapter 2.

Adjusting Base Frame Influence

When you draw an initial Roto Brush stroke, the current frame becomes a *base frame*. The mask definition, as determined by the Roto Brush strokes, is automatically propagated forward and backwards 20 frames. If you look closely at the Layer panel's timeline, a small, arrow-laden, base frame span bar extends from the frame you are working on (Figure 3.13). The direction of the arrows (< or >) on the span bar indicates the direction of the base frame propagation. In essence, the base frames function as keyframes for the Roto Brush tool.

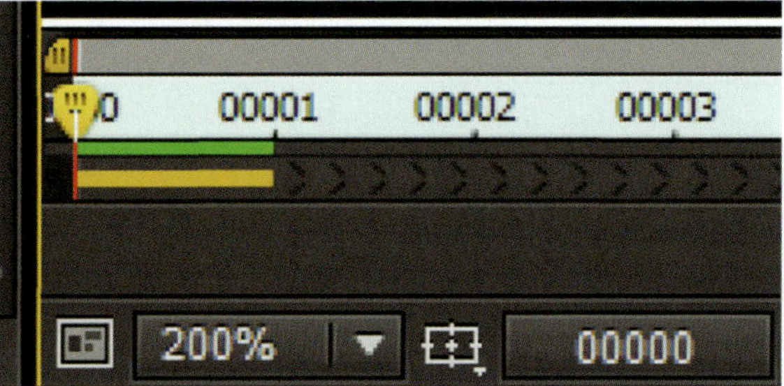

FIG 3.13 Close-up of Layer panel timeline. The gold line indicates a Roto Brush base frame. A span bar extends to the right with small > arrows.

If you draw corrective strokes at a later frame, the influence of the strokes is carried in the direction of the arrows. Each time you draw a corrective stroke, the base frame span bar extends. You can limit the effect of a base frame by LMB-dragging the end of the span bar. This may be useful if the object you're rotoscoping leaves the frame or is occluded. If you move to a frame that is not covered by a base frame span bar, no mask is drawn. You can lengthen or shorten a span bar at any point.

Any frame of the timeline can hold a single Roto Brush base frame and a single Roto Brush mask. However, if you move to a frame where no base frame span exists, you can draw a brand new base frame that receives its own span bar in the forward and backward direction. This produces a brand new mask. Once again, you can determine the length of any base frame span bar by LMB-dragging its left or right end.

Note that rotoscoping with Roto Brush may be significantly slower than rotoscoping with the Pen tool. The Roto Brush tool must calculate the mask shape along the span bar whenever you update the mask and move to a different frame. That said, you might save time with the Roto Brush because you have to lay down fewer manual keyframes (again, you can think of base frames and corrective strokes as a unique form of keyframes).

Roto brush mini-tutorial

The following steps represent the general approach you can take when applying the Roto Brush tool. For practice, apply these steps to the *mini_roto_brush.aep* project saved in the *\ProjectFiles\aeFiles\Chapter3* directory.

1. Open the sole layer carried by Comp 1 in the Layer view. You can do this by double-clicking the layer name in the layer outline (which is named after the image sequence). You can distinguish the Layer view panel by its built-in timeline.
2. Click the Roto Brush Tool icon in the main toolbar. The button carries an icon of a man and a paintbrush and is to the right of the Eraser Tool button. In the Layer view, roughly LMB-drag a roto paint stroke to define what you wish to rotoscope. With this example, concentrate on one part of the actress. For example, roughly draw a line to establish where her right hand and arm are (Top) (Figure 3.11). The stroke is colored green, indicating the foreground area. When you let go of the mouse button, the stroke is converted into a mask (also called a *segmentation boundary*). The edge of the hand and arm are detected, although the detection may not be perfect due to the tool's inability to distinguish some of the foreground and background pixels.
3. LMB-drag the brush again to better define where the edge should be. For example, draw smaller, shorter strokes to define the fingers. You can interactively change the brush size by Ctrl/Cmd-LMB-dragging in the Layer view.

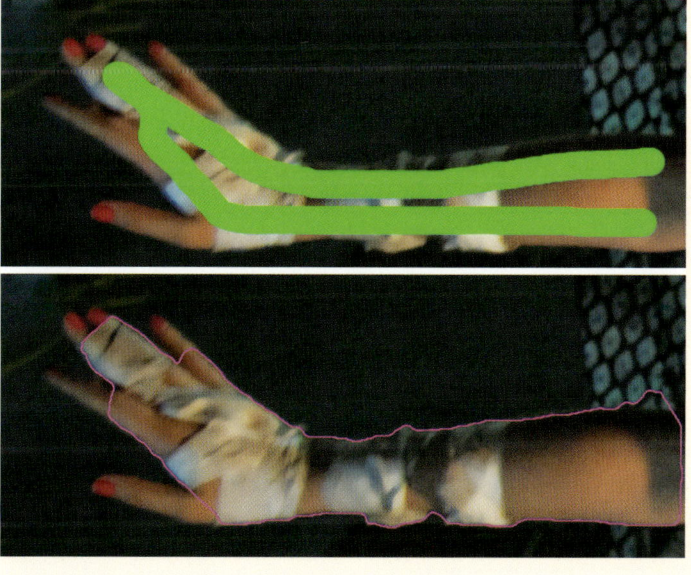

FIG 3.11 Top: A green stroke is drawn with the Roto Brush tool, roughly indicating the position of an arm and hand. Bottom: The resulting mask is drawn in pink. Note that the mask does not encompass all the fingers at this point.

4. If the mask extends too far and encompasses the background, you can shrink the mask by Alt/Opt-LMB-dragging negative strokes. These strokes are colored red and the brush receives a negative sign in its center. Continue to refine the mask by painting additional foreground and background strokes (Figure 3.12).

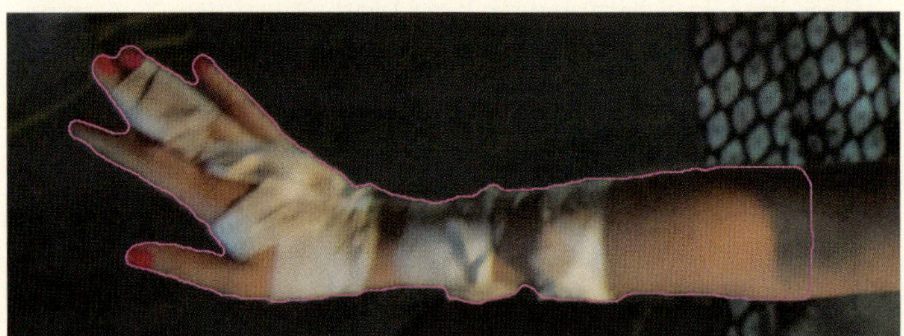

FIG 3.12 Additional positive and negative Roto Brush strokes better define the arm and hand.

5. After the mask is properly formed, step forward one frame on the timeline. Note that the mask automatically updates. Should the mask become inaccurate, you are free to apply additional foreground and background strokes.
6. Play the timeline forward. The mask is calculated for each frame. If low contrast exists between the foreground and background, the mask becomes inaccurate. Heavy motion blur also confuses the tool. Hence, a significant amount of adjustment may be necessary to create a clean mask. When the mask is satisfactory, you can click the Freeze button at the lower right of the Layer view panel to prevent the Roto Brush tool from recalculating the frames as you play back the timeline.

The Roto Brush tool attaches itself to the layer as an effect. It carries properties that control the mask propagation over the timeline, which can have significant effect on the success of the resulting mask. These are discussed in the next section. A finished version of this project is saved as *mini_roto_brush_finished.aep* in the *\ProjectFiles\aeFiles\Chapter3* directory.

Adjusting Propagation and Refining Edges

Each base frame carries its own unique set of property values. Creating multiple base frames is useful for rotoscoping footage where the rotoscoped object suffers significant changes in silhouette shape, carries different degrees of motion blur, and transitions through different pools of light. The properties for the Roto Brush are stored in the Roto Brush & Refine Edge section of the layer outline and are grouped into Roto Brush Propagation and Refine Edge Matte properties (Figure 3.14).

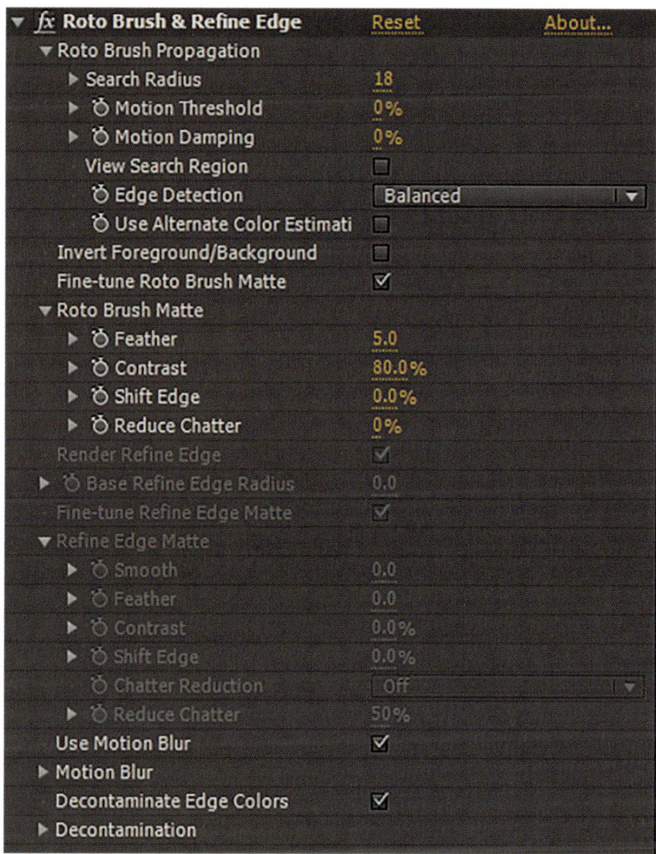

FIG 3.14 Roto Brush & Refine Edge options with Roto Brush Propagation and Roto Brush Matte sections expanded.

Descriptions of base frame propagation properties follow:

View Search Region and Search Radius

View Search Region, when set to on, displays a yellow area that represents the search region— the region in which the tool searches for foreground pixels that match the foreground pixels of a prior frame. If your object is moving quickly or is constantly changing shape, it may pay to expand the search region by increasing the Search Radius property value. If the rotoscoped object is moving slowly or doesn't change its shape, you can reduce the Search Radius to avoid chatter (the fluctuation of the mask around the object edge).

Motion Threshold and Motion Damping

Together, these two properties constrict or expand the search region based on detected motion. Motion Threshold sets it namesake, where areas of the search region that have less motion than the threshold are removed (and assumed to be part of the background). This leads to smoothing of the search region shape, which is most noticeable when the Motion Damping value is low. Shrinking the areas with no or little motion can help prevent chatter. If you increase the Motion Damping value, the search region is constricted again, with areas containing little or no motion removed from the search region.

Edge Detection

This menu provides three options for calculating the mask edge on new frames. The Favor Predicted Edges option biases the overall shape of the mask on a base frame and is less sensitive to matching colors among pixels. This mode is useful when the rotoscoped object carries similar color values as the background. The Favor Current Edges option does the opposite and biases matching pixel values regardless of the resulting mask shape. This option works better in high-contrast situations. The default option, Balanced, combines these techniques equally.

If the Fine-Tune Roto Brush Matte property is selected and View Search Region is deselected, additional properties for the Refine Edge effect become available. Descriptions of key properties follow:

Roto Brush Matte

This subsection provides basic properties for refining the resulting alpha matte. The Feather property works in a similar fashion to the Mask Feather property of a standard mask. (You can return to the Composition view to see the result.) The Contrast option, on the other hand, controls the taper from 100 percent opaqueness to 0 percent transparency. High-contrast values create a sharp edge while low values create a soft edge. If the Contrast value is high, raising the Feather value will smooth the mask, reducing the number of small undulations. The Shift Edge property works as a choker, eroding or expanding the matte (Feather must be a non-0 value for this property to take effect). The Reduce Chatter property attempts to reduce mask undulations by averaging the mattes of the surrounding frame together. If Chatter is 0, the function is off.

Use Motion Blur

If selected, the property applies motion blur to the alpha matte, taking into account the matte's prior position in the frame. This may be useful for rotoscoping fast-moving objects with blurred edges.

Decontaminate Edge Colors

If selected, this property attempts to remove the background color from the edges of the foreground. The Decontamination Amount property controls the aggressiveness of the removal.

Note that you can interactively refine small sections of the matte edge by applying the Refine Matte Tool (located in the drop-down menu visible when you click and hold the Roto Brush Tool button). When you LMB-drag the Refine Matte tool brush over the mask edge in the Layer view, it softens the alpha matte edge under the brush. Alt/Opt+LMB-dragging in the same area removes the softness.

Importing Masks

You are not limited to masks that are generated within After Effects. You can import a variety of masks from other programs such as Adobe Photoshop, Adobe Illustrator, and Mocha AE.

Importing Bitmap and Vector Masks

You can import a bitmap in any common file format and use it as a mask in After Effects. In addition, After Effects supports vector-based Adobe Illustrator files. You can import an Illustrator .ai, .eps, or .pdf file directly into After Effects. The result is an alpha matte cut in the shape of the closed vector shapes. The vectors themselves are not immediately accessible. Whether you are working with bitmaps or vectors, you can add the imported mask to a composition as a hidden layer and transfer alpha information from it to another layer with the Track Matte option or a channel effect. (For examples using Track Matte and the Set Matte effect, see Chapter 2.)

You can convert an imported vector file into a shape layer. A shape layer combines solid colors with one or more masks (called *paths*). To make the conversion, place the imported mask in a composition as a layer, select that layer, and choose Layer > Create Shapes From Vector Layer. A new layer is created with one mask for each closed vector shape (Figure 3.15). The original layer is hidden. You are free to adjust the resulting paths by moving vertices and tangent handles as you would with masks created by the Pen tool. Each shape is assigned a Contents > Group section of the layer in the layer outline. The shape is broken down into a path, a fill color, and a set of transforms. You can change any of these properties.

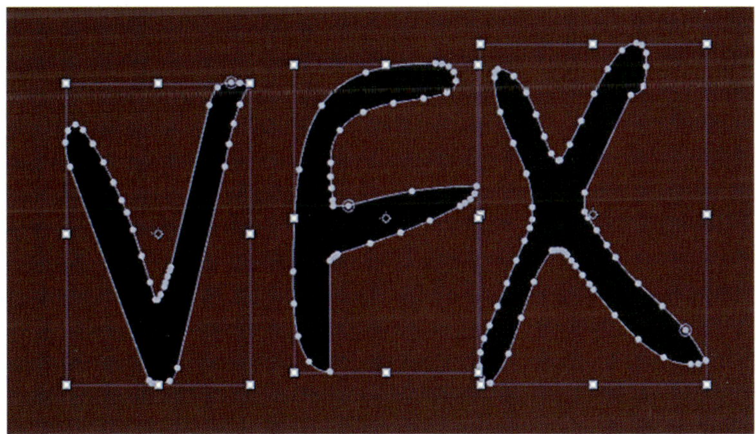

FIG 3.15 An Illustrator .ai file is imported into After Effects and converted to a shape layer. There is one path for each closed-vector letter. The Fill Color for each path is set to black. A sample project file is saved as *ai_shape_layer.aep* in the *\ProjectFiles\aefiles\Chapter3* directory.

Working with Mocha AE Masks

Imagineer Systems Mocha AE is bundled with recent editions of After Effects. Mocha AE offers a planar-based motion tracking and masking system. Mocha AE is able to automate many tracking and masking tasks that would normally take a significant amount of time inside After Effects. You can import motion tracking data and mask into After Effects from Mocha. The following tutorial walks you through the basic steps of creating and importing a mask. (Motion tracking is demonstrated in Chapter 4.)

Mocha masks mini-tutorial

The following steps represent the general approach you can take when using Mocha AE to rotoscope. You can apply these steps to the *mini_mocha_ae.aep* project saved in the *\ProjectFiles\aeFiles\Chapter3* directory.

1. Select the sole layer carried by Comp 1, which is named after the image sequence. Choose Animation > Track In Mocha AE. Mocha AE opens.
2. In Mocha AE, the New Project window opens and states the footage frame range and frame rate. If this information is incorrect, you are free to change it. Click the OK button to close the window. The footage appears in the Mocha viewer. You can play the footage with the viewer's playback controls. You can zoom in and out by selecting the Zoom tool from the top toolbar (Figure 3.16) and LMB-dragging up and down in the viewer. You can scroll by MMB-dragging. To escape a tool, you can select the Pick tool.

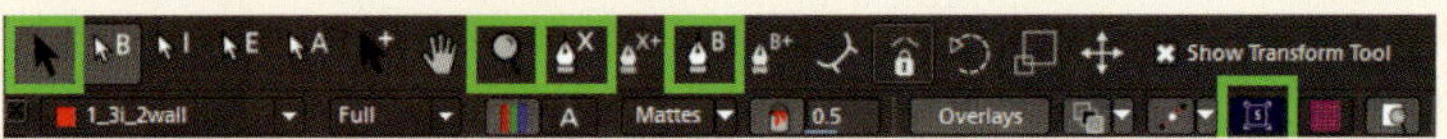

FIG 3.16 The Mocha AE CC 2014 toolbar. The Pick, Zoom, Create X-Spline Layer, and Create Bezier Layer tools and Show Planar Surface button are highlighted. Note that Mocha AE CC 2015 uses the same tools and buttons, although there are minor variations in the toolbar layout.

3. Mocha is a planar tracker, which means that it tracks shapes that are defined as planar (a flat, two-dimensional surface that may rotate or change in scale). To define the tracked shape, you use one of several spline tools to loosely form a spline "cage" around the shape. For this tutorial, we'll use the X-Spline tool, which is perhaps the easiest to apply. We'll track a section of unpainted drywall surrounded by the white paint lines.
4. Return to the first frame. Select the Create X-Spline Layer tool from the top toolbar (Figure 3.16). This features a pen tip and a small X as part of the icon. LMB-click near the bottom left of the rightmost unpainted drywall area. You can place the vertex within the painted white line. An X-Spline vertex is drawn. The vertex does not have to touch the exact corner of the unpainted drywall; in fact, the tracking works better if there is a small gap (Figure 3.17). LMB-click at another corner near the drywall area. A new vertex is laid down with a spline span in between. Click two more times to form two more corners slightly out of frame at the top of the area.

A rounded-corner, rectangular cage is formed. RMB-click over the shape to finish it. Note that Mocha is able to track planar shapes that extend past the frame edge. You can adjust the vertex positions after the cage is drawn by LMB-dragging them.

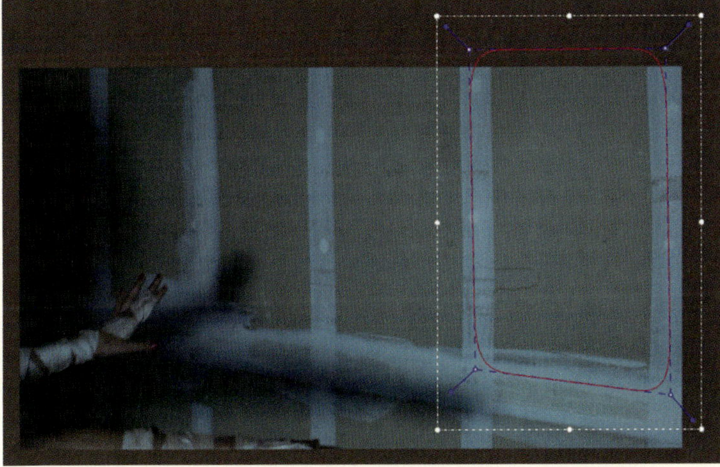

FIG 3.17 An X-spline cage is drawn around an unpainted section of drywall.

5. Mocha AE will attempt to track the caged shape over time. The application of tracking is similar to After Effects motion tracking (discussed in the next chapter). To activate the tracking, click the Track Forward button. The tracking buttons sit to the right of the playback buttons and feature a small *T* in the icons. You can also track backwards or track in either direction one frame at a time. When you click the Track Forward button, the timeline moves forward and Mocha updates the X-spline cage vertex positions to follow the chosen shape. With this example, the unpainted drywall area is tracked. Complex organic shapes can also be planar tracked if there are no drastic changes (such as large rotations, significant silhouette shape changes, heavy motion blur, and so on). Minor occlusions, such as the crossing of shadows, do not prevent the success of the tracking. Heavy occlusions, however, can interfere with the accuracy of some of the vertex positions, causing the cage to drift away from the chosen shape. After the tracking has completed, you can use the standard playback controls to gauge the tracking success.
6. If the spline cage drifts, you can correct it by creating reference points. To do this, return to the first frame and click the Show Planar Surface button in the top toolbar (see Figure 3.16 earlier in this section). A blue rectangle is drawn in the center of the cage. You can LMB-drag the

rectangle corners and place them over specific reference points in the footage. For example, you can LMB-drag the bottom-left corner and place it over the bottom-left corner of the unpainted drywall area (Figure 3.18). You can choose to keyframe the rectangle corners over time by switching to the Adjust Track tab at the bottom left of the program window, moving to a later frame, and updating the corner positions. The corner positions, in turn, force the cage to be placed more accurately over time. When you move a corner, a zoomed view of the mouse area is presented at the top left of the viewer. This is labeled *Current Frame*. For comparison, a zoomed-in view of the same area is presented for the *Master Frame*—the frame on which the initial corner position was established (Figure 3.19). This allows you to better judge the precision of the corner placement. Note that the planar vertices carry a small X on the master frame.

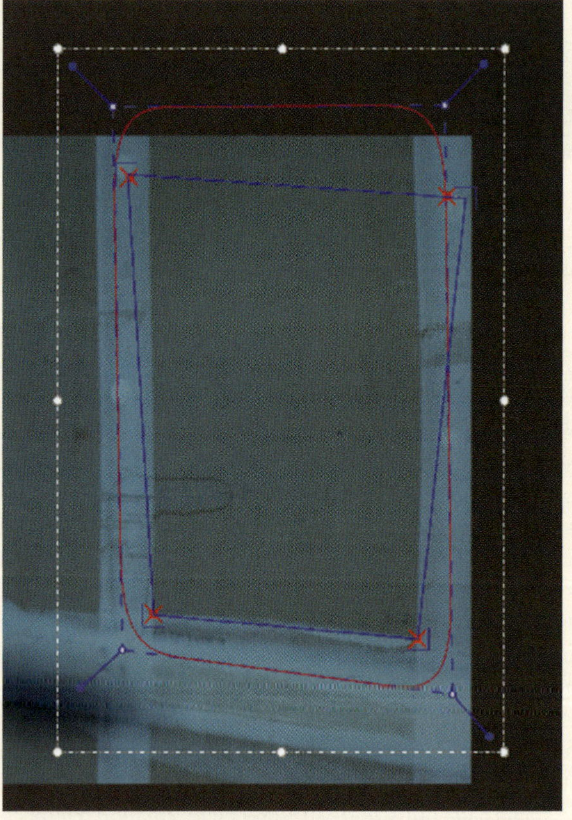

FIG 3.18 The planar reference surface is revealed. Its corners are positioned over the corners formed by the paint lines and several circular nail hole patches. The Xs indicate that the frame is a master frame.

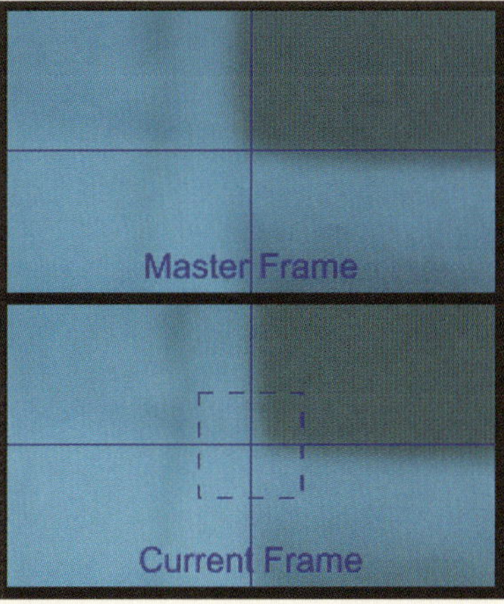

FIG 3.19 Zoomed-in views of a planar corner as seen on the current frame and the master frame.

7. As soon as the cage is following the chosen shape in an accurate fashion, you can combine the tracked shapes with more traditional masking. To create a mask around the drywall area, choose the Create Bezier Layer tool from the top toolbar (Figure 3.16 earlier in this section). LMB-click in the viewer at one corner of the drywall area. A vertex is laid down. LMB-click at the opposite corner. A second vertex appears with a Bezier segment and tangent handles at the vertex positions. LMB-click a third time at the right top of the area outside the frame. LMB-click a fourth time at the left top of the area outside the frame. LMB-click a final time over the top of the first vertex to finish the mask. LMB-drag the tangent handle ends to better follow the drywall edges. You can shorten the tangent handles to create tighter corners (Figure 3.20).
8. Note that the new Bezier and the X-spline cage are listed as *Layer 1* and *Layer 2* in the Layer Controls panel at the top left of the program window (Figure 3.21). Rename *Layer 2* by double-clicking the name and entering **Mask** into the field. Rename *Layer 1* by double-clicking the name and entering **Track** into the field. You can attach the Mask layer to the Track layer by linking them. This prevents the need to manually update the mask shape over time. To do so, select the Mask layer in the Layer Controls panel and change the Link To Track menu to Mask. Play back the timeline. The mask follows the cage and covers the drywall area without drifting. Should you need to adjust the mask shape at a later frame, you can LMB-drag the mask vertices or tangent handles. A keyframe is automatically created and indicated on the timeline as a green triangle.
9. To transfer the mask to After Effects, select the Mask layer in the Layer Controls panel and click the Export Shape Data button in the Track tab

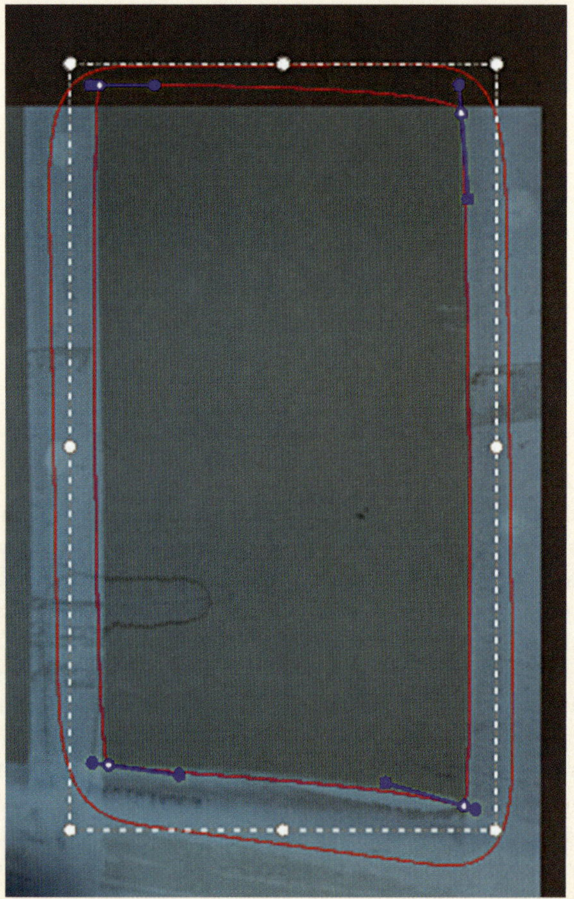

FIG 3.20 An adjusted Bezier shape (red inner lines with blue tangent handles) forms a mask.

at the bottom right of the program window. In the Export Shape Data window, select the Selected Layer radio button and click the Copy To Clipboard button. Return to the After Effects program window. Select the layer to which you want to add the mask, and choose Edit > Paste. The mask is added to the layer as an effect named after the Mocha layer. The After Effects layer is cut out, although no spline shape is visible in the Composition view. The transform properties carried by the effect are pre-animated for every frame of the timeline. The properties include Shape Data (mask shape information), Translation, Scale, Rotation, Shear, and Perspective. You are free to edit the keyframes as you would any other animation in After Effects.

There are numerous ways to adjust the tracking and masking within Mocha AE. Unfortunately, these can't be covered in this book due to space limitations. For more information on Mocha AE functionality,

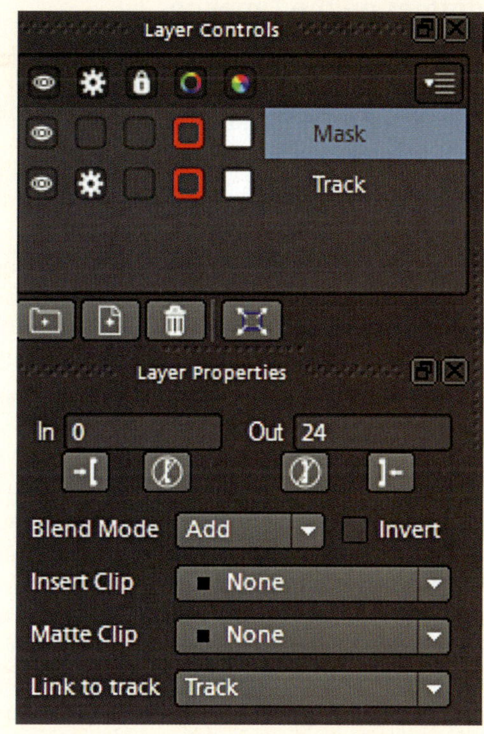

FIG 3.21 Layer Controls panel with renamed layers. The Link To Track menu is at the bottom of the panel.

visit the Mocha AE Help files. Note that you can save Mocha AE project files by choosing File > Save Project in the Mocha program window. A finished Mocha project is saved as *mini_mocha_ae_finished.mocha* in the *\ProjectFiles\aeFiles\Chapter3\ directory*. A finished After Effects project is saved as *mini_mocha_ae_finished.aep* in the *\ProjectFiles\aeFiles\Chapter3* directory.

Basic Keyframing

A *keyframe* or *key* is stored value associated with a particular frame. In After Effects, the value may belong to an effect, mask, or transform property. There are two places keyframes appear: on the timeline and in the Graph Editor. You can edit the keyframes in either location. To set a keyframe, move to the frame where you'd like to place the key and click the Time icon beside the property you wish to keyframe. At that point forward, changes to the property result in an updated keyframe (if the frame remains the same) or a new keyframe (if you've moved to a different frame). If two or more keyframes exist for a property, an animation curve is threaded through the keyframes; this is used to determine what property values should exist on inbetween frames.

Editing Keyframes on the Timeline

When a keyframe is created, a symbol is placed on the timeline for the current frame. By default, this appears as a small diamond to indicate that the keyframe is using linear spans. You can alter existing keyframes in the following ways:

- You can delete a keyframe by selecting it on the timeline and pressing the Delete key. Selected keyframes turn yellow. The associated animation curve updates to ensure that it threads through the remaining keyframes.
- You can remove animation from a property by clicking the property's Time icon so that it turns off.
- You can move keyframes in time by LMB-dragging them on the timeline. You can select more than one keyframe by Shift-LMB-clicking them or LMB-dragging a selection marquee around them.
- You can force a keyframe at the current point of the timeline by RMB-clicking over the property name and choosing Add Key from the menu. You can do this without changing the current property value or changing the current mask shape.
- You can enter a precise numerical value for a keyframe by RMB-clicking the keyframe icon on the timeline and choosing Edit from the menu. You can then enter the value into the property window that pops up.
- You can copy and paste one or more keyframes. To do this, select the keyframes, press Ctrl/Cmd+C, move to a different frame, and press Ctrl/Cmd+V. If multiple keyframes are selected, the group of keyframes is pasted at the current frame but maintain their original spacing. You can also copy and paste keyframes between similar properties on different layers. To do this, select the keyframes, press Ctrl/Cmd+C, move to the frame where you would like to paste, select a similar property on a different layer by clicking its name, and press Ctrl/Cmd+V.

Separating Dimensions

Several After Effects properties have two dimensions. That is, they have X and Y values. Each dimensional value receives its own curve and set of keyframes. To access the individual curve, you must use the Graph Editor. Despite this, only a single keyframe is placed on the timeline for both dimensions. For example, if you keyframe the Scale property, both the X and Y Scale dimensions receive a single keyframe symbol for any given frame on the timeline. In Figure 3.22, the Position and Scale properties of a layer are animated, producing keyframes at frame 1, 2, and 3. The Scale property is unlinked so that X and Y can carry different values; however, there is only a single timeline keyframe symbol for both X and Y. (The Scale link button appears to the immediate left of the X and Y fields.)

In Figure 3.22, the Position property is separated into X and Y properties so that each carries its own timeline keyframe symbol. To split the Position into

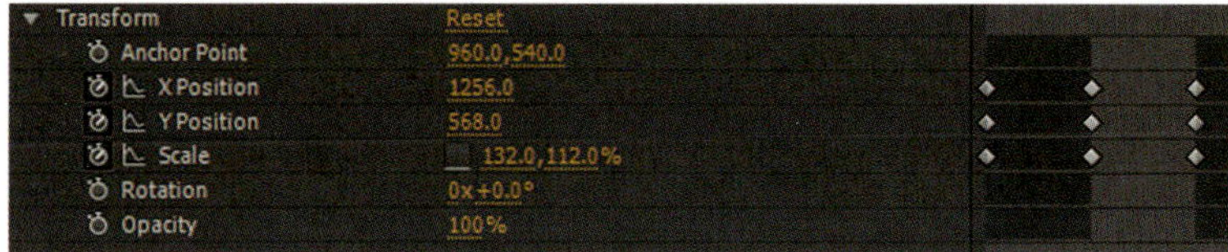

FIG 3.22 Position and Scale properties are keyframed for a layer.

X and Y, RMB-click over the Position property name and choose Separate Dimensions. To recombine the X and Y, RMB-click and choose Separate Dimensions again so the option becomes deselected. Note that 3D layers cause some properties to take on a third dimension, Z. 3D layers are discussed in Chapter 5.

Working in the Graph Editor

The Graph Editor provides the most powerful means of altering keyframe animation. In the editor, you can access and fine-tune the animation curves, thus controlling how the inbetween frame values are generated.

To open the Graph Editor, click the large Graph Editor button at the top right of the layer outline. To see a property curve in the editor, click the property name while the editor is open. You can also click the Include This Property In The Graph Editor Set button beside the property name. You can display more than one curve in the editor at a time.

The Graph Editor carries two display modes: a speed graph and a value graph. The speed graph mode displays the rate of value change. Because this mode is difficult to interpret and adjust, I suggest that you use the value graph mode. The value graph mode displays property values and is similar to what you would find in the curve editor of 3D programs such as Autodesk Maya. To choose a display mode, click the Choose Graph Type And Options button at the bottom left of the Graph Editor (Figure 3.23) and choose either Edit Value Graph or Edit Speed Graph.

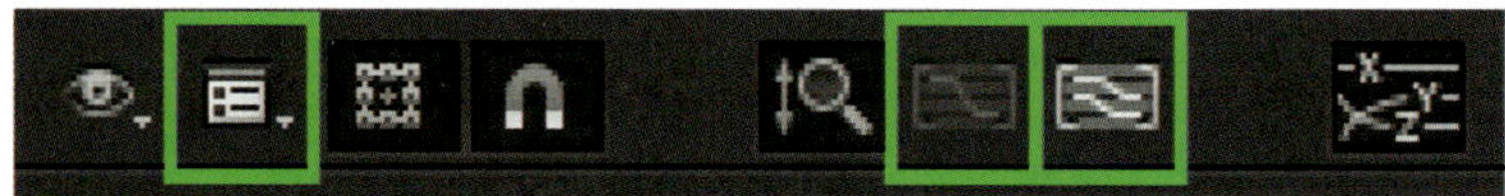

FIG 3.23 Graph Editor buttons. Choose Graph Type And Options, Fit Selection To View, and Fit All Graphs To View are highlighted.

Altering Curves

If two or more keyframes exist for a property, an animation curve is threaded through them. Any given frame produces a value for the property. For example, if you go to frame 10 and read the value for the curve, that value is then given to the property at frame 10. To read a curve value at any given frame, place your mouse over the curve. The value is printed in a small readout box (Figure 3.24). In the Graph Editor, time runs left to right and property values run down to up. The property values are incrementally displayed along the left side of the editor.

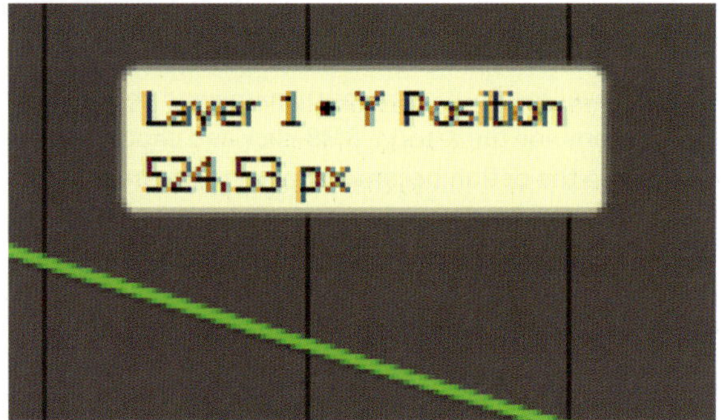

FIG 3.24 The mouse is placed over a curve at frame 5. The yellow readout box displays the layer name, the property name, and the property value for that frame (524.53). *px* stands for *pixels*.

You can alter animation curves in the following manner:

- To move a keyframe, LMB-click on the yellow keyframe dot and LMB-drag it. Up-down motion creates a property value change and left-right motion creates a time change. By default, the keyframe "sticks" to whole frame numbers.
- To add a new keyframe along a curve at the current mouse position, Ctrl/Cmd+LMB-click on the curve. The new keyframe also appears on the timeline.
- To delete a keyframe, select it and press the Delete key. You can click on the keyframe or LMB-drag a marquee box around multiple keyframes.
- To frame a curve (or curves) so it is fully seen in the Graph Editor, click the Fit All Graphs To View button (Figure 3.23 in the previous section). To frame selected keyframes, click the Fit Selection To View button.
- If more than one keyframe is selected, a gray transform box is displayed (Figure 3.25). You can move the selected keyframes by LMB-dragging the gray area of the box. You can scale the keyframes by LMB-dragging any of the white dots on the box edges. If you scale the keyframes vertically, the value range is compressed or expanded. If you scale the keyframes horizontally, the frame range is compressed or expanded. The shorter the frame range, the faster the value change (for Position, this equates to faster motion).

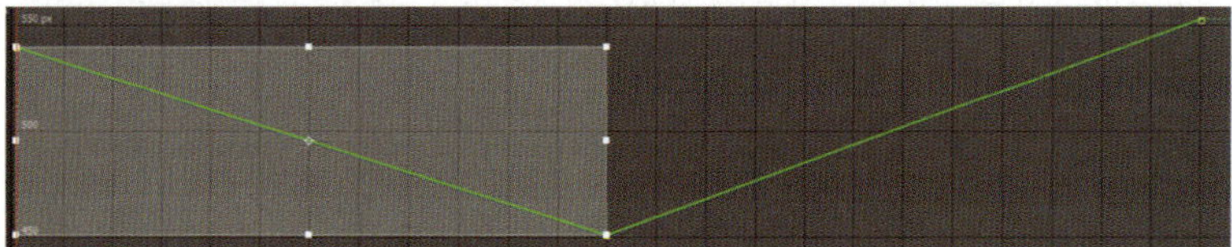

FIG 3.25 A V-shaped animation curve with three keyframes appears in the Graph Editor. The left two keyframes are selected, producing the gray transform box.

Changing Tangent Types

One of the most significant changes you can make to an animation curve is changing the tangent types of its keyframes. By default, the curve spans are linear—that is, they run in perfectly straight lines between keyframes. This creates a mechanical motion that is not particularly suited for animation that needs to appear organic. To change the tangent type of a keyframe, place your mouse over the keyframe icon, RMB-click, and choose Keyframe Interpolation from the menu. In the Keyframe Interpolation window, change the Temporal Interpolation menu to the tangent type of your choice. Descriptions of the tangent types follow:

Linear produces straight spans between keyframes with no tangent handles (Figure 3.26). This type is suitable for mechanical animation where there are abrupt changes in speed.

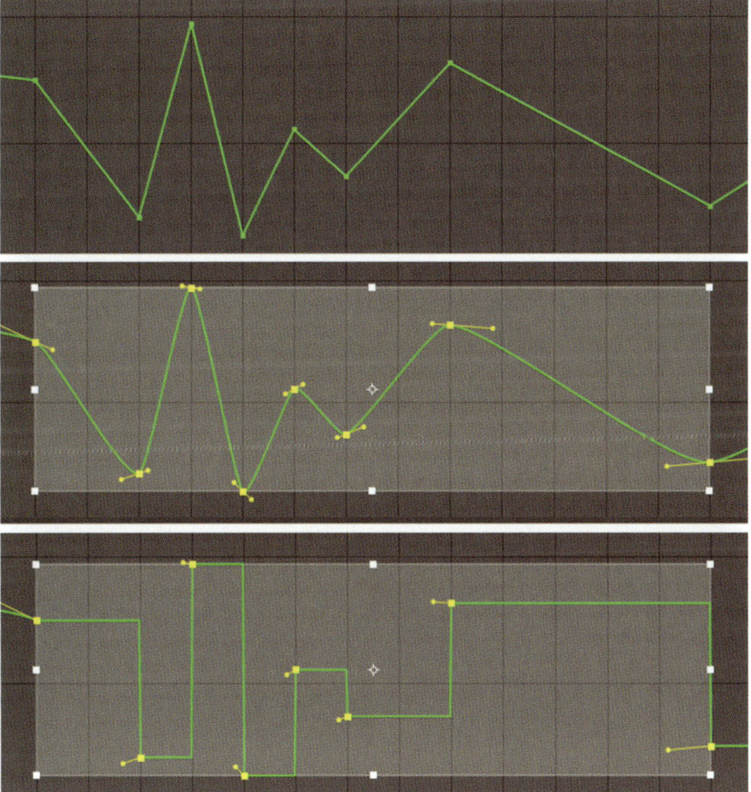

FIG 3.26 Top: Complex curve with default Linear spans. Middle: Same curve converted to Bezier tangents. Bottom: Same curve converted to Hold tangents.

Bezier creates a tangent handle that extends in both directions from the keyframe (Figure 3.26). (To see the handles, you must select the keyframes.) You can LMB-drag the tangent ends to rotate the tangent handle, lengthen the tangent handles, or shorten the tangent handles to alter the curve span flow. This type of fine-tuning is not available to the timeline view and is often mandatory for creating quality animation, whether it's for transform, mask shape, or effect property changes.

Hold forces the current keyframe value to be carried forward until the next keyframe is encountered (Figure 3.26). This type is rarely used but may be appropiate for rough key pose animation where the character or object "jumps" from one key pose to the next.

Auto Bezier creates tangent handles but keeps the handles short to force tight and smooth transitions at the "peaks" and "valleys" (Figure 3.27). This type often prevents excessive curve values from forming when a Bezier curve shoots too high or too low.

Continuous Bezier is identical to Auto Bezier but carries manual adjustments. Auto Bezier automatically switches to Continuous Bezier as soon as you edit the keyframes.

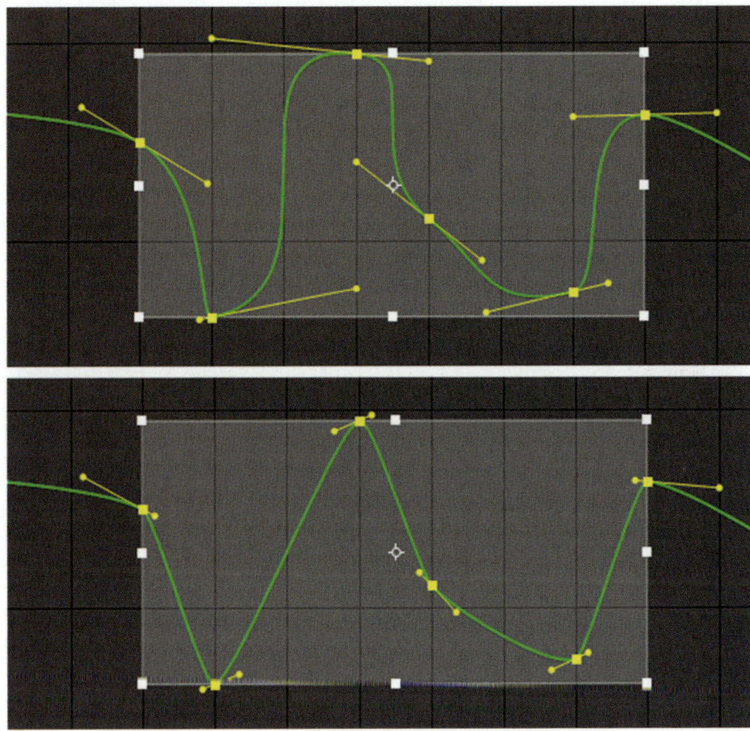

FIG 3.27 Top: Curve with manually adjusted Bezier tangents. Bottom: Same curve converted to Auto Bezier.

Each tangent type produces a different keyframe symbol on the timeline. Linear keyframes use diamonds. Auto Bezier keyframes use circles. Bezier and Continuous Bezier keyframes use an hourglass symbol. Hold keyframes use a square symbol with notched squares appearing for surrounding keyframes.

Note that the Spatial Interpolation menu, available in the Keyframe Interpolation window, sets the tangent type for motion paths that appear in the view panels. Spatial Interpolation is further explored in Chapter 4.

Graph editor mini-tutorial

The following steps allow you to practice editing curves in the Graph Editor. With this tutorial, we'll create a mask in the shape of a leaf and animate the leaf slowing "flitting" down through the air.

1. Create a new After Effects project. Create a new composition. Make the composition 60 frames long with a frame rate of 30 fps. Choose any of the larger resolutions, such as 1920x1080.
2. Choose Layer > New > Solid. In the Solid Settings window, click the Make Comp Size button. Change the color swatch to a leaf-like color (green, brown, or red). See Figure 3.28.

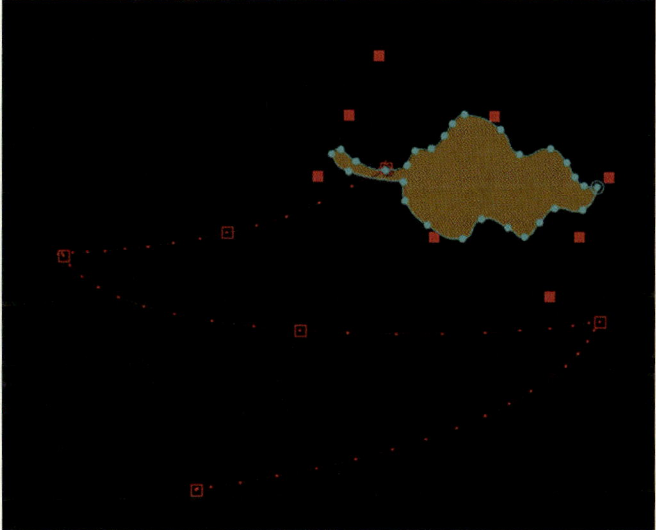

FIG 3.28 A leaf is cut out of a solid layer with a mask. The red line is the final motion path created by the Position animation.

3. Using the Pen tool, draw a closed mask on the new solid layer that forms the shape of leaf. Position the mask so that the leaf stem corresponds with the layer center (the small red crosshair in the center of the frame). Use any of the masking methods discussed in this chapter to refine the mask shape.
4. On the first frame, click the Time icon beside the Position and Rotation properties for the layer. Keyframes are laid down. Proceed to the last frame of the timeline. Change the position and rotation of the leaf so that it sits at the bottom of the frame (as if it has fallen). New keyframes are automatically laid down.

5. Proceed to other frames and add additional keyframes to make the falling animation more interesting, For example, make the leaf "flit" left and right as it falls. You can use any of the keyframe techniques discussed in the "Rotoscoping Approaches" section earlier in this chapter. Even though we're not changing the mask shape, you can apply bisecting or key pose techniques to transform animation.
6. Play back the timeline and adjust the keyframes. After the basic animation is roughed in, open the Graph Editor. Click on the Position property name and choose Separate Dimensions from the menu. If the Position X and Y are left merged, you cannot alter the tangent handles of individual keyframes.
7. Proceed to adjust one curve at a time. To see a property curve, click on the property name in the layer outline. Convert all the keyframes to Bezier-style tangents (Figure 3.29). For example, click on the Rotation property name, select all the Rotation keyframes in the Graph Editor, LMB-click one of those keyframes, choose Keyframe Interpolation from the menu, and change the Temporal Interpolation menu to Bezier. Proceed to adjust tangent handles and play back the timeline to see the result.

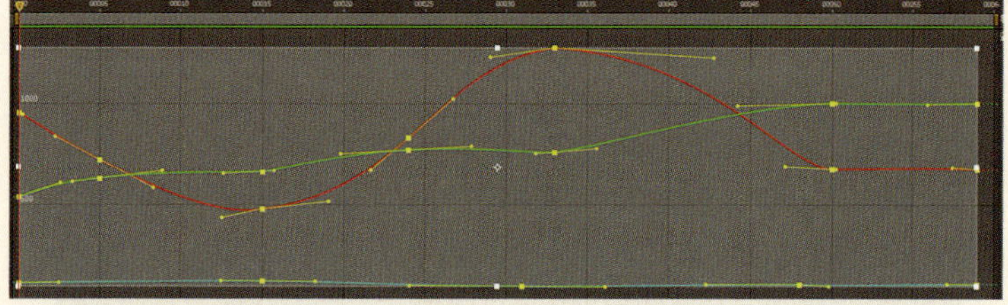

FIG 3.29 A final version of the animation. X Position is red. Y Position is green. Rotation is cyan. Note the different shapes of the curve spans and different positions and lengths of tangent handles.

As you alter the animation curves, keep these guidelines in mind:

- The steeper a curve span, the faster the change in value. With Position or Rotation, it means the leaf is moving faster.
- The more shallow a curve span, the slower the change in value. With Position or Rotation, it means the leaf is moving slower.
- If a curve span becomes perfectly flat, it means there is no change in value. With Position or Rotation, it means the leaf has stopped moving.

A finished After Effects project is saved as *mini_graph_editor_finished.aep* in the *\ProjectFiles\aefiles\Chapter3* directory.

Chapter Tutorial: Keying a Difficult Green Screen, Part 2

In Chapter 2, we keyed the green screen of a shot with an actress. Although we spent time working on a clean alpha matte around her body and hair, there are still several improvements we can make to the shot.

1. Open the *tutorial_2_1.aep* file located in the *\ProjectFiles\aeFiles\Chapter2* directory.
2. Go to the first frame. Select the footage layer and create a new mask with the Pen tool that surrounds the actress, but removes the X-shaped tracking marks. You can extend the mask outside of the bottom and top of frame. This is a holdout mask, as it retains the actress but throws away the marks (Figure 3.30). Animate the mask over time to take into account the motion of the camera. You can use the bisecting method to determine keyframe locations. Play back the timeline to make sure no part of the actress is cut off. In the finished version, keyframes are placed approximately every 8 to 10 frames.

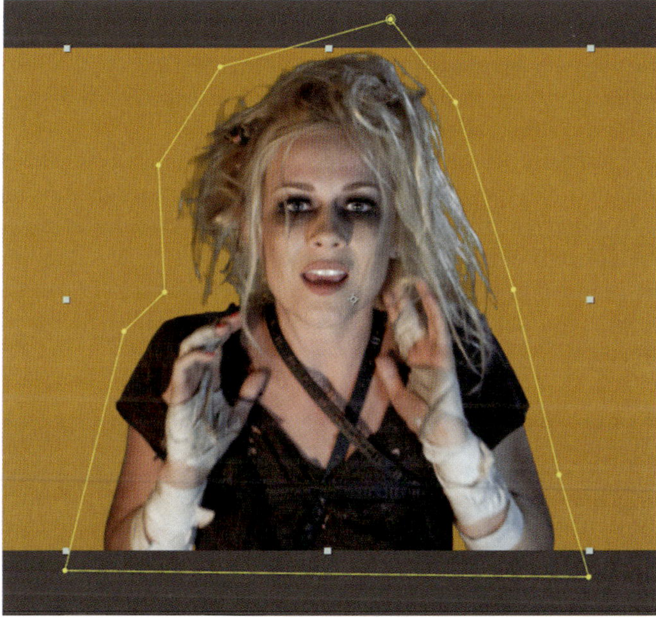

FIG 3.30 A holdout mask, as seen on frame 8, is created to retain the actress but remove the tracking marks. The Refine Soft Matte effect is disabled.

3. Go to the Effect Controls panel for the footage layer. Turn off the Refine Soft Matte effect and Keylight by clicking the small *fx* buttons beside the effect names. As an alternative, we'll create a custom luma matte to retain the fine hairs.
4. Duplicate the footage layer by selecting it and choosing Edit > Duplicate. Select the new top layer and choose Effect > Color Correction > Hue/Saturation. Reduce the Master Saturation to –100. The layer becomes grayscale. Choose Effect > Color Correction > Curves. Click the Curves line in two places to add two new points. LMB-drag the points to form a severe S-curve (Figure 3.31). This creates a large amount of contrast, which differentiates the hair from the background. Many of the fine hairs become visible.

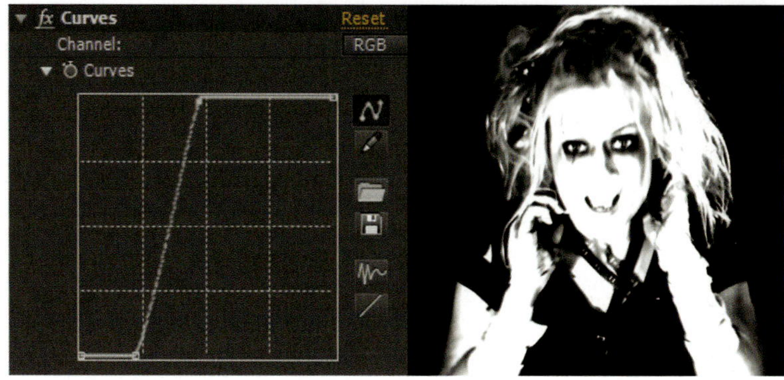

FIG 3.31 Left: The adjusted Curves effect. Right: The resulting custom luma matte.

5. Hide the new top layer by clicking off the Video eye icon beside the layer name. Change the lower footage layer's Track Matte menu to Luma Matte. (Track Matte is described in detail in Chapter 2.) The footage is cut out by the top layer. Although the edge of the hair is acceptable, the center of the actress is adversely affected.
6. Duplicate the lower footage layer. Because the old top layer is hidden, the duplicated layer is moved to the top of the layer outline. Select the new top layer and reactivate its Keylight effect. The keyed version of the actress is thus placed over the luma matte version (Figure 3.32). This allows fine hairs retrieved by the luma matte to appear along the previously eroded hair edge. You can hide the solid layer to better judge the new hair integration.

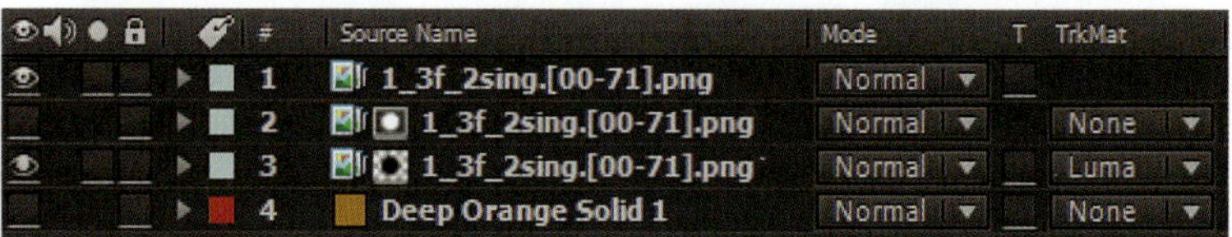

FIG 3.32 The revised layer outline with the keyed layer on top, the luma matte hidden in the middle, and the matted layer at the bottom over the solid.

7. The new hair is tinted green due to green screen spill. Select the matted layer (now numbered *3*) and choose Effect > Color Correction > Hue/Saturation. Reduce Master Saturation to –75 and increase Master Lightness to 20. The new hair is now better integrated (Figure 3.33).

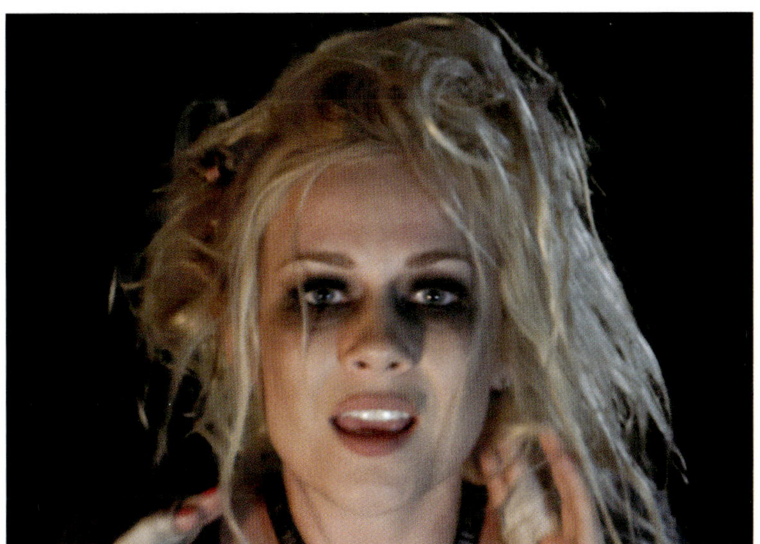

FIG 3.33 Updated hair, which is more detailed and subtle than what was provided by the Refine Soft Matte effect.

We're now ready to integrate a new background behind the actress. We'll do this in Chapter 4. This version of the project is saved as *tutorial_2_2.aep* in the *\ProjectFiles\aeFiles\Chapter3* directory.

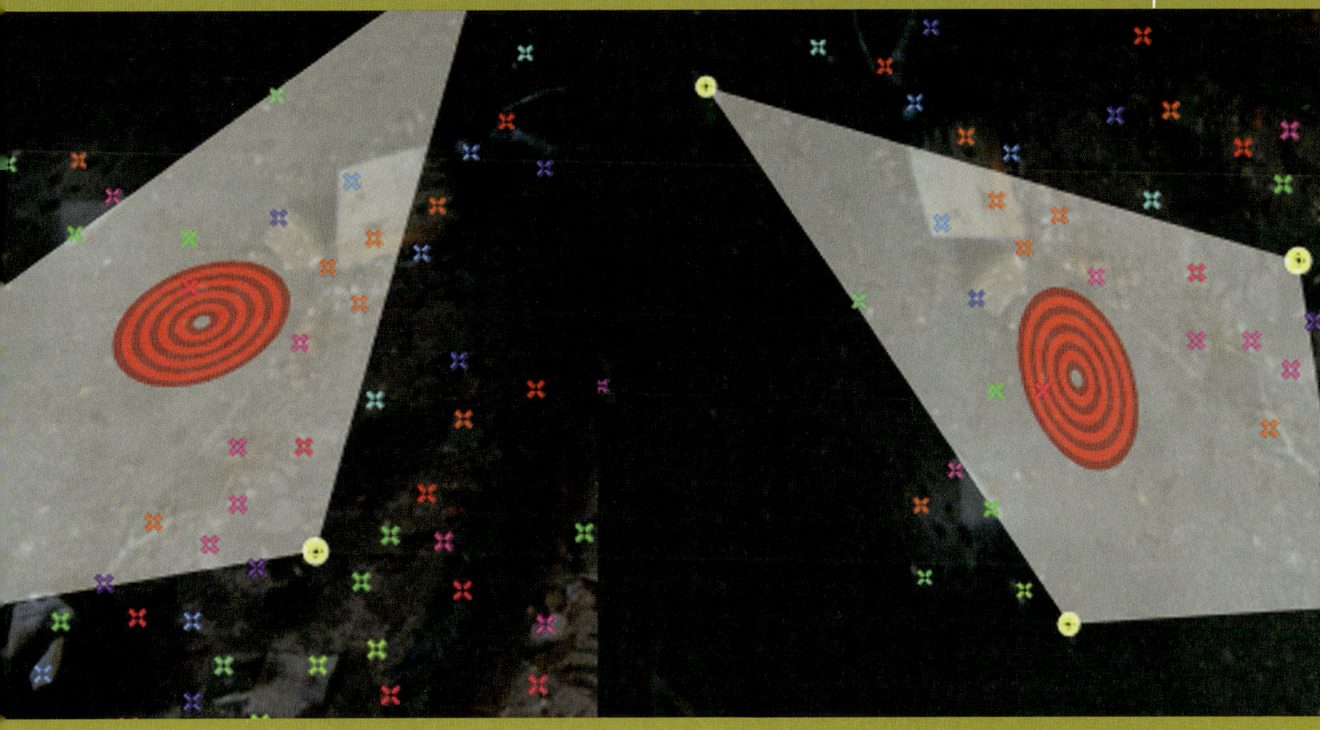

Transforming and Motion Tracking

There are many opportunities to apply animation inside a compositing program such as After Effects. That is, you're not limited to the motion contained within imported renders or footage. You can animate the layer transforms, which include position, rotation, and scale. When transform animation is present, you can activate motion blur to mimic the way a real-world camera captures its images. You can also add motion by motion tracking. Motion tracking captures the movement of features within footage and applies that motion to nonmoving layers (Figure 4.1). This creates the illusion that the affected layers were shot with the original camera.

This chapter includes the following critical information:

- Overview of layer transformation, parenting, and nesting
- Applying motion tracking, including transform, corner-pin, and stabilization tracking
- Introduction to planar and 3D camera motion tracking

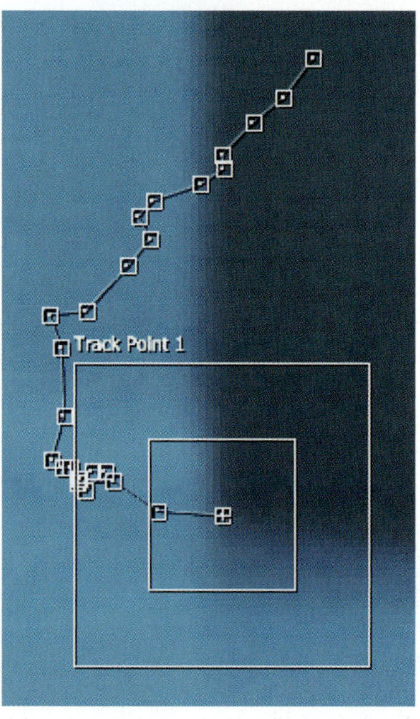

FIG 4.1 Close-up of a motion path automatically created by the Track Motion motion-tracking tool.

Transforming Layers

Each layer in After Effects receives a set of properties in the layer's Transform section. These include Anchor Point, Position, Scale, Rotation, and Opacity.

Working with the Anchor Point

By default, the Anchor Point value is set to the layer center and is indicated by a small crosshair icon in the view panel when the layer is selected (Figure 4.2). For example, a 1920 × 1080 layer has an Anchor Point value of 960, 540 and a 100 × 100 layer has an Anchor Point value of 50, 50. In contrast, the Position is set to the center of the composition. Thus, a layer that is 100 × 100 has a default position of 250, 250 in a 500 × 500 composition (Figure 4.2).

Keep in mind that After Effects screen space places 0, 0 at the top left of the frame. Thus, moving a layer to 0, 0 places the layer's Anchor Point crosshair at the top left. As such, X runs left to right and Y runs from top to bottom.

Changing the Anchor Point value changes the pivot point of the layer. The pivot is the point from which and around which all transforms occur. Hence, changing the Rotation value causes the layer to spin around the current Anchor Point location. Altering the Anchor Point is often useful for offsetting motion-tracked animation, which is demonstrated later in this chapter.

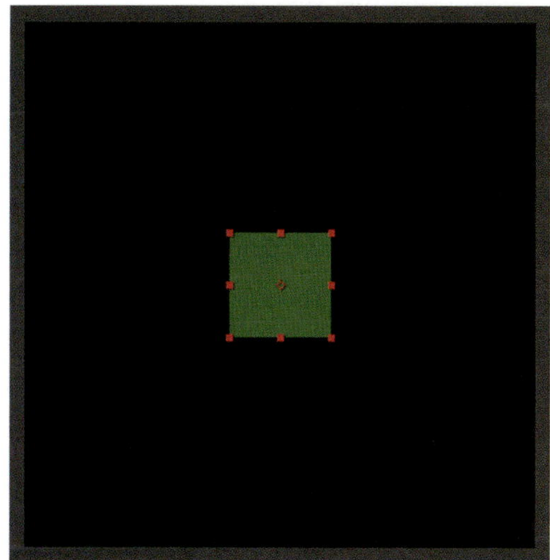

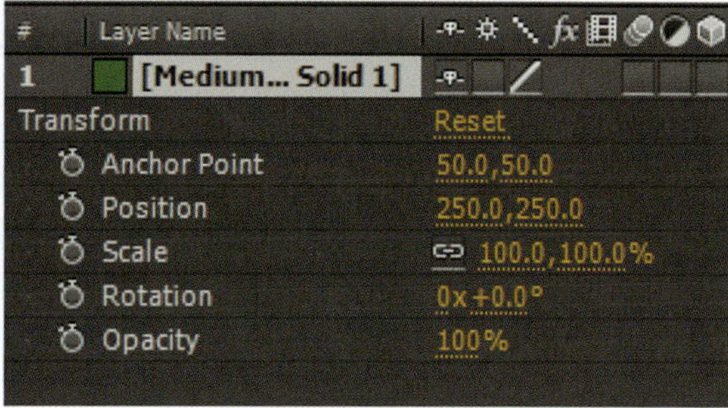

FIG 4.2 Left: A 100 × 100 solid layer in a 500 × 500 composition (the Anchor Point is indicated by the small crosshair at the layer center). Right: The corresponding Transform section of the layer.

Working with Additional Transform Properties

Here are a few tips for working with properties in the Transform section:

Dual Properties

Properties with two values always include the X value on the left and the Y value on the right. This follows the same logic as resolution where X (width) comes before Y (height).

Linked Scale

Scale is linked by default. To change the Scale X and Y values individually, click the link icon (see Figure 4.2) so it disappears. You can re-click the link icon at any time to relink the current X and Y values.

Rotation Revolutions

Rotation carries two numeric values: revolution and degrees. Each time degrees surpasses 360, the revolution value is increased by 1.0, and the degrees are reset to 0. However, when working with a Rotation curve in the Graph Editor, the total number of degrees is stored by keyframes. For example, if the Rotation property reads 2x90, the curve value is stored as 810, which is equal to (360 × 2) + 90.

Keyframing

You can keyframe any transform property. Each property carries a Time icon. To jump between keyframes, click the small forward and backward buttons to the left of the keyframed property.

Linked Position

By default, Position X and Position Y are linked and cannot be keyframed separately. At the same time X and Y cannot be edited separately in the Graph Editor. However, you can RMB-click over the *Position* name in the Transform section and choose Separate Dimensions from the menu. For a demonstration, see the previous chapter.

Resetting

You can return the transforms of a layer to their defaults by clicking the word *Reset* at the top of the Transform section.

For more specific techniques covering keyframing and working within the Graph Editor, see Chapter 3.

Parenting

You can parent one layer to another by changing the Parent menu to the name of the parent layer (Figure 4.3). (If the Parent menu is not visible, click the Toggle Switches/Modes button at the bottom of the layer outline.) This forces the "child" layer to adopt the transforms of the parent. If both the child and parent layer possess unique transforms or transform animations, the net transformation values are used. For example, if the child layer is rotated 45 degrees and the parent layer is rotated 10 degrees, the net rotation for the child layer is 55 degrees. That said, the transforms passed to the child layer occur at or around the parent layer's Anchor Point position and not the position of the child's Anchor Point. Nevertheless, parenting offers a convenient means to have one layer "follow" another.

Nesting and Transform Collapsing

When creating a complex project in After Effects, you often wind up with a large number of layers in a single composition. A large stack of layers can make it difficult to fine-tune the result. One way to avoid this is to use additional compositions. In order to pass the result of one composition to the next, you can *nest* compositions. To nest one composition into a

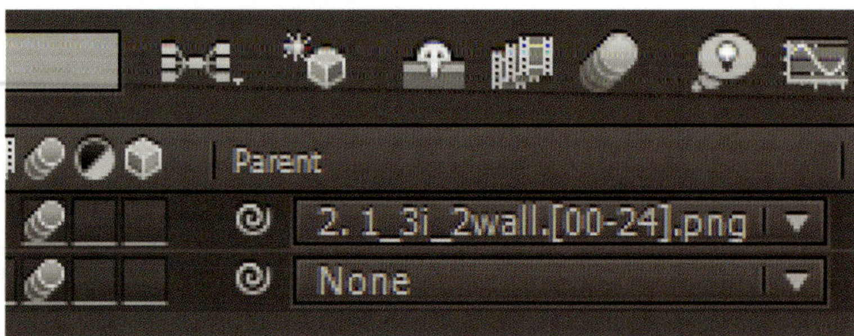

FIG 4.3 The Parent menu for two layers appears at the bottom right of this figure. With this example, the top layer is parented to the bottom layer. The Motion Blur switch sits to the left of the menus and is activated for both layers. However, the Enables Motion Blur switch for the composition (at the top center) has not yet been activated.

second composition (referred to as a *containing composition*), LMB-drag the composition from the Project panel and drop it into the second, containing composition on the timeline. When a composition is nested, it's essentially flattened and appears as a single, new layer (Figure 4.4).

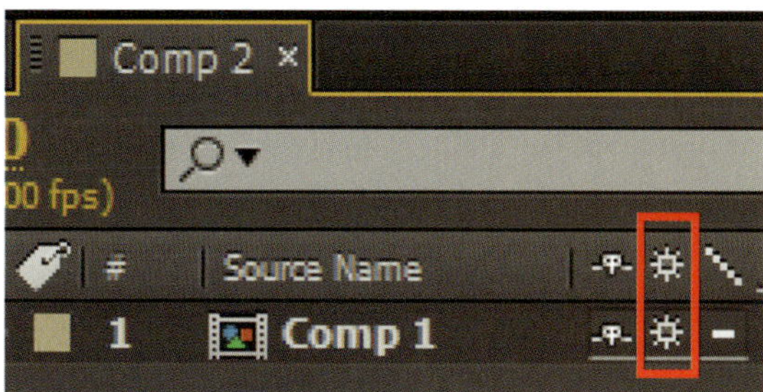

FIG 4.4 A nested composition, named Comp 1, is nested in Comp 2. Note the Collapse Transformations switch (outlined in red).

Nesting offers several advantages:

Transform and Effect Application You can apply transformations or effects to a nested composition in one step (as opposed to applying the transformations or effects to numerous layers).

Linked Compositions The original composition remains intact with all its layers, transforms, and effects. If you adjust the original composition, the nested version updates automatically.

Simplification Nesting allows you to create a series of compositions with fewer contained layers. This simplifies the management of complex projects and prevents a single composition from becoming crowded and difficult to see within the timeline area.

One potential danger of nesting comes in the form of redundant transformations that create a loss of quality. For example, the following scenario produces a degraded result:

- Layer 1 within Comp 1 is scaled by 50 percent.
- Comp 1 is nested within Comp 2.
- The Comp 1 layer within Comp 2 is scaled by 150 percent.

With this scenario, the net scale applied to Layer 1 is 75 percent (50 percent scale in Comp 1 and 150 percent scale in Comp 2). Because the scale transformation happens in two steps, the resulting pixels are blurrier. If a single transformation were applied (75 percent scale), the result would be sharper. The combination of transformations to preserve quality is called *concatenation*. With After Effects, concatenation is achieved with the Collapse Transformations switch, which each nested composition carries (see Figure 4.4).

If the Collapse Transformations switch is selected for a nested composition, the transformations are applied *after* the effects and masks are applied. This allows the transformations of the nested and containing composition to be combined. If you nest a vector layer, such as a shape or text, the Collapse Transformations switch is replaced with a Continuously Rasterize switch.

Precomposing and Pre-Rendering

As an alternative to manually nesting a composition within a second composition, you can precompose specific layers. *Precomposing* moves selected layers into a new composition; the new composition is then nested into the original composition. To precompose in After Effects, you can follow these steps:

1. Select the layer or layers you wish to precompose. Choose Layer > Pre-Compose through the main menu.
2. In the Pre-Compose window, enter a name for the new composition to be created. If you've selected more than one layer within the composition, the Move All Attributes Into New Composition is selected by default. Click the OK button to close the window. The new composition is created and the selected layers are placed within it. The layers are moved with their transforms, masks, and effects. The new composition is nested within the original composition.
3. If you've only selected one layer, you have the option to choose the Leave All Attributes In Comp option (Figure 4.5). With this option, the selected layer is placed within the new composition, but the transforms, masks, and effects are applied to the nested composition layer.

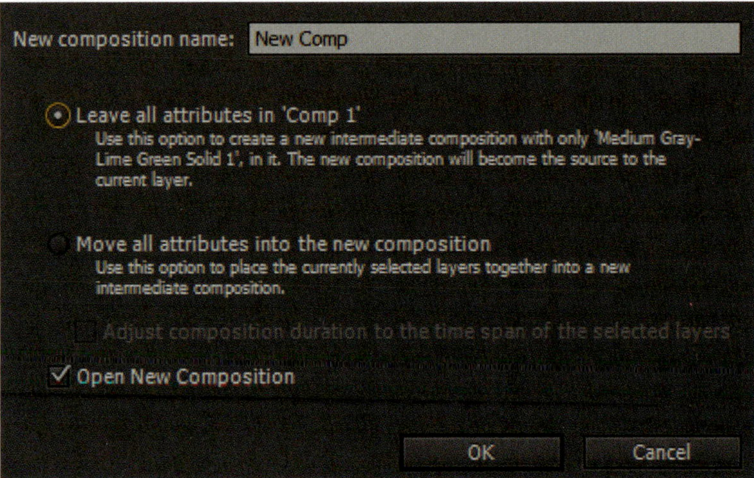

FIG 4.5 The Pre-Compose window with one layer selected.

In contrast, *pre-rendering* allows you to render out a movie or image sequence and thus permanently flatten a composition. To pre-render in After Effects, select a composition and choose Composition > Pre-Render. The Composition is added to the render queue. Set the Output Module and Output To options to select an appropriate render format and location and press the Render button. After the completion of the render, the rendered movie or image sequence is imported automatically. Any nested iteration of the rendered composition is replaced with the movie or the image sequence. Pre-rendering a complex composition can save a significant amount of rendering time as you continue to build the project. However, you should not pre-render until you feel a composition has been thoroughly adjusted and is complete or close to completion. When you choose the Pre-Render option, the Post-Render Action menu, in the Output Module Settings window, is set to Import & Replace Usage.

Motion Blur

Any layer that carries transform animation, whether it's through changes in position, rotation, or scale, can gain motion blur. Motion blur is a natural artifact of real-world cameras that require a small period of time to expose a single frame (referred to as *shutter speed*). For example, if the shutter speed is 1/30th of a second, the motion blur trail of a moving object corresponds to the distance the object moves in 1/30th of a second.

To activate the motion blur in After Effects, click the small Motion Blur switch beside the layer name (see Figure 4.3 earlier in this chapter). The switch carries three small circles. If the switch does not appear, click the Toggle Switches/Modes button at the bottom of the layer outline. In addition, you must activate motion blur for the entire composition by clicking Enables Motion Blur For All Layers at the top of the layer outline.

The length of the motion blur trail is determined by the distance the layer moves during one frame and the Shutter Angle and Shutter Phase property values. Shutter Angle and Shutter Phase are located in the Advanced tab of the Composition Settings window (Figure 4.6). (Each composition may carry unique Shutter Angle and Shutter Phase values.)

By default, Shutter Angle is set to 180 degrees, which emulates common video camera shutters. However, you can increase this value to lengthen the motion blur trail or reduce the value to shorten the motion blur trail. You can determine the virtual shutter speed (as measured in After Effects frames), and the length of the corresponding motion blur trail, with the following formula:

$$\textit{Shutter Speed} = 1/(360/\textit{Shutter Angle})$$

Thus, to create a blur trail equivalent to a shutter speed that lasts 1 frame, set Shutter Angle to 360 degrees. In contrast, Shutter Phase determines when, in

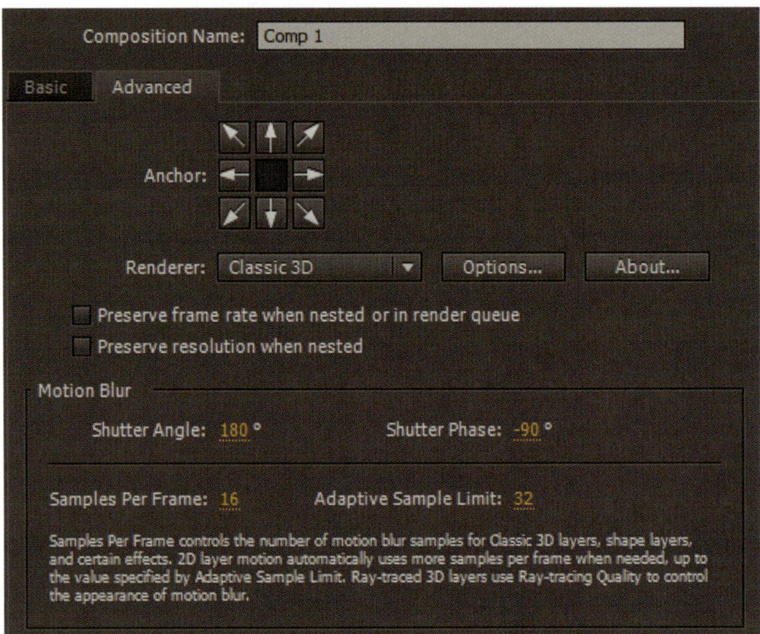

FIG 4.6 The Advanced tab of the Composition Settings window.

time, the motion blur trail starts and ends. You can use the following formula to determine the blur start and end frames, which remain dependent on the Shutter Angle:

Start Frame = Current Frame – (1/(360 / (Shutter Angle + Shutter Phase)))

End Frame = Current Frame + (1/(360 / (Shutter Angle + Shutter Phase)))

Thus, if Shutter Angle is 180, Shutter Phase is –90, and the current frame is 2, the motion blur start frame is 1.75 and the motion blur end frame is 2.25. To center the motion blur trail at the layer's current position (so the trail extends backwards and forwards in time), set the Shutter Phase value to (Shutter Angle/2) * –1. The ability to adjust the start and stop of motion blur trails, as well as the motion blur trail length, is useful for matching After Effects blur to the motion blur contained within live-action film or video footage.

The Advanced tab of the Composition Settings window also includes quality settings in the form of Samples Per Frame and Adaptive Sample Limit. The higher the Samples Per Frame and Adaptive Sample Limit, the smoother the resulting blur but the longer the render time. Standard 2D layers use sample values between the Samples Per Frames and Adaptive Sample Limit, depending on the aggressiveness of the blur. (3D layer rendering is discussed in Chapter 5.)

Motion Tracking

Motion tracking is a process through which the motion of a feature within a piece of footage is determined. You can apply the motion-tracking data to a different layer and thereby have the layer pick up the same motion. In general, the main goal of motion tracking is one of the following:

- To impart motion to a different layer so that it looks like the layer was shot with the same real-world camera. The layer may take the form of a 3D render, a static piece of artwork, or video footage. For example, if you shoot a television with a moving camera, you can use motion tracking to place new video footage onto the television screen. This type of motion tracking is commonly known as *matchmoving*. (Matchmoving is sometimes used to refer to all forms of motion tracking.)
- To impart motion to a different layer so that the layer appears to follow a particular feature. The camera need not move in this case. For example, you can use motion tracking to add a 3D object to the hand of a person who is gesticulating.
- To remove motion. You can use motion tracking to remove camera jitter or minor movement so that it appears as if the camera is static. This process is known as *stabilization*.

Transform Tracking

Transform tracking is a variant of motion tracking where the motion is only detected in the X and Y directions. Transform tracking can detect changes in position, rotation, and scale (scale changes may occur as a camera "zooms" in or out or an object moves closer or farther from the camera). After Effects supports transform tracking through the Track Motion tool. The Track Motion tool allows you to select a particular feature within the frame. A feature is a set of identifiable pixels. A feature might be a motion-tracking tape mark, the corner of a poster, a pebble on the ground, a rivet on a machine, a sticker, or any other small pattern. To apply the Track Motion tool, use the following tutorial as a guide.

Track motion mini-tutorial

With this tutorial, we'll detect the motion within a shot and apply the motion-tracking data to a null object as a test. Follow these steps:

1. Create a new After Effects project. Import *1_31_2wall.##.png* from the *\ProjectFiles\Plates\MotionTracking\1_3i_2wall* directory. Set the frame rate interpretation to 24 fps. LMB-drag the image sequence into a new composition.

2. Choose Layer > New > Null Object. A Null 1 layer is added to the composition. Null objects do not render, but carry a set of transforms. You can apply motion-tracking data to a null as a test.
3. With the footage layer selected, choose Animation > Track Motion. The Layer view opens. The Tracker panel also opens at the bottom right of the program (Figure 4.7). Note that the Position radio checkbox is selected by default.

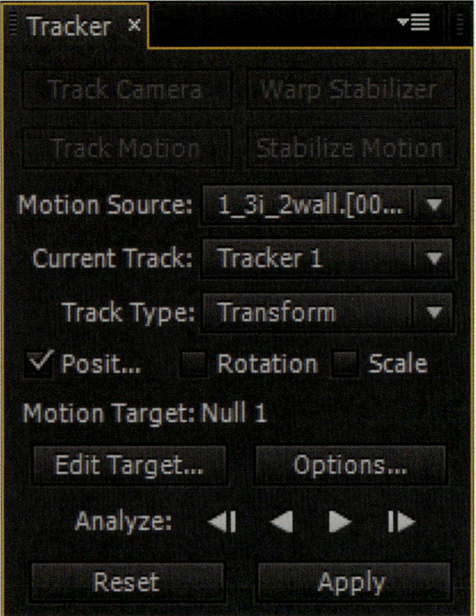

FIG 4.7 The Tracker panel.

4. A track point, Track Point 1, is displayed in the Layer view. LMB-drag the track point (place the mouse over an empty space within the nested point boxes) and place it over a corner where horizontal and vertical tape marks meet (Figure 4.8). When you LMB-drag the track point, a zoomed-in view of the pixels within its feature region (the center box) is displayed.
5. In the Tracker panel, press the Analyze Forward button. The timeline is played forward and the motion of the feature within the Anchor Point feature region (the inner box) is detected. A motion path is laid down in the viewer to indicate this motion (see Figure 4.1 at the start of this chapter).
6. When the timeline reaches the final frame, click the Tracker panel's Edit Target button. In the Motion Target window, change the Layer menu to Null 1. Click the Tracker panel's Apply button. Press the OK

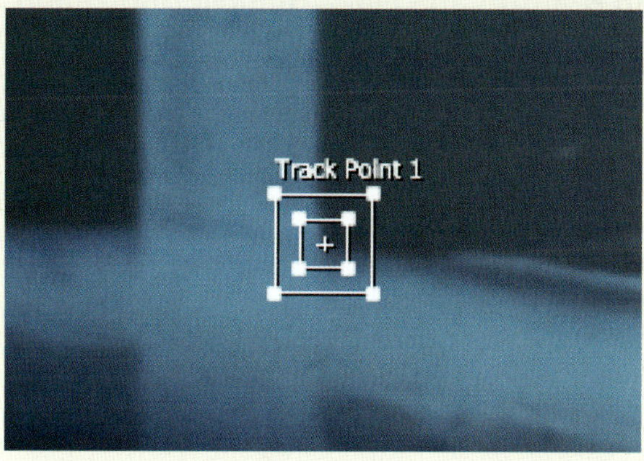

FIG 4.8 Track Point 1 is positioned over a corner formed by tape marks on the wall.

button when the Motion Tracker Apply Options window opens. The view panel switches back to the Composition view. The Null 1 layer's Position is keyframed automatically to follow the tracked feature.

7. Manually scrub the timeline by LMB-dragging the Current Frame Indicator bar in the timeline. The red square of the null follows the tape corner as if it was shot by the same real-world camera (Figure 4.9). Note that the null's upper-left corner is pinned to the motion path.

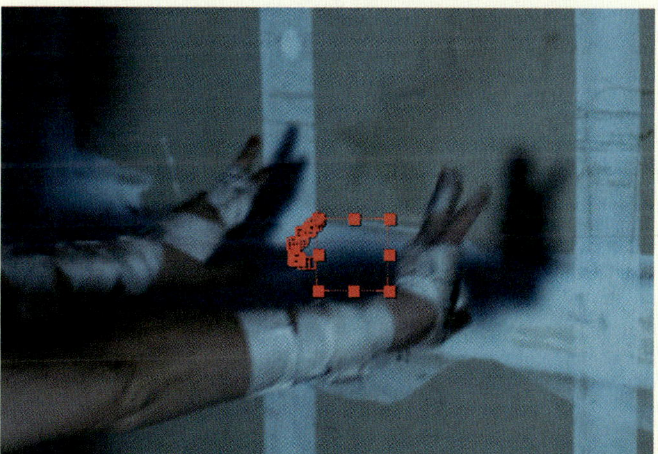

FIG 4.9 Motion-tracking data is applied to a null object, which appears as a red box when the null layer is selected. The null layer's animated Position property creates a red motion path in the view panel.

Although this tutorial uses footage with easy-to-track motion, other shots may be more difficult. Hence, there are numerous ways to adjust track points, add additional track points, and manipulate the resulting motion paths. These techniques are discussed through the remainder of this chapter. A completed version of this tutorial is saved as *mini_transform_tracking.aep* in the *\ProjectFiles\aeFiles\Chapter4* directory.

Selecting Features and Fine-Tuning Motion Paths

When choosing a feature to track, look for the following traits:

Small Pattern Although you can increase the size of the track point region boxes, large regions slow the motion-tracking calculation.
High-Contrast Features that include high-contrast edges produce the best tracking results.
Low Motion Blur The heavier the blur, the more difficult it is to accurately track a feature over time.
No Occlusion Features that enter or exit the frame or are covered by other objects will cause the motion tracker to fail.
Stable Lighting Features that enter or exit light fields or shadows are more difficult to track due to the change in color values.

It may not be possible to find a feature that fulfills all the listed criteria. As such, you may need to fine-tune the resulting motion paths. There are various ways to do this, which are discussed here.

Reanalyze

You can write over previously tracked motion paths by reanalyzing. You are free to analyze forward or backward. You can also analyze in both directions one frame at a time. Hence, Analyze Forward, Analyze Backward, Analyze 1 Frame Forward, and Analyze 1 Frame Backward buttons are included in the Tracker panel.

Choose a New Feature

If a feature produces an inaccurate motion path or causes the tracker to consistently fail, choose a new feature and reanalyze. Note that you should set the Composition panel's Resolution/Down Sample Factor menu to Full—otherwise, the Layer view will display a simplified version of the frame (where pixels are skipped) and it will be more difficult to accurately track features.

Analyze from a Mid-Point

You are not obligated to track from frame 0 or frame 1 forward. You can position the track point on any frame where the feature is easily seen. You can then analyze forward and/or analyze backward. The order of analysis is up to you.

Adjust the Anchor Point Regions

At any phase of the tracking process, you are free to adjust the Anchor Point regions. To do so, LMB-drag a box corner point. The inner region, indicated by the inner box, is the feature region. The feature region defines the pattern of pixels that is tracked. The outer region, indicated by the outer box, is the search region, and defines the area in which the program searches for the feature should the feature be temporarily lost due to occlusion, rapid motion, change in lighting, and so on.

Manually Adjust Keyframes

A keyframe is laid down for each frame of the timeline that is tracked. The keyframes appear on the motion path in the Layer view as hollow boxes. You can LMB-drag the keyframe boxes to new positions. This is particularly useful if the motion path suddenly moves off the feature. Use manual adjustment sparingly, however, as it can lead to jitter.

Track a Different Channel

If you click the Options button in the Tracker panel, the Motion Tracker Options window opens (Figure 4.10). Here, you can choose to track a particular channel through the Channel section. The Luminance option compares pixel brightness and is suitable for high-contrast footage. The RGB option compares red, green, and blue pixel values and ignores brightness; this is useful for footage that carries distinct colors, such as green screen footage. The Saturation option examines its namesake, which is the amount of contrast that exists between color channels.

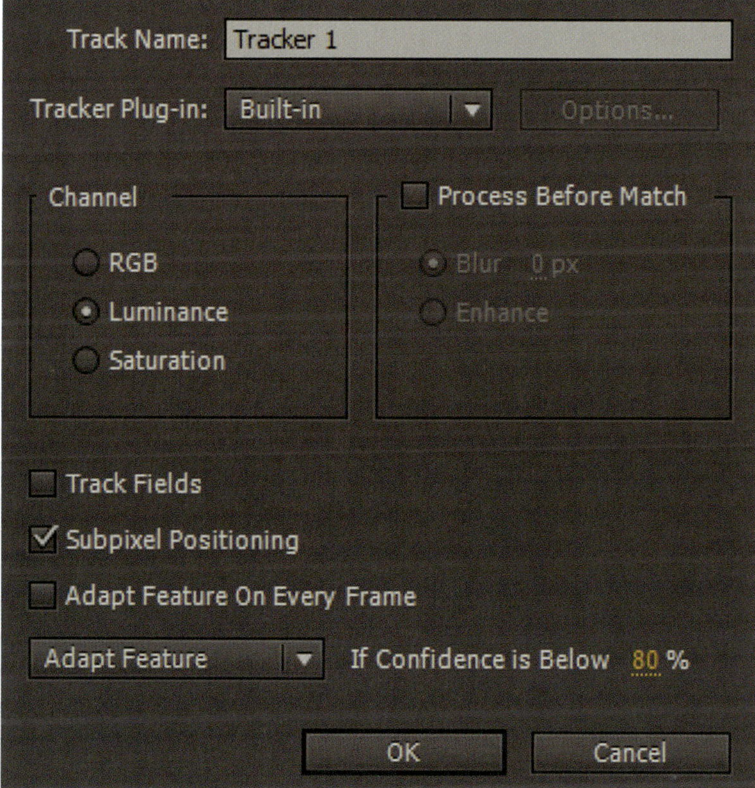

FIG 4.10 The Motion Tracker Options window, as seen in CC 2014.

Pre-Process the Footage

In the Motion Tracker Options window, you can select the Process Before Match checkbox. You then can choose Blur or Enhance. Enhance sharpens the footage before the motion tracking is applied. This is useful for soft or blurry footage. Blur applies a blur filter with a strength set by the accompanying field. Blur can improve the tracking results for footage that carries heavy film grain or video noise. Note that After Effects CC 2015 removes the Process Before Match section. Instead, CC 2015 offers an Enhance Before Match checkbox. Nevertheless, you can apply your own pre-process by applying effects to a footage layer, nesting the layer's composition into a second composition, and then applying Track Motion to the nested composition in the containing composition.

Alter the Tracker Behavior

In the Motion Tracker Options window, you can choose what the tracker does when its confidence drops. *Confidence* is the mathematical certainty with which the tracker has found the correct feature pattern for a frame. With the behavior menu set to Adapt Feature, the tracker allows for variations in the feature pattern over time. Although the tracker is less likely to fail with this setting, it may cause the track point to suddenly "jump" to a feature pattern that is roughly equivalent to the original. Despite this, Adapt Feature generally produces good results with a wide range of footage. Nevertheless, you can set the behavior menu to Continue Tracking, which ignores a loss in confidence and presses ahead, or Extrapolate Motion, which estimates the position of the feature by deleting low-confidence keyframes (hence, some positions are inbetweened). You can also set the menu to Stop Tracking, which simply kills the tracking when the confidence reaches a value below the percentage set by the If Confidence Is Below field. It may be useful to raise the percentage value when working with difficult footage to prevent the tracker from dying on each and every frame.

Transform Tracking with Rotation and Scale

By default, the Track Motion tool only detects positional changes. However, you can choose to track rotation and/or scale changes. To do so, select the Rotation and Scale checkboxes in the Tracker panel before analyzing. The addition of the Rotation or Scale dimensions adds a second track point, Track Point 2, to the Layer view. The two track points are connected by a "rubber band" and are needed to determine if the camera or particular objects undergo rotation, become larger, or become smaller (Figure 4.11).

You can position and scale Track Point 2 as you would place Track Point 1. For example, if you want to detect the rotation and zoom of a handheld camera, place the two track points along the edge of a door or window or similar straight edge. Optimally, the pixel pattern below each point's feature region should possess the traits listed in the prior section. When you apply

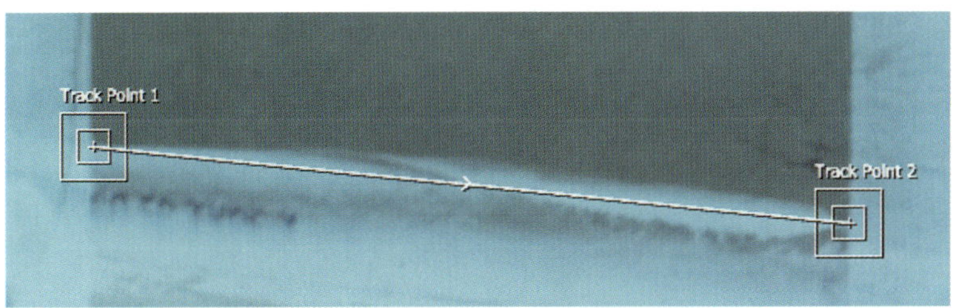

FIG 4.11 The addition of Rotation to the tracker creates Track Point 2. Here, the track points are lined up along a tape edge. Each track point is centered over a high-contrast corner.

the motion-tracking data with Rotation and Scale selected, the target layer's Position, Scale, and Rotation properties are keyframed automatically.

Adjusting Applied Tracking Transforms

As discussed, applying the motion-tracking data creates keyframes for the Position, Rotation, and/or Scale properties of the target layer. Although you can alter the resulting animation curves in the Graph Editor, this becomes difficult due to the large number of keyframes. Alternatively, you can use the techniques in this section to refine the animation.

Adjusting the Anchor Point

If the target layer suddenly "jumps" to an undesirable location when the motion-tracking data is applied, you can correct its position by altering its Anchor Point values. This adjustment does not harm the motion-tracking data and does not alter the Position animation. When you apply motion-tracking data, the Anchor Point of the target layer is lined up with the attach point of Track Point 1 (which is indicated by a small + icon at the track point's center).

Deleting Keyframes

You can delete Position, Scale, and Rotation keyframes to make the corresponding curves easier to work with in the Graph Editor. You can also decimate a curve by using the Smoother tool (Figure 4.12). To apply the Smoother, choose Window > Smoother, select keyframes of a curve in the Graph Editor or timeline view, and press the Apply button in the Smoother panel (the panel appears at the bottom right of the program). You can increase the aggressiveness of the decimation by raising the Tolerance value in the Smoother panel.

Updating the Motion Paths

At any time, you can return to the Tracker panel and refine the motion-tracking motion paths. You can reapply the data and thus overwrite the old transform animation of the target layer.

If the Tracker panel is closed, choose Window > Tracker. If a prior tracking session is not visible in the Tracker panel, change the Motion Source menu to the layer to which Track Motion was applied. Note that each time you choose

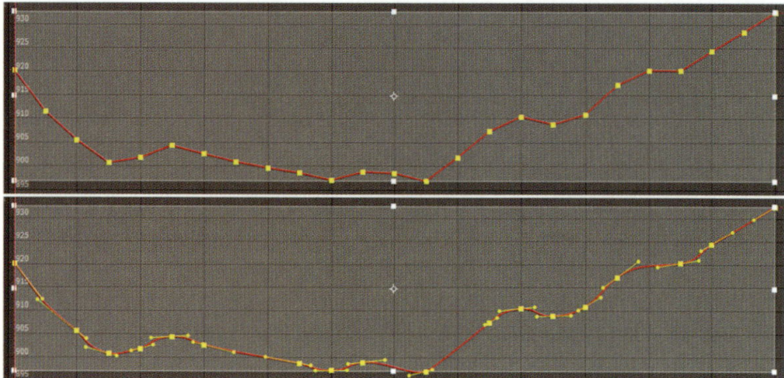

FIG 4.12 Position X curve created by motion tracking. The top view shows the curve before decimation, with one keyframe per frame. The bottom view shows the curve after the decimation provided by the Smoother tool with a Tolerance value of 0.5.

Animation > Track Motion, a new tracker is created and named Tracker *n*. You can choose to work with a specific tracker by changing the Current Track menu to the tracker name. Each tracker is listed in the Motion Trackers section of the layer (above the Transform section). Keyframes for the track point position (named Feature Center), track point attach point position (same as Feature Center unless manually moved), and confidence value are stored in this section.

Tracking Multiple Features

Occasionally, it may be necessary to motion track multiple features. This is generally required when no single feature is clearly visible throughout the entire duration of the composition. For example, features may enter or leave the frame, become occluded, or suffer from heavy motion blur. You can follow these basic steps to track multiple features:

1. Determine what feature is available at the start of the footage. Place the track point over the feature. Analyze Forward until the feature is no longer viable. You can stop the analysis by pressing the Stop button in the Tracker panel.
2. Locate a new feature that is visible from that point forward. If the last few frames of previous tracking are inaccurate, back up to an earlier frame by LMB-dragging the Current Time Indicator bar.
3. Alt/Opt + LMB-drag the track point to the new feature. If you use Alt/Opt while dragging, the track point attach point remains along the original motion path. Analyze forward. Repeat steps 2 and 3 if you need to jump to additional new features.
4. After you've analyzed the entire timeline, apply the data by clicking the Apply button. After Effects takes into account the multiple features with their offset motion path segments and applies a single, continuous keyframe animation to the target layer. The target layer's Anchor Point is lined up with the Track Point 1 attach point, which remains along the motion path created for the first feature that was tracked.

Stabilizing Footage

You can use the Track Motion tool to stabilize a plate and thus make it appear as if the camera is not moving. To practice stabilization techniques, use the following tutorial.

Stabilization mini-tutorial

1. Create a new After Effects project. Import *shake.##.png* from the *\ProjectFiles\Plates\MotionTracking\Shake* directory. Set the frame rate interpretation to 24 fps. LMB-drag the image sequence into the timeline to create a new composition. Play back the timeline. Note that the shot features two types of camera motion: smooth tilts and high-frequency jitter.
2. With the new layer selected, choose Animation > Track Motion. The Layer view opens. The Tracker panel also opens at the bottom right. Change the Track Type from Transform to Stabilize.
3. A track point, Track Point 1, is displayed in the Layer view. While on the first frame of the timeline, LMB-drag the track point and place it at the corner of the left-hand tracking tape mark. Place the Anchor Point's attach point over at the border between the white tape and the green screen. Scale the feature region and search region boxes so that they cover most of the tape X (Figure 4.13).

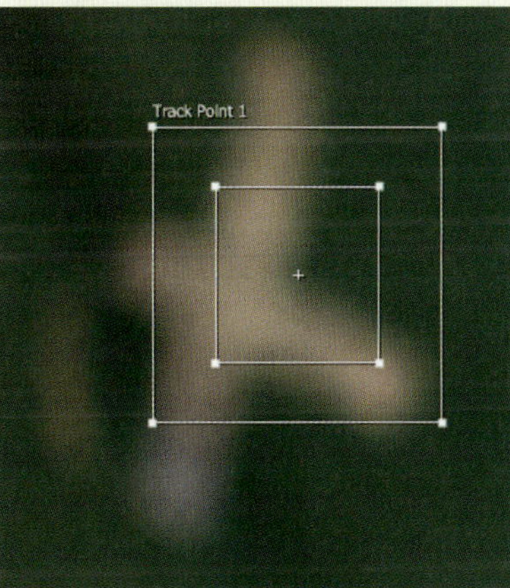

FIG 4.13 Track Point 1 is placed and scaled over the left-hand tracking mark.

4. In the Tracker panel, press the Analyze Forward button. The timeline plays forward and the motion of the feature within the Anchor Point feature region (the inner box) is detected. A motion path is laid down in the viewer to indicate this motion.
5. When the timeline reaches the final frame, click the Tracker panel's Apply button. The motion-tracking data is applied to the same layer. The view panel switches to the Composition view. The layer's Anchor Point is keyframed automatically.

6. Play back. The layer is moved left/right and up/down in order to pin the position of the tracking tape mark so it does not move. Thus, in turn, the camera appears static.
7. The stabilization reveals the frame edges as the frame is repositioned (Figure 4.14). This leads to black gaps at the bottom and right sides. To avoid this, create a new composition with the same resolution, frame rate, and duration, and nest the first composition into it. Go to the nested layer and change the Scale to 110 percent and the Position Y value to 567. Play back. The gaps are no longer visible.

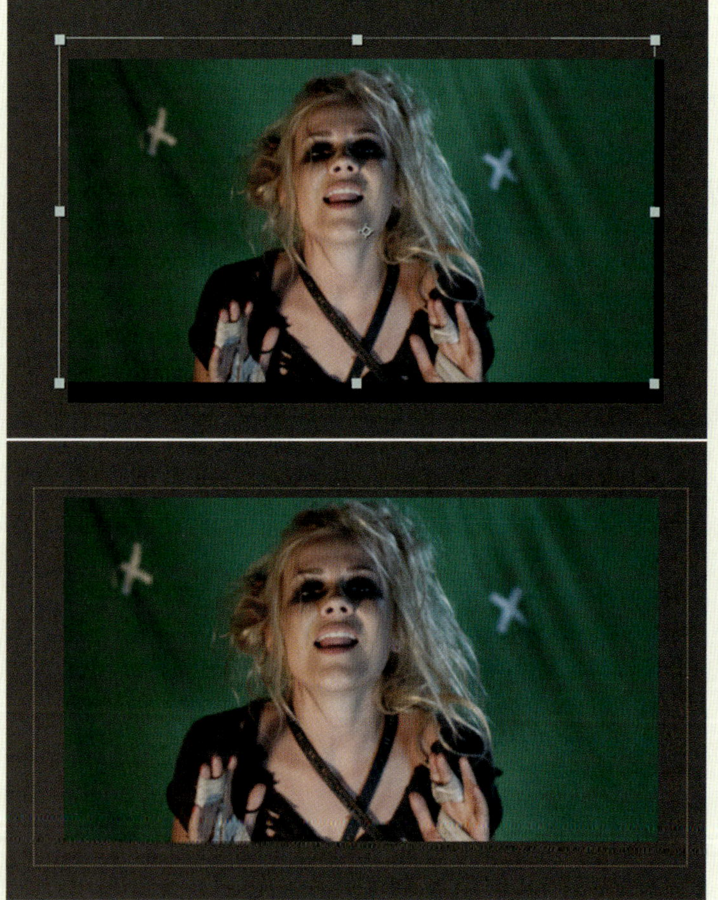

FIG 4.14 Top: The stabilization of the layer reveals the layer edges and black gaps at the edge of the composition. Bottom: The composition is nested and scaled, removing the gaps.

Note that stabilization is unable to remove motion blur created by the moving camera. A completed version of this tutorial is saved as *mini_stabilization.aep* in the *\ProjectFiles\aeFiles\Chapter4* directory.

Corner-Pin Tracking

Corner-pin tracking utilizes four track points to follow a rectangular feature. For example, you can use corner-pin tracking to track the four corners of a window, door, picture frame, cell phone screen, billboard, and so on. When you apply corner-pin motion-tracking data to a layer, the four corners of the layer are moved to the track point positions, thus fitting the layer to the tracked rectangle. To apply corner-pin tracking, you can use the following tutorial.

Corner-pin mini-tutorial

You can use the Track Motion tool to apply corner-pin tracking. To practice this form of tracking, follow these steps:

1. Create a new After Effects project. Import *wallpov.##.png* from the *\ProjectFiles\Plates\MotionTracking\WallPOV* directory. Set the frame rate interpretation to 24 fps. LMB-drag the image sequence into the timeline to create a new composition.
2. With the *wallpov.##.png* footage layer selected, choose Animation > Track Motion. The Layer view opens. The Tracker panel also opens at the bottom right.
3. Change the Track Type menu from Transform to Perspective Corner Pin. Four track points, connected by "rubber bands," are added. Play back the timeline to determine which frame contains a minimal amount of camera motion blur. For example, frame 10 is relatively sharp.
4. Position the track points over the four corners formed by overlapping paint lines (Figure 4.15). Select corners that contain good contrast. You can move each point independent of the other. Note that the track points are numbered in the following fashion (starting at the top left and moving clockwise): 1, 2, 4, 3. It's best to maintain that order. Moving the track points past each other so that the bands become twisted and the track point order changes may cause tracking errors.

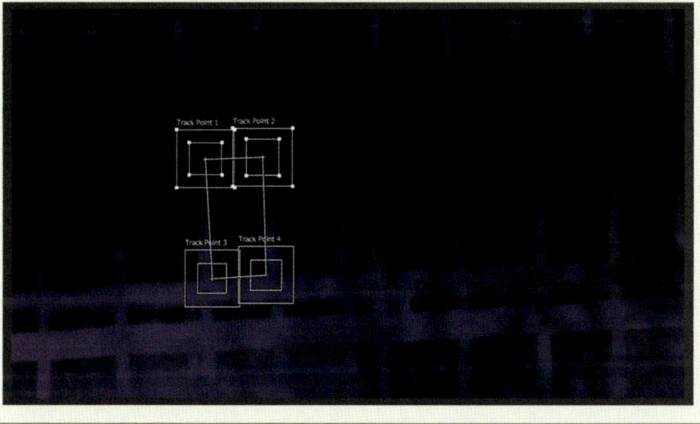

FIG 4.15 Positioned and scaled track points.

Feel free to adjust the feature and search region boxes of the track points. Larger boxes will improve the tracking when the footage is dimly lit or otherwise low contrast.

5. Use the Analyze buttons to create motion paths for the track points. Use the suggestions in the "Selecting Features and Fine-Tuning Motion Paths" section earlier in this chapter to maximize the quality of the motion paths. Note that the relatively dim lighting and heavy camera blur contained within the first few frames makes the motion tracking particularly difficult in that area. Hence, it may be necessary to manually place the track points in the correct locations for those few frames.
6. When the motion paths are complete, import the *warning.png* file from the *\ProjectFiles\Art* directory. LMB-drag the warning image to the top of the layer outline. Click the Edit Target Button in the Tracker panel and check that the drawing layer is selected. Click the Apply button. The view panel returns to the Composition view. A Corner Pin effect is added to the warning layer and appears in the Effects section. The effect carries four sets of keyframes that determine the new positions of the layer's corners. Thus, the layer is distorted to fit the tracked rectangular shape. Play back the timeline. The four layer corners are placed at the attach point positions of the track points. In addition, the warning layer's Position property is animated.
7. Although the sign layer now carries transform animation, there is no motion blur. Activate the blur by clicking the layer's Motion Blur switch. Make sure that the composition's Enables Motion Blur For All Layers switch is also activated. Play back. The sign gains heavy motion blur that matches the footage. Feel free to adjust the motion blur settings in the Advanced tab of the Composition Settings window

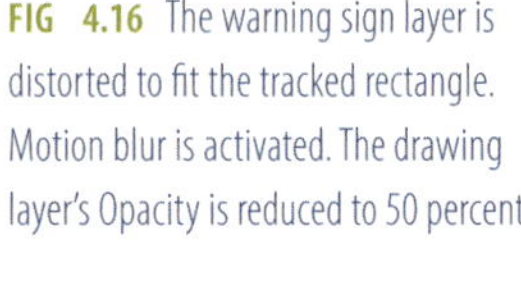

FIG 4.16 The warning sign layer is distorted to fit the tracked rectangle. Motion blur is activated. The drawing layer's Opacity is reduced to 50 percent.

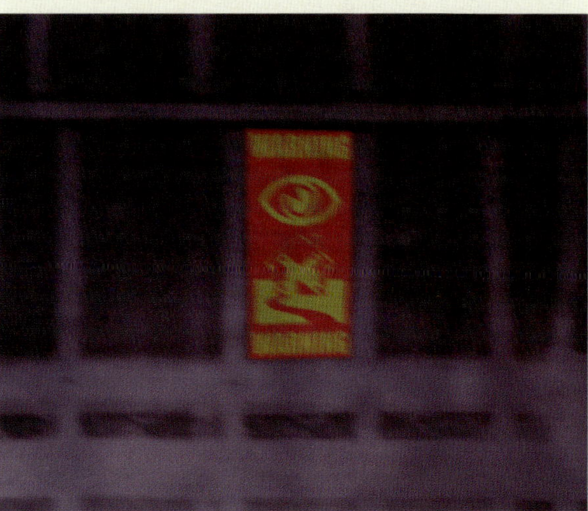

(see the "Motion Blur" section earlier in this chapter). To better integrate the sign, reduce the warning layer's Opacity to 50 percent. This allows the purple of the wall to mix with the paper colors (Figure 4.16). A finished version of this tutorial is saved as *mini_corner_pin.aep* from the *\ProjectFiles\aeFiles\Chapter4* directory. (To better integrate the sign, we'll also apply color-grading techniques in Chapter 9.)

If the distortion of the targeted layer prevents the layer from retaining a rectangular or square shape, you can offset the corner pin animation and "push" the corners back into a more desirable location. To make the warning sign wider and a bit more rectangular, you can follow these additional optional steps:

1. Expand the Corner Pin section of the warning layer. Select one of the corner names, such as *Upper Left*. Open the Graph Editor. LMB-drag a selection marquee around all the keyframes of either the X (red) or Y (green) curve. Place your mouse over one of the selected keyframes and LMB-drag straight up or straight down. The values of the keyframes are increased if you drag up or decreased if you drag down. The corner of the layer is moved in the viewer. Be careful not to drag the keyframes left or right in the Graph Editor, which offsets the animation curve in time.
2. Repeat this process with other curves and other corners until the layer appears rectangular once again. You can also alter the scale of the layer by offsetting the corners (Figure 4.17). This does not affect the quality of the motion tracking. However, the farther you push the corners, the most potential there is to see subtle flaws in the tracking in the form of

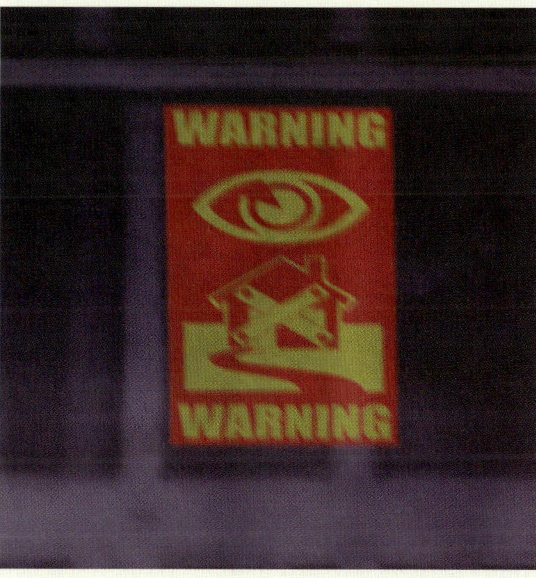

FIG 4.17 The sign is widened and made more rectangular and by offsetting the Corner Pin effect's corner animation curves.

sliding. That said, you can adjust individual corner pin X or Y keyframes to smooth out the result. An offset version of this tutorial is saved as *corner_pin_offset.aep* from the *\ProjectFiles\aeFiles\Chapter4* directory.

Note that the Track Type menu of the Tracker panel also provides the Parallel Corner Pin option. This is similar to Perspective Corner Pin but makes the Track Point 4 position dependent on the other three points. For example, if you move Track Point 2, Track Point 4 follows at the same distance. This form of corner pin is suitable for rectangular shapes that undergo predictable or subtle perspective changes.

3D Camera Tracking

3D camera tracking separates itself from 2D tracking methods, such as transform tracking, by operating in a 3D space. The goal of 3D camera tracking systems is the creation of a virtual camera within a 3D space that emulates the original real-world camera. 3D camera tracking attempts to match the real-world lens and any camera motion, such as tilts, pans, and dollies. Hence, 3D tracking is suitable for complex shots where the camera moves in multiple directions (as opposed to a camera that's locked to a tripod).

A basic introduction to 3D camera tracking is included in the following two tutorials. After Effects provides the Track Camera tool for this task. In addition, The Foundry provides its own plug-in. (Note that the program's 3D environment is discussed in great detail in Chapter 5.)

3D camera tracking mini-tutorial

In After Effects, you can use the Track Camera tool to apply 3D camera tracking. You can follow these basic steps:

1. Create a new After Effects project. Import *1_3b_4stand.##.png* from the *\ProjectFiles\Plates\MotionTracking\1_3b_4stand* directory. Set the frame rate interpretation to 24 fps. LMB-drag the image sequence into the timeline to create a new composition.
2. With the footage layer selected, choose Animation > Track Camera. A 3D Camera Tracker effects is added to the layer. A blue "Analyzing" bar appears over the frame in the Composition view. Stop the analysis by clicking the Cancel button at the top of the 3D Camera Tracker section in the Effect Controls panel (Figure 4.18).
3. Note that the Shot Type menu is set to Fixed Angle Of View. This setting is suitable if the camera used a fixed (nonzoom) lens, but the exact lens field of view is not known. If you are aware of the camera field of view, you can switch this menu to Specify Angle Of View and change the Horizontal Angle Of View slider to the correct value. A field-of-view value

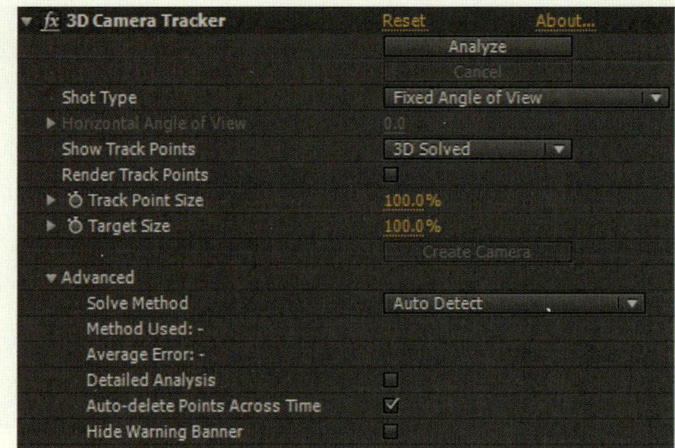

FIG 4.18 The 3D Camera Tracker effect with default values.

is derived through a trigonometric calculation involving the lens focal length and the physical size of the film aperture or image sensor:

*2 * arctan ((film frame or image sensor width/2)/focal length)*

If the camera uses a zoom lens, where the focal length changes during the shot, set the menu to Variable Zoom. With this tutorial, the default Fixed Angle Of View option is appropriate.

4. Go to the Advanced section. Note that the Solve Method menu is set to Auto Detect. This forces the effect to determine the style of camera motion. The Solve Method menu offers three additional camera motion types: Typical, Mostly Flat Scene, and Tripod Pan. Tripod Pan assumes the camera is fixed but pans or tilts. Mostly Flat Scene allows for camera motion forwards, backwards, or sideways, but assumes the motion is limited to a single plane. Typical is appropriate for more aggressive camera moment such as a handheld camera that moves forward. For this tutorial, leave the menu set to Auto Detect.
5. Click the Analyze button. The blue bar changes back to "Analyzing." The footage is analyzed in two passes (playing forward and playing backward). Upon the completion of the analysis, a number of track points are displayed in the viewer (Figure 4.19). These are points that are identified as specific positions in 3D space. Play back. A few points disappear as their associated feature disappears. A few may slide incorrectly. Others remain fixed to features throughout the duration of the timeline. The ones that stay fixed should be considered successful. The effect is able to determine the relative positions of the features in 3D space through parallax calculations. To view the points in perspective, the effect "solves" a virtual 3D camera and looks though

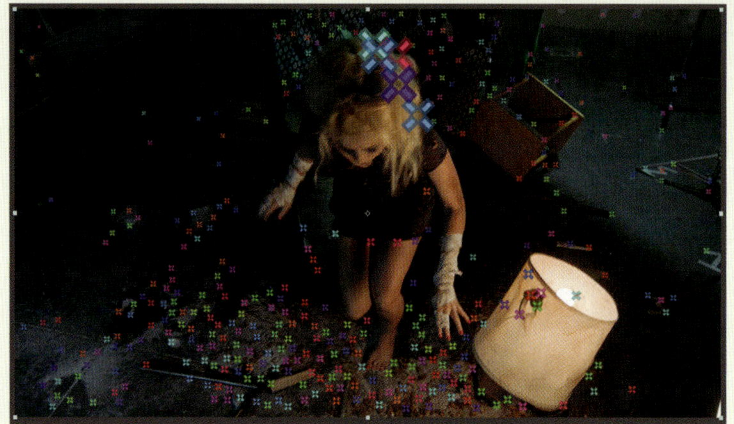

FIG 4.19 Track points displayed after analysis. Larger points represent features that are closer to the real-world camera. The large points on the head of the actress disappear as she moves and are not useful for motion tracking. Track Point Size is set to 150 percent.

it. During the analysis, the effect automatically identifies features that contain high-contrast, trackable patterns.

6. If the track points are difficult to see, you can scale them by raising the Track Point Size value. If necessary, you can enter a large value into the Track Point Size field. (Track points are only visible if the effect is selected in the Effect Controls panel.) Track points that follow features close to the camera appear larger than those that follow features far from the camera (hence, this is one way to determine if the tracking is accurate). You are free to delete inaccurate or unneeded track points. To do so, LMB-click a track point center in the viewer, so that the track point is given a yellow circle, and press the Delete key. (Be careful not to delete the entire effect.) For example, consider deleting track points that appear over features on the body or clothing of the actress.
7. LMB-drag the mouse between track points. Note that a gray triangle and a red and black bullseye appears between sets of three. This indicates a plane in 3D space where the three track points intersect. You can use this knowledge to place a 2D layer on the identified plane. On the first frame of the timeline, drag your mouse between the points along the floor at the bottom left of frame. Due to the density of the points, the bullseye sometimes appears with incorrect rotation. As an alternative, you can manually select three or more points. To do so, Shift+LMB-click the point centers. Manually selecting points allows you to choose points that are further apart and more appropriate for representing the ground plane orientation (Figure 4.20).
8. With points selected, RMB-click over the bullseye and choose Create Text And Camera. This creates a 3D camera, which appears as a new layer. The transforms of the camera are animated to replicate the real-world camera. In addition, a text layer is created and converted to a 3D layer (the 3D Layer switch is on). The default text, *Text*, appears at the

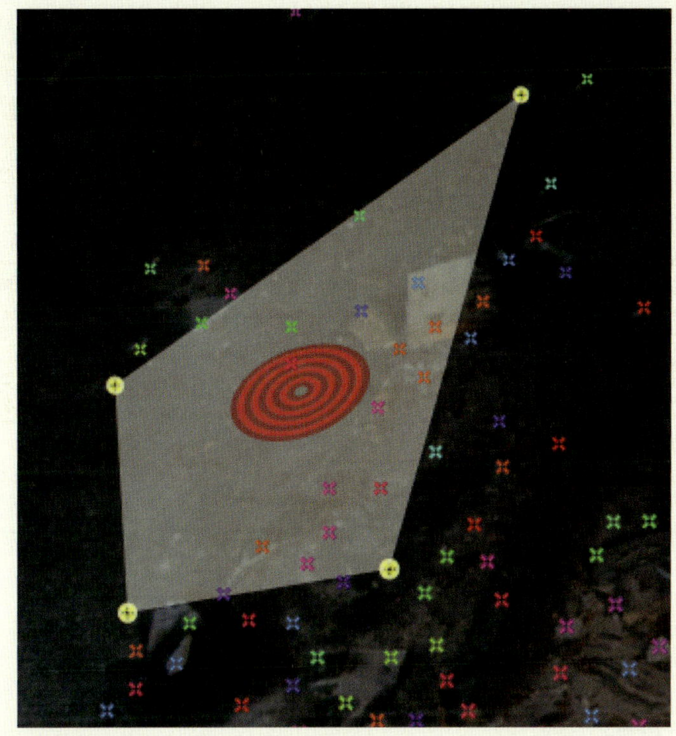

FIG 4.20 Four track points are manually selected. The resulting gray shape and bullseye represents the orientation of the floor.

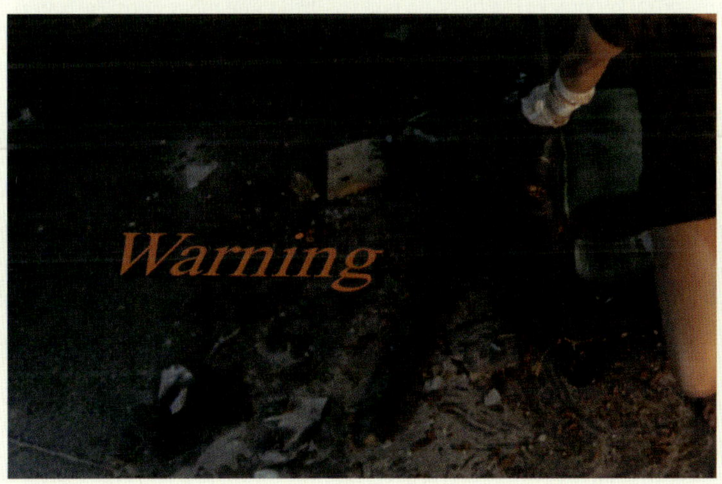

FIG 4.21 A text layer, converted to a 3D layer by the 3D Camera Tracker effect, is automatically positioned so that it appears to lie on the floor. A 3D camera, created and animated by the 3D Camera Tracker effect, creates the appropriate depth and perspective.

bullseye center and takes on the orientation of the bullseye. To hide the track points, simply deselect the 3D Camera Tracker effect.

9. Play back the timeline. The text appears to lie on the floor as if it was shot with the original camera (Figure 4.21). Optionally, you can alter

any of the text options for the text layer (through the Window > Character panel). For example, with this tutorial, the text appears very small; change the text Font Size field to 1200. You can also activate motion blur for the text layer, as well as offset the text by altering its transforms. As a 3D layer, the text has X, Y, and Z (depth) transform values.

Optionally, you can return to the 3D Camera Tracker and reanalyze with different settings. If you reanalyze, you have the additional option to create a brand new camera by clicking the Create Camera button. You are not limited to placing text in the scene. When you select three or more track points, you have the option to create a solid layer or a null object through the RMB menu. You can drive a custom 3D layer if you parent it to the null layer or link the transforms through expressions. More complex uses of 3D layers and 3D cameras are explored in Chapter 5. Expressions are covered in Chapter 10. A finished version of this tutorial is saved as *mini_3d_camera.aep* in the *\ProjectFiles\aeFiles\Chapter4* directory.

Introduction to The Foundry's CameraTracker

The Foundry offers the CameraTracker plug-in for After Effects to undertake the task of 3D camera tracking. Although the logic is similar to the After Effects Track Camera tool, the plug-in offers additional features. An overview of the plug-in is included in this section.

CameraTracker breaks the tracking process into three main steps. Each step is given a button with the step name and a section of options you can adjust before applying the step (Figure 4.22).

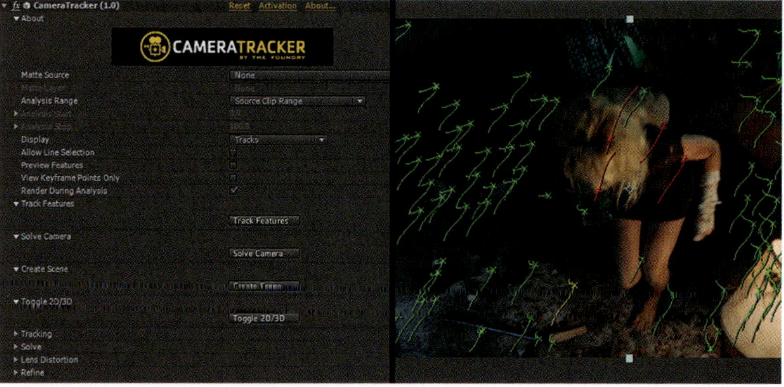

FIG 4.22 Left: CameraTracker properties. Right: Portion of solved tracking points and their partial motion paths.

The steps are designed for application in the following order:

1. **Track Features** This step identifies track points and tracks forwards and backwards across the entire timeline. When the tracking is complete,

each track point is drawn in the viewer with a small x with a partial motion path trail. You can set the number of desired track points in the scene and adjust tracking sensitivity in the Tracking section before applying Track Features. You can choose one of two camera styles through the Track Validation menu: Free Camera, which is suitable for handheld shots, and Rotating Camera, which is suitable for tripod-based tilting and panning.

2. **Solve Camera** This step "solves" or creates an internal, virtual camera based on the tracking point data. When the camera is solved, the tracking points are color-coded (Figure 4.22). Green points are valid for the solution. Red points are unsuitable and generally represent points that disappear over time. The Solve section contains additional camera options. Here, you can set the Focal Length Type and Film Back Size before solving. If you know the real-word camera focal length, you can Set Focal Length Type to Known, set Units to mm, and choose the correct Focal Length size. (A camera's film back represents the physical size of the camera sensor or exposed film frame.)
3. **Create Scene** This step creates a 3D camera layer that matches the solved camera. In addition, a null object is created as a 3D layer. The camera layer is parented to the null layer. Hence, the camera's animated transforms are relative to the null layer, which is placed at the frame center.

In addition, the plug-in provides a Toggle 2D/3D button. Pressing this button switches to a view of the internal 3D space. The tracking appears as a cloud of dots. Looking at the 3D view is useful for determining if the track points are correctly oriented to a particular feature, such as the ground. (You can use the Unified Camera tool to alter the view to examine the points.) In fact, you can select points and define which axis or axes they belong to. For example, return to the 2D view by clicking the Toggle 2D/3D button again, draw a selection marquee box in the viewer over a group of points along the floor at the left of frame, and use the CameraTracker menu (embedded into lower left of the Composition view when the effect is selected) to choose Ground Plane > Set To Selected. The entire point cloud is reoriented in 3D space to align the selected points with the XZ plane. The camera position is also updated to keep the points aligned with the tracked features.

After the scene is created, you have the option to attach a new null object or solid layer to a track point. To do so, select a track point in the viewer and choose CameraTracker menu > Create > Null Object or CameraTracker menu > Create > Solid. The new null or solid layer is parented to the initial null layer and is given transform values that align them with the selected track point. You can drive a custom 3D layer if you parent it to the new null layer or link the transforms through expressions. More complex uses of 3D layers and 3D cameras are explored in Chapter 5. See The Foundry's "CameraTracker" PDF user guide for more specific details on the plug-in (www.thefoundry.co.uk).

A Note on Hand Tracking

Occasionally, you may find that a particular shot is untrackable with the motion-tracking effects and plug-ins available to After Effects. This may be due to aggressive camera movement that prevents location of a usable feature. Extremely heavy motion blur, film grain, or video noise may also prevent the motion-tracking tools from producing usable motion paths. In this situation, you can apply hand tracking. Hand tracking uses these basic steps:

1. A mock-up of the real-world set or location is created as simple geometry in a 3D program, such as Autodesk Maya.
2. An image plane containing the footage is attached to the 3D camera.
3. The camera is animated to match the real-world camera motion. Lining up the geometry to the features within the footage aids in the positioning of the camera. For example, matching the edges of a building to a 3D mock-up of the building helps determine where the camera should be positioned and how it should be rotated.
4. The element that needs to be tracked, such as a 3D prop, is placed in the 3D scene and rendered with a 3D camera. The render is then composited on top of the original footage in After Effects or a similar compositing program.

With this scenario, the motion tracking actually occurs in the 3D program and not the compositing program. This is most likely to occur when a 3D object needs to gain the real-world camera motion. To maximize the quality of the hand tracking, it's necessary to build the mock-up geometry as accurately as possible. Hence, real-world measurements and similar notes are useful. At the same time, real-world camera information is extremely valuable, such as the millimeter size of the lens, image sensor size, distance from the ground to the lens, and so on.

You can also hand track with After Effects. For example, it you need to track a label so that it follows an object in an actor's hand, you can manually keyframe the label layer's Position, Scale, and Rotation.

Motion Tracking Masks and Facial Tracking

The rotoscoping process can be time consuming due to the manipulation of the mask shape at numerous points across the timeline. You can simplify the rotoscoping, however, by using the Track Mask motion tracking option. To apply this option, you can follow these steps:

1. Create a mask over the feature you wish to isolate. The mask need not follow the feature tightly, but can loosely surround the feature. For example, you might draw a mask around a desired element, such as a face,

or unwanted elements, such as motion tracking marks (in which case, you can invert the mask to remove the features).

2. RMB-click over the mask name in the layer outline and choose Track Mask. The Tracker panel opens with a set of Analyze playback buttons and a Method menu.
3. Set the Method menu to the style of motion tracking you prefer. If the feature is moving left/right or up/down with no rotation or scale change, set Method to Position. If the feature is rotating and changing size, set Method to Position, Scale & Rotation. If the feature goes through changes in perspective, set Method to Perspective.
4. Use the Analyze buttons to analyze the timeline. When the analyzation is complete, the Mask Path property is automatically keyframed. Play back the timeline. The mask follows the feature.

After Effects CC 2015 includes two facial tracking options: Face Tracking (Outline Only) and Face Tracking (Detailed Features). These options are available through the Method menu of the Tracker panel when the Track Mask option is chosen. To apply facial tracking, follow these steps:

1. Create a mask over the face you wish to motion track. Draw the mask loosely around the face.
2. RMB-click over the mask name in the layer outline and choose Track Mask. The Tracker panel opens with a set of Analyze playback buttons and a Method menu. Set Method to Face Tracking (Outline Only) or Face Tracking (Detailed Features).
3. Use the Analyze buttons to analyze the timeline. If Method is set to Outline Only, the Mask Path property is automatically keyframed. Play back the timeline. The mask follows the edges of the visible face. If Method is set to Detailed Features, the mask is animated and a Face Track Points section is created and added to the Effects section of the layer (Figure 4.23).

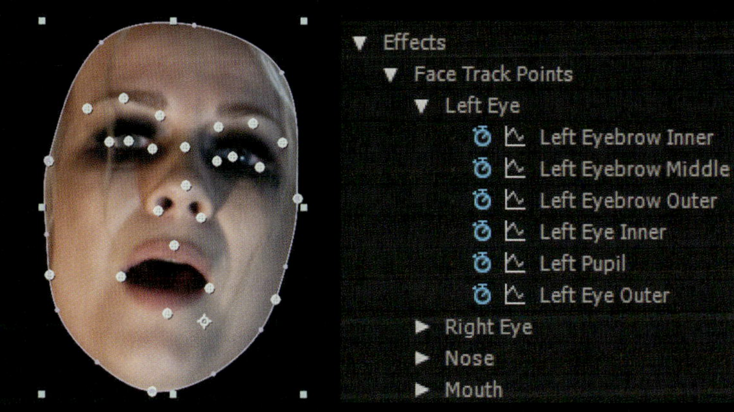

FIG 4.23 Left: A face is automatically masked with the Face Tracking (Detailed Features) motion tracking option. In addition, face track points follow important facial details over time. Right: A portion of the resulting Face Track Points section in the layer outline. An example project is saved as *facial_tracking.aep* in the *\ProjectFiles\aeFiles\Chapter4* directory.

The Face Track Points section includes many properties that plot the X and Y positions of various facial details, including the upper and lower eyelids, corners of the nose, corners of the mouth, and upper and lower lips. You can copy the keyframe animation of any Facial Track Point property and paste it onto a different layer. In this way, you can force a different layer to follow a particular facial detail over time. You can also use the Facial Track Points properties as part of an expression. (Expressions are discussed in Chapter 10.) The track points appear in the Composition view as circles with crosshairs but will not appear as part of the final render.

Planar Tracking with Mocha AE

Planar tracking is a motion-tracking variation that tracks the location and rotation of a planar shape. Although superficially similar to corner-pin tracking, planar tracking is aware of the planar shape as a whole and is able to follow a shape whose corners may be temporary occluded and briefly leave the frame. Although you can use planar tracking to follow a rectangular shape, you can use it to track *any* shape that exists within a single two-dimensional plane (in other words, any shape that is essentially flat in the real world). You can use planar tracking to track a wall, the side of a box, a lined parking space, an irregular wooden cutout, a gear ringed with teeth, and so on. The following tutorial takes you through the basic steps of planar motion tracking.

Chapter Tutorial: Planar Motion Tracking

The following steps represent the general approach you can take when using Mocha AE to planar track. You can apply these steps to the *tutorial_4_start.aep* project saved in the *\ProjectFiles\aeFiles\Chapter4* directory.

1. Select the sole layer carried by the 1_3i_2wall composition. Choose Animation > Track In Mocha AE. Mocha AE opens. In Mocha AE, the New Project window opens and states the footage frame range and frame rate. The Location field lists the directory in which the initial Mocha project file will be saved. You can change the location if necessary. Click the OK button to close the window. The footage appears in the Mocha viewer. You can play the footage with the viewer's playback controls. (See the "Mocha Masks Mini Tutorial" section in Chapter 3 for more information on the Mocha interface.)
2. Mocha is a planar tracker, which means that it tracks shapes that are defined as planar (a flat, two-dimensional surface that may rotate or change in scale). To define the tracked shape, you use one of several spline tools to loosely form a spline "cage" around the shape. For this tutorial, we'll use the X-Spline tool. Return to the first frame. Select the Create X-Spline Layer tool from the top toolbar. This features a pen tip and a small X as part of the icon. LMB-click four times around the center section

of wall. Place three of the vertices outside circular spots formed by nail hole patches. Place the fourth vertex outside a dirt spot. Use Figure 4.24 as a guideline. It's best to form the resulting cage so that it does not include a part of the footage where the lighting or shadows change. For example, the hand of the actress crosses over one of the lower nail hole spots, which makes it difficult to use for tracking. Note that a vertex can sit outside the frame edge. RMB-click over the shape to finish it. You can adjust vertex positions after the cage is drawn by LMB-dragging them.

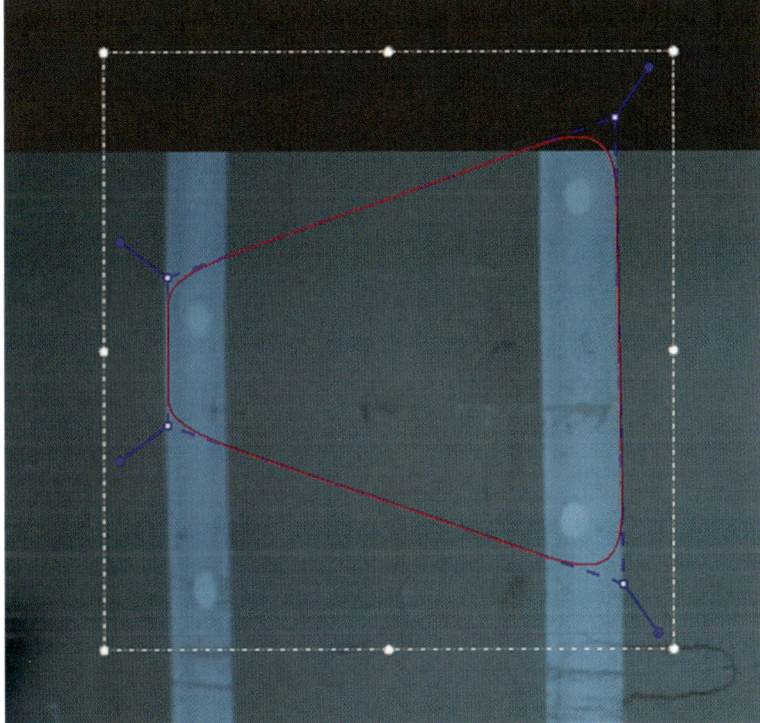

FIG 4.24 An X-spline cage is drawn around the three nail hole spots and a dirt streak. Note that the vertices do not have to touch a specific feature. A vertex can also sit outside the frame edge.

3. Click the Track Forward button. The tracking buttons sit to the right of the playback buttons and feature a small *T* in the icons. When you click the Track Forward button, the timeline moves forward and Mocha updates the X-spline cage vertex positions to follow the chosen shape. With this example, the overall pattern within the cage is tracked. When the tracking is complete, play back to gauge the accuracy of the cage placement.
4. If the spline cage drifts, you can correct it by creating reference points. After the adjustment, you can reanalyze forwards or backwards from any frame. For information on creating reference points, see the "Mocha Masks Mini-Tutorial" section in Chapter 3. Adjusting the X-spline cage for rotoscoping is the same process as adjusting the cage for planar motion tracking.

5. When the tracking of the cage is acceptable, click the Show Planar Surface button in the Toolbar. The button features a blue background with a white square and small letter S. This displays a blue planar reference square in the viewer (assuming the X-spline layer is selected in the Layer Controls panel). The square shows where four corners of a 2D surface will be placed when the Mocha AE tracking data is exported back to After Effects. Although Mocha AE uses planar tracking techniques, the exported data is most often used by the Corner Pin effect in After Effects.
6. While on the first frame of the timeline, LMB-drag the corners of the planar surface square to form a taller, more rectangular shape. Use Figure 4.25 as a reference. Play back. Note that the planar surface keeps its new shape and moves relative to the X-spline cage.

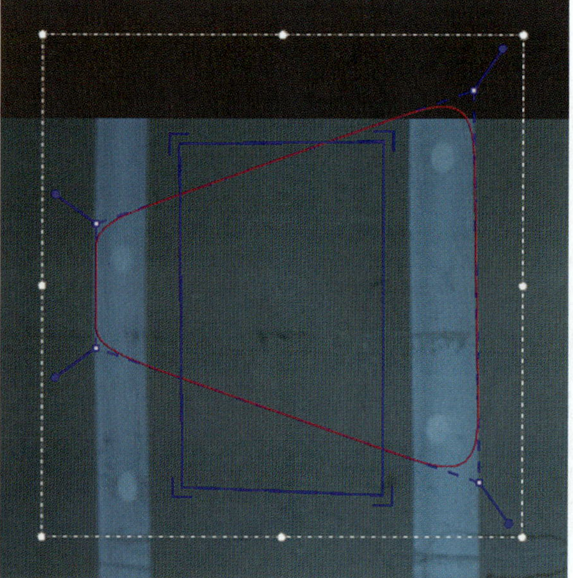

FIG 4.25 The blue planar surface square is adjusted to take on a more rectangular shape.

7. Click the Export Tracking Data button, which is located at the bottom right of the lower Track tab. In the Export Tracking Data window, change the Format menu to After Effects Corner Pin. Click the Copy To Clipboard button. The window closes and the tracking data, in the form of the corner positional data, is copied to the operating system clipboard.
8. Save the Mocha project by choosing File > Save. Switch back to the After Effects program window. Import the *warning.png* file from the *\ProjectFiles\Art* directory. LMB-drag the warning layer to the top of the layer outline. Expand the warning layer's Transform section. Change

the Anchor Point so that it matches the current layer position—in this case 960, 540. This is necessary to align the layer with the Mocha AE planar shape. Choose Edit > Paste. The Mocha data is pasted from the clipboard to the sign layer and appears as a new Position, Scale, and Rotation animation, as well as a new Corner Pin effect with animated corner positions.

9. Play back. The sign layer is distorted to fit the area designated by Mocha's planar surface (Figure 4.26). In addition, the layer takes on the motion of the camera. Note that the sign is allowed to appropriately drift outside of the frame edge. To better integrate the sign, lower its opacity to 75 percent and activate motion blur. A finished Mocha project is saved as *tutorial_4_finished.mocha* in the *\ProjectFiles\aefiles\Chapter4* directory. A finished After Effects project is saved as *tutorial_4_finished.aep* in the *\ProjectFiles\aefiles\Chapter4* directory. (To better integrate the sign, we'll apply color-grading techniques in Chapter 9.)

FIG 4.26 The Mocha planar tracking data is applied to a sign layer. The data is converted to Corner Pin and transform animation.

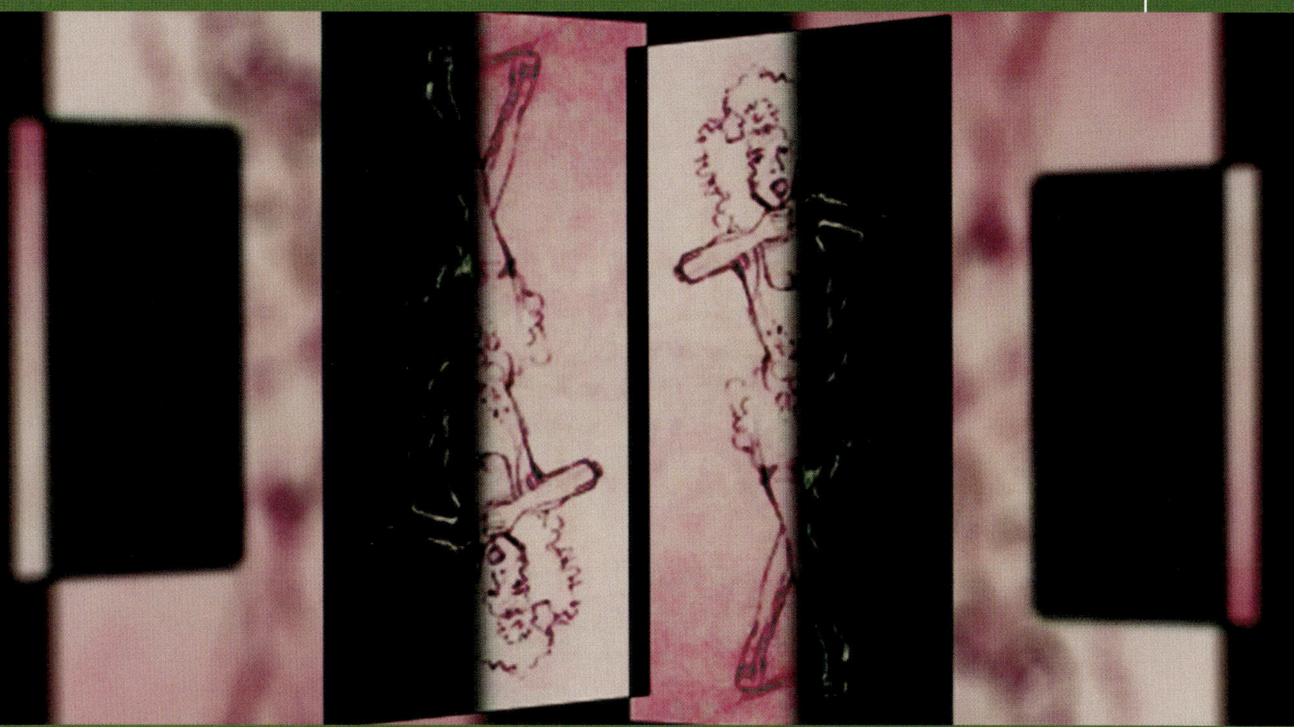

CHAPTER 5

Working with the 3D Environment

Due to increasingly short postproduction times in film, television, and commercial production, 2D and 3D software package features have begun to overlap. After Effects, which is mainly designed for 2D compositing, nevertheless has a full 3D environment with cameras, lights, materials, and more recently, the ability to render 3D geometry (Figure 5.1). This adds even more power to the compositor as he or she has the option to work in 2D, 2.5D, 3D, or go back and forth between all three spaces. *2.5D* refers to 2D layers in a 3D space and is useful for giving depth to otherwise flat matte paintings and similar backdrops.

This chapter includes the following critical information:

- Creating and transforming 3D layers, cameras, and lights
- Working with 3D layer material properties and shadows
- Importing elements from Cinema 4D Lite and other 3D programs

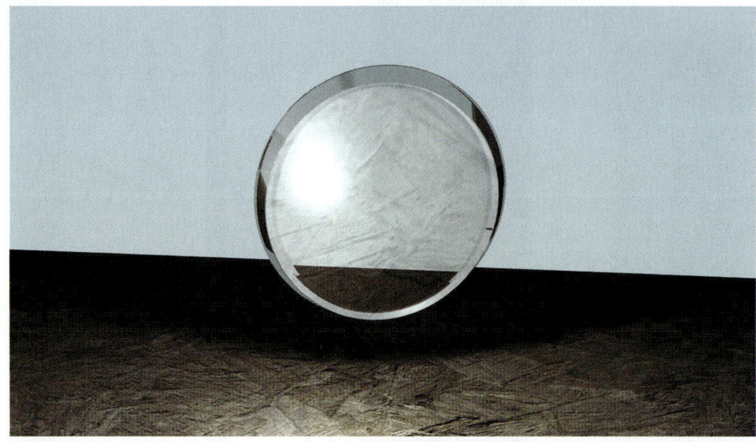

FIG 5.1 A glass-like disc is created and rendered in After Effects using 3D layers, an environmental layer, a 3D camera, and the Ray-Trace 3D renderer.

Creating and Transforming 3D Layers

In After Effects, you can convert any layer to a 3D layer by clicking the 3D Layer switch beside the layer name. This carries a small cube for an icon. With the conversion, the layer gains a third dimension for its transforms and a Material Options section. In addition, if the layer is selected, a 3D transform handle is displayed with the handle located at the Anchor Point (Figure 5.2). Like standard 3D programs, the transform handle has three axis arrows, where the green arrow is Y, the red arrow is X, and the blue arrow is Z.

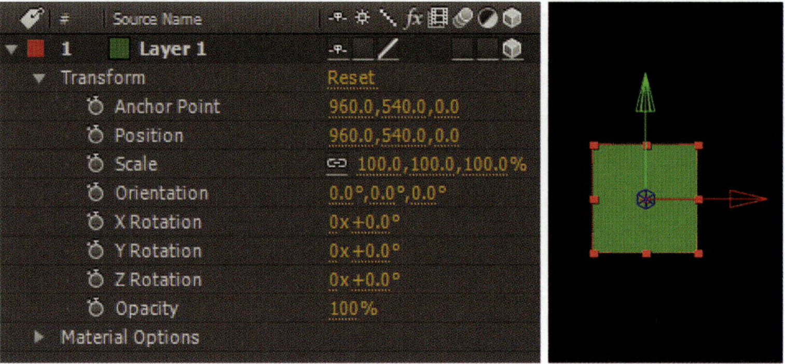

FIG 5.2 Left: The Transform section of a 3D layer. Right: The transform handle of a 3D layer, as seen in the Composition view.

The 3D layer's Anchor Point, Position, and Scale receive a Z field (the field order is X, Y, Z, from left to right). Note that the Z Scale has no effect on the layer as it remains two-dimensional in a 3D space (much like a piece of paper). Rotation is broken into three separate properties—one for each axis. A new property, Orientation, is added. Orientation rotates the layer. However, Orientation does not use revolutions and degrees; instead, Orientation simply offers X, Y, and Z degrees with no upper or lower limit. You can use Rotation, Orientation, or both properties to rotate the layer. You can rotate a 3D layer in three dimensions without a 3D camera.

Using Multiple Viewports

By default, the Composition view panel shows a single view. You have the option to lay out the panel as you would a 3D program, with multiple orthographic and/or perspective viewports. To do this, change the Select View Layout menu to a layout. For example, to mimic the default layout of Autodesk Maya, change the menu to 4 Views. This adds a Top, Front, and Right orthographic viewport along with the original view, which is labeled Active Camera (Figure 5.3). If you haven't created a 3D camera, the Active Camera viewport shows the standard Composition view. If you've created a 3D camera, the Active Camera becomes a perspective view similar to standard 3D programs. To make a particular viewport active, LMB-click within its border. The viewport receives a orange triangle at each corner to indicate that it's active.

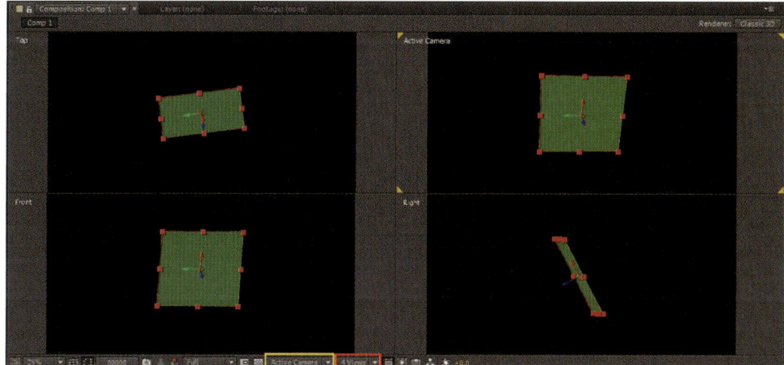

FIG 5.3 The Select View Layout menu, indicated by the red box, is set to 4 Views. With this example, the Active Camera viewport is active, as indicated by the orange corner triangles. At this point, there is no 3D camera but there is a green 512×512 3D layer with rotation. The 3D View Popup menu is indicated by a yellow box.

The black field of the perspective viewport indicates the frame that renders. The orthographic viewports also possess these; however, you cannot render orthographic viewports through the Render Queue.

You can adjust the view of any viewport by using one of the camera tools. For example, if you select the Unified Camera tool from the camera tools menu in the main toolbar (Figure 5.4), you can MMB-drag in an active viewport to scroll up/down or left/right (i.e., track XY). You can RMB-drag in an active viewport to dolly in and out (i.e., track Z). If you use the Unified Camera tool in a perspective viewport with a 3D camera, you can LMB-drag to rotate (orbit) the camera.

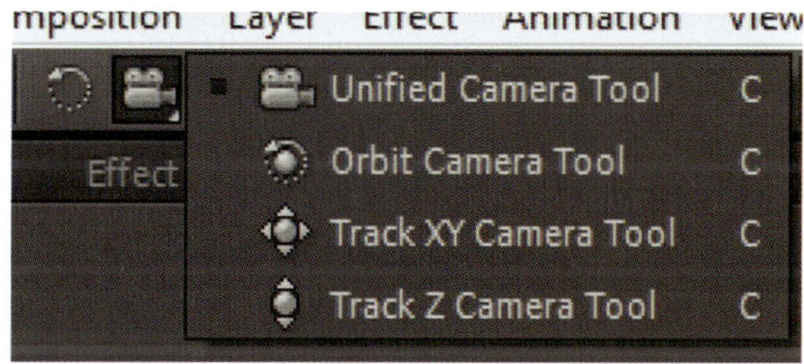

FIG 5.4 The camera tools menu, which sits to the right of the Rotate tool.

You can interactively transform a 3D layer in a viewport. To move a 3D layer, select the layer and use the Selection tool to LMB-drag one of the axis arrows in a positive or negative direction. You can also interactively rotate a 3D layer by selecting the Rotate tool from the main toolbar (Figure 5.4) and LMB-dragging along or over one of the axis arrows.

Creating and Transforming a 3D Camera

The best way to take advantage of the 3D environment is to create a 3D camera. 3D cameras emulate real-world cameras and give you a wide range of looks by selecting different lenses or applying different transforms. To create a 3D camera, choose Layer > New > Camera. The Camera Settings window opens (Figure 5.5).

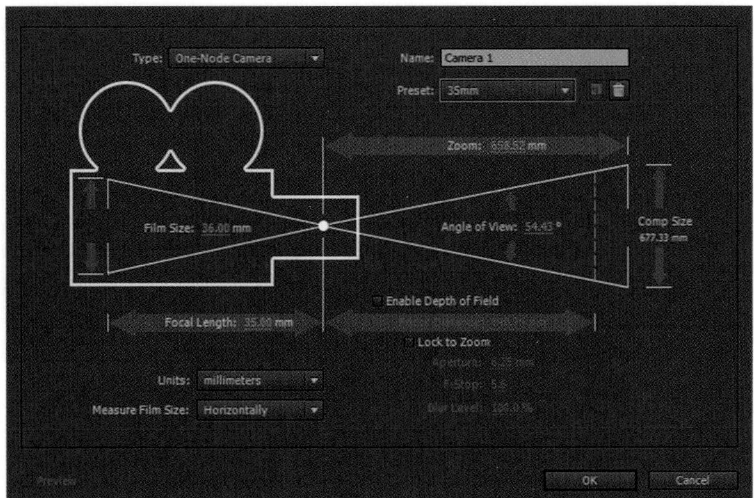

FIG 5.5 The Camera Settings window.

You can choose a lens by selecting a common focal length through the Preset menu. You also have the option to enter a custom focal length through the field below the camera body icon. If you have information pertaining to the angle of view or film size (horizontal aperture) of a real-world camera, you can enter those values into the namesake fields. The default camera style creates a two-node camera with a camera body and a point of interest (each of which has its own transforms). Alternatively, you can set the Type menu to One-Node Camera to prevent the creation of the point of interest. When you press OK, a new camera layer is created and placed at the top of the layer outline.

The camera receives an icon, which is visible in the orthographic viewports (Figure 5.6). If a 3D camera exists, you can move 2D layers closer or farther away from the camera. The After Effects 3D space uses a Y-up system, where positive-X runs right, positive-Z runs towards the camera's default position, and positive-Y runs up.

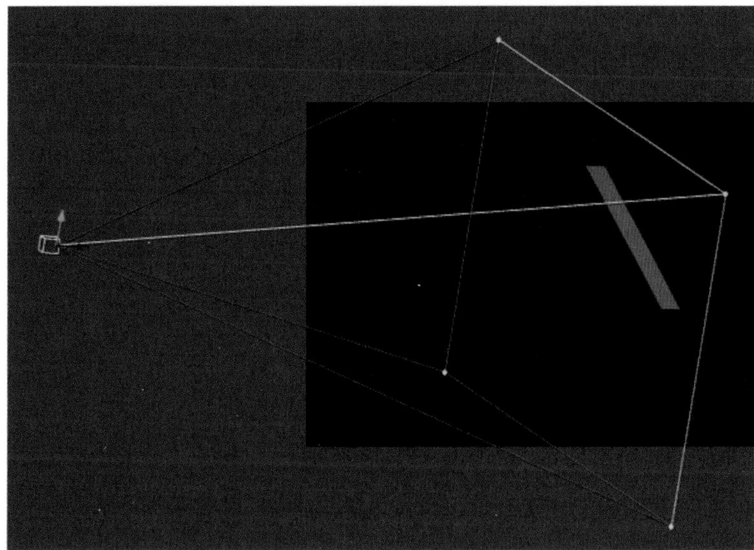

FIG 5.6 A selected one-node 3D camera, as seen in the Right viewport. The camera is given nondefault rotational values.

Transforming a 3D Camera

There are several ways to transform a 3D camera. You can use the Unified Camera tool to change the view by LMB-, MMB-, or RMB-dragging in the perspective viewport. You also have the option to use the Orbit, Track XY (scroll), and Track Z (dolly) tools (see Figure 5.4 earlier in this chapter); with these, you need only LMB-drag in the perspective viewport.

In addition, you can interactively transform the camera icon. To transform the camera body, select the camera layer, go to a viewport, and LMB-drag one of the three axis arrows in the positive or negative direction. To move the point of interest of a two-node camera, LMB-drag its point in a viewport (it does not receive a transform handle). Moving the point of interest rotates the camera body (Figure 5.7). If the body axis arrows are difficult to see, you can dolly closer to the camera by RMB-dragging with the Unified Camera tool. If your mouse has a middle scroll button, you can use it to dolly in and out. If you are using a one-node camera, you can also interactively rotate it with the Rotate tool.

You can alter the transform values of the camera layer as you would any other layer. The transforms include a Position X, Y, Z, an Orientation X, Y, Z, and separate Rotate properties for each axis (Figure 5.8). If you interactively rotate a one-node camera in a viewport, the Orientation values of the camera body are changed. You can separate Position into three properties by RMB-clicking over the *Position* name and choosing Separate Dimensions. Two-node cameras also carry a Point Of Interest X, Y, Z.

You can create more than one 3D camera. To choose a camera to look through, select a viewport, and change the 3D View Popup menu to the

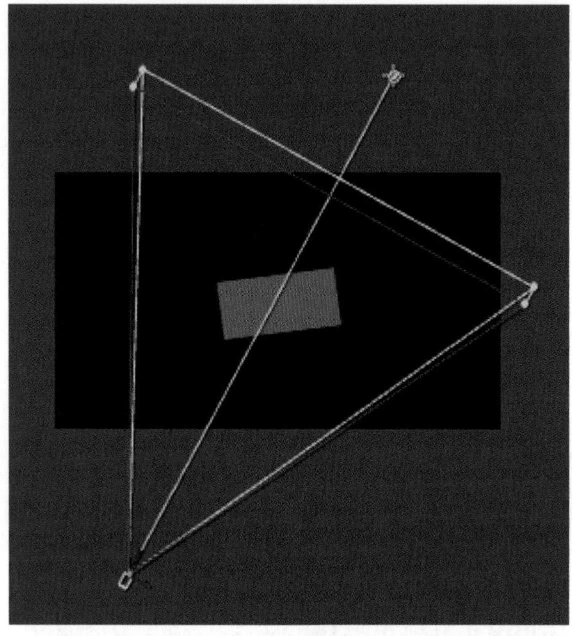

FIG 5.7 A two-node camera, as seen in the Top viewport. The point of interest is moved out in front of the camera's rectangular image plane.

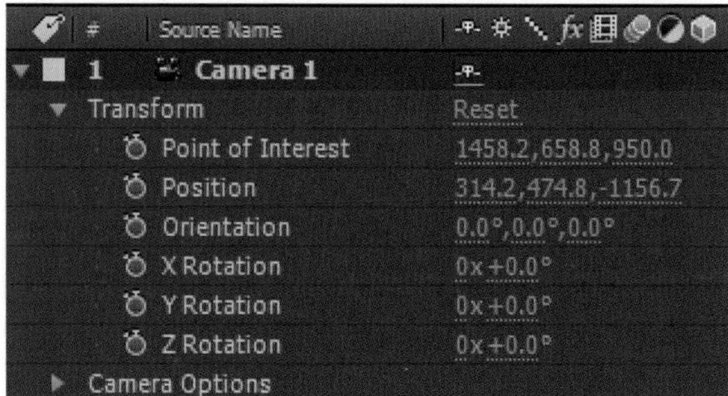

#	Source Name	
1	Camera 1	
	Transform	Reset
	Point of Interest	1458.2,658.8,950.0
	Position	314.2,474.8,-1156.7
	Orientation	0.0°,0.0°,0.0°
	X Rotation	0x+0.0°
	Y Rotation	0x+0.0°
	Z Rotation	0x+0.0°
	Camera Options	

FIG 5.8 The Transform section of a two-node 3D camera layer.

camera of choice (see Figure 5.3 earlier in this chapter). Similarly, you can change an orthographic viewport to a different view, such as Left or Bottom. You can store a specific custom perspective view by selecting a viewport and changing the 3D View Popup menu to one of the custom bookmarks, named *Custom View* and numbered 1, 2, and 3.

Altering 3D Camera Properties

Each 3D camera layer includes a Camera Options section (Figure 5.9). The Zoom property controls the focal length of the lens. This is represented by a pixel distance value, which indicates the distance the camera lens is from the image plane. The image plane is visible as the rectangle at the end of the camera icon frustum (the pyramid-like structure indicating the camera's field of view). See Figures 5.6 and 5.7 in the previous sections. If you alter the Zoom value, the horizontal angle of view updates automatically (this value appears in parenthesis to the right of the Zoom property). If you raise the Zoom value, the lens becomes "longer" and the camera "zooms in." If you lower the value, the lens becomes "shorter" and "zooms out" and the view is widened.

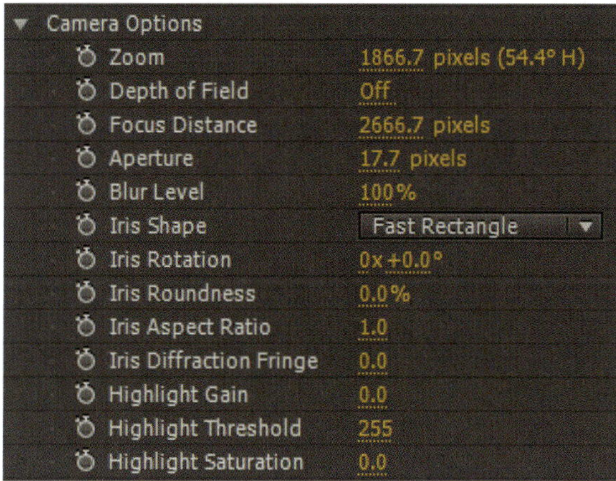

FIG 5.9 The Camera Options section of a 3D camera layer.

Because the Zoom pixel distance and the horizontal angle of view values are nonintuitive, you have the option to alter the camera lens by selecting the camera layer and choosing Layer > Camera Settings. In the Camera Settings window, you can select a new focal length preset or enter an mm value into the Focal Length field. Smaller mm values produce a wider lens while larger mm values produce a "long" or telephoto lens.

The remaining properties in the Camera Options section control the depth of field, which is described in the next section. Note that 2D layers remain visible to a 3D camera. However, the 2D layers are fixed to the default, non-3D view.

Working with Depth of Field

Depth of field refers to the "out-of-focusness" of a camera. That is, depth of field indicates the distance range within which objects are in focus. Objects outside of this range are out of focus or blurry. By default the Depth Of Field property is set to Off. If you switch the property to On, the following additional camera properties affect the result:

> **Focus Distance** The pixel distance from the lens to the center of the "in focus" range. This is represented by a second rectangle inserted into the camera icon frustum. If you alter the Focus Distance value, you can see this rectangle move in the viewports. Alter this value so that the rectangle bisects the 3D layer or layers that you want to remain sharply in focus.

Aperture The size of the lens opening in pixels. As with a real-world camera, the larger the aperture value, the smaller the in-focus range.

Blur Level Sets the degree of blurriness in the out-of-focus areas. The higher the value, the greater the blurriness.

Iris Shape Sets the shape of the camera's *bokeh*, which is the shape of an out-of-focus point of light. Common real-world lenses produce octagon or other *n*-sided polygon bokehs.

Iris Rotation, Iris Roundness, and Iris Aspect Ratio These further alter the bokeh shape.

Iris Diffraction Fringe This creates a halo around the bokeh when the value is raised. The halo is visible around small, high-contrast areas.

Highlight Gain, Highlight Threshold, and Highlight Saturation These alter the look of bright areas when Depth Of Field is on.

The camera properties that control depth of field are similar to those carried by Effect > Blur & Sharpen > Camera Lens Blur. You can apply Camera Lens Blur to a 2D layer when no 3D camera is present and therefore emulate a real-world camera by creating realistic bokehs. Depth of field is demonstrated in the following tutorial.

Depth of field mini-tutorial

To practice the creation of depth of field, you can follow these steps:

1. Create three 3D layers in a composition. You can use three unique layers or three copies of the same layer. To better see the eventual depth of field, create layers that are smaller than the composition resolution. For example, import artwork or create a new solid layer with a smaller size. An example piece of artwork is included as *drawing.jpg* in the *\ProjectFiles\Art* directory.
2. Create a new camera by choosing Layer > New > Camera. You can create a one-node or two-node camera. Switch the Select View Layout menu to 4 Views so you have access to the orthographic viewports.
3. Position the layers so they are spread out along the Z-axis. You can interactively LMB-drag the Z-axis handle when a 3D layer is selected. (When you first create the 3D layers, they overlap in the same position in 3D space.)
4. Adjust the camera position and rotation so that the three layers are seen through the Active Camera perspective view (Figure 5.10). Expand the camera layer's Camera Options section. Switch Depth Of Field to On. Adjust the Focus Distance value. You'll see the focus distance plane move back and forth in the orthographic views. Line up the Focus Distance plane so that it bisects the central layer (the layer that is midway between the other two layers in 3D space).

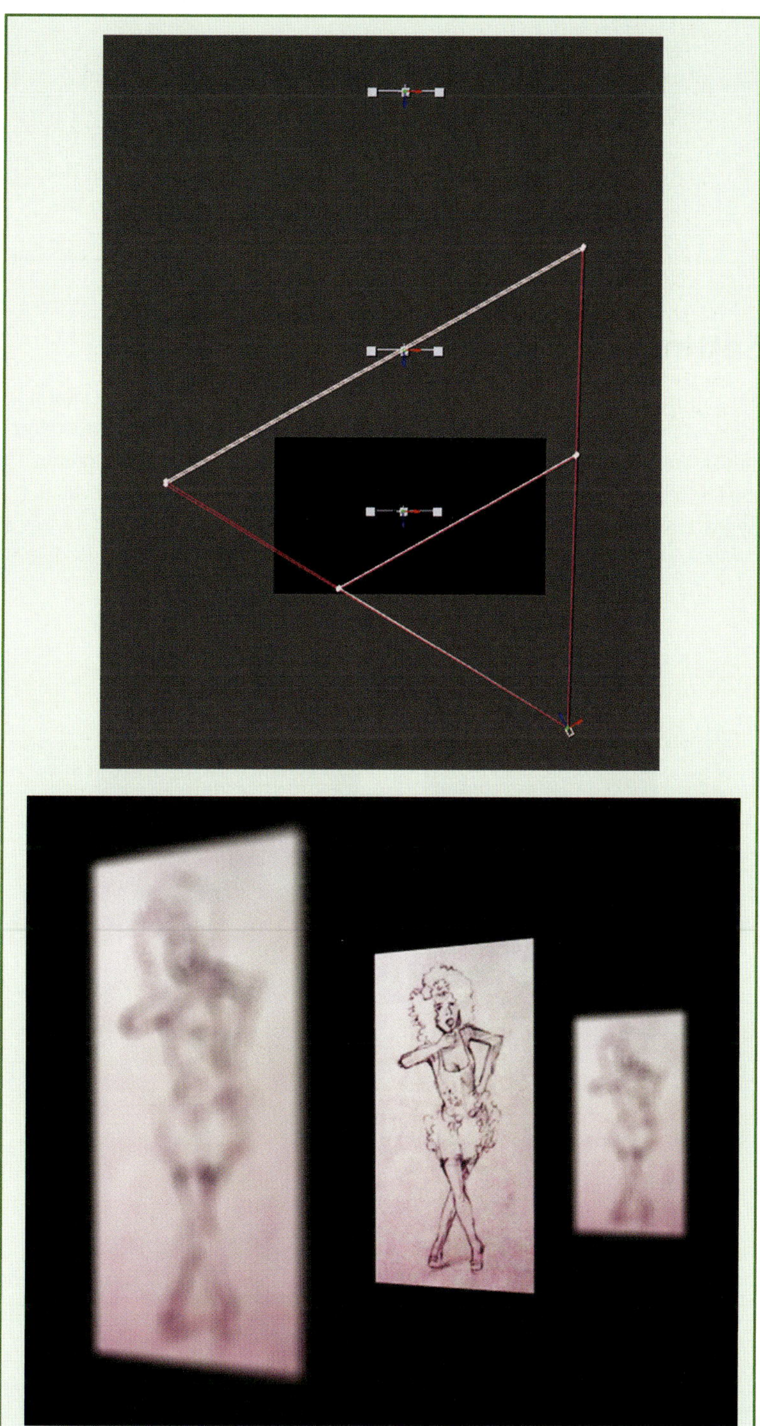

FIG 5.10 Three 3D layers, seen as horizontal lines in the Top viewport, are spread out along the Z-axis. The camera is rotated and positioned to look at them from the right side. The Focus Distance plane bisects the central 3D layer.

FIG 5.11 The resulting depth of field.

5. Slowly raise the Aperture value. The higher the value, the more out of focus the near and far layers become (Figure 5.11). Experiment with different Iris Shape menu settings and other iris properties. Each change alters the bokehs of the out-of-focus points. Alter the Focus Distance value to place the focus area at different points, such as the foreground layer. A sample project is saved as *mini_depth.aep* in the *\ProjectFiles\aeFiles\Chapter5* directory.

Setting Up Lights

If no lights are present in an After Effects 3D environment, 3D layers maintain their original pixel brightness. That is, there are no highlights or shadows. You can create a light at any time, however, by choosing Layer > New > Light. In the Light Settings window, you can choose between one of four lights, as set by the Light Type menu (Figure 5.12).

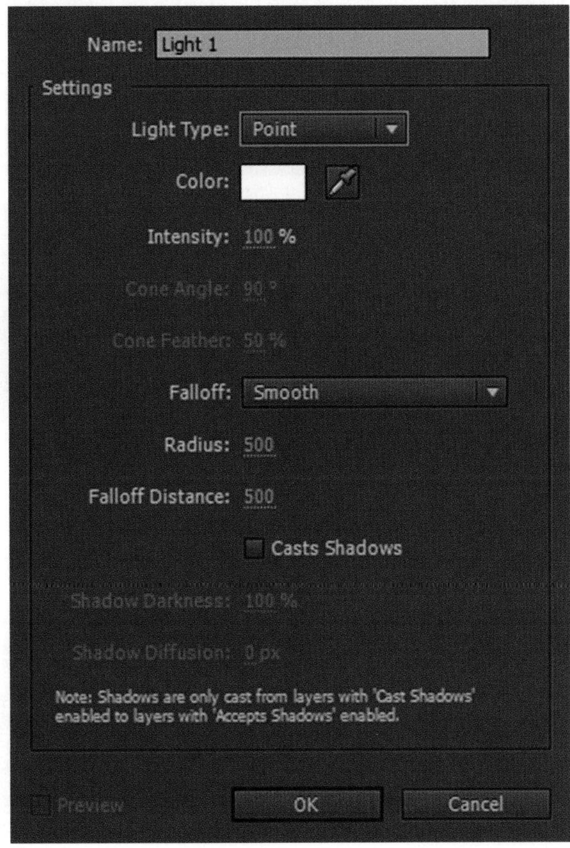

FIG 5.12 The Light Settings window.

Descriptions of the light types follow:

Parallel A directional light whose light rays are parallel. Ultimately, the light's rotation affects the light quality, but its position does not (Figure 5.13).

Spot Emulates a real-world spot light that produces a conical light throw.

Point An omnidirectional light that originates from the light icon. This is similar to a light bulb.

Ambient This light has no position and no light icon, but arrives from all directions.

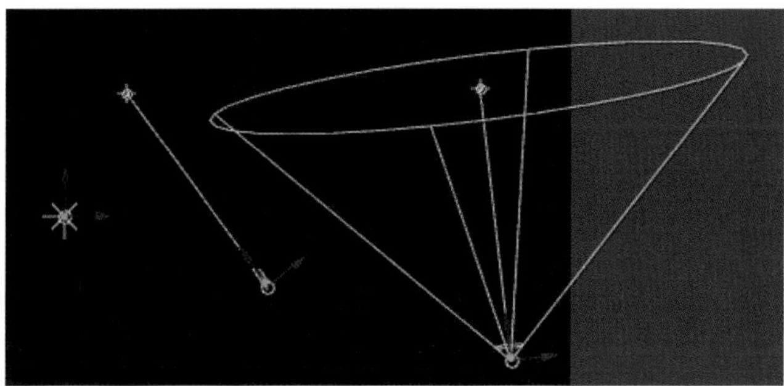

FIG 5.13 Left to Right: Point light, Parallel light, and Spot light.

You can choose a light color, intensity (brightness), and whether the light casts shadows for all the light types. Additionally, Parallel, Spot, and Ambient lights include a Falloff menu. If Falloff is set to Smooth, the light decays (loses intensity) over distance in a linear fashion. The decay starts at the Radius distance and ends at the Falloff Distance. If Falloff is set to Inverse Square Clamped, the light decay is an inverse of the square of the distance from the light, replicating light decay within the Earth's atmosphere. In this case, the decay starts at the Radius value. Spot lights also include a Cone Angle value, which sets the width of the light cone, and a Cone Feather value, which sets the decay at the cone edge. High Cone Feather values create a softer cone edge, as seen when the spot light strikes a 3D layer.

When you click the OK button in the Light Settings window, the light is created as a new light layer is added to the layer outline. The light layer carries its own set of transforms and a Light Options section, which carries the light properties discussed in this section. You can change the Light Options properties values at any time.

You can interactively transform a light as you would a 3D layer or camera. Parallel lights carry a light icon and a point of interest, each with its own position property. Spot lights possess a point of interest but also include Orientation and Rotation properties for the light icon. You can move the point of interest of a light by LMB-dragging the point in a viewport. Point lights only possess a Position property. Ambient lights lack transforms and are considered to be equally intense everywhere at once. You are free to create as many lights within a composition as you like.

Working with Materials

As soon as a light is present in the After Effects 3D environment, 3D layers gain surface shading qualities controlled by the 3D layer's Material Options section (Figure 5.14).

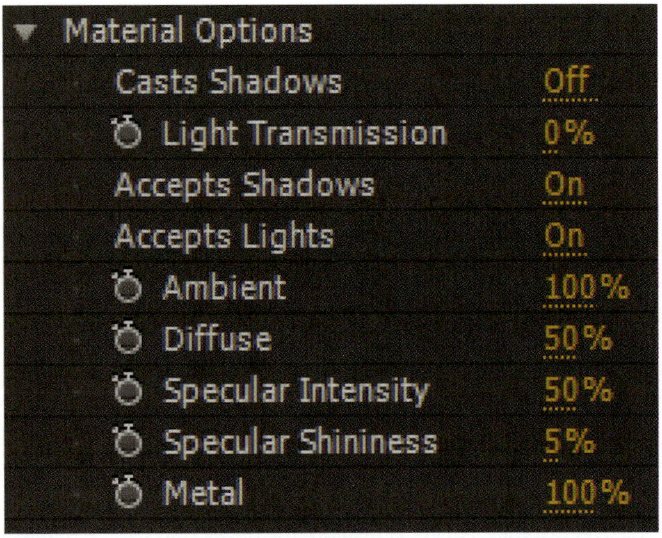

FIG 5.14 The Material Options section of a 3D layer.

Material Options	
Casts Shadows	Off
Light Transmission	0%
Accepts Shadows	On
Accepts Lights	On
Ambient	100%
Diffuse	50%
Specular Intensity	50%
Specular Shininess	5%
Metal	100%

Descriptions of these Material Options properties are laid out in the following sections.

Ambient

This is the ambient shading component, which represents the net sum of all secondary (fill) light reaching the surface. The higher the Ambient value, the brighter the non-lit areas of the layer become.

Diffuse

This represents the diffuse shading component, which controls the brightness or darkness of the surface (that is, how much light the surface reflects back to the camera). The higher the value, the brighter the layer.

Specular Shininess, Specular Intensity, and Metal

Specular Shininess controls the size of the surface's specular highlight (Figure 5.15). A *specular highlight* is a focused light reflection that appears as a "hot spot" on the surface. The higher the Specular Shininess value, the smaller the specular highlight, which is similar to smooth surfaces such as glass. The lower the Specular Shininess value, the broader the highlight, which is similar to rough surfaces. If a specular highlight is not visible, it indicates that a surface is *diffuse*, whereby light is reflected in all directions and in a random manner. (Paper and cardboard are examples of diffuse surfaces.) The Specular Intensity property sets the brightness of the specular highlight. The Metal property determines the color of the specular highlight. Low Metal values favor the color white while high Metal values favor the colors contained within the layer (which emulates some metals, such as copper).

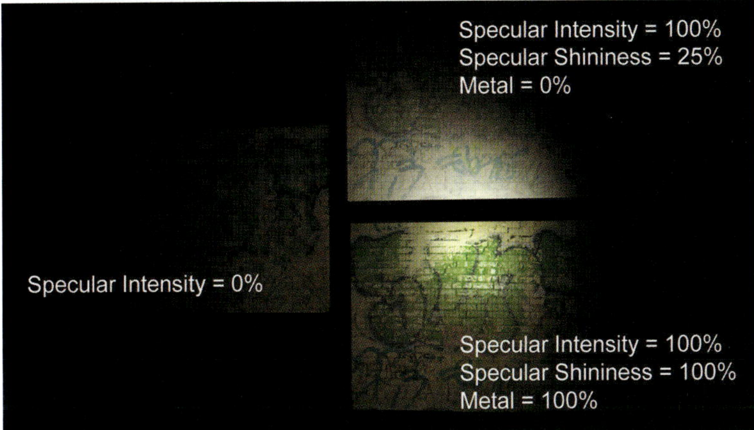

FIG 5.15 Three different specular properties for three 3D layers. The layers are lit by a single Spot light. This project is saved as *specular.aep* in the *\ProjectFiles\aeFiles\Chapter5* directory.

Light Transmission

This controls the translucence of a layer. If a surface is translucent, light is transmitted *through* the surface. Real-world translucent surfaces include flesh, wax, soap, and so on. You can see the effect by pressing a flashlight to your hand. You can see the effect in After Effects if the Light Transmission value is high and a light sits *behind* the 3D layer relative to the rendering camera (Figure 5.16).

Casts Shadows, Accepts Shadows, and Accepts Lights

These are on/off switches that determine their namesake qualities. Note that Cast Shadows is off by default. Each 3D layer can carry its own unique shadow and light settings. If a 3D layer has its Accepts Lights property set to Off, it receives its default pixel values—as if there are no lights in the scene. Note that shadows understand transparency. If a 3D layer casts a shadow and has transparent areas due to an alpha channel, the shadow gains the correct shape (Figure 5.17). (By the same token, you can mask 3D layers, which is discussed in the next section.) The darkness of cast shadows is set by the Shadow Darkness property in the Light Options section of the shadow-casting light. If you use a Point or Spot light, you can soften the shadow edge by raising the Shadow Diffusion value, also found in the Light Options section.

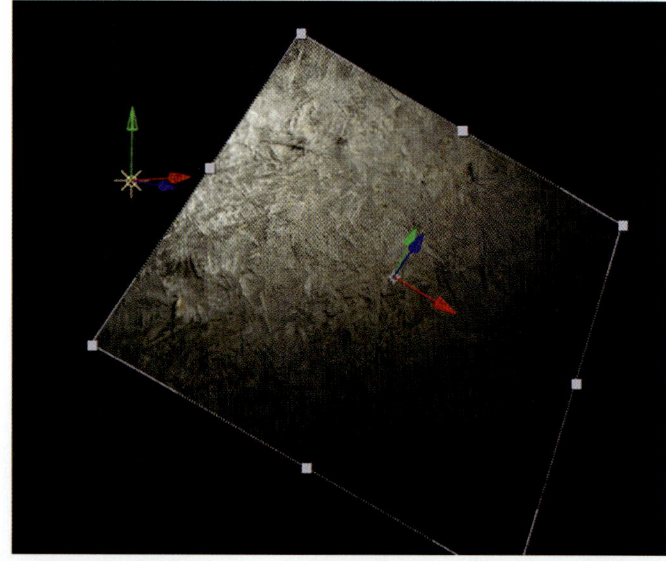

FIG 5.16 A Point light sits behind a 3D layer but transmits *through* the surface thanks to a Light Transmission value of 100 percent.

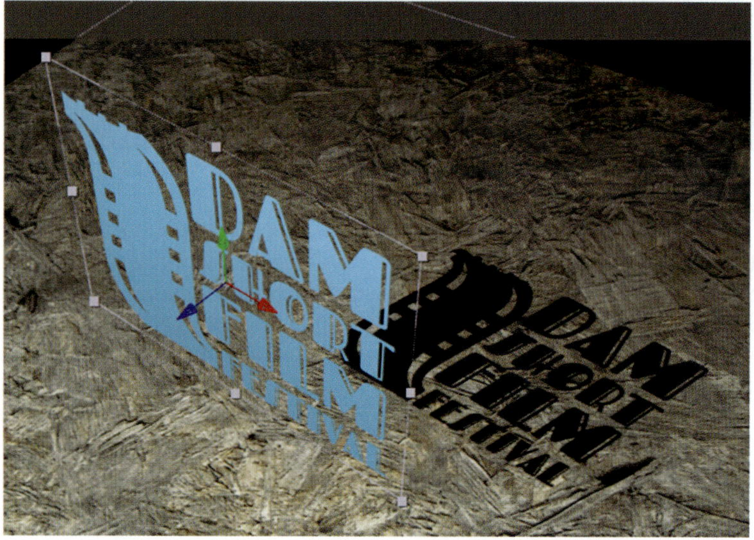

FIG 5.17 A Parallel light casts the shadow of a 3D layer that possesses transparency through its alpha channel. This project is saved as *shadow_trans.aep* in the *\ProjectFiles\aeFiles\Chapter5* directory.

By default, shadow map resolution is set to the size of the current composition. You can alter the resolution, however, by choosing Composition > Composition Settings, switching to the Advanced tab of the Composition Settings window, and clicking the Options button. In the Classic 3D Renderer Options window, you can change the Shadow Map Resolution menu to a smaller size. This may be useful for speeding up renders while you are setting up the composition.

Masking 3D Layers

You can apply standard masking and rotoscoping techniques to 3D layers. When you draw a mask, it's drawn from the perspective of the viewport you're working in. From that point forward, the mask is "stuck" to the 2D plane of the 3D layer. If you rotate or position the layer, the mask follows and keeps its size and shape relative to the layer. Masking techniques are demonstrated in the following tutorial.

Lighting, shadowing, and masking 3D layers mini-tutorial

Use this tutorial to practice creating and arranging 3D layers and 3D cameras, adjusting layer material properties, and masking 3D layers. Follow these steps:

1. Create a new project. Import the *wall2.tif* file from the *\ProjectFiles\Art* directory.
2. Create a new composition with a resolution of 1920x1080, a frame rate of 24, and a duration of 48. LMB-drag the wall file into the composition.
3. Initially, the wall artwork is larger than the composition. Scale the layer down to 25 percent. Click the 3D Layer switch for the layer. Change the Select View Layout to 4 Views. Proceed to move the artwork layer along the negative Z direction so it recedes from the default camera. You can interactively LMB-drag the Z handle in a view or change the Position values in the layer outline. When the Z value increases, the layer recedes from the camera.
4. Using the Front orthographic viewport, draw a rectangular mask so that a thin vertical portion of the left side of the layer is saved (Figure 5.18). Adjust the layer position in the perspective camera viewport. Note how the mask sticks to the layer and takes on the perspective of the layer.
5. Duplicate the wall layer using Edit > Duplicate. Adjust the mask on the new layer so that it cuts out a right portion of the wall. Rotate and position the new layer so that it forms a right angle with the original layer and thus creates a pillar-like shape. Create a new 3D camera via Layer > New > Camera. Position and rotate the camera so that you can see the 3D layers better (Figure 5.19).
6. Import the *rock.tif* file from the *\ProjectFiles\Art* directory. Place it at the bottom of the layer outline. Convert it to a 3D layer. Rotate it to lie flat (90, 0, 0). Position the layer so it forms a floor below the pillar.
7. Create a Spot light via Layer > New > Light. Position and rotate the light so that it points down towards the pillar and floor. If the scene becomes dark, raise the light's Falloff Distance. Further raise the light's

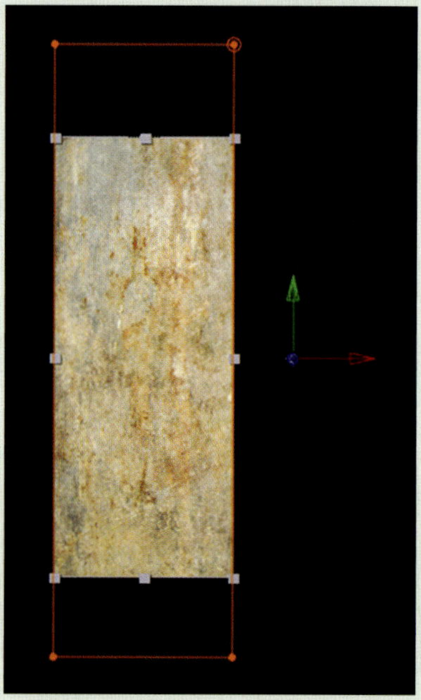

FIG 5.18 A rectangular mask (orange) cuts out a vertical portion of the wall 3D layer. Note that the transform handle remains at the original Anchor Point.

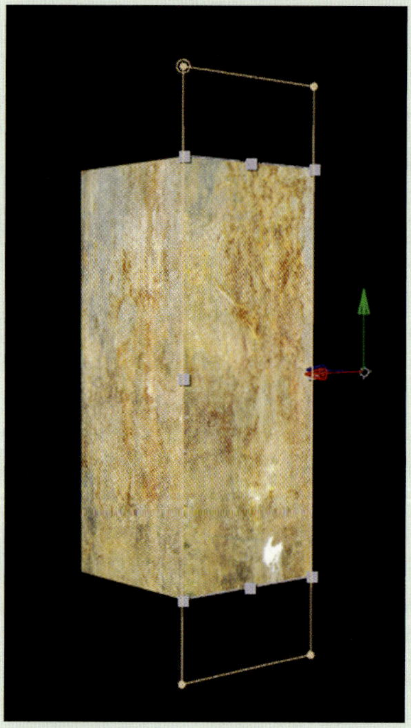

FIG 5.19 A 3D camera is created and positioned to look at the new pillar shape created by placing the two cut out 3D layers at right angles to each other. Note that the mask "sticks" to the 3D layers when they are rotated.

Intensity. For example, set the Falloff Distance to 5000 and Intensity to 200 percent. The 3D layers should be visible but not be so bright that their textures become white. Turn the light's Cast Shadows to On.

8. Go to each 3D layer and turn the Cast Shadows, Accepts Shadows, and Accepts Lights properties to On. A cast shadow of the pillar appears on the floor. Adjust the light position and rotation to form an interesting shadow shape.
9. Fine-tune each 3D layer's Diffuse, Specular Intensity, Specular Shininess, and Metal property value. Adjust the light's Cone Angle and Cone Feather values so that the edge of the light prevents the top of the pillar or the back of the floor from becoming visible (Figure 5.20).

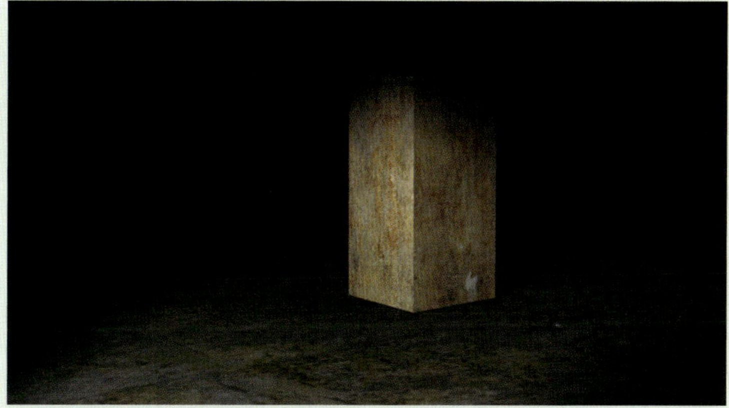

FIG 5.20 A Spot light casts light and shadows on the pillar and floor.

Feel free to add additional lights or additional 3D layers to create additional architecture (such as walls or a ceiling). A sample project is saved as *mini_3d.aep* in the *\ProjectFiles\aeFile\Chapter5* directory.

Arranging 2D Layers as Visual Effects Cards

In addition to traditional motion graphics, the After Effects 3D environment is often used to create 2.5D scenes. *2.5D*, or *2 1/2D*, refers to 2D layers arranged within a 3D space, which occurs when you activate a 3D Layer button for a layer in After Effects. These layers are sometimes called *cards*. 2.5D scenes are useful for adding additional depth and perspective to otherwise flat backgrounds. For example, 2.5D may be used to add more depth to a static matte painting. Matte paintings may come in the form of a painted piece of static art, static art created by combining photograph of real locations, or rendered image sequences produced by a 3D program. To create your own 2.5D matte painting, use the following tutorial.

2.5D matte painting mini-tutorial

For this tutorial, we'll arrange cards to form a room that will eventually include video footage of an actress. We'll take the cards from several static Maya 3D renders. You can follow these steps:

1. Open the *2.5_set_start.aep* project file located in the *\ProjectFiles\aeFiles\Chapter5* directory. Examine the contents. Two compositions are set up. Five static renders of a 3D room are imported.
2. Open Comp 1. LMB-drag the static artwork into the composition. Follow this order, from top to bottom: right wall, left wall, ceiling, back wall, and floor. Note that Comp 1 is an extra-large 3000x4000, while the renders are 2400x3000 and 3200x4000. The large resolution will allow a camera to be animated within the final set but maintain a final output resolution of 1920x1080.
3. Double-click the new right wall layer to open it, by itself, in the Layer view. The finished 3D render takes up a portion of the render while much of it is left as a wireframe. Draw a mask to isolate the wall. The black part of the render corresponds with transparent alpha, so you need only draw a rectangular mask (Figure 5.21). You can draw a mask in the Layer view as you normally would in the Composition view.

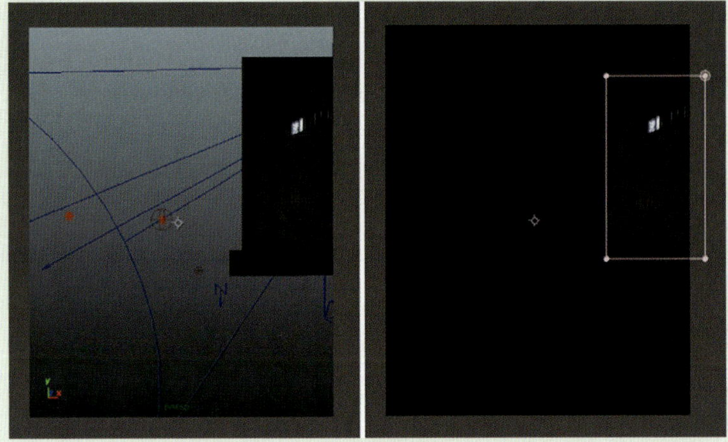

FIG 5.21 Left: Unmasked layer showing the Maya-generated partial render and wireframe. Right: Masked layer that isolates the completed render of right wall.

4. Open the remaining render layers, one at a time, and draw masks to isolate the finished portions while throwing away the wireframe areas. Convert all the layers to 3D layers.
5. Go back to the Composition view. Change the Select View Layout to 4 Views. Use the Unified Camera tool to arrange the orthographic views so you can see the layers. At this point, all of the layers overlap.

6. Go to the floor layer and change X Rotation to –45. The rotation will generate the illusion of parallax shift when a 3D camera is added and animated. This process is similar to creating a forced-perspective miniature. Unlink the Scale property and change the values to 120, 85, 100. This widens the layer.
7. Go to the ceiling layer and change X Rotation to 45. Unlink Scale and change the values to 150, 120, 100. Go to the left wall layer and set the Y Rotation to –45. Unlink the Scale and change the values to 100, 135, 100. Go to the right wall layer and change the Y rotation to 45. Unlink the Scale and set the values to 100, 135, 100. Note that the floor has the opposite rotation of the ceiling. The left wall layer has the opposite rotation of the right wall layer. This will create a box-like shape that widens. At this stage, however, the layers continue to intersect.
8. Move the layers apart so that the corners line up. For example, move the left wall left. Move the right wall right. Move the back wall away from the camera view along Z. Move the ceiling up. Move the floor down. You have several choices when positioning layers. You can interactively LMB-drag the transform axis handles in the viewports when the layer is selected. This alters the layer's Position values. You can also alter the Position fields in the layer outline. You have the option of changing the Anchor Point values. However, this may move the Anchor Point handle away from the layer. Because this virtual set is intended to be static, altering a combination of Position and Anchor Point values is acceptable. If animation or motion tracking data was to be applied, then it would be better to alter the Position values and leave the Anchor Point with default values so the Anchor Point doesn't wind up too far from the layer.
9. Continue adjusting the layer positions until you create with a forced-perspective layout that looks similar to Figure 5.22. Create a new

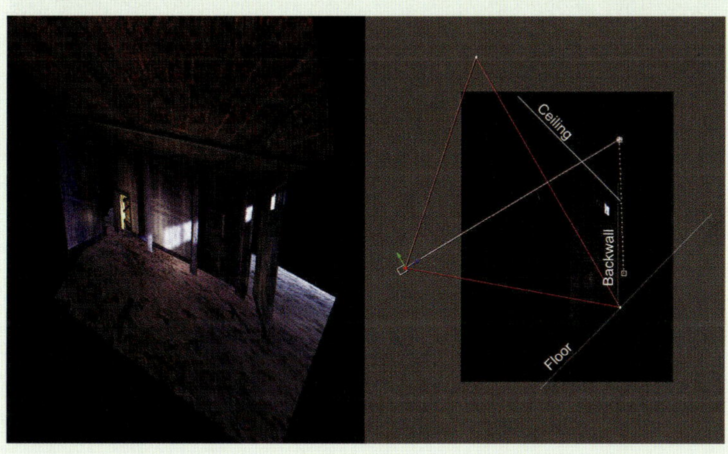

FIG 5.22 Left: The final arrangement of 3D layers, creating a shallow, forced-perspective room with a floor, ceiling, side walls, and back wall. Right: Right orthographic view showing camera position. The vertical dotted line is the point of interest motion path. The camera starts in a tilted-up position.

two-node camera by choosing Layer > New > Camera. Set the lens to 28 mm. Position the camera so that its view plane intersects the front of the floor layer (Figure 5.22). While on the first frame of the timeline, position the point of view near the top of the back wall layer so that the camera is looking up at the ceiling. Keyframe the point of interest. Go to the last frame. Position the point of interest near the base of the back wall so that the room is centered.

10. Open Comp 2. Comp 1 is already nested inside. Comp 2 is 1920x1080, which is the desired output resolution. Comp 1 overhangs Comp 2 thus creating a usable final frame. Play back the timeline. Note the parallax shift (that is, changing perspective) due to a combination of the wide 3D camera lens and the forced-perspective construction of the room.

Optionally, apply color correction effects, such as Curves, Hue/Saturation, and Color Balance, to adjust the renders to create a more cohesive room. For example, give the overall lighting a dark, purplish-blue look (Figure 5.23). Also, you can return to Comp 1, activate motion blur for the layers, and play back Comp 2 again. A final version of this project is saved as *2.5_set_finished.aep* in the *\ProjectFiles\aeFiles\Chapter5* directory.

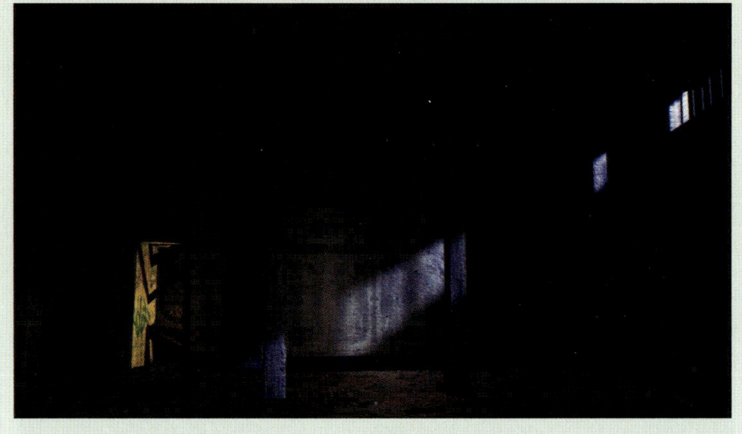

FIG 5.23 The final assembled room, as seen in Comp 2. The layers carry color correction effects, such as Curves and Color Balance, to make the overall lighting look purplish-blue.

Importing Cameras, Lights, and Geometry

You can import cameras from Autodesk Maya and 3D programs that support the RLA and RPF format. You can import cameras, lights, and geometry from Cinema 4D Lite. Cinema 4D Lite is bundled with After Effects CC. The ability to incorporate 3D scenes from 3D programs adds additional power and flexibility to the compositing process.

Importing Maya Cameras

You can import an Autodesk Maya camera into After Effects as a 3D camera layer. To do so, follow these steps:

1. Export a camera from Maya by selecting the camera and choosing File > Export Selection. Choose the .ma format, which is a text file. An example camera .ma file is included as *camera.ma* in the *\ProjectFiles\Data* directory.
2. In After Effects, choose File > Import > File and browse for the .ma file. The camera is imported as a new 3D camera layer within a new composition named after the camera node. Note that 0, 0, 0 in Maya space is lined up with 0, 0 in After Effects screen space. Thus, if the camera is at 0, 0, 0 in Maya, the 3D camera body appears at 0, 0 in the After Effects Front viewport. Nevertheless, if the camera is animated, the animation curves are imported and matching keyframes appear on the timeline. A motion path is also drawn in the viewport. The new composition is the same duration as the duration of the Maya animation. The camera icon inside After Effects does not necessarily correlate to the camera icon inside Maya (in fact, it may appear significantly larger in After Effects relative to its motion path).
3. You are free to copy and paste the 3D camera layer to a different composition. The Zoom property of the 3D camera is converted from the Maya focal length value. Maya one-node cameras become one-node cameras in After Effects. A two-node or three-node Maya camera, however, is imported as a one-node camera but is parented to a new null object layer.

Using the RLA and RPF Formats

If you render an image sequence in the RLA or RPF (Rich Pixel File) format, you can retrieve the contained camera information within After Effects. To do so, import the RLA or RPF image sequence and drop it into a composition. Select the new layer and choose Animation > Keyframe Assistant > RPF Camera Import. A new 3D camera layer is created with keyframed transforms. You can then manipulate the camera as you would any other 3D camera.

At a minimum, the RLA or RPF image sequence must contain a Z-Depth pass so that the camera information is stored. An example RPF image sequence is included in the *\ProjectFiles\Data\camera* directory. The image sequence was created with an empty Autodesk 3ds Max scene.

Working with Cinema 4D Lite

After Effects CC can read Maxon Cinema 4D Lite files through the Cineware plug-in. Although it's beyond the scope of this book to cover Cinema 4D Lite in depth, a tutorial is included here to demonstrate the creation and importation of cameras, lights, and geometry.

Cinema 4D lite mini-tutorial

Follow these steps to create primitive objects, lights, materials, and animation in Cinema 4D Lite and bring those elements into After Effects:

1. Create a new Cinema 4D Lite scene file by choosing File > New > Maxon Cinema 4D File. The file browser window opens. Choose a name and location for the new Cinema 4D scene and click the Save button.
2. Cinema 4D Lite launches as an external program. The program starts with a large perspective viewport (the viewport area is known as an Editor window). You can manipulate the camera through this view by using the Alt/Opt keys and the mouse buttons (the same functionality as Maya). You can choose different viewport panel layouts by choosing Panel > Arrangement > *layout* from the viewport menu. See Figure 5.24 for an overview of the interface.

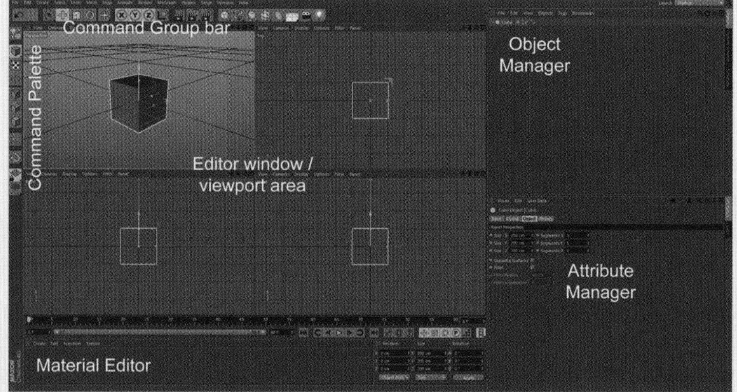

FIG 5.24 The Cinema 4D Lite program window with key interface components.

3. To create a piece of test geometry, use the Create menu, located in the main menu. For example, choose Create > Object > Cube to place a primitive cube at 0, 0, 0. To transform a primitive, select the transform tools located along the Command Group bar at the top left of the program and LMB-drag the associated axis handle in the viewport.
4. If you wish to alter a primitive object, you can make it editable. To do so, click the Model mode button, click the object in a viewport so it receives an orange outline, and RMB-click over the object and choose Make Editable from the menu. The Model mode button and Object mode button share the second-from-the-top position in the Command Palette. To see both buttons, click and hold the current button. After you make the object editable, you can then select subcomponents by switching to the Points, Edges, or Polygons tools along the Command Palette bar, and LMB-clicking on the object in

a viewport. The Points tool selects vertices and the Polygons tool selects faces. When one or more subcomponents are selected (you can additively add selections by Shift+LMB-clicking them), you can transform them using the standard transform tools. Note that polygon modeling tools are not included with Cinema 4D Lite. However, if you have access to a full version of Cinema 4D, you are free to prepare models for importation into After Effects.

5. To assign a material to the object, choose Create > New Material from the Material Manager panel at the bottom left of the program window. This panel is empty by default. A new material, named Mat, is created. The material icon is shown in the panel. If you select the icon, the material attributes appear in the Attribute Manager panel (Figure 5.25). These include attributes common to 3D programs, such as Color, Brightness (diffuse quality), and various specular controls. To map a texture to an attribute, such as Color, click the path bar beside the *Texture* attribute name in the Color tab and browse for the texture file. If you click the small arrow beside the attribute name, you can select a procedural texture, such as Noise or Gradient, from the menu. To assign a material to an object, LMB-drag the material icon and drop it on top of the object in a viewport. The object updates in the viewport to reveal the assigned material.

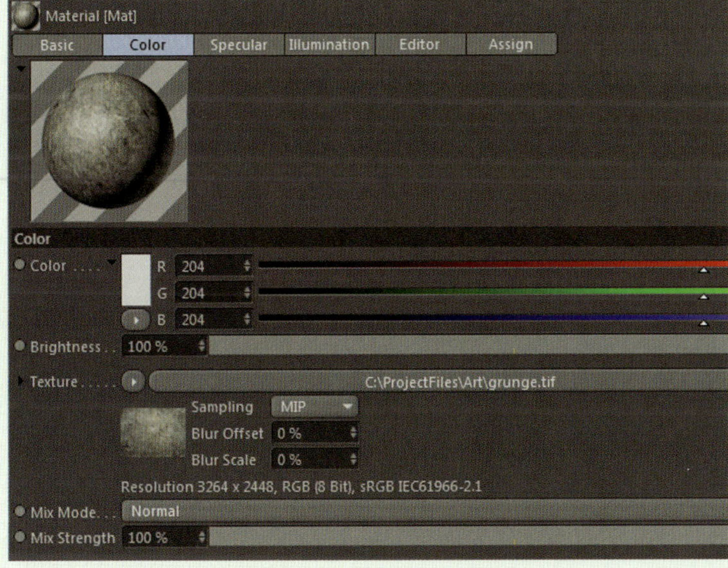

FIG 5.25 A new material in the Attribute Manager. A bitmap is mapped to the Texture attribute of the Color tab.

6. To animate an object, select it, move the timeline to the specific frame, transform the object, and press the Record Active Objects button (this features a key icon inside a red circle at the right side of the timeline).

Repeat this process at different frames. If you are editing the object as a model, reselect it as an object before keyframing it. To do so, click the Object mode button in the Command Palette and click the object in the viewport.

7. To create a light, choose Create > Light > *light* from the main menu. To alter the basic light attributes, select the light and go to the Attribute Manager. For example, to alter the brightness, adjust the Intensity slider. To activate shadows, choose a shadow type through the Shadow menu. You can use the standard transform tools to position the light in the viewports.
8. To save a Cinema 4D scene, choose File > Save. The file is saved in .c4d format with the name and location selected when you chose File > New > Maxon Cinema 4D File in After Effects. To see the scene in After Effects, LMB-drag the Cinema 4D scene, automatically added to the Project panel, into a composition. You can return to Cinema 4D Lite to update the scene. If you re-save, After Effects automatically detects the changes and updates the associated layer. (Optionally, you can import a different Cinema 4D file by choosing File > Import > File.) The Cinema 4D scene carries a resolution, duration, and frame rate set by the Cinema 4D program. When the scene is added to a composition, the Cinema 4D Lite perspective camera view in shown the Composition view panel (Figure 5.26). The view is shaded and includes wireframes of lights and the XZ axis grid. Imported components include lights, animation curves, materials, and textures. You can play back the timeline to see the animation.

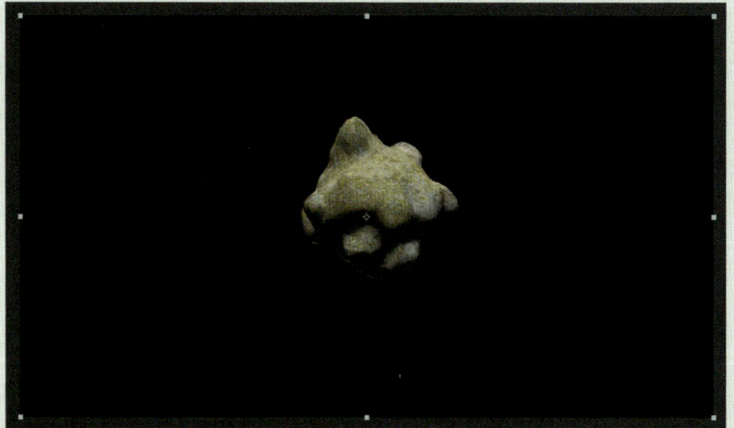

FIG 5.26 A Cinema 4D Lite scene is added to a composition and is viewed through the Composition view. With this example, the scene includes an animated polygon meteorite that is textured with a color bitmap and procedural bump map.

9. To see the final render quality, open the Cineware effect, which is added to the Cinema 4D layer (Figure 5.27). Change the Renderer menu to Standard (Final) and play back. The render quality is based on the render settings within Cinema 4D. You can change the render settings before saving the Cinema 4D file—this is described in the next section.

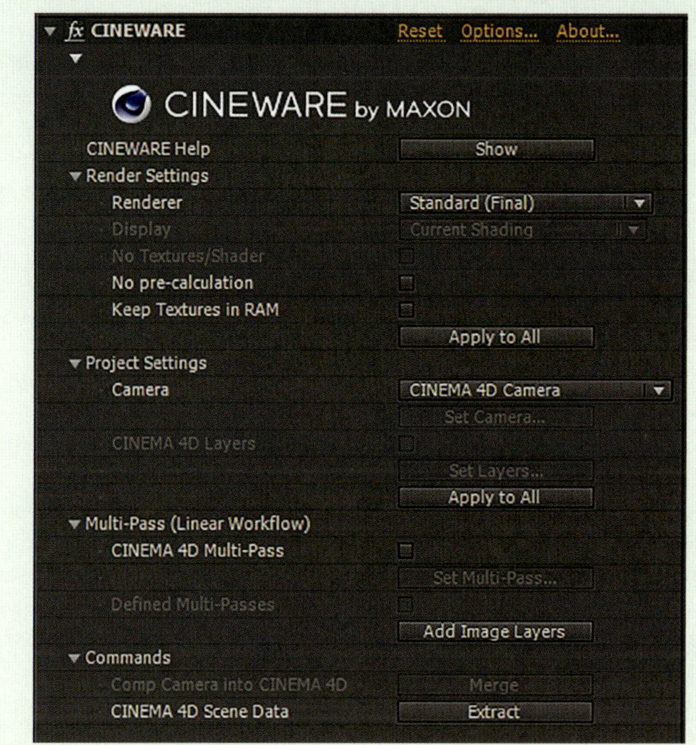

FIG 5.27 The Cineware effect properties.

10. Empty space with Cinema 4D Lite becomes transparent inside After Effects. Therefore, you can combine the Cinema 4D footage with standard 2D and 3D layers (Figure 5.28). Note that the Cinema 4D scene is not a 3D layer inside After Effects—it's treated like a 2D layer.

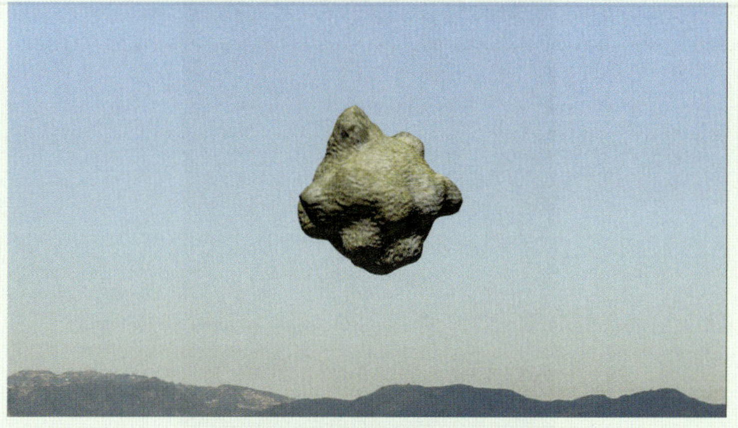

FIG 5.28 Render using Standard (Final) quality. A 2D layer featuring a sky image is placed under the Cinema 4D layer. The wireframe view of objects disappears when the final render quality is chosen.

A sample After Effects project is included as *cinema4D.aep* in the *\ProjectFiles\aeFiles\Chapter5* directory. A matching Cinema 4D file is included as *meteor.c4d* in the *\ProjectFiles\Data* directory.

Working with Cinema 4D Multi-Passes

When setting up a render in Cinema 4D, you have the option to create multi-passes, which are also known as render passes. Render passes break a single frame into separate shading components. For example, you can render the diffuse, specular, and shadow components of a surface as different image sequences. Using render passes gives you greater control in the composite as you can add unique effects, such as blurs or color corrections, to each shading component layer. When you import a Cinema 4D file into After Effects, you have the option to read the individual multi-passes.

To set up multi-passes in Cinema 4D Lite, you can follow these basic steps:

1. From the main menu, choose Render > Edit Render Settings. In the Output section of the Render Settings window, set common render attributes such as resolution, frame rate, and duration. Note that the Lite version has a resolution size limit of 800x600.
2. To activate multi-passes, click the Multi-Pass check box in the left column (Figure 5.29). To add a render pass, click the Multi-Pass menu button at the left center of the window and select the pass. Common render passes include Diffuse, Specular, Shadow, Ambient Occlusion, and Depth. You can add as many render passes as may be useful. (Render passes are discussed in more detail in Chapter 7.)
3. Close the window and save the Cinema 4D scene.

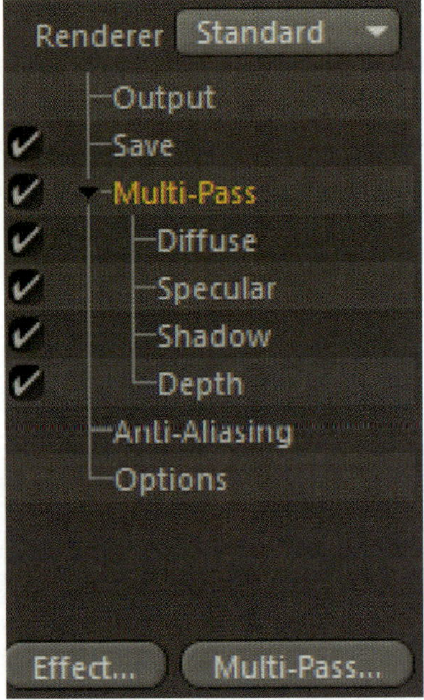

FIG 5.29 Detail of the Cinema 4D Lite Render Settings window with four multi-passes listed. The Multi-Pass menu button is at the bottom of the figure.

To use multi-passes inside After Effects, follow these steps:

1. Follow the basic steps outlined in the "Cinema 4D Lite Mini-Tutorial" section earlier in this chapter to import the Cinema 4D scene into After Effects. A sample scene is saved as *multi_pass.c4d* in the *\ProjectFiles\Data* directory.
2. Place the imported Cinema 4D file into a new composition. Open the Cineware effect in the Effect Controls panel. Change the Renderer menu to Standard (Final). Select the Defined Multi-Passes check box. Click the Add Image Layers button. A new layer is added for each multi-pass. The blending modes menu for each layer is set to a mode commonly associated with the pass. (Blending modes as they pertain to render passes are discussed in more detail in Chapter 7.) The new multi-pass layers are ordered to re-create the original 3D render (Figure 5.30).
3. Go to frame 11. A 3D meteor appears along a falling trajectory. Feel free to solo any layer to examine it in the Composition view. Import the *sky.png* file from the *\ProjectFiles\Art* directory and place it at the bottom of the layer outline.

FIG 5.30 Extracted multi-pass layers share the composition with a 2D layer of a sky. Note the preset blending mode menus.

At this stage, the multi-passes occlude any lower 2D layers even though the 3D geometry only takes up a small portion of the frame. As a workaround, you can reorder the layers and use the Track Matte tool to borrow alpha information from a Depth multi-pass render. To do this, follow these steps:

1. Reorder the multi-pass layers by LMB-dragging them up and down. Use the following order, starting at the top and working downwards: Shadow, Specular, Depth, and Diffuse.
2. Hide the Depth layer and original multipass.c4d layer (numbered *5*) by clicking the Video eye icons. The Shadow layer blending mode menu is set to Multiply, which blends the shadow pass without need of alpha. The Specular layer blending mode is set to Add. Change the Specular blending mode to Screen (Figure 5.31). Like Add, Screen blends the bright spots of the layer over lower layers; however, Screen prevents superwhite values and allows the specular highlights to look similar to the original render.

FIG 5.31 The multi-pass layers are reordered. The Depth layer and original multipass.c4d layer are hidden. The Specular layer's blending mode is changed to Screen.

3. Change the Diffuse layer's Track Matte menu to Luma Matte. This converts brightness information of the Depth layer to alpha information for the Diffuse layer. The sky layer appears below the meteorite (Figure 5.32).

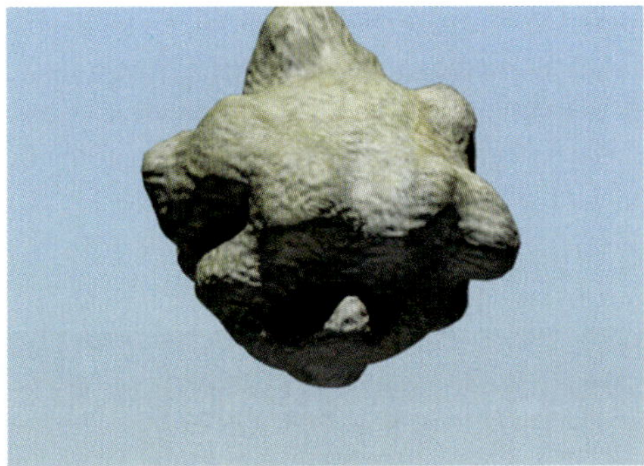

FIG 5.32 The Diffuse layer gains alpha from the Track Matte tool, allowing it to appear over the sky layer.

A finished project file is included as *multi_pass.aep* in the *\ProjectFiles\aeFiles\Chapter5* directory.

Extracting Cinema 4D Scene Elements

You can convert Cinema 4D cameras and lights so they are accessible in the After Effects 3D environment. To do this, click the Cinema 4D Scene Data Extract button, found with the Cineware effect properties. Each light is converted to an equivalent After Effects light, complete with standard transforms and light options. A one-node camera is also created as a new 3D camera layer. You are free to transform, animate, or adjust the lights and cameras.

Initially, the Cinema 4D layer continues to use the internal Cineware Cinema 4D camera. However, you can change the Cineware effect's Camera menu to Use Comp Camera. With this setting, Cineware renders the Cinema 4D scene with the new, converted 3D camera layer. Unfortunately, the converted lights no longer affect the Cinema 4D layer.

Motion Blurring Cinema 4D Scenes

Motion blur does not carry over from Cinema 4D to After Effects. However, you can add the Pixel Motion Blur effect (Effect > Time > Pixel Motion Blur) to the Cinema 4D layer to emulate the blur. The effect includes the following properties:

Shutter Control determines whether the shutter angle is automatically or manually set.

Shutter Angle sets the length of the motion blur trail. The higher the value, the longer blur trail. 180 degrees matches many film and video cameras (Figure 5.33).

Shutter Sample sets the quality of the blur. A higher value results in smoother blur trails.

Vector Detail determines the number of motion vectors used to track pixels between frames. A value of 100 produces one vector per pixel. The higher the values, the more accurate the blur and the longer the render takes.

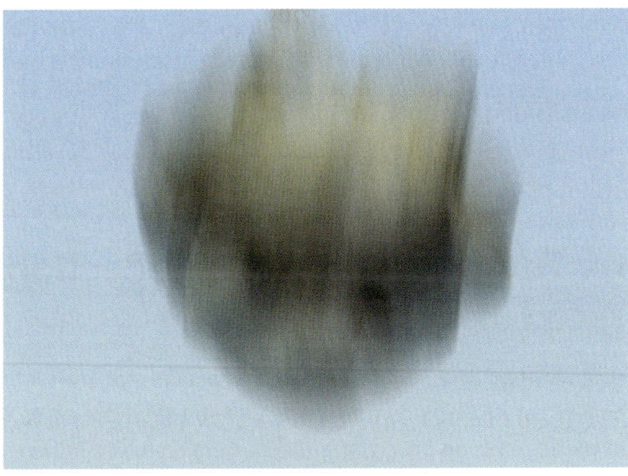

FIG 5.33 A Cinema 4D scene is given motion blur with the Pixel Motion Blur effect. Shutter Control is set to Manual, Shutter Angle is set to 180, Shutter Sample is set to 64, and Vector Detail is set to 50. A sample project is saved as *pixel_motion.aep* in the *\ProjectFiles\aeFiles\Chapter5* directory.

Pixel Motion Blur may not produce perfect results, particularly when objects cross over each other or cross the frame edge. In such situations, it may be necessary to render an image sequence inside Cinema 4D with motion blur and import the sequence into After Effects (thus bypassing the importation of the Cinema 4D scene).

Switching to Ray-Traced 3D

By default, compositions are rendered with the After Effects Classic 3D renderer. However, you have the option to switch to the Ray-Traced 3D renderer by changing the Renderer menu in the Advanced tab of the

Composition Settings window. In addition to the general features of the Classic 3D renderer, the Ray-Traced 3D renderer supports reflections, refractions, environment textures, and semitransparent translucency. The renderer is also able to extrude and bevel text and shape layers. The renderer adds a number of extra properties to the Material Options section of 3D layers. The renderer also adds a new Geometry Options section to each 3D layer. The new options included in the Material Options section are described here:

Reflection Intensity and Reflection Sharpness These properties produce reflections on the 3D layer. The higher the Reflection Intensity and Reflection Sharpness, the stronger and sharper the reflection.

Transparency and Index Of Refraction Set the amount of transparency and light distortion as light passes through the 3D layer. An Index Of Refraction set to 1.0 is equivalent to nondistorting air. An Index Of Refraction of 1.33 emulates water. An Index Of Refraction of 1.4 or 1.5 emulates glass.

Reflection Rolloff and Transparency Rolloff These properties determine the Fresnel quality of a 3D layer, whereby the viewing angle affects the transparency or strength of reflection. The higher the values, the less visible the reflection and the more transparent the glass.

Despite the expanded features, Ray-Traced 3D is unable to support blending modes or Track Matte operations. To utilize the Ray-Traced 3D renderer, you can use the following tutorial.

Chapter Tutorial: Rendering Reflections with Ray-Traced 3D

1. Using the 3D layer and 3D camera techniques demonstrated throughout this chapter, rotate and position a 3D layer so that it becomes a floor or ground plane. Position and rotate the camera so that it looks down at the layer. You can use any of the images included in the *\ProjectFiles\Art* folder as a source for the 3D layer or use your own artwork.
2. With no layer selected, use the Ellipse tool to draw an oval shape in a viewport. The Ellipse tool is in the shape menu in the main toolbar and is below the Rectangle tool. When you use a shape tool without selecting a layer, a new shape layer is created.
3. Convert the shape layer into a 3D layer. Move the shape layer so it sits above the floor layer. Readjust the camera so that the shape is centered. Rotate the shape so that it is tipped down toward the floor (Figure 5.34).
4. Choose Composition > Composition Settings. Switch to the Advanced tab of the Composition Settings window. Change the Renderer menu to Ray-Traced 3D. As soon as the renderer is switched, the Material Options section gains new ray-tracing and transparency properties (these are described in the previous section).

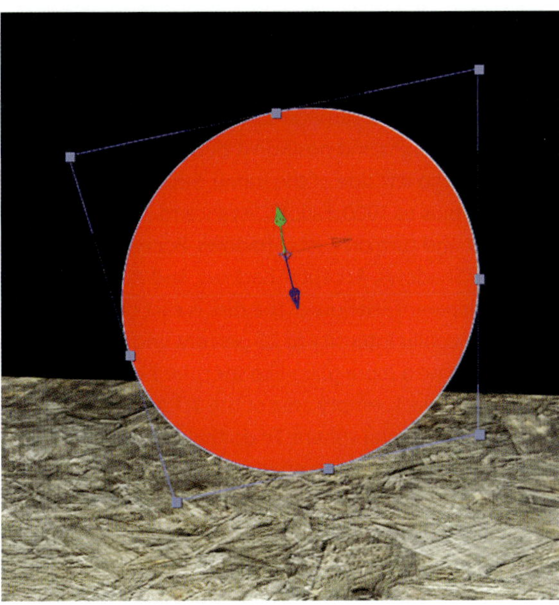

FIG 5.34 A shape layer is cut with an ellipse mask, converted to a 3D layer, and rotated to point down at a second 3D layer serving as a floor.

5. Expand the Contents > Ellipse 1 > Fill 1 subsection of the shape layer. Change the Color to white. Go to the Material Options section for the shape layer and change Reflection Intensity to 100 percent. The renderer takes some time to update the frame. After completion, the solid reflects the floor. If the renderer refresh is too slow, you can temporarily reduce the quality by setting the Resolution/Down Sample Factor Popup menu, in the view panel, to lower quality, such as Quarter.
6. Changing the renderer also adds a Geometry Options section to the shape layer. To emulate a 3D object, you can bevel or extrude the shape. For example, set Bevel Style to Angular and Bevel Depth to 20. A bevel appears on the edge of the shape and also reflects the floor (Figure 5.35). Note that the reflection includes the black of the After Effects empty 3D space.

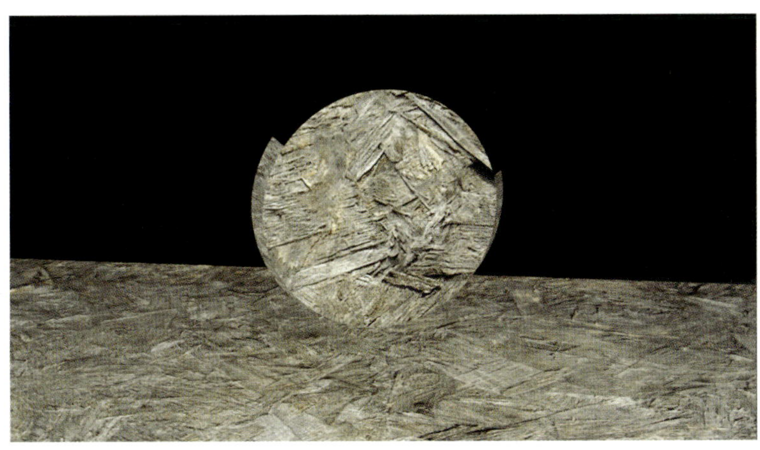

FIG 5.35 The shape is given a bevel and reflectivity by switching the renderer to Ray-Traced 3D.

7. Reduce the shape layer's Reflection Sharpness to 75 percent to blur the reflection. Reduce the Transparency to 90 percent. Increase the Index Of Refraction to 1.5. Reduce the Reflection Intensity to 15 percent. The resulting render creates a semitransparent, glass-like disc.
8. Create a new Point light and position it between the camera and the shape along the left side of the frame. Set the light's Intensity to 200 percent, Radius to 1000, Falloff Distance to 5000, and Shadow Diffusion to 25, and turn on Casts Shadows. For each 3D layer, make sure that Casts Shadows, Accepts Shadows, and Accepts Lights is set to On. A semitransparent shadow of the disc is cast on the floor. Set the shape layer's Specular Intensity to 20 percent and Specular Shininess to 50 percent to create a more glass-like specular highlight.
9. You can fill in the black, empty area of the 3D space by converting a layer to an environmental sphere. To do this, import a still image, image sequence, or movie and drop it on top of the layer outline. For example, use *sky.png* located in the *\ProjectFiles\Art* directory. Select the new layer and choose Layer > Environment Layer. The environment layer replaces the previously empty black space (see Figure 5.1 at the start of this chapter). If the environment layer appears grainy, feel free to add a blur effect, such as Fast Blur, to soften it.
10. To produce a render with the final quality that lacks the wireframe icons of lights, add the composition to the Render Queue. You can choose to render a single frame by clicking the Queue's *Best Settings* link (beside Render Settings) and entering a new frame range by clicking the Custom button at the bottom right of the Render Settings window. Before you render, you can increase the render quality by clicking the Options button of the Advanced tab of the Composition Settings window. In the Ray-Traced 3D Renderer Options window, gradually increase the Ray-Tracing Quality. You can also choose more accurate anti-aliasing by changing the Anti-Aliasing Filter menu to Cubic.

Optionally, you can animate the shape layer or light moving and render the entire timeline as a movie or image sequence. You can also add additional lights or 3D layers. Although the Ray-Traced 3D renderer and its associated options are not as robust as similar tools found in dedicated 3D programs, it is able to produce simple surfaces with complex surface qualities. Hence, it may be suitable for creating small props or debris for visual effects shots. A final version of this project is saved as *reflection_finished.aep* in the *\ProjectFiles\aeFiles\Chapter5* directory.

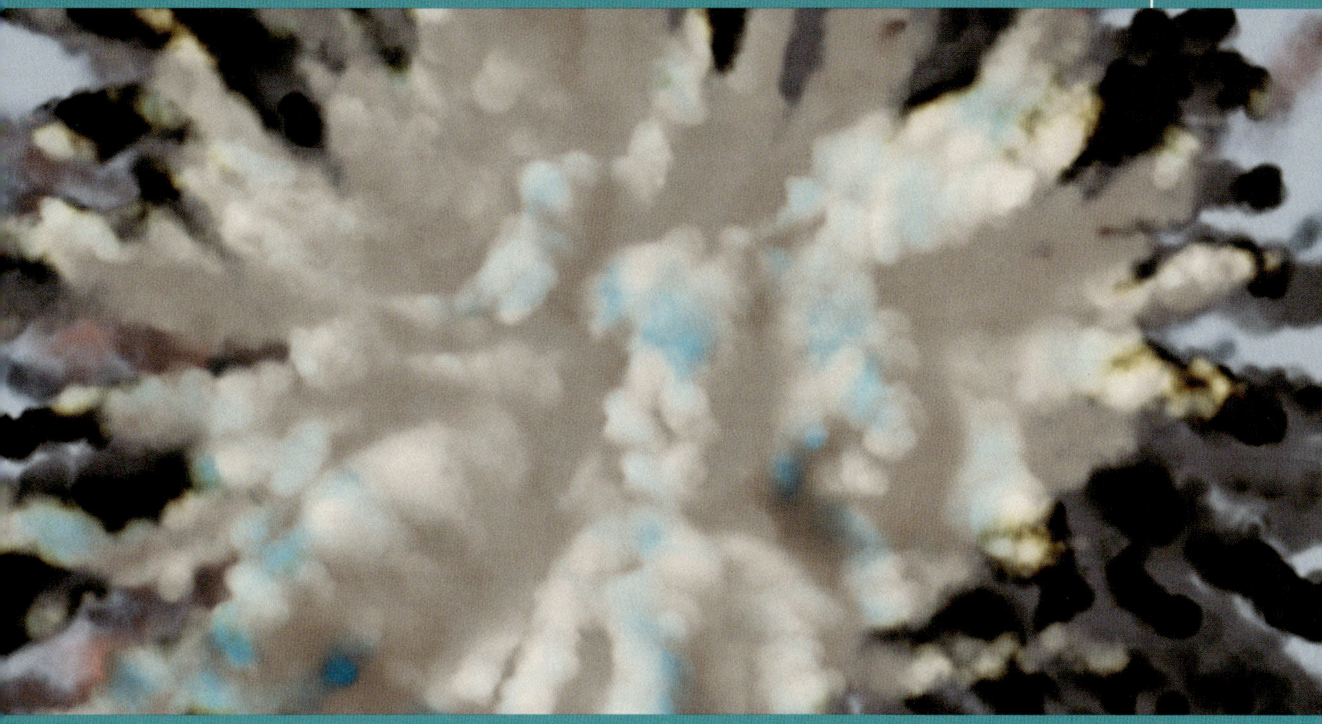

CHAPTER 6

Creating Particle Simulations

Particle simulations are a mainstay of visual effects work and are generated within 3D and compositing programs. Particle simulations are able to recreate a wide range of fluid, semi-fluid, vaporous, combustive, and shattered-surface substances and events. For example, particle simulations are used to create water, mud, sparks, fire, smoke, dust, explosions, and debris (Figure 6.1).

This chapter includes the following critical information:

- Review of built-in particle plug-ins
- Creating dust puffs, sparks, smoke, and water with particle effects
- Review of third-party plug-ins and an introduction to Trapcode Particular

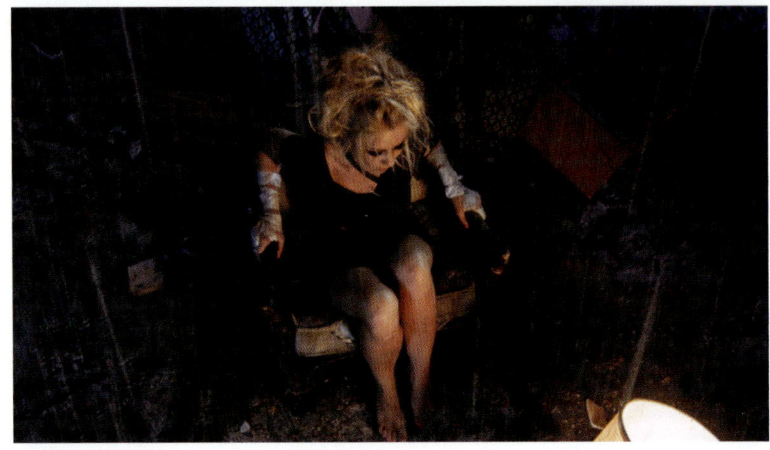

FIG 6.1 Raindrops, puddles, and ripples are added to a shot using particle and blur effects, as well as masking and 3D layers.

General Particle Workflow

Whether particles are simulated in After Effects or a 3D program such as Autodesk Maya, the basic workflow is generally the same. The steps include:

1. An emitter is created and positioned. The emitter generates *n* number of particles per second. The emitter may be an omnidirectional point, have a geometric volume, or may take the form of a plane or piece of geometry.
2. The particles, at their moment of birth, are given various attributes, such as size (measured as a radius), initial velocity, initial direction, and so on.
3. Optionally, forces are added to simulate the physical world and alter the particle movement. Most often, gravity is applied, but other forces (also called *fields*) may be added to simulate natural events such as turbulence or wind. If no forces are applied, the simulation acts as if the particles are in a vacuum.
4. Optionally, particles are made to "die" off within a certain number of seconds, frames, or randomly within a time range. Some particle systems allow for particle collisions with boundaries or with geometry. The collisions may cause particle death or the spawning of additional sub-particles.
5. Particles are rendered with a chosen shading quality and lighting. Particles can emulate a wide range of materials, including vaporous smoke, cohesive liquids, embers, and so on.

3D programs such as Autodesk Maya, Autodesk 3ds Max, and Side Effects Houdini can create incredibly complex particle simulations. Therefore, particle simulations are often delivered to visual effects compositors as completed renders. Nevertheless, the renders often need additional adjustment to make them usable. In fact, the renders may appear crude or incomplete until effects are applied within After Effects or similar programs. For example, particle renders may require additional blur effects or color grading.

Using Built-In Particle Effects

After Effects includes several particle simulation effects. These include Particle Playground, CC Particle World, and CC Particle Systems II. (*CC* stands for the software developer, Cycore Effects.) Although the effects are not as advanced as some third-party particle plug-ins, they are often suitable for simple phenomena, such as dust puffs, smoke, and sparks. The following sections and tutorials demonstrate the use of these plug-ins.

Additional Cycore Effects plug-ins are designed for specific simulations that require a particle-like motion. These include CC Drizzle, CC Bubbles, CC Snowfall, and CC Rainfall. You can find these in the Effect > Simulation menu. CC Drizzle and CC Rainfall are demonstrated as part of the tutorial at the end of this chapter.

Creating Dust Puffs with Particle Playground

A common visual effect element is a dust puff. Such puffs are often used to indicate an object's connection with the ground, wall, or some other surface. The object may be a piece of falling debris or the foot of a character. If the character comes in the form of green screen footage or a 3D render, the puffs help strengthen the connection of the character to the ground. You can also add dust puffs to live-action footage to accentuate the footsteps. For example, an included example uses the Particle Playground effect to add dust to a close-up of an actor's feet. The main steps needed to create the puffs follow:

1. A solid layer the same size as the composition is placed on top of the layer outline. The layer color is not important as the particle effect eventually replaces the solid. The live-action shot is placed at the bottom of the layer outline.
2. The Particle Playground effect is added to the solid. (Choose Effect > Simulation > Particle Playground.)
3. The effect's emitter is placed below a foot at the point that the foot touches the ground. With this example, the right foot steps down on frame 19. The emitter location is set by the Position property in the Cannon section. The Cannon section also holds properties for critical qualities like size, velocity, direction, and particle numbers (Figure 6.2).
4. The particles are scaled up with the Particle Radius property so they overlap. To make a short puff, the Particles Per Second property is animated off to on to off over a short period of time. For example, the property is keyed to change from 0 to 5000 to 0 over a period of 6 frames.
5. The Barrel Radius property is increased to create the particles over the width of the foot. The Velocity value is increased to create greater particle speed. The Direction Random Spread and Velocity Random Spread are increased to create greater variety in the particle motion.
6. By default, the particles drift upwards, which works for a footstep. You can change the particle direction by altering the Direction property. You can

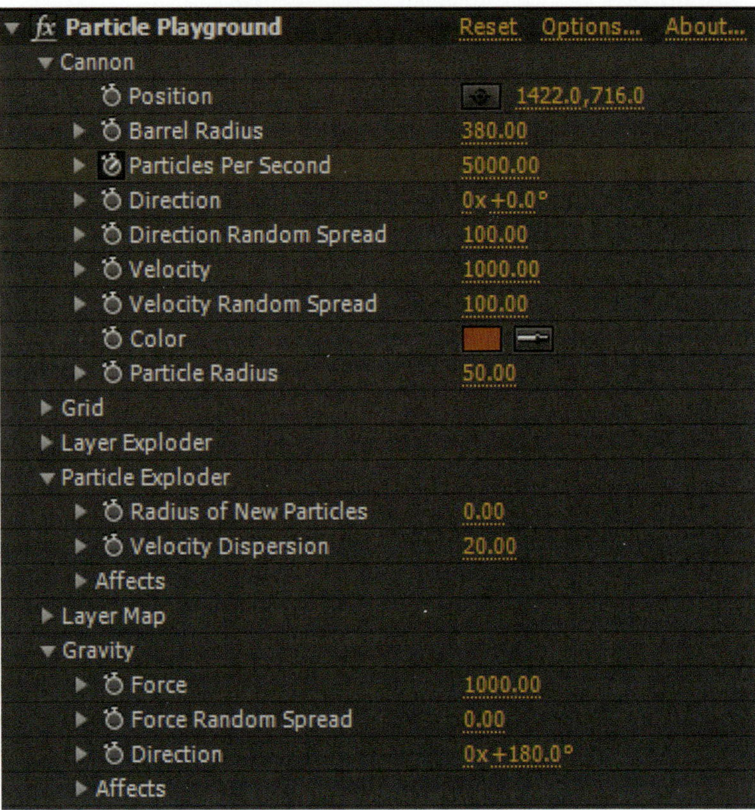

FIG 6.2 Adjusted properties of the Particle Playground effect.

also strengthen gravity by raising the Force value in the Gravity section. By default, the built-in gravity pulls the particles downwards.

7. The particle color is changed to brown through the Color property (in the Cannon section). By default, the particles are square and live forever. Hence, additional effects and adjustments are needed to make the particles more dust-like.
8. To remove the squarish nature of the particles, a blur effect is added. For example, a Fast Blur with Bluriness set to 100 blends and softens the particle mass (Figure 6.3).
9. The solid layer's Opacity is keyed to change from 0 percent to 10 percent. The particles are "killed off" by setting a later keyframe back to 0 percent. With a low Opacity value, the particles appear like a thin, undulating dust. You can alter the Opacity animation to create thinner or thicker dust (Figure 6.4).

In general, dust puff effects can remain subtle. As long as the particle color matches the ground material or general scene lighting and the particles take on believable motion (i.e., puffing, drifting, or wafting), a simple particle simulation is all that is necessary. You can add complexity to the simulation by adding multiple iterations of the particle effect and giving each iteration a

FIG 6.3 The particles are made brown and blurred with the Fast Blur effect. The live action is temporarily hidden.

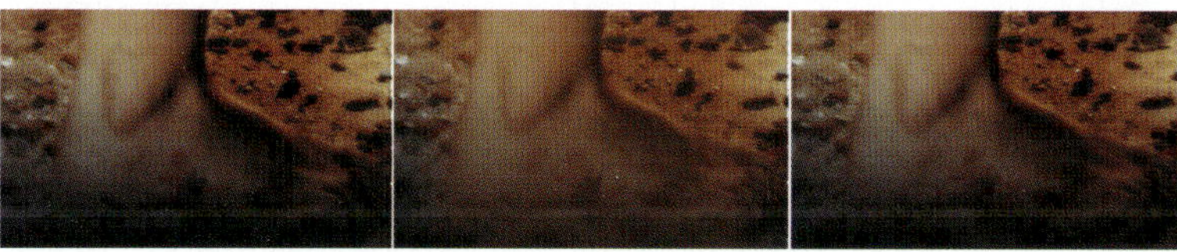

FIG 6.4 Left to right: Particles layered over the live-action footage with 0 percent, 30 percent, and 10 percent Opacity.

unique emitter location and property values. An example project file is saved as *particle_playground.aep* in the *\ProjectFiles\aeFiles\Chapter6* directory.

Creating Sparks with CC Particle Systems II

Sparks are another visual effect element that is commonly used. Sparks may be added to explosions, electrical short circuits, collisions between metal and other surfaces, or futuristic gun blasts. The following steps detail the creation of generic sparks with the CC Particle Systems II effect.

1. A new solid layer is created and placed on top of the layer outline. The layer color is not important as the particle effect eventually replaces the solid.
2. The CC Particle Systems II effect is added to the solid. (Choose Effect > Simulation > CC Particle Systems II.)
3. The default simulation creates a burst of particles, which fall downwards. You can see this by playing back the timeline. To reduce the number of particles, the Birth Rate property is reduced (Figure 6.5). You can also turn

the particle emitter off by keyframing the value at 0. With this example, the Birth Rate is animated, changing from 0 to 1.0 to 0 over a span of 4 frames. Birth Rate is kept below 1.0 to create a small number of particles.

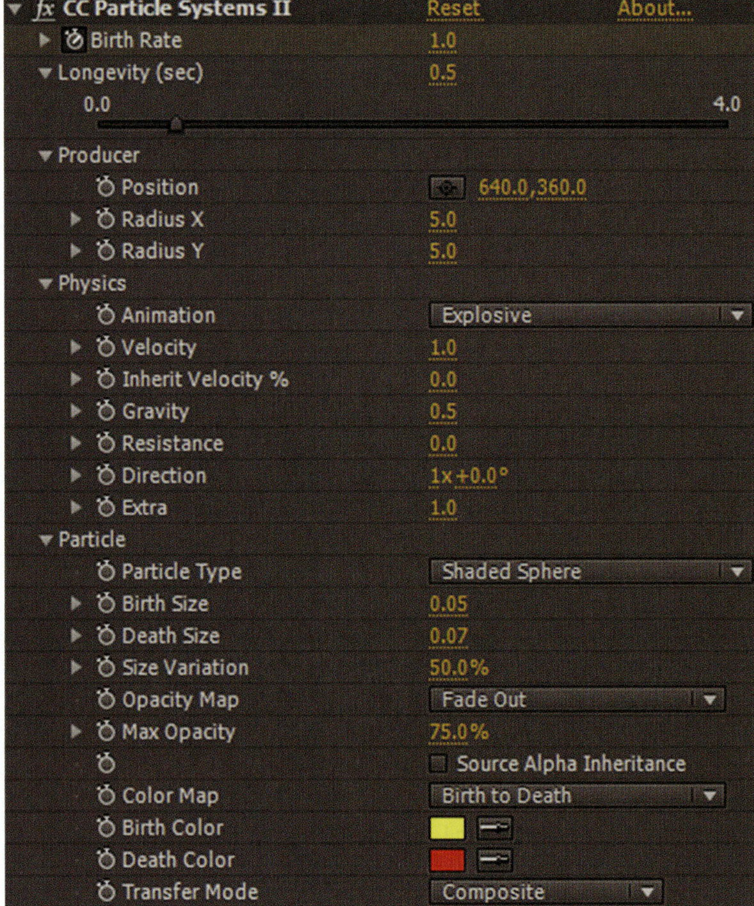

FIG 6.5 Adjusted Particle Systems II properties.

4. You can time the particle burst so that it corresponds to a particular event in the live-action footage by animating the Birth Rate property. As an alternative, you can create the particle simulation in its own composition and nest the result within a different composition that carries the live-action footage. This allows you to "slide" the nested particles back and forth on the timeline to line the particle birth with a particular event.
5. You can place the emitter in a different position by altering the Position X and Y values in the Producer section. With this example, the emitter is left in its default position. To enlarge the area in which the particles are born, the Radius X and Y values are increased.

6. By default, the particle burst is omnidirectional. However, the particles quickly fall due to gravity. You can alter the basic forces through the Physics section. For this example, the Gravity property is reduced to 0.5.
7. By default, any particle that is born lives forever. To force them to "die" within 12 frames (half a second at 24 fps), Longevity (Sec) is set to 0.5.
8. Particle Systems II supports different particle types. To create a more three-dimensional look to the sparks, the Particle Type menu, in the Particle section, is set to Shaded Sphere. To reduce the particle size, Birth Size is set to 0.05 and Death Size to 0.07. With these settings, the particles shrink over their lifetime. If you change the particle type, you may need to adjust the Birth Rate values.
9. By default, the particle Birth Color is yellow and Death Color is red. This is suitable for sparks, although you are free to change the color swatches.
10. To make the particles more spark-like, a Glow effect is added (Effect > Stylize > Glow). Glow Threshold is set to 0 percent, Glow Radius is set to 15, and Glow Intensity is set to 3. The Glow Colors menu is changed to A & B Colors; Color A is set to orange, and Color B is set to dark red. This produces a glowy halo around each spark (Figure 6.6).
11. You can add motion blur to particle simulations in After Effects. Hence, motion blur is activated for the solid layer and the entire composition.

When the solid layer is placed over a live-action footage layer, you can set the solid layer's blending mode menu to Screen. The Screen mode ensures that only

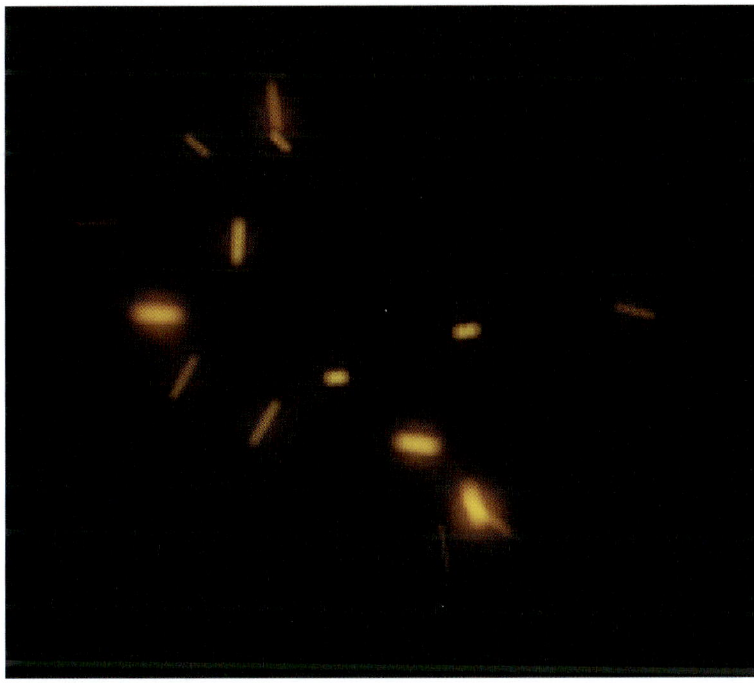

FIG 6.6 The final spark simulation. The Glow effect and motion blur add realism to the particles.

the bright areas of particles appear over lower layers. An example project file is saved as *particle_systems.aep* in the *\ProjectFiles\aeFiles\Chapter6* directory.

Creating Smoke with CC Particle World

You can create smoke with particle effects in After Effects. So long as the smoke does not require a rounded, three-dimensional quality, a simple particle simulation will suffice. (If a more volumetric smoke is required, a simulation created in a 3D program or a more advanced plug-in, such as Trapcode Particular, will create a better result.) The following tutorial demonstrates the creation of simple smoke.

CC Particle World mini-tutorial

You can follow these steps to create rising smoke with CC Particle World:

1. Create a new project. Import the *\ProjectFiles\Plates\Particles\Factory.##.png* image sequence. Interpret the sequence as 30 fps by RMB-clicking the sequence name, choosing Interpret Footage > Main, and setting Assume This Frame Rate to 30.
2. LMB-drag the sequence to the timeline to create a new composition. The sequence features an aerial shot of a factory. Several of the smokestacks produce a brownish smoke. However, in the foreground, the shorter smokestack does not (see Figure 6.11 at the end of this tutorial). We'll add smoke to this stack.
3. Create a new solid layer (Layer > New > Solid Layer). Make the solid the same size as the composition. The solid color does not matter. The solid layer is placed automatically at the top of the layer outline.
4. With the solid layer selected, choose Effect > Simulation > CC Particle World. The solid color is replaced with a spherical emitter (called a producer), a shower of particles, a reference grid, and an axis control cube at the top left.
5. To more easily see the emitter and axis cube, temporarily turn off the particles by setting the effect's Birth Rate property to 0. While on the first frame of the timeline, LMB-drag the axis reference cube. This rotates the effect's built-in camera view of the emitter. Roughly orient the emitter and grid so that the camera is looking down on the emitter. You can move the emitter left/right and up/down by LMB-dragging the emitter in the Composition view. Continue to adjust the axis cube and emitter position until the emitter is slightly lower than the top of the foreground smokestack (Figure 6.7).
6. Expand the Particle World sections in the Effect Controls panel. Set Birth Rate to 25 and Longevity (Sec) to 6. Note that the emitter position is stored by the Position X, Y, and Z values in the Producer section. Set Radius X, Y, and Z to 0.025. Radius determines the width of the emitter.

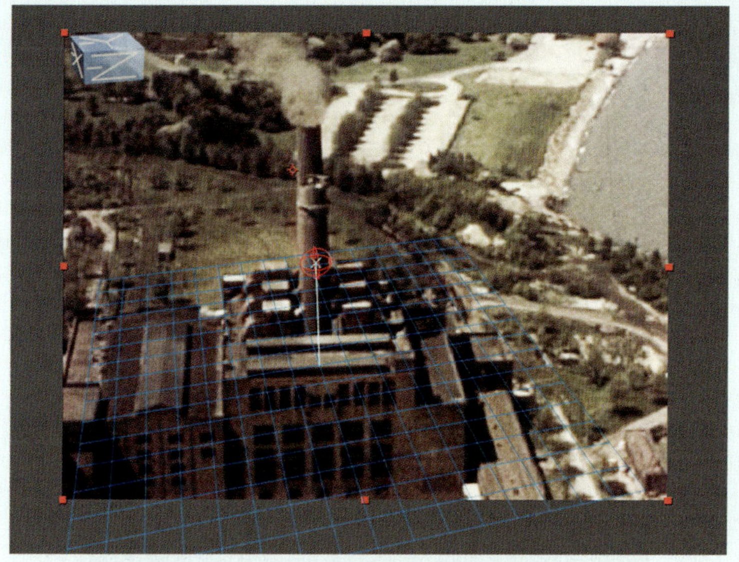

FIG 6.7 The particles are temporarily hidden to show the emitter (producer) sphere, reference grid, and axis cube. The axis cube is adjusted so that the effect camera looks down on the emitter and grid.

7. In the Physics section, change the Animation menu to Cone Axis. This generates a widening column of particles as opposed to the default explosive pattern. Change Velocity to 0.4 and Resistance to 5. This betters matches the speed of the particles to the smoke that exists in the image sequence. Reduce Gravity to 0.1 so the particles do not fall back to the bottom of the frame. Play back the timeline to see the simulation. Stop at a middle frame. Interactively adjust the Gravity Vector X, Y, and Z values. This points the gravity vector in a different direction to bias the direction the particles are moving. Leave Gravity Vector X, Y, and Z set to −0.2, −1.0, −0.2. Play back. This makes particles flow in a slight right-to-left and upward direction.
8. In the Particle section, change Particle Type to Faded Sphere. This converts the particle simulation into a soft-edge mass. Change Birth Size to 0.2 and Death Size to 0.6. Reduce Max Opacity to 3 percent to give the particles a semitransparent look that matches the smoke in the footage. Slight changes to Max Opacity cause significant differences in the final look of the particles. Change the Birth Color to tan and Death Color to brown. You can use the eyedropper to sample the smoke in the image sequence. To better see the particles with low Opacity, temporarily hide the image sequence layer.
9. In the Extras section, change the Depth Cue Type menu to Fade. This affects the way the particles are combined from the view of the camera. The Fade setting fades the particles based on distance so that the particle mass is less opaque (Figure 6.8).
10. Unhide the image sequence and play back. At this point, the particle smoke location does not correspond with the smokestack opening.

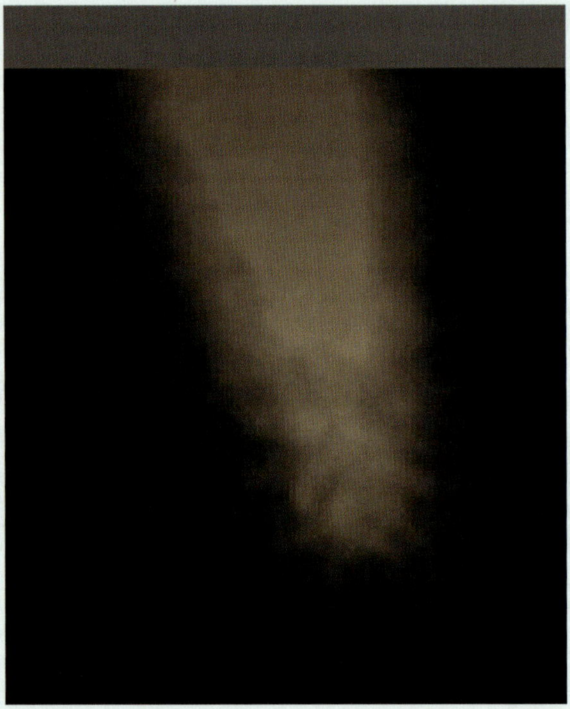

FIG 6.8 The particle mass, as seen on frame 50 with the image sequence hidden.

You can animate the emitter's Position X, Y, and Z to match the emitter location to the smokestack opening. However, this leads to sudden "bends" in the flow of smoke. As such, it's better to motion track the footage and apply the motion tracking data to the solid layer. With the factory layer selected, choose Animation > Track Motion. In the Layer view, position Track Point 1 so it sits over a detail of the smokestack opening. Analyze to produce a motion track for the entire timeline. Click the Edit Target button in the Tracker panel and choose the solid layer. Click the Apply button in the Tracker panel. The solid layer gains position animation. To better line up the smoke with the stack, adjust the solid layer's Anchor Point values. You can temporarily raise the Max Opacity of the particle effect to better see where the particles are born (Figure 6.9). If necessary, you can also adjust the solid layer's Scale. For example, set Scale to 100 percent, 125 percent to stretch the particles vertically and prevent the solid layer edge from becoming visible in the frame. (For more information on motion tracking, see Chapter 4.)

11. Despite the addition of motion tracking, the particles may continue to overlap the top of the smokestack. To prevent this, you can add a mask that either cuts off the bottom of the particles or creates a "patch" that covers up the bottom of the particles. With this project,

a patch creates a cleaner result. To create a patch, copy the image sequence layer with Edit > Duplicate and place the copy on top of the layer outline. With the Pen tool, draw a mask on the new top layer that occludes the particles that are lower than the smokestack (Figure 6.10). Return the Max Opacity of the particles back to 3 percent to see an accurate result. Animate the mask shape over time to follow the smokestack.

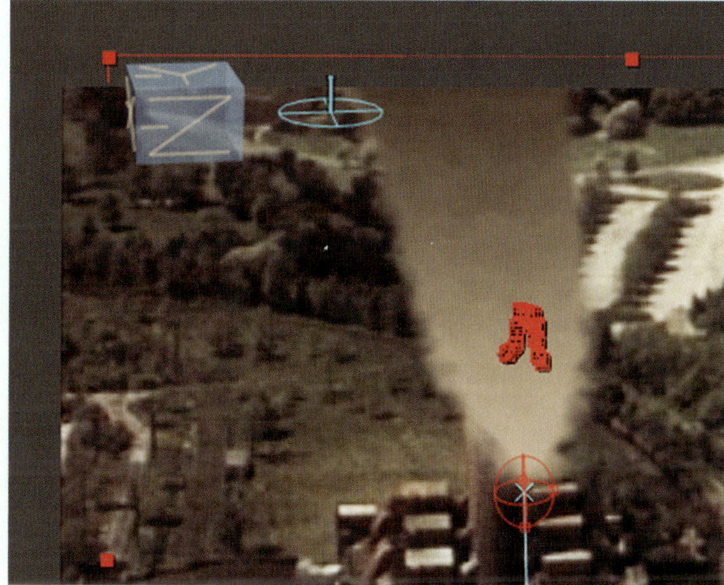

FIG 6.9 The solid layer, which carries the particles, is motion tracked. The red motion path is visible. The Max Opacity of the particles is temporarily set to 50 percent.

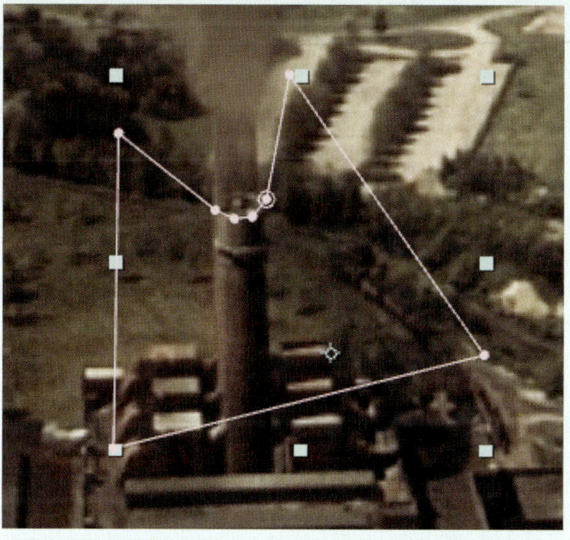

FIG 6.10 A mask is drawn to create a patch, which covers up any particles lower than the smokestack opening.

Although the particles are subtle and somewhat hard to see on a single frame, the playback reveals an undulating mass that looks like rising smoke (Figure 6.11). A finished version of this project is saved as *mini_particle_world.aep* in the *\ProjectFiles\aeFiles\Chapter6* directory. The image sequence is taken from "The Power to Serve," an industrial film from the Prelinger Archives, made available via a Creative Commons Public Domain license. For more information, visit www.archive.org/details/prelinger.

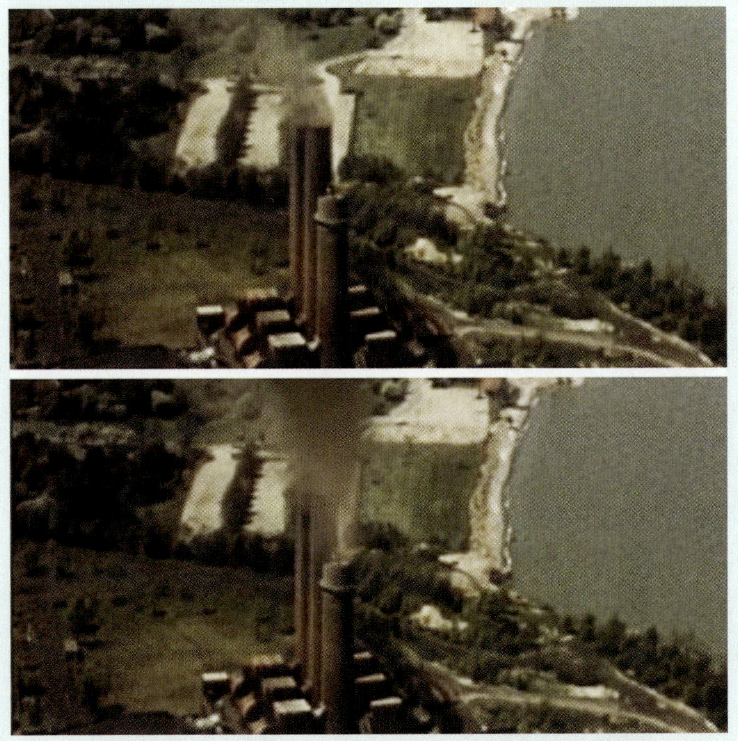

FIG 6.11 Top: The footage without particles. Bottom: The footage with the final particle simulation.

Using Particle Plug-Ins

There are many third party plug-in effects that create particle simulations within After Effects. Here's a partial overview of those available at the time of this writing.

Red Giant Trapcode Particular

Trapcode Particular supports simulations with millions of particles and offers the ability to move a camera through the particle simulations, create long-exposure particle trails, and add natural lighting and shading that emulates a wide range of natural phenomenon. This plug-in is discussed further in "An Introduction to Trapcode Particular" later in the chapter.

Video Copilot Element 3D

Element 3D supports particle/geometry arrays, whereby you can distribute 3D geometry across a particle simulation. (Visit www.videocopilot.net.)

Wondertouch particleIllusion

This plug-in provides a large set of ready-made particle emitters that simulate a wide range of natural phenomena, including water, fire, smoke, explosions, and so on. (Visit www.wondertouch.com.)

Rowbyte Plexus 2

Plexus 2 integrates the particle simulations with After Effects cameras and lights and offers algorithms to build organic particle-based structures. (Visit www.rowbyte.com.)

Digieffects Phenomena

Phenomena provides particle simulation tools to create such effects as fire, bubbles, rain, snow, electrical arcs, muzzle flashes, sparks, and so on. (Visit www.digieffects.com.)

Motion Boutique Newton 2

Newton 2 supports complex, physics-based simulations with a wide range of dynamic forces and body types. As opposed to working within a 3D environment, Newton 2 converts After Effects 2D layers into dynamic bodies. (Visit motionboutique.com.)

An Introduction to Trapcode Particular

The Red Giant Trapcode Particular plug-in shares some of the basic functionality of the standard particle plug-ins that come with After Effects. The Trapcode Particular effect generates particles with emitters and dynamic simulations. You can choose different styles of particles and alter qualities such as size, velocity, and shading. However, Particular offers a much larger set of properties that you can adjust. In addition, Trapcode Particular offers sub-particle generation, where each initial particle generates additional particles based on specific events. Sub-particles are ideal for creating light streaks or smoke trails. Trapcode Particular also provides built-in motion blur and depth-of-field rendering properties.

When you install Trapcode Particular, it includes a large number of animation presets. To apply a preset, add a solid layer to your current composition, go to the first frame of the timeline, select the new solid layer, go to the Effects & Presets panel (along the right side of the program window), and double-click a preset name. For example, double-click Animation Presets > Trapcode Particular Ffx > Trapcode HD Presets > t2_explodeoutdark_hd. The Particular effect is added to the layer with its properties altered (Figure 6.12). You are free to change any of the property values or change any of the keyframe animation. In fact, starting with a preset can save a significant amount of time when setting up a complex simulation. Although many of the presets are designed for motion graphics tasks, many others are suitable for visual effects work. These include explosions, fireworks, smoke trails, flames, snow, star fields, and welding sparks (the presets carry these descriptions as part of the preset names).

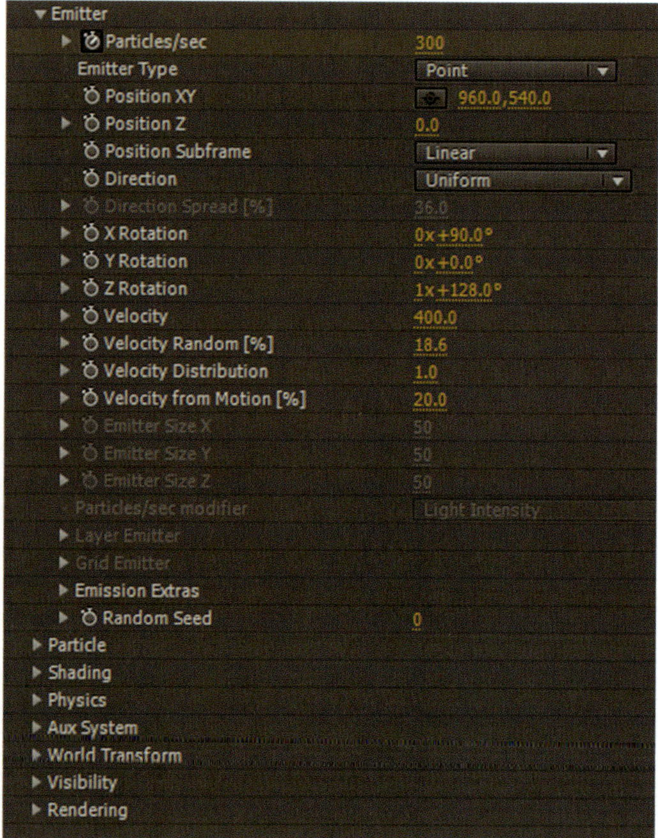

FIG 6.12 Portion of Trapcode Particular properties as set by the t2_explodeoutdark_hd preset.

Like other particle effects, Trapcode Particular renders the particles to a 2D layer. However, Particular offers various means to make the particles appear three-dimensional. These are briefly discussed here.

3D Camera Awareness

You can move and rotate a 3D camera around the particle mass. The perspective shifts appropriately. The layer carrying the particles does not have to be a 3D layer. (For more information on 3D cameras, lights, and layers, see Chapter 5.) By default, the particles render with depth of field, as per the camera settings. By default, the particles exhibit motion blur if motion blur is activated for the composition.

Volumetric Emitters

You can set the Emitter Type menu, in the Emitter section, to Box or Sphere. This generates particles within a volume area. The size of the emitter is set by Emitter Size X, Y, Z. Regardless of the emitter type, you can also set the Direction property to determine the particle's initial direction. For example, if you set Direction to the default Uniform, the emitters kick out particles in an omnidirectional fashion. If you set the Direction menu to Directional, the particles flow in the direction determined by the X, Y, Z Rotation properties. When compared to built-in particle effects, such as Particle Systems II, Trapcode creates a more convincing sense that particles are receding in depth along the Z-axis, even if no 3D camera is present in the composition.

Soft Particles

Particular provides several different particle types. Sphere, Cloudlet, and Streaklet types support edge feathering. These are ideal for creating smoke, explosions, and other soft-edged phenomena (Figure 6.13). You can set the

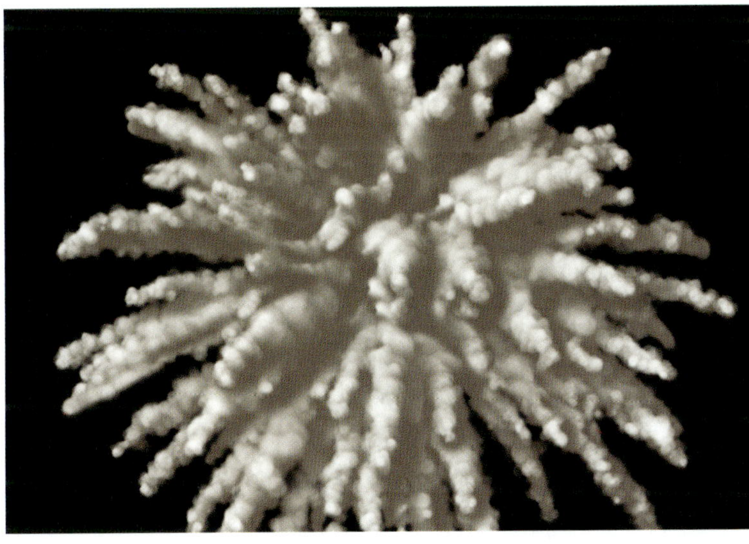

FIG 6.13 The Cloudlet particle type with Shadowlets activated creates puffy smoke trails.

type though the Particle Type menu, found in the Particle section. The Feather is set by the property with the *Feather* suffix.

Self-Shadowing

By default, Particular particles are flat-shaded with a color set by the Color property in the Particle section. However, you can activate self-shadowing and create a sense of three-dimensionality by changing the Particle Type to Cloudlet or Streaklet and setting the Shadowlet For Main menu, in the Shading section, to On.

Light Awareness

Initially, Particular particles are self-illuminated. However, you can light the particles with After Effects lights. To do so, change the Shading menu, in the Shading section, to On and create at least one light through the Layer > New > Light menu. The result is similar to lighting 3D layers. By default, the self-shadows ignore the light position. However, if you change the Placement menu to Project, the self-shadows are based on the actual light position or direction in XYZ. You can find the Placement property in the Shading > Shadowlet Settings subsection. You must add the **Shadow** prefix to the light layer name for the Project option to take effect.

Life Color

You can force particles to shift to specific colors as they age by setting the Set Color menu to Over Life and altering the Color Over Life ramp graph (Figure 6.14). (Note that the particle death color is at the ramp left while the particle birth color is at the ramp right.) By default, particles become less opaque over their life. However, you're free to alter the Opacity Over Life ramp graph to make the particles more or less opaque. Particle lifespan is set by the Life [Sec] property. All of these properties are found in the Particle section.

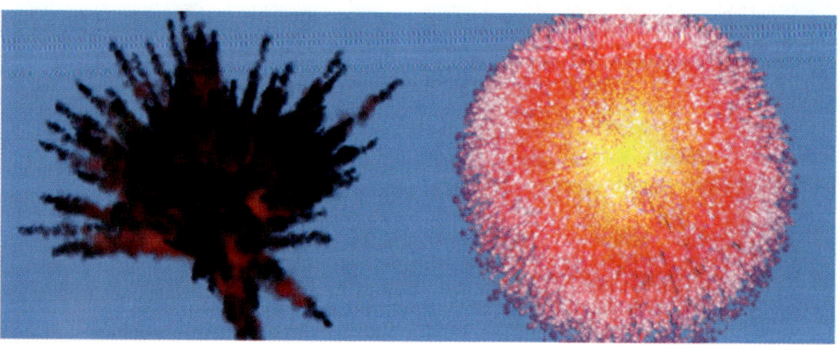

FIG 6.14 Two simulations using different Color Over Life ramps.

Textured Particles

If you set the Particle Type menu to a type with a *Sprite* or *Textured* suffix, you can map a layer to each particle. The layer is selected through the Layer menu, found in the Particle > Texture subsection. Sprite particles are flat, rectangular, and always face the camera. Sprites are able to read layer opacity. Textured particles are similar to sprites but are allowed to rotate.

Sub-Particles

The Aux System section is designed to create sub-particles as the primary particles move through the scene. If the Emit menu is set to Continuously, you can create steaks and trails. You can choose a sub-particle type through the Life > Type menu. The sub-particles carry their own size, color, opacity, and feather properties in this section.

For additional information on the Trapcode Particular effects, visit www.redgiant.com.

Chapter Tutorial: Creating Particle Rain

While real-world rain can be difficult to shoot in, particle rain is fairly easy to add to a shot as part of the post process. You can use almost any particle system within After Effects to create streaked raindrops. However, Cycore Effects provides two effects specifically for this task: CC Rainfall and CC Drizzle. That said, the effects may not be realistic when used as is. Hence, you can combine the effects with 3D layers, blur effects, and masking to create more complex results. To add rain to a shot, follow these steps:

1. Create a new project. Import *Chair.##.png* from the *\ProjectFiles\Plates\Particles\Chair* directory. Make sure the frame rate is interpreted as 24 fps. LMB-drag the sequence to the timeline to create a new composition. Play back. The sequence features a short, high-angle shot of an actress. Although After Effects work has already been applied to the shot in a previous project, we can add an additional rain effect.
2. Create a new solid layer. Make the solid the same resolution as the composition. Set the solid color to black. The solid is placed automatically on top of the layer outline. With the new layer selected, choose Effect > Simulation > CC Rainfall. Vertical, gray streaks are added to the frame with each representing a raindrop blurred by a camera exposure. In the Effect Controls panel, deselect the Composite With Original check box. The rain is placed over the lower layers and the black areas are ignored. Play back. The rain is pre-animated.
3. Change the solid layer's blending mode menu to Screen. This brightens the drops slightly. Change Drops to 500 and Size to 10 to alter the rain density and apparent closeness to camera. Change Speed to 20,000

to speed up the drop falls. Change Scene Depth to 20,000 to create a greater variety of drop widths and thus create the illusion that the drops are spread out in depth away from the camera.

4. Convert the layer into a 3D layer. Set the layer's X Rotation to 45. This "tips" the layer towards the camera. Scale the layer to 400 percent to create the illusion that the drops are close to the camera lens (Figure 6.15). (For more information on 3D layers and the 3D environment, see Chapter 5.)

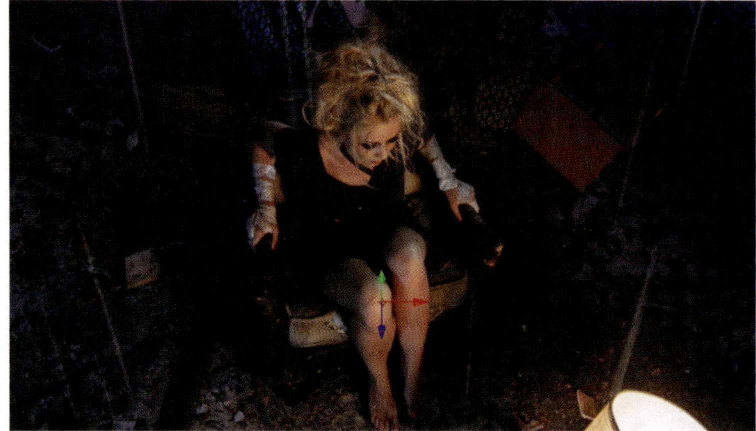

FIG 6.15 The CC Rainfall effect creates streaked raindrops in the foreground. The drops are oriented to the camera by rotating the 3D layer along the X-axis. The layer is scaled up to 400 percent.

5. To soften the drops, select the 3D layer and choose Effect > Blur & Sharpen > Directional Blur. Set the Blur Length to 50.
6. Rename the 3D layer **FGRain**. You can rename a layer by RMB-clicking the layer name in the layer outline and choosing Rename from the menu. Select the 3D layer and choose Edit > Duplicate. Rename the new layer **MidRain**. Interactively move the layer backwards along the Z-axis so it serves as a mid-ground layer of raindrops. Open MidRain's CC Rainfall effect in the Effect Controls panel (all effects are copied when you choose Edit > Duplicate). Set Drops to 5000 and Size to 5 to make a denser field of thinner drops. Set the layer's Rotation X to 35. Change the Scale to 200 percent. Reduce the effect's Opacity, in the Transform section, to 50 percent.
7. Select the MidRain layer and choose Edit > Duplicate. Rename the new layer **BGRain**. Open BGRain's CC Rainfall effect in the Effect Controls panel. Set Drops to 2500 and Size to 2 to make a semi-dense field of even thinner drops. Interactively move the layer backwards along the Z-axis so it serves as a background layer of raindrops (Figure 6.16). Set the layer's Rotation X to 25. Change the Scale to 150 percent. Set the layer's Opacity to 25 percent. Play back.
8. Although the raindrops are now more complex, there is no interaction with the ground. You can create a set of fake puddles with reflections with masking. To do so, duplicate the image sequence layer. Rename

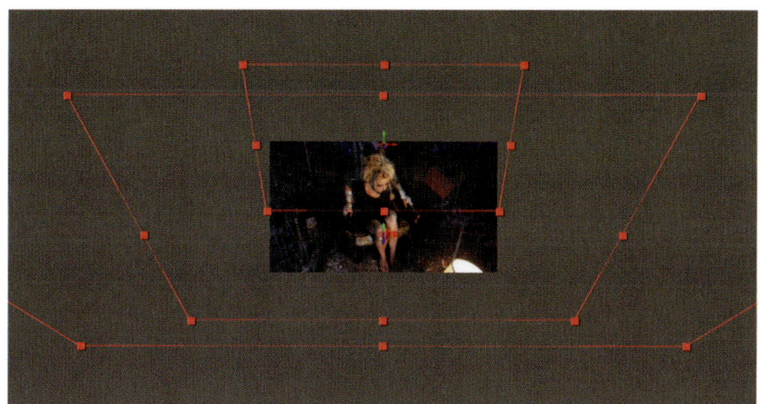

FIG 6.16 Two additional copies of the rain layer are created and moved backwards in Z. Each 3D layer has unique Scale, X Rotation, and CC Rainfall values, creating a more complex, layered rain effect.

the new layer **Reflection**. Unlink the Scale property for Reflection and change the values to 100, –100. This mirrors the layer in the Y up/down direction. Move the Reflection layer downwards (a Position Y of roughly 1060). Draw a series of masks with the Pen tool to create puddle-like shapes (Figure 6.17). With the Reflection layer selected, choose Effect > Blur & Sharpen > Directional Blur. Set the Blur Length to 25. This vertically streaks the puddle areas, creating the illusion of a reflection. (For more information on masking, see Chapter 3.)

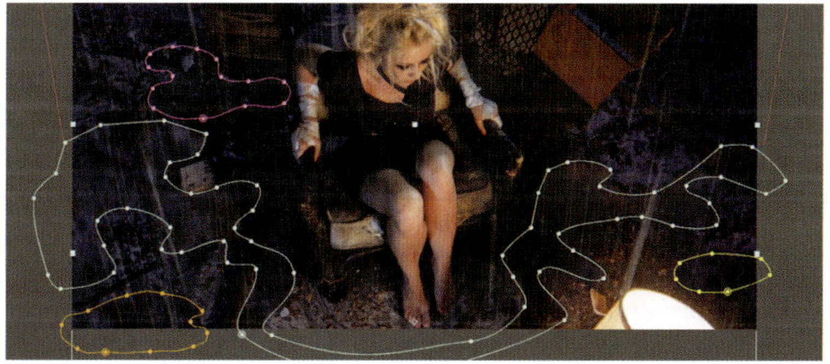

FIG 6.17 A series of puddles are created by masking a copy of the image sequence layer. A Directional Blur effect streaks the areas inside the puddle masks.

9. To create motion within the puddle areas, as if the pooled water is hit by raindrops, choose Effect > Distort > Turbulent Displace. Turbulent Displace distorts a layer by moving pixels based on the intensity of a built-in fractal noise. Set the effect's Amount property to 50 and Size to 10. To animate the distortion, go to the first frame of the timeline and click the Time icon beside Evolution. Go to the last frame of the timeline and change Evolution to 3 revolutions. Play back. The puddles undulate.
10. To further strengthen the interaction of the raindrops with the ground, you can apply the CC Drizzle effect, which creates a series of circular ripple patterns. To do so, create a new solid layer. Set the solid resolution

to 4000×4000. Set the solid color to mid-gray. Name the solid **Ripples**. Choose Effect > Simulation > CC Drizzle. White, circular ripples are added to the gray solid (Figure 6.18). To remove the gray color, go to the effect in the Effect Controls panel. Expand the Shading section and set Ambient to 0. Set the Ripple layer's blending mode menu to Screen. Reduce the layer's Opacity to 33 percent to make the ripples barely visible.

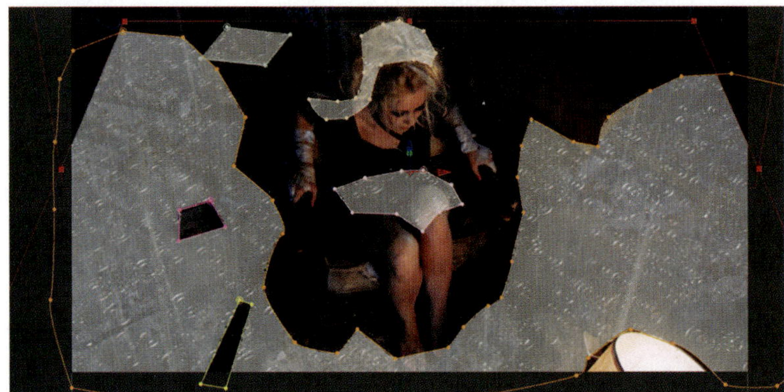

FIG 6.18 Circular ripples are added with the CC Drizzle effect. The ripples are tilted back by converting the solid layer to a 3D layer. The ripples are limited to specific areas by masking.

11. Set the CC Drizzle effect's Drip Rate to 100 and Longevity (Sec) to 0.5. This increases the number of ripples while making them disappear quicker. Convert the Ripple layer to a 3D layer. Change the layer's X Rotation to –50. This leans the layer back to roughly match the ground in the image sequence. Using the Pen tool, draw one or more masks to limit the ripples to areas on the ground while keeping them off vertical objects or parts of the scene that should otherwise be dry. Play back. Ripples randomly appear, helping to make the shot look wet from rain (see Figure 6.1 at the beginning of this chapter).

A finished project is included as *particle_rain.aep* in the *\ProjectFiles\aeFiles\Chapter6* directory.

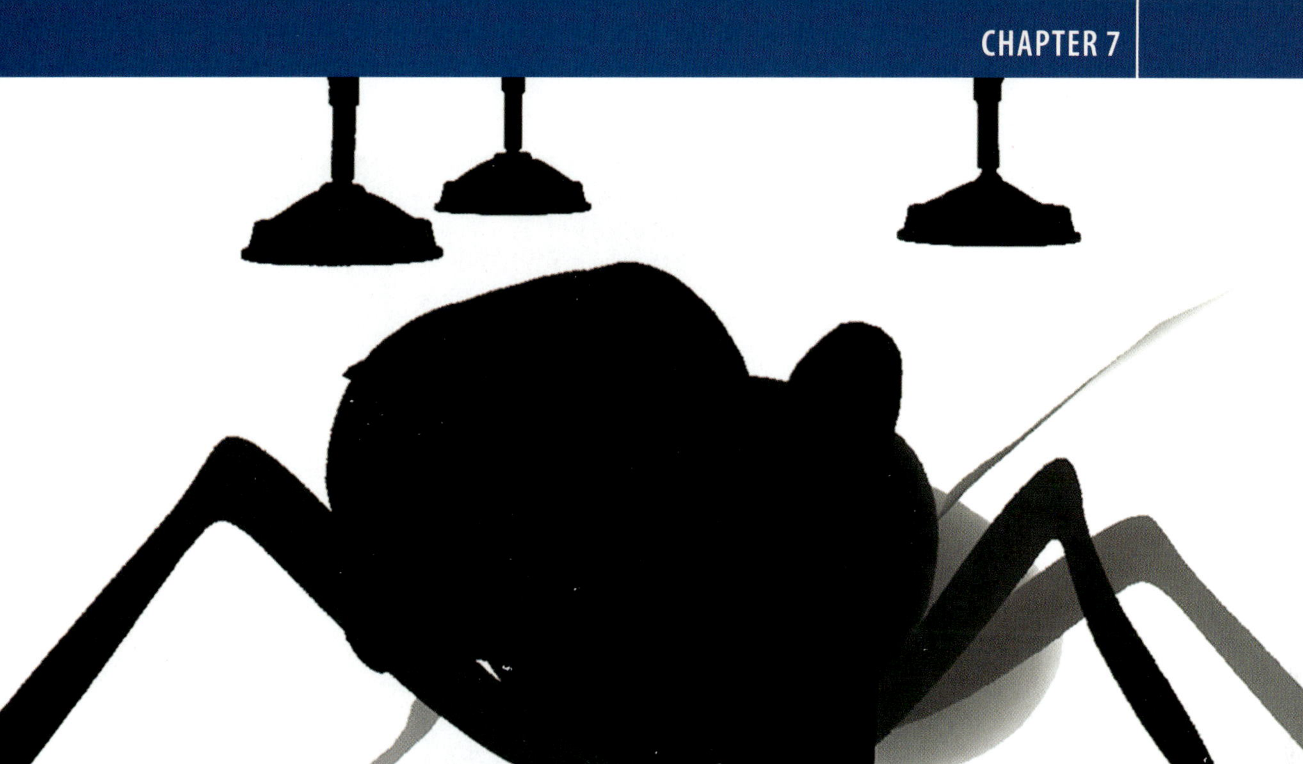

CHAPTER 7

Integrating Render Passes

A common task of visual effects compositing is the integration of 3D renders. Although these may be delivered to the compositor as completed "beauty" renders, they may also be delivered as render passes. Render passes often split the shot content into multiple image sequences. That is, objects within a single shot may be rendered separately. At the same time, individual objects may be further split into multiple shading component passes (Figure 7.1). As such, care must be taken to recombine the passes so that the final result appears equivalent to the original render seen in the 3D program. This requires the judicious use of After Effects blending modes, layer order, masking, and channel manipulation.

This chapter includes the following critical information:

- Overview of common render passes
- Techniques for combining passes in After Effects
- Utilizing multichannel OpenEXRs

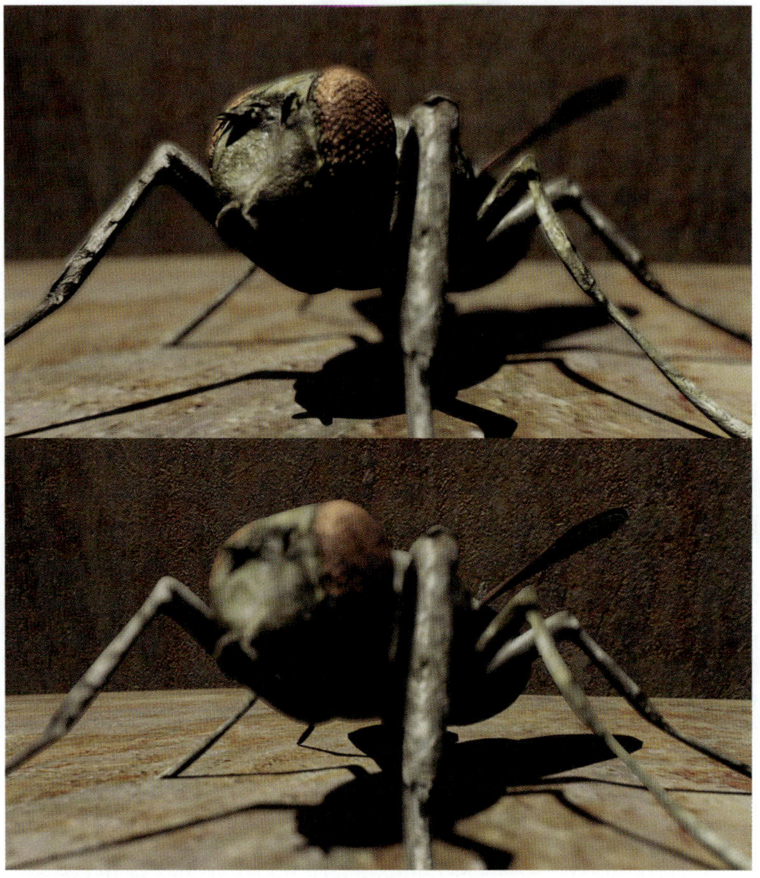

FIG 7.1 Top: The Camera Lens Blur effect and a depth render pass causes the background of a 3D render to go out of focus. Bottom: The effect is reversed so the foreground goes out of focus.

Identifying Render Passes and Blending Modes

There are two styles of render passes: object and shading. Shading render passes include a wide variety of forms that represent surface shading qualities. As such, shading render passes often require special blending modes within After Effects.

Using Object Render Passes

A simple form of render pass setup separates the objects within a scene. For example, character A is added to one pass, character B is added to a second pass, and the background is added to a third pass. No pass contains all the objects. Separating the objects allows the individual renders to become more efficient. Optionally, an object can be used as a static frame. For example, a single, static frame of a background can be used in conjunction with fully rendered character passes.

Review of Blending Modes

Every layer in After Effects is given a blending mode menu (Figure 7.2). These are set to Normal by default, which means that the upper layers occlude the lower layers unless the upper layers include transparency through an alpha channel. (If you don't see the menu, click the Toggle Switches/Modes button at the bottom of the layer outline.)

Normal
Dissolve
Dancing Dissolve
Darken
Multiply
Color Burn
Classic Color Burn
Linear Burn
Darker Color
Add
Lighten
Screen
Color Dodge
Classic Color Dodge
Linear Dodge
Lighter Color

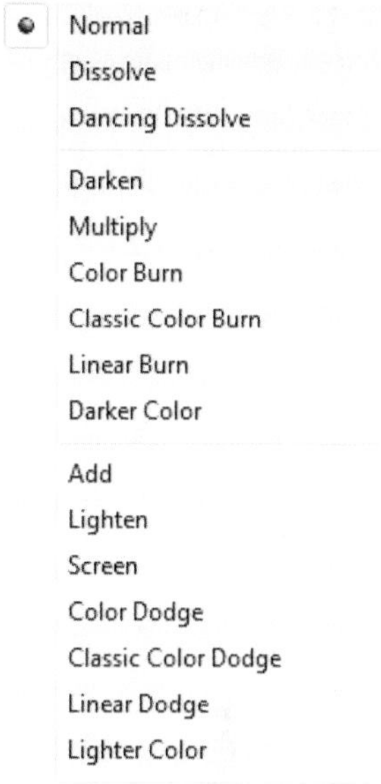

FIG 7.2 A small portion of available blending modes.

Many other blending modes are available. Each blending mode represents a mathematical formula by which a pixel of an upper layer is combined with the corresponding pixel of a lower layer or net result of lower layers. If there are more than two layers in a composition, the layers are combined in pairs, starting at the bottom of the layer outline and working upwards. It's not necessary to remember the mathematical formula for each blending mode, but it pays to be familiar with the result of commonly used modes. For example, the Screen, Lighten, Multiply, and Darken modes are used over and over. In fact, these modes are often associated with specific render passes. The render passes and corresponding modes are described in the following section. You can see the result of other modes by simply changing the blending mode menu—the result is shown immediately in the Composition view.

Overview of Common Shading Passes

Shading render passes break the render up into to individual shading components. Shading components are associated with specific surface shading qualities, such as diffuse, specular, shadow, and so on. In 3D programs, these shading components are controlled by the properties of materials or shaders.

The following represents shading render passes that are commonly used in the visual effects industry. In addition, appropriate After Effects blending modes are listed for each pass.

Beauty

A beauty pass is one that includes all the shading components available to the 3D renderer. Beauty passes are generally produced by the renderer when no render passes are established. For example, if you test render in Autodesk Maya with the Render View window, the result is a beauty pass. Nevertheless, some batch renderers, such as mental ray, include a beauty pass in addition to any requested render passes. If you are using render passes, it's not mandatory to use the beauty pass. Depending on the render settings, the beauty pass may or may not include motion blur (Figure 7.3).

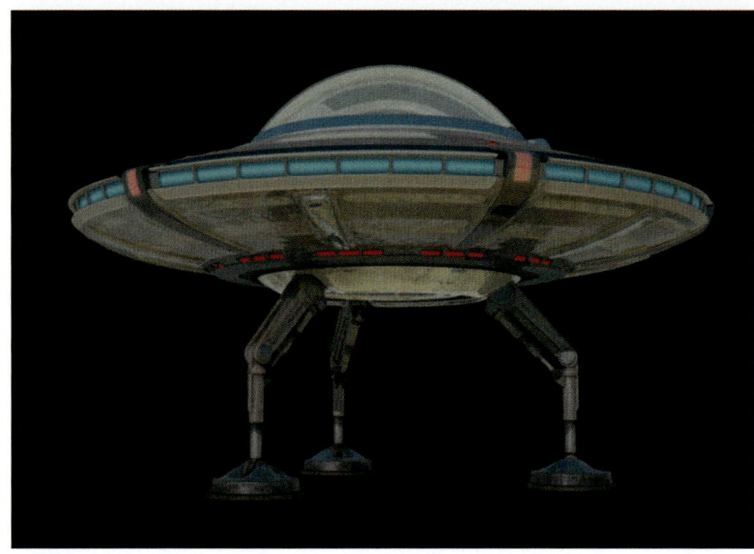

FIG 7.3 Beauty render pass of a spaceship. Motion blur is turned off.

Diffuse

The diffuse pass represents the surface color without specularity or shadows. Some diffuse pass variations include basic shading, where the surface is dark in areas of low light (Figure 7.4). Some diffuse passes do not include shading—hence, the surface appears self-illuminated or "toon" shaded. Generally, diffuse passes require no special blending mode.

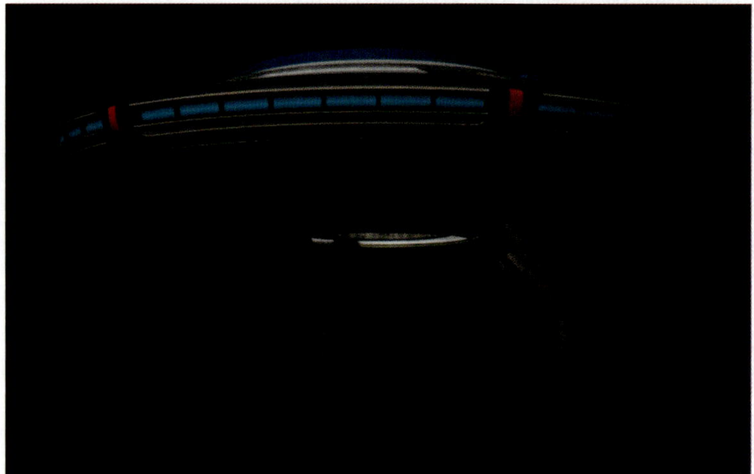

FIG 7.4 A diffuse render pass. The pass includes basic shading but ignores cast shadows, specular highlights, and reflections. The lack of specularity and reflectivity causes the surfaces to appear darker. The glass dome does not appear due to its high transparency.

Specular

This pass captures the specular component. In the real world, a specular highlight is the intense, coherent reflection of light off a surface. Specular highlights appear as "hot spots" on shiny surfaces. Specular passes render the hot spot over black.

In general, no alpha channel is present. Therefore, you can choose the Screen or Lighten blending mode to place this pass over lower passes, such as a diffuse pass (Figure 7.5). Screen differs from Lighten in that it clamps high values and prevents superwhite values (*superwhite* is any value that exceeds the working bit depth color range, such as 0 to 255 in 8-bit). Specular passes do not include reflectivity and may or may not take into account cast shadows.

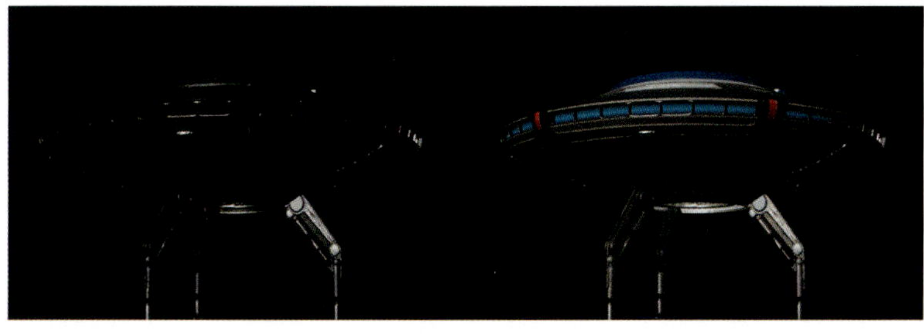

FIG 7.5 Left: Specular render pass. Right: Specular render placed over diffuse pass with Screen blending mode.

Depth

Depth passes encode the distance from objects to the cameras as grayscale values (Figure 7.6). Depth passes are also referred to as *Z-depth* or *Z-buffer* passes. Different renderers record the values in different ways.

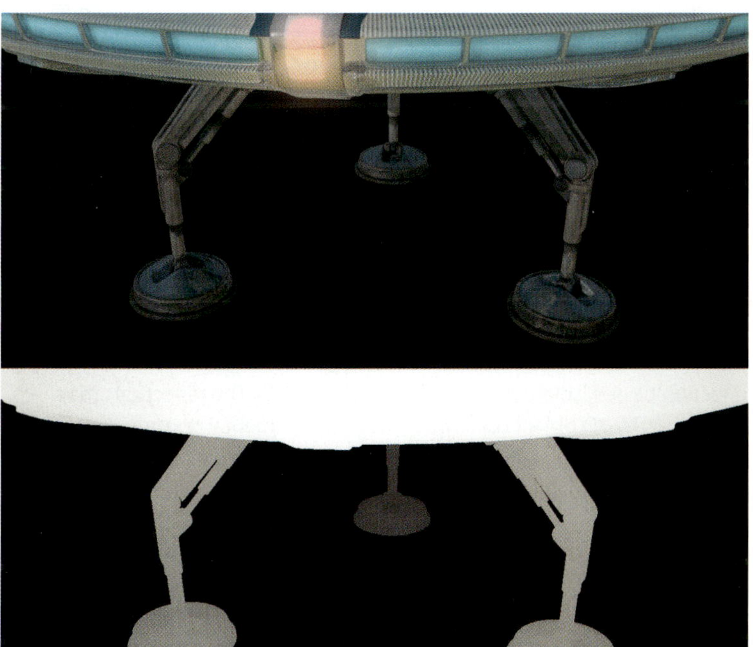

FIG 7.6 Top: Beauty pass render of ship's landing gear. Bottom: Depth pass from the same camera.

Hence, alteration of the depth values may be necessary to make the pass useful. Depth passes are generally used to composite an element in virtual depth. For example, you can add an artificial depth of field to a shot with this pass. This technique is demonstrated in the "Z-Buffer Depth of Field Mini-Tutorial" later in this chapter. You can also composite a virtual fog or atmosphere into a shot using a similar technique.

Matte

This pass, also called a *holdout*, assigns white pixels to opaque objects and black pixels to empty space (Figure 7.7). Although matte passes look similar to alpha channels, the matte passes store the information in RGB. Matte passes are useful for lending transparency information to layers that lack alpha. For example, you can use the Track Matte tool to borrow alpha information from a matte layer. This is demonstrated in the "Supplying Alpha to Nonalpha Passes" section later in this chapter.

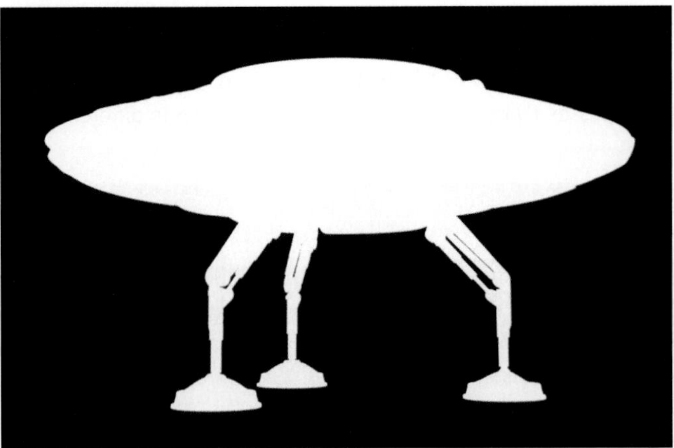

FIG 7.7 A matte pass.

Reflection

Reflection passes isolate their namesake (Figure 7.8). The reflections may include nearby 3D objects or surrounding environmental textures. Due to the lack of alpha, these passes require the use of the Screen or Lighten blending mode, additional rotoscoping, or the use of a matte pass.

Ambient Occlusion

Ambient occlusion passes, also known as AO passes, capture shadow information (Figure 7.9). In particular, the passes capture the soft shadows that appear where surfaces are in close approximation or where a surface has many intricate convolutions that prevent light from returning to the viewer. AO passes appear white or gray with soft gray or black shadows. You can place

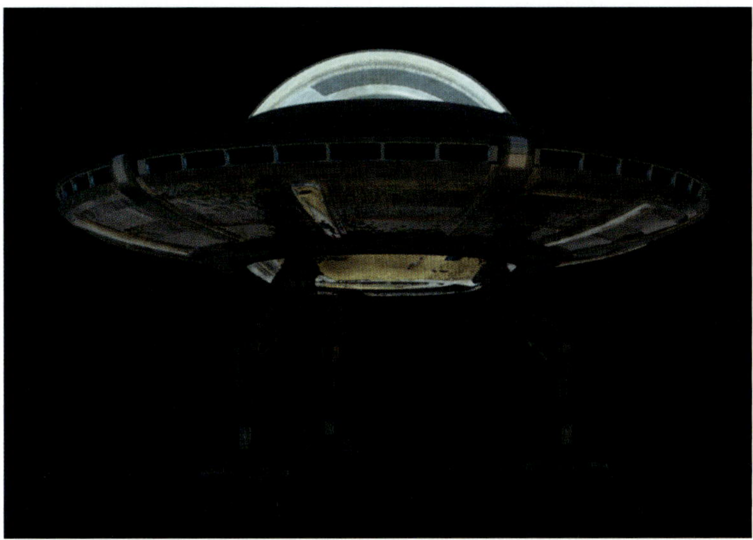

FIG 7.8 A reflection pass.

an AO pass over lower layers with the Multiply or Darken blending mode. You may need to adjust the brightness and contrast of the pass to make the nonshadow areas white.

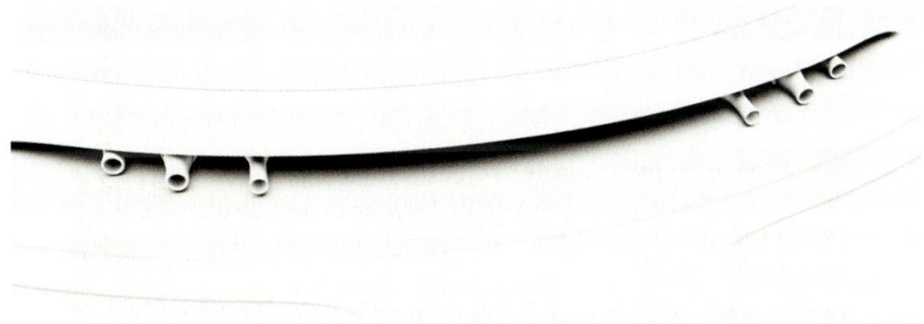

FIG 7.9 Close-up of an ambient occlusion pass showing that soft shadows render where surfaces are close together or surfaces have small grooves and ridges.

Incandescence and Glow

With many 3D materials, it's possible to create incandescence, which creates the illusion that the surface is a light source. Incandescent passes isolate this shading information. In a similar fashion, glow passes separate post-process glows, which are bright, blurry halos created by the render. You can combine incandescent and glow passes using the Lighten or Screen blending modes. For an example of an incandescence pass, see the "Common Render Pass Combination Mini-Tutorial" later in the chapter.

Shadow

A shadow pass isolates the shadow. Shadow passes may capture an opaque shadow within an alpha channel. You can place this type of pass over lower layers without a special blending mode. If the resulting shadow is too dark, you are free to lower the shadow layer's Opacity. Another variation of the shadow pass captures the shadow shape in the RGB channels (Figure 7.10). The application of this pass is demonstrated in the following tutorial.

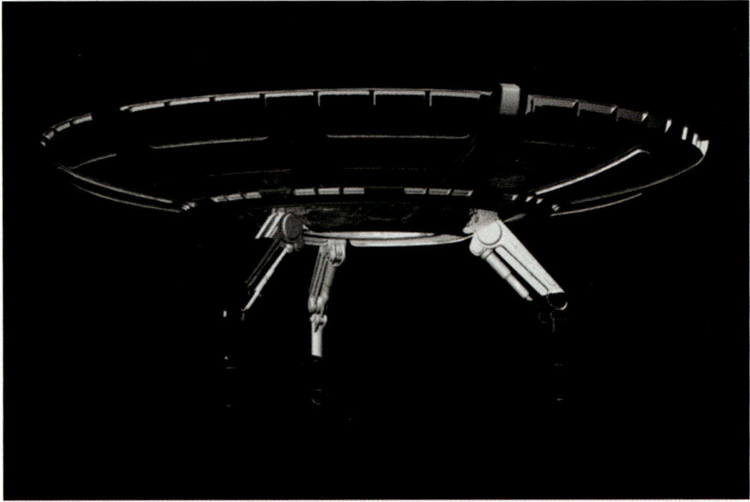

FIG 7.10 A shadow pass that captures the shadow shape in RGB. Where the pixels are the brightest, the shadow is the darkest in the associated beauty pass render.

Common render pass combination mini-tutorial

In this tutorial, we'll recombine common render passes to create a result similar to the corresponding beauty pass. You can follow these steps:

1. Create a new project. Import the following image sequences, all of which are located in the *\ProjectFiles\Renders* directory:

   Diffuse\diffuse.##.tif
   Specular\spec.##.tif
   Reflection\ref.##.tif
   Shadow\shadow.##.tif
   Incandesence\incan.##.tif

   Any sequence that carries an alpha channel causes After Effects to open the Interpret Footage window. When it does, select the Premultiplied radio button. This ensures that the alpha Is correctly interpreted. Autodesk Maya, which was used to create these renders, premultiplies the RGB values by the alpha values when rendering. If the alpha interpretation is left at the default Straight, a grayish line will be trapped at the alpha edge (this is created when the black background is trapped along the semitransparent matte edge).
2. Create a new composition that is 1280x720, 24 fps, and 10 frames in duration. LMB-drag the diffuse sequence into the composition. LMB-drag the spec (specular) sequence into the composition, placing

it on top. Change the specular layer's blending mode menu to Screen. (If you don't see the menu, click the Toggle Switches/Modes button at the bottom of the layer outline.) The specular render appears over the diffuse layer without occluding it.

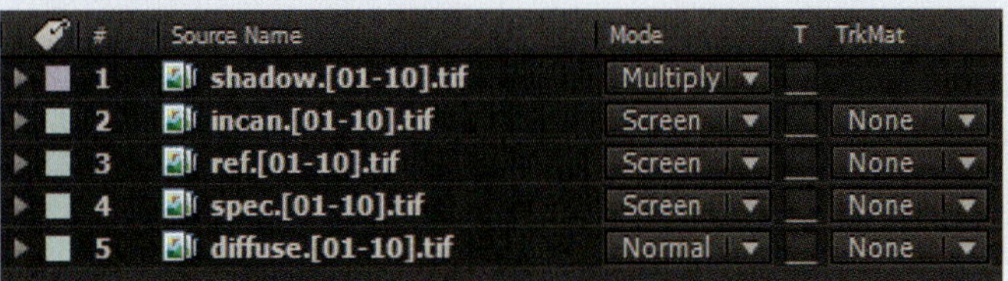

#	Source Name	Mode	T	TrkMat
1	shadow.[01-10].tif	Multiply		
2	incan.[01-10].tif	Screen		None
3	ref.[01-10].tif	Screen		None
4	spec.[01-10].tif	Screen		None
5	diffuse.[01-10].tif	Normal		None

FIG 7.11 The final layer arrangement used to reconstruct the spaceship with render passes.

3. Place the ref (reflection) pass on top of the layer outline (see Figure 7.11 for the final layer arrangement). Change its blending mode to Screen. Place the incan (incandescence) sequence on top of the layer outline. Change its blending mode to Screen.
4. Place the shadow pass on top of the layer outline. A white shadow over black appears. With the layer selected, choose Effect > Channel > Invert. The layer is inverted so the shadow becomes black. Change the layer's blending mode to Multiply. The values of the shadow layer are multiplied by the values of the layers below it. This causes the shadow layer to darken the ship in the shadow areas.
5. The composite now looks similar to the associated beauty pass render (Figure 7.12). (A beauty pass render is included in the *\ProjectFiles\Renders* directory for reference.) Nevertheless, you are free to adjust

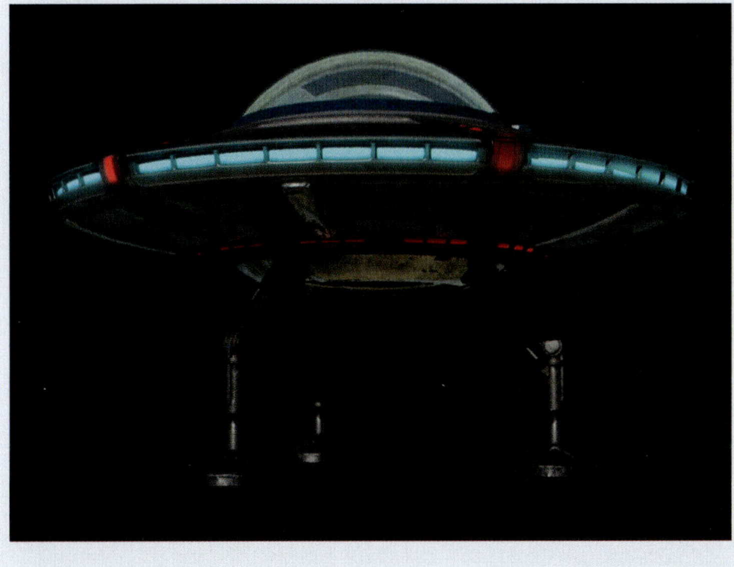

FIG 7.12 The recombined render passes.

any of the layers to improve the final quality of the composition. For example, add a Glow effect (in the Effect > Stylize menu) to the incandescence layer to make the ship's lights softer and more intense. Add a Curves or Brightness & Contrast effect (in the Effect > Color Correction menu) to the specular layer to increase the intensity of the specularity.

At this point, the alpha channel of the composite is completely opaque. This is due to the solid alpha given to some render passes, such as the specular pass. There are several methods by which you can recreate an appropriate alpha channel. These methods are discussed in the "Supplying Alpha to Nonalpha Layers" section later in this chapter. A sample project file is included as *mini_passes_combine.aep* in the *\ProjectFiles\aeFiles\Chapter7* tutorial directory.

Applying Advanced Shading Passes

Several additional render passes require special manipulation in After Effects. These are described in this section.

Motion Vector

Motion vector passes encode the XY motion of 3D objects in RGB as red and green values (Figure 7.13). The magnitude of the motion is encoded in the blue channel. You can use this pass to create motion blur in the composite, which is potentially more time-efficient than rendering the motion blur as part of a beauty pass. Motion vector application is demonstrated in the "Motion Vector Blur Mini-Tutorial" later in this chapter.

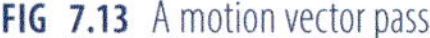

FIG 7.13 A motion vector pass.

UV

UV passes encode the UV texture values of surface points in RGB. UV passes appear various shades of red and green, which corresponds with the UV texture values in the U and V directions. You can use UV passes to re-texture an object in the compositing program, although this requires a complex process. You can also use a UV pass to distort a background. For example, in Figure 7.14, a UV pass of the spaceship distorts video of a landscape. The Displacement Map effect is added to the landscape layer with its Displacement Map Layer menu set to the hidden UV pass layer. The brighter the pixels in the UV pass, the farther the pixels are pushed in the landscape. The distortion is divided between the vertical and horizontal directions. You can drive each direction with a different channel of the UV pass. For example, you can set Use For Horizontal Displacement to the red channel and the Use For Vertical Displacement menu to the green channel. An example project using this technique is included as *uv_distort.aep* in the *\ProjectFiles\aeFiles\Chapter7* directory. You can find the Displacement Map effect in the Effect > Distort menu.

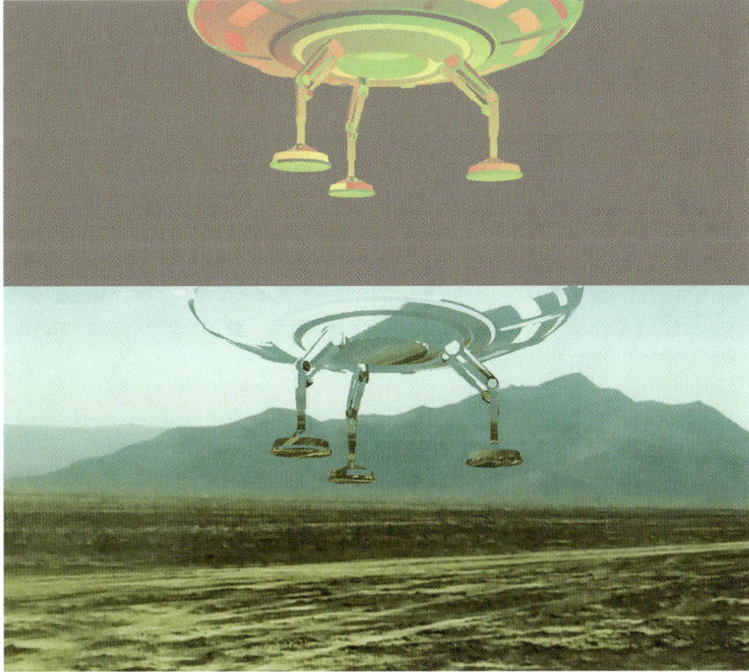

FIG 7.14 Top: UV pass. Bottom: Landscape distorted with the UV pass using the Displacement Map effect.

Normal

A normal pass encodes the geometry surface angle vectors in the RGB channels. The encoding may occur in one of several 3D coordinate spaces, such as object, world, or camera space. You can use a normal pass to affect a particular portion of a render based on the surface angle. For example, in Figure 7.15, a world-space normal pass renders the spaceship so that the polygon faces facing to the right (towards positive X in the 3D program) are rendered more intensely red. Polygon faces facing up (towards positive Y in the 3D program) are rendered more intensely green. Polygon faces facing the camera (towards positive Z in the 3D program) are rendered more intensely blue. To access this axis color information, you can shift the colors within the render pass. For example, if you apply the Shift Channels effect to the normal pass and set the Take Red From, Take Green From, and Take Blue From menus to Green, a grayscale image is produced with the brightest area of the ship along the top where they face the positive Y axis. You can find Shift Channels in the Effect > Channel menu.

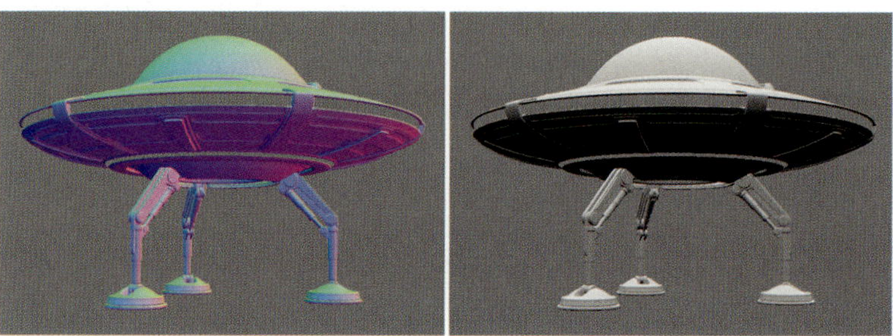

FIG 7.15 Left: Normal pass. Right: Normal pass with RGB sourced from its green channel using the Shift Channels effect.

You can use the normal passes with shifted channels as a source for a luma matte operation. Alternatively, you can place the adjusted normal pass over a lower beauty layer with the Multiply blending mode and thereby darken the underside of the ship (Figure 7.16). An example project using this technique is included as *normal_vector.aep* in the *\ProjectFiles\aeFiles\Chapter7* directory. Note that the empty space of the normal pass is mid-gray; you may need to brighten this area or cut it out with a Track Matte or luma matte operation so that it doesn't interfere with lower layers.

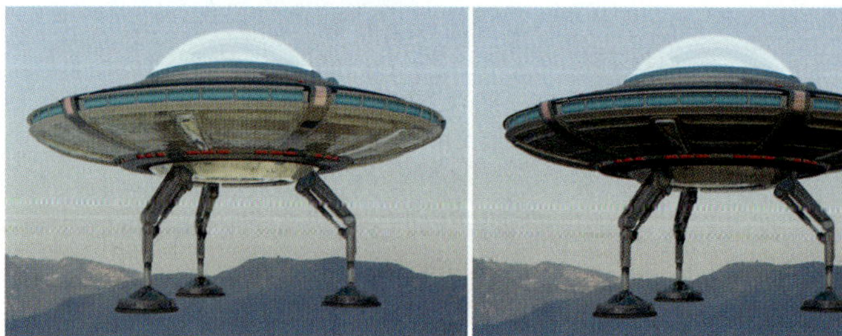

FIG 7.16 Left: Beauty pass and reflection pass placed over background. Right: Normal pass placed on top with the Multiply blending mode darkening the underside of the ship.

Supplying Alpha to Nonalpha Passes

Some render passes may not carry an alpha channel. In this situation, the pass occludes lower layers unless you use a blending mode such as Screen or Multiply. Nevertheless, there are several methods in After Effects you can use to borrow alpha information from a matte pass, another layer, or a different channel.

For example, you can use the TrkMat menu of the layer to take alpha information from a matte pass. Place the matte pass one layer higher and set the TrkMat menu to Luma Matte (Figure 7.17). The RGB information of the matte pass is transferred to the alpha channel of the TrkMat layer and transparency is achieved. You're free to add a new background as the lowest layer in the composition.

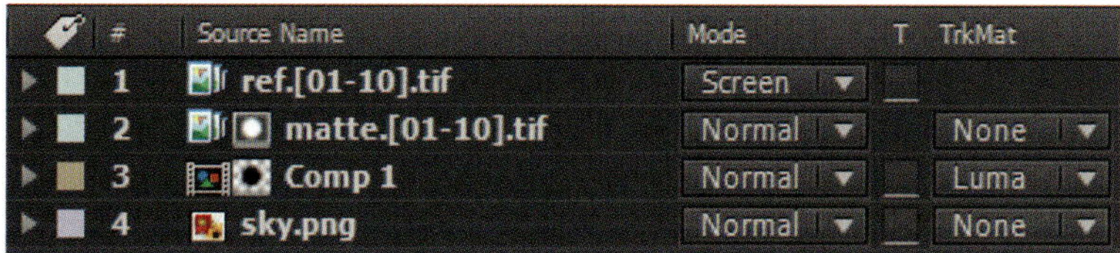

FIG 7.17 A matte pass cuts out a nested composition through the TrkMat menu. The nested composition carries the recombined ship. To restore the transparent but reflective dome, a reflection pass is placed on top of the layer outline.

Note that matte passes recognize transparency. Hence, the matte pass render of the ship used in Figure 7.17 is missing the dome because the dome's material is 100 percent transparent. You can restore the dome, however, by placing a reflection pass at the top of the layer outline and choosing the

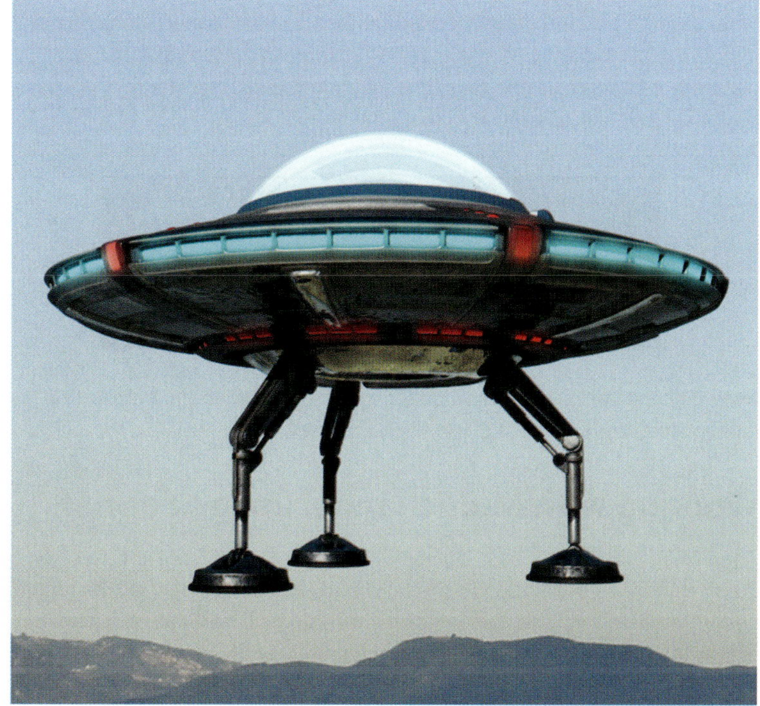

FIG 7.18 Alpha is restored to the ship with a matte pass and the TrkMat tool so that a lower sky layer shows behind the ship.

Screen blending mode. To prevent the reflection from appearing over the entire ship, you can draw a mask to limit the reflection layer to the dome area (Figure 7.18). A sample project is saved as *passes_matte.aep* in the *\ProjectFiles\aeFiles\Chapter7* directory.

You can also use the Set Matte effect to borrow alpha information from a different layer and/or a particular channel. To use Set Matte, follow these guidelines:

1. Select the layer that lacks alpha and choose Effect > Channel > Set Matte.
2. In the Effect Controls panel, change the Take Matte From Layer menu to the layer that contains the matte pass. The matte pass may be at a lower layer or higher layer. The matte pass layer should remain hidden.
3. Set the effect's Use For Matte menu to Luminance. In this way, Set Matte functions like the Track Matte tool.
4. You also have the option to generate alpha based on the values of RGB channels. For example, if you set Use For Matte to Red Channel, the red values are converted to alpha values. The layer you choose for the Take Matte From Layer need not contain the matte pass but can be any layer that contains video footage, still footage, or artwork. However, unless the chosen layer contains solid colors, otherwise opaque alpha areas will become semitransparent.

A better solution for generating alpha information from a nonmatte layer is to use a layer that carries serviceable alpha. For example, set the Take Matte From Layer to a beauty pass layer and set the Use For Matte to Alpha Channel (Figure 7.19). A beauty pass may not be desirable for its look in RGB, but it generally contains a usable alpha channel that you can transfer to a render pass layer that has no alpha information.

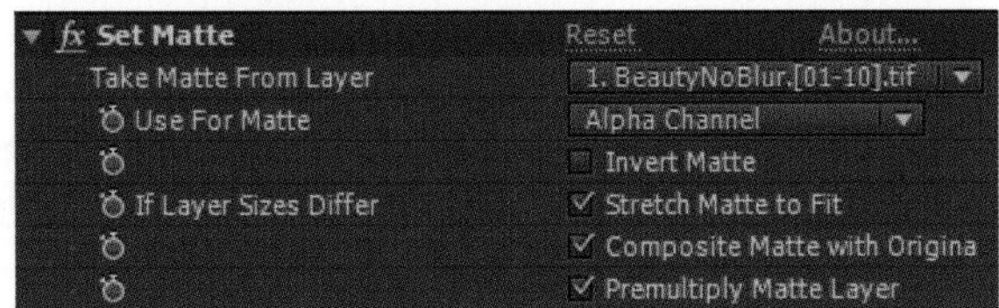

FIG 7.19 The Set Matte effect borrows alpha information from a beauty pass layer.

Note that you can also set the TrkMat menu to Alpha Matte to borrow the alpha values from the above layer if it has an alpha channel.

Working with Multichannel Image Formats

A few image formats, such as OpenEXR, RLA, and Maya IFF, are able to carry custom channels in addition to standard RGB and alpha. In fact, all the renders passes required for a shot can be carried by a single OpenEXR sequence. To access these channels in After Effects, you must transfer them to RGB using the EXtractoR plug-in. For example, to retrieve a matte pass from an OpenEXR sequence, you can follow these steps:

1. Import the sequence and place it on a new layer. With the layer selected, choose Effect > 3D Channel > EXtractoR.
2. Open the effect's properties. Click one of the channel names, such as Blue. A dialog window opens. Click the Blue menu. The available passes and associated channels are listed (Figure 7.20). The rendering program assigns the channel names. For example, the matte pass rendered in Maya with mental ray is named MATTE:matte.*camera* with R, G, and B suffixes that represent the red, green, and blue channels of the matte pass. An example sequence following this naming convention is included as *ship.##.exr* in the *\ProjectFiles\Renders\EXR* directory.
3. You can skip the channel menus and choose the pass name from the Layers menu, which automatically selects the correct channel names for red, green, and blue. Click the OK button to close the window. The channels are transferred and the grayscale matte pass becomes visible in the Composition view. Note that the ship rises up into the frame in the *ship.##.exr* image sequence.

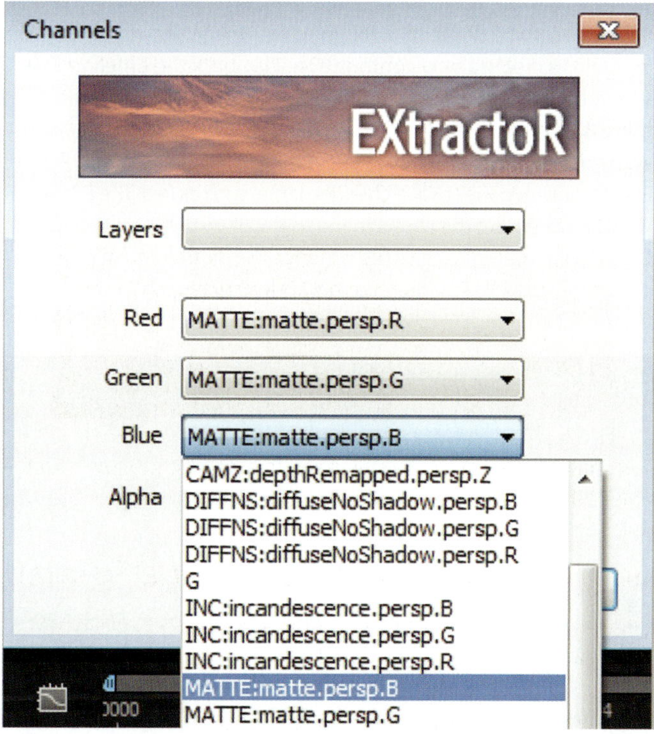

FIG 7.20 EXtractoR plug-in window with partial list of passes and channels carried by an OpenEXR sequence.

If you wish to extract an additional pass, you must create a new layer with the sequence, add a new EXtractoR effect to that layer, and set the Layers menu to the desired pass name. Some render passes, such as the depth pass, may only have one channel in the OpenEXR. In such a situation, you can set the Red, Green, and Blue menus to the same channel. A sample project that retrieves a matte pass is saved as *exr_matte.aep* in the *\ProjectFiles\aeFiles\Chapter7* directory.

Creating Motion Blur in the Composite

You can add motion blur during the compositing phase if you have a nonblurred version of the animation and a motion vector render pass. However, you must use a third-party plug-in to read the motion vectors in After Effects. For example, you can use the RE:Vision Effects ReelSmart Motion Blur plug-in. The following tutorial explains the process.

ReelSmart motion blur mini-tutorial

To apply motion blur using an OpenEXR sequence and a normalized motion vector render pass created in Autodesk Maya, follow these steps:

1. Create a new project. Import *Lemons.###.exr* from the *\ProjectFiles\Renders\Lemons* directory. LMB-drag the image sequence to the timeline to create a new composition. Play back the timeline. The sequence features a large number of falling 3D lemons. At this point, there is no motion blur.
2. With the layer selected, choose Effects > 3D Channel > EXtractoR. In the Effect Controls panel, click a channel name, such as *Red*. The EXtractoR window opens. Set the Layers menu to MV2N:mv2DNormRemap.persp. Click the OK button to close the window. The motion vector pass becomes visible. Yellow-green colors appear within the lemons (Figure 7.21).

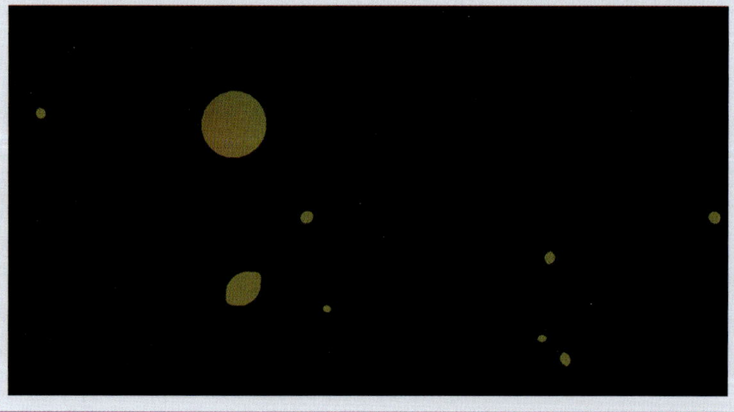

FIG 7.21 Motion vector pass, made visible with the EXtractoR plug-in and cut out with TrkMat and a matte pass.

3. These channels were created with a mental ray normalized motion vector pass. The normalization keeps the contained values within a predictable range (0 to 1.0). With this type of motion vector pass, the X object motion is stored in the MX (red) channel and the Y object motion is stored in the MY (green) channel. The blue channel is not used and is empty. Note that the OpenEXR sequence is in 32-bit floating point; a high bit-depth is critical for storing accurate motion blur vectors.
4. To make the motion vector layer useful, it must be cut out by a matte pass. Duplicate the current layer upwards by choosing Edit > Duplicate. Open the EXtractoR window for the top layer. Change the Layers menu to MATTE:matte.persp. Hide the matte layer by turning off the layer eye icon. Change the TrkMat menu for the lower motion vector layer to Luma Matte. The motion vector pass is cut out by the matte pass. This prevents values within the empty 3D space (which carry no RGB values) from interfering with the motion vector interpretation.
5. Create a new composition. LMB-drag the first composition into the new composition. Hide the nested layer. LMB-drag a new copy of the *lemon.##.exr* sequence into the new composition and place it at the bottom of the layer outline. By default, if no channels are chosen within the OpenEXR files, the default RGB channels are used. To ensure that the correct RGB channels are used, add a new EXtractoR effect to the lower layer. Set the EXtractoR Layers menu to BEAUTY.beauty.persp.

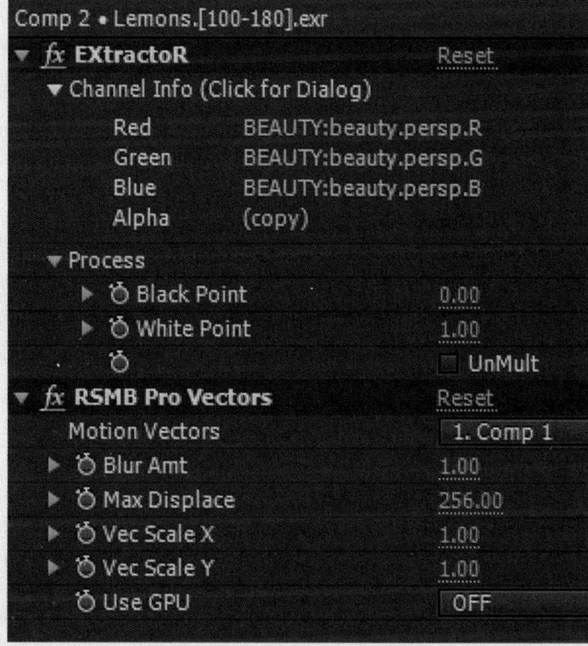

FIG 7.22 EXtractoR and RSMB Pro Vectors effects settings for the motion blurred layer.

6. With the lower layer selected, choose Effect > RE:Vision Plug-ins > RSMB Pro Vectors. This is the ReelSmart Motion Blur motion vector tool. Open the effect in the Effect Controls panel. Change the Motion Vectors menu to the nested comp layer (*1. Comp 1*). Change the Max Displace to 256 (see Figure 7.22). 256 matches the maximum displacement setting carried by the normalized motion vector render pass in mental ray. The motion blur appears. Play back the timeline. Note that the blur takes into account spinning, as well as differences in foreground and background motion blur streak lengths (Figure 7.23).

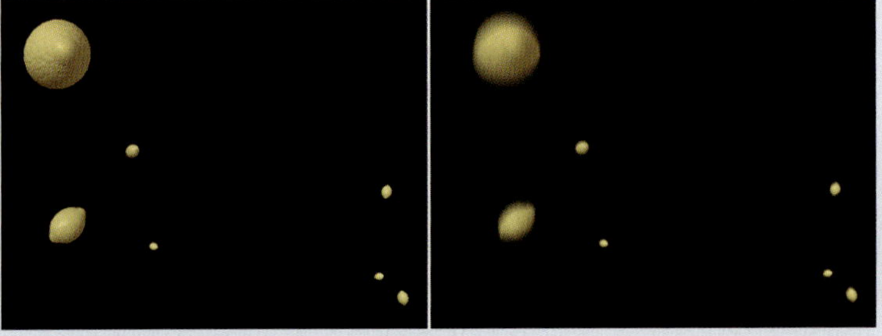

FIG 7.23 Left: Lemons with no blur. Right: Lemons with blur created by RSMB Pro Vectors. The Blur Amt property is set to 1.0.

7. You can adjust the length of the blur streaks by adjusting the Blur Amt value. 0.5 is equivalent to common camera exposures. Higher Blur Amt values lengthen the blur trails.

A finished project is saved as *mini_motion_vector.aep* in the *\ProjectFiles\aeFiles\Chapter7* directory. For more information on ReelSmart Motion Blur, visit www.revisioneffects.com.

Chapter Tutorial: Using OpenEXR Depth Channels for Depth of Field

You can add a narrow depth of field, where parts of the screen are out of focus, to a render as part of the compositing process. This requires a depth pass and the use of the Camera Lens Blur Effect. To add depth of field to an OpenEXR image, follow these steps:

1. Create a new project. Import the *fly.exr* render from the *\ProjectFiles\Renders\EXR* directory. It is a single frame and not a sequence.
2. Create a new composition that's 1280x720, 24 fps, and 24 frames in duration. LMB-drag *fly.exr* into the new composition. Although the render is a single frame, the frame is repeated the entire duration of the timeline. The render features a fly sitting on a surface.
3. With the new layer selected, choose Effect > 3D Channel > EXtractoR. Open the effect in the Effect Controls panel and click on one of the

channel names, such as *Red*. The EXtractoR window opens. Set the Red, Green, and Blue menus to CAMZ:depthRemapped.persp.Z. The depth channel appears as a grayscale image in the Composition view (Figure 7.24).

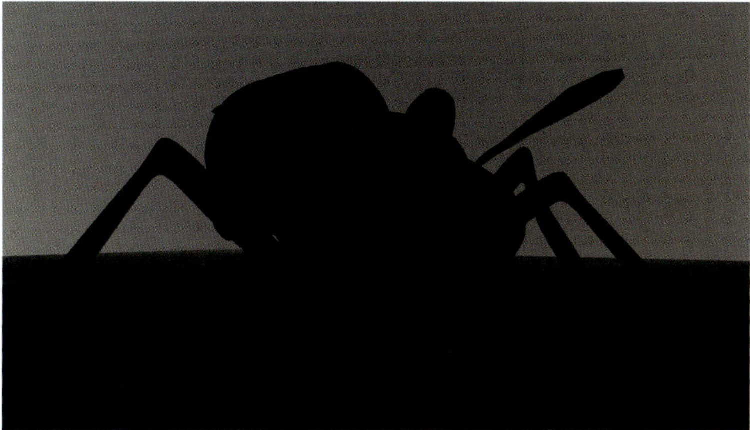

FIG 7.24 The depth pass revealed with the EXtractoR plug-in.

4. With this depth channel, the far wall is brighter gray while the close parts of the fly are darker. Overall, the contrast is low. You can increase the contrast by remapping the range of values with the Black Point and White Point properties. Go to the Info panel at the top right of the program window and click the panel's upper-right menu arrow. Switch the menu from 8-bpc (0–255) to Decimal (0.0–1.0). This causes the Info panel to display RGBA values in decimal form (Figure 7.25). This matches the 0–1.0 values contained in the depth pass. This particular style of depth pass normalizes the values, forcing the values to stay between 0 and 1.0. (Other depth pass variations create extremely large values.) Place the mouse over the head of the fly and note the value of the red channel (the RGB channels are identical). The value is roughly 0.01. Place the mouse over the background wall and note the value. The value is roughly 0.04.

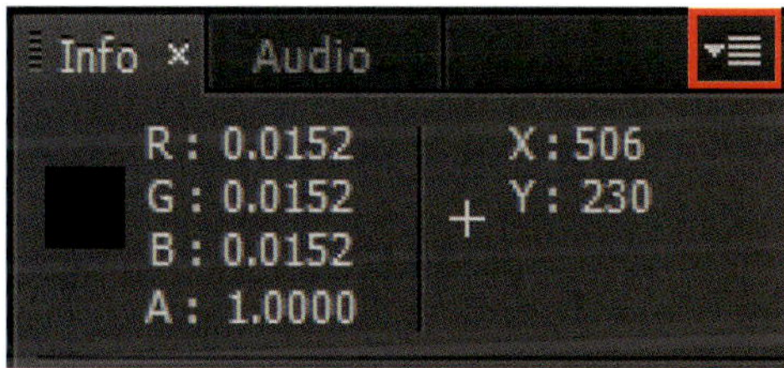

FIG 7.25 The Info panel with the RGBA readout when the mouse is placed over the head of the fly. The readout is set to Decimal. The menu that sets the readout style is indicated by the red box.

5. Enter 0.02 into the EXtractoR effect's Black Point field. This forces values between 0 and 0.02 to be remapped to 0. The contrast increases slightly. Enter 0.04 into the White Point field. Values between 0.4 and 1.0 are forced up to 1.0. The depth image gains contrast (Figure 7.26).

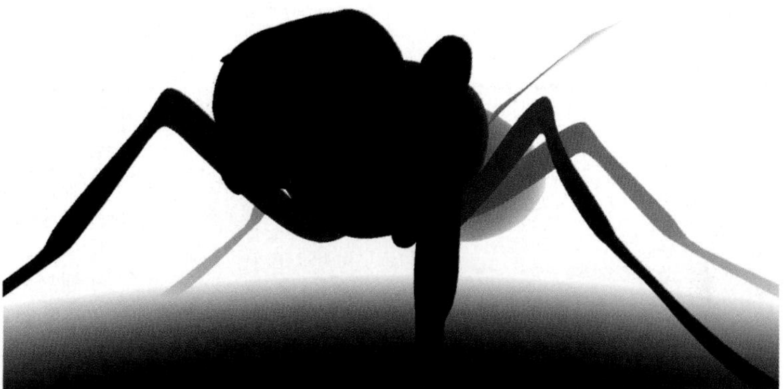

FIG 7.26 The depth pass gains contrast by adjusting the Black Point and White Point values.

6. Create a new composition with the same resolution, frame rate, and duration as the first composition. LMB-drag the first composition into the new composition. Hide the nested composition layer by turning off the eye icon.
7. LMB-drag *fly.exr* into the new composition and place it at the bottom of the layer outline. With the new fly layer selected, go to Effect > 3D Channel > EXtractoR. Open the effect in the Effect Controls panel and click on one of the channel names, such as *Red*. The EXtractoR window opens. Set the Layers menu to BEAUTY.beauty.persp. With this OpenEXR render, a separate beauty render pass was added in addition to the default RGB render. Click the OK button to close the window.
8. Select the fly layer, and choose Effect > Blur & Sharpen > Camera Lens Blur. In the Effect Controls panel, expand the blur effect's Blur Map section. Change the Layer menu to the nested comp layer (*1.Comp 1*). Increase the Blur Radius to 10. The background wall, the back of the floor plane, and the back of the fly become out of focus (see Figure 7.1 at the start of this chapter). You can adjust the intensity of the "out-of-focusness" by altering the Blur Radius value. To reverse the depth so that the foreground is out of focus, select the Invert Blur Map radio button in the Blur Map section.
9. To make the area that's in focus more narrow, return to the first composition and lower the White Point value. To increase the in-focus range, raise the White Point value. The part of the depth pass that is white receives the maximum amount of blurriness. The part that is black receives no blurriness.

A finished version of this project is saved as *depth_blur.aep* in the *\ProjectFiles\aeFiles\Chapter7* directory.

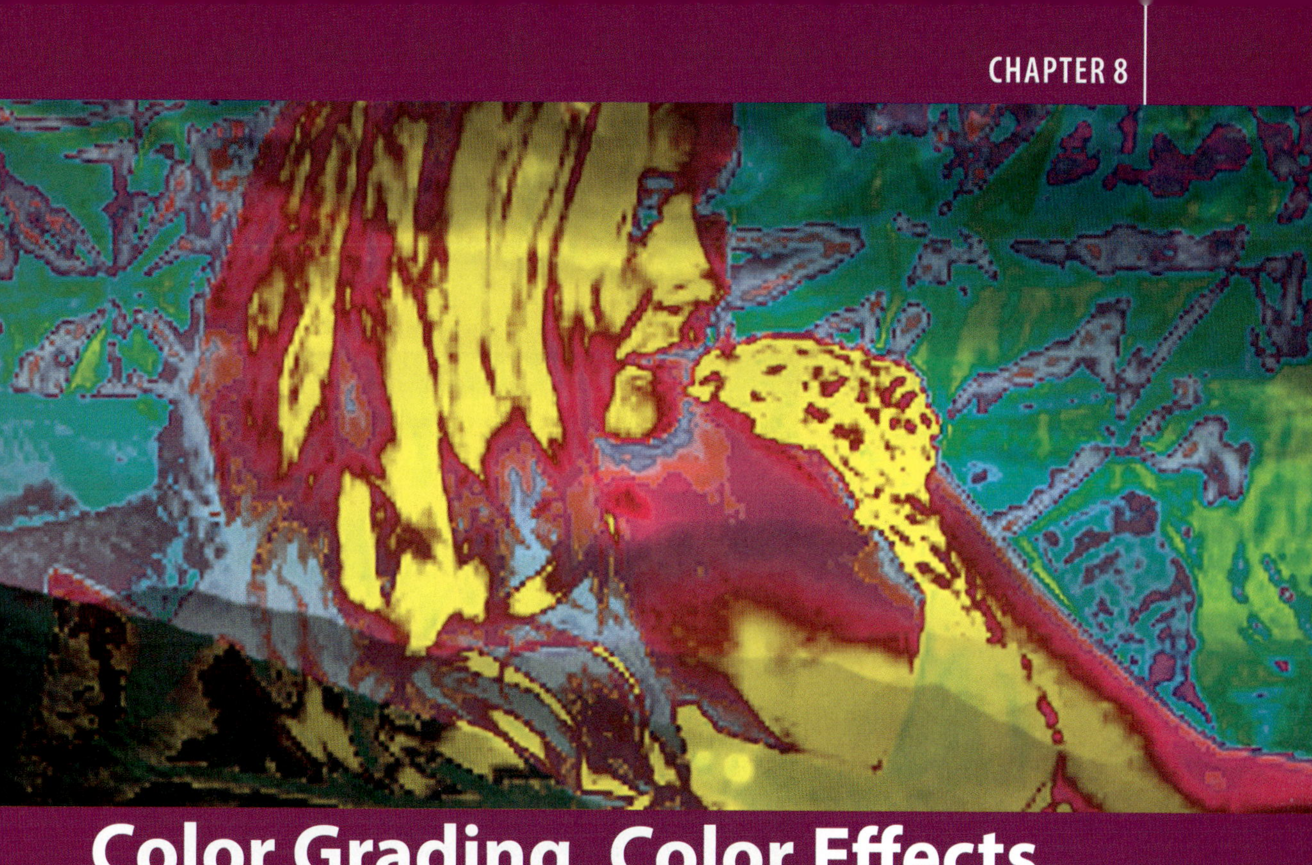

CHAPTER 8

Color Grading, Color Effects, and HDRI

Digital composites are ultimately dependent on the three color channels: red, green, and blue. Hence, color grading and the use of color effects is an important part of the compositing process. Color effects allow you to alter the balance of colors. You can shift colors, reduce a particular color, replace colors with other colors, increase contrast between color channels, creatively "re-light," and so on (Figure 8.1). Although After Effects provides numerous color effects, many of them provide similar results with different methodologies. If you understand the underlying functionality of these effects, you can make educated decisions on their use. Color grading, on the other hand, is a process by which colors are altered with a particular goal. For example, color grading can help ensure that multiple shots match within a scene or that a particular shot takes on a different mood through the adjustment of color. Beyond that, After Effects supports the ability to work with 8-bit, standard images or 32-bit High-Dynamic Range Imagery (HDRI).

This chapter includes the following critical information:

- Overview of color grading goals and techniques
- Functionality of useful color effects
- Overview of HDRI support

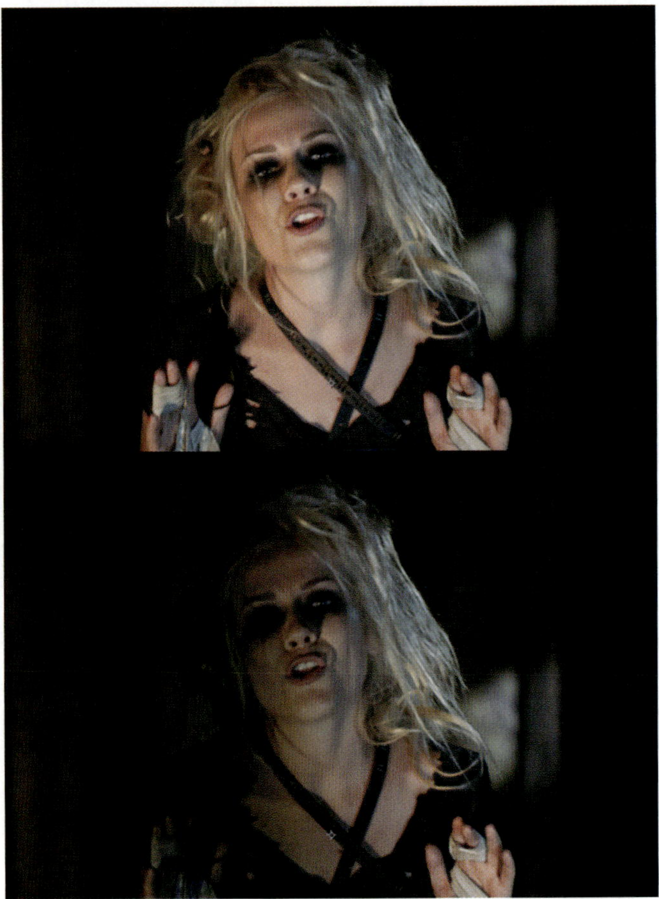

FIG 8.1 Top: An ungraded shot. Bottom: Color grading is limited to the left side of an actress, which creates a new, artificial shadow.

Color Grading

Color grading, as it's applied to film, video, animation, and visual effects industries, has several main functions, which are discussed in this section. (Note that the terms *color grading* and *color correction* are often used interchangeably.)

Aesthetic Adjustment

Colors are adjusted to create pleasing results. This may involve shifting the main color tone of a shot to alter the mood. For example, you can desaturate an otherwise bright, saturated shot to make the mood more somber (Figure 8.2).

Time of Day Change

Colors are shifted to match a different time of day. For example, you can color grade an afternoon shot to look more like sunset (Figure 8.2).

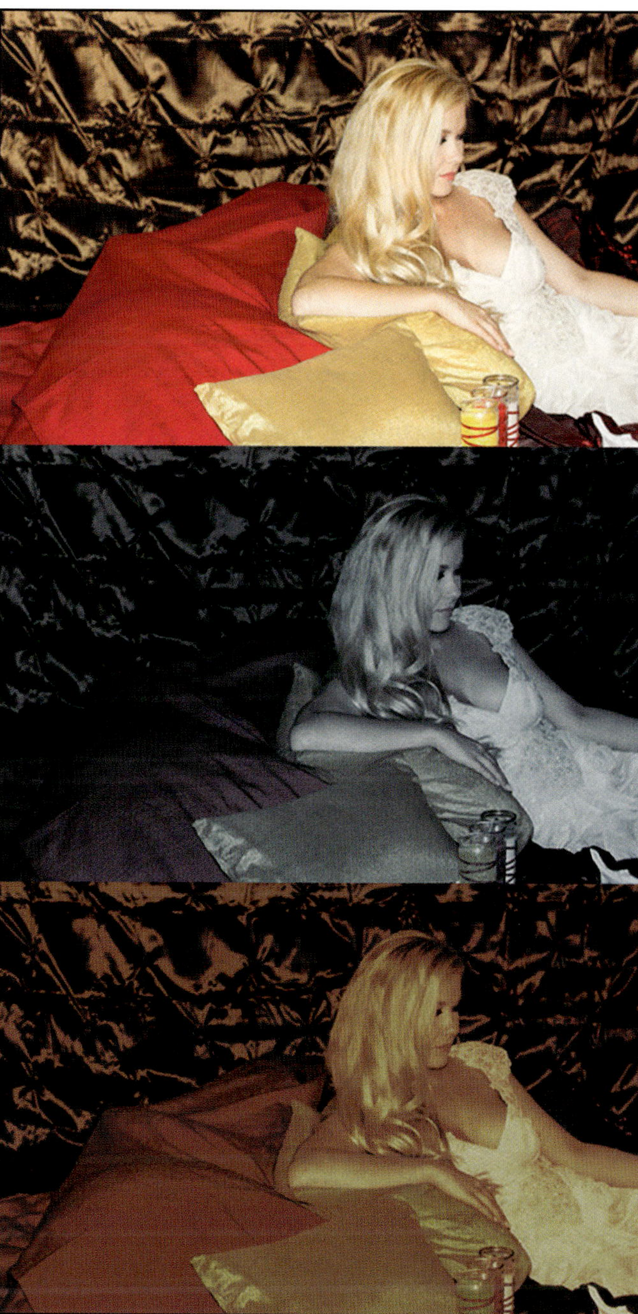

FIG 8.2 Top: Ungraded frame. Middle: Frame graded to make the scene more somber. Bottom: Frame graded to approximate sunset. This image is included as *ungraded.png* in the *\ProjectFiles\Art* directory.

Shot Consistency

Shots are graded so they match each other and are consistent across a scene. Before color grading, each shot may vary slightly due to differences in lighting setups or shifting natural light.

Element Integration

When 3D renders digital matte paintings, and other 2D artwork are integrated with live-action footage, it must be graded to match. For example, the darkest areas of a 3D render are often significantly different from similar areas captured on video.

Stylistic Changes

Colors are adjusted to create psychedelic, fanciful, or otherwise unnatural results. Such changes may be suitable for equally fantastic subjects, such as dream sequences, science-fiction or horror plots, and so on.

You can apply color grading with any effect or tool that alters colors within the image. Color grading generally involves the alteration of red, green, and blue ratios within an entire frame or a portion of a frame (through masking or rotoscoping).

Working with Blacks, Whites, and Color Cast

Color grading is only successful if it can be properly gauged. Aside from simply looking at the resulting frame, you can measure color values for each channel. After Effects provides the Info panel, at the top right of the program, for this purpose. When you drag your mouse over any of the view panels, the red, green, blue, and alpha channel values are printed out. The readout reflects the current color space bit depth. The 8-bit setting reads out values between 0 and 255, with 255 the maximum white value. The 16-bit setting reads out from 0 to 32,768. (Note that After Effects "16-bit" color space is actually 15-bit, or 2^{15}, with one extra color level; see Chapter 1 for more information.) The 32-bit setting, due to its floating-point architecture, reads out from 0 to 1.0. With 32-bit, 1.0 is the maximum value an 8-bit display can show; however, 32-bit files often carry superwhite values above 1.0. In addition to a space-centric readout, you can choose different scales through the panel's upper-right arrow menu (CC 2014) or panel tab menu (CC 2015). For example, you can switch to 10-bit, which runs from 0 to 1023. The 10-bit scale is a common bit-depth for logarithmic formats originally designed for motion picture scanning, such as Cineon and DPX.

When checking color values, a common task of color grading is matching blacks and whites. In this case, *blacks* refers to the darkest values within the frame. This may be a shadow area, an object that has a dark surface color, or the dark area of an actor's hair or eyes. *Whites* refers to the brightest area of a frame. These may be specular highlights, bright sky, and so on. For example, in Figure 8.2 in the previous section, the blacks are found within the wrinkles of the background while the whites are found within the dress. Within After Effects, matching blacks and whites requires matching color values between two different layers. For example, if the shadow area in layer A has a value around 35, 20, 15 in RGB, then the goal for grading layer B is to move the layer B shadow values into the same approximate range.

Along similar lines, another common color grading task is the matching of color casts. A color cast is the overall tint of a shot—that is, the specific hue the shot is biased towards. Some shots may have reddish casts, others may have blueish casts, and so on. Color casts may be a product of the natural lighting (e.g. blue daylight) or a film/video camera filter (e.g. a filter to shift the natural green of specific fluorescent lighting). As such, if shots within a scene must be matched, color grading a consistent color cast across shots is important.

Choosing Color Effects

You can find After Effects color effects within the Effect > Color Correction menu.

It's important to remember that color effects are dependent on the current color space. As discussed in Chapter 1, After Effects supports three color spaces: 8-bit, 16-bit, and 32-bit floating point. The higher the bit-depth is, the more accurate the color calculations are. Nevertheless, higher accuracy may not be discernible on screen. Thus, it may be more efficient to work at a lower bit-depth unless there is a noticeable degradation. That said, not all effects are designed to work at higher bit-depths. If an effect is intended for 8-bit color space, a warning icon appears when in 16-bit or 32-bit space (Figure 8.3).

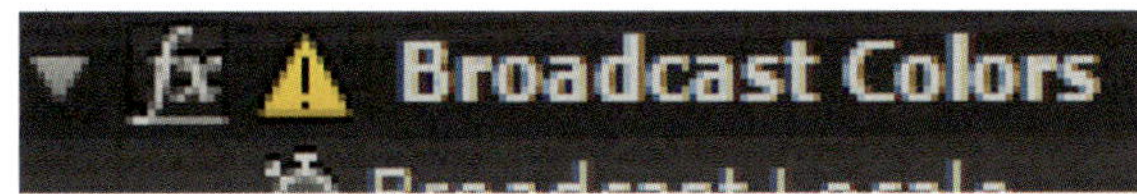

FIG 8.3 The bit-depth warning appears as a yellow triangle. With this example, the Broadcast Colors effect, designed to limit the color range of footage intended for video broadcast, does not function properly in 16- or 32-bit space.

Color Theory Terminology

Before familiarizing yourself with the functionality of color effects, it's helpful to understand basic color theory terminology. Here are a few critical definitions.

Hue/Color

As a general term, *hue* refers to pure spectrum colors that have specific names, such as red, blue, yellow, and so on. Within a digital color system, *hue* is the degree to which a color is similar or dissimilar to those pure spectrum colors. Although *hue* and *color* are often used interchangeably, you can think of hue as a more specific subset of all potential colors.

Saturation

Saturation is intrinsically linked to colorfulness and chroma. *Colorfulness* is the difference between the color and gray. *Chroma* is the difference between the color and what is considered white. *Saturation* is the colorfulness of a color as compared to white. You can equate saturation to the mixing of a hue with white. High saturation leads to a more intense color (more hue and less white) while low saturation leads to a pale color (less hue and more white). In After Effects, saturation is adjusted by altering the contrast between color channels.

Contrast

Contrast is the ratio of brightness to darkness within an image. A high-contrast image contains dark areas and bright areas with few mid-range values. A low-contrast image contains values evenly spread across the entire color range. Low-contrast images appear "washed out."

Brightness/Intensity/Lightness/Luminance

With a digital color system, brightness is the numeric value of a pixel within a color channel. A "bright" value is closer to the top of the current scale. For example, a pixel with a red value of 200 on a 0-to-255 scale is fairly bright while a pixel with a value of 20 is fairly dark. If a pixel has equal red, green, and blue values, it appears desaturated; that is, the pixel appears gray. If the channels share the same maximum value, they appear white. (The white may carry a color cast based on the color temperature of the monitor—see Chapter 1 for more information.) Brightness is also referred to as *intensity*, *lightness*, and *luminance*. Although these terms carry specific scientific or mathematical connotations, they are often use interchangeably by artists. Some color models incorporate these terms into their channels. For example, HSV stands for Hue Saturation Value. HSL stands for Hue Saturation Lightness. (HSL is sometimes called *HLS*.) You can graphically represent HSV and HSL with a conical of cylindrical shape where hue is plotted around the circumference, lightness/value is plotted along the height, and saturation is plotted from the central core to the outer surface (Figure 8.4).

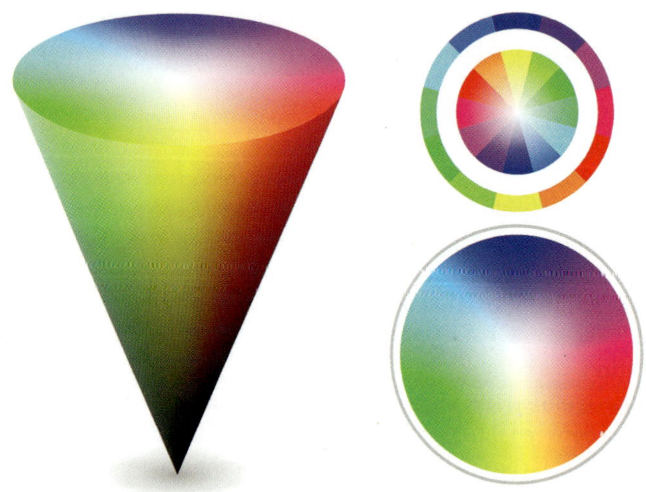

FIG 8.4 Left: HSV/HSL color space represented with a cone. Right: Same space represented with 2D color wheels. Note how red, green, and blue are positioned 120 degrees apart. Secondary colors are visible as cyan, magenta, and yellow. *Graphic © 2014 Mikrobius/Dollar Photo Club.*

Black Point, White Point, and Midtone

A *black point* is a value that is considered black, or the lowest possible value. Although this is usually 0, you can select a different black point by applying effects. A *white point* is a value that is considered white. Although this is generally the maximum value available to a color space, you can select a new white point value. This is sometimes necessary for color grading intended for a particular output medium. For example, "broadcast safe" video requires a white point below the available maximum. A midtone point is a value in the center of the range available to the color space. For example, on a 0-to-1.0 32-bit floating point space, 0.5 is the midtone. Note that a white point is established for an operating system through monitor calibration—this is separate from the compositing process. For more information on monitor calibration, see Chapter 1.

The RGB color model, which digital imaging software employs, is additive. That is, equal additions of red, green, and blue produce gray. Maximum additions of red, green, and blue produce white. This is the opposite of subtractive color models, where the absence of colors produces white (as with the white of the unprinted page with CMYK printing).

Working with Hue, Saturation, Tint, and Color Balance

The Hue/Saturation effect allows you to shift the hue and alter the saturation and brightness (Figure 8.5).

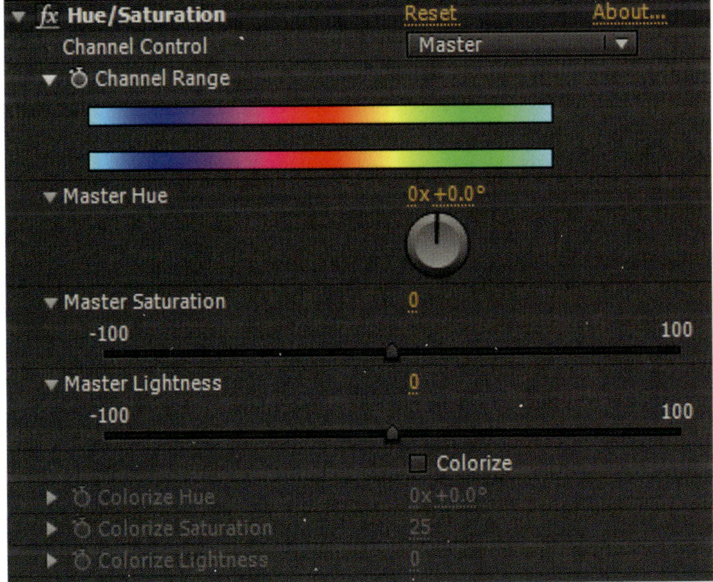

FIG 8.5 The Hue/Saturation effect properties with their default values.

With this effect, you can carry out the following tasks:

- You can shift the hues contained within the layer by altering the Master Hue color wheel. Essentially, the Hue/Saturation converts the color space to HSL, where hue is separated from saturation and lightness. In terms of the mathematical color model, hue is identified as a position on a conical or cylindrical representation of all hues available to the model. Thus, you can "spin" the cone or cylinder to shift all the hues within the layer. For example, setting the Master Hue to –50 shifts the layer's orange colors to violet and blue colors to blue-green (Figure 8.6). Note that you can go either direction on the color wheel. The 0 setting is equivalent to 360 and –50 is equivalent to 310.

FIG 8.6 Left: Ungraded layer. Middle: Same layer with the Master Hue wheel set to –50. Right: Same layer with the Master Hue wheel set to 30. *Photo © 2014 Kevron2001/Dollar Photo Club.*

- The Master Saturation and Master Lightness sliders control their namesakes. Increasing the saturation has the practical effect of increasing the contrast between color channels in favor of the brightest channels. For example, if the red channel has slightly higher values than the green and blue channels, increasing the saturation exaggerates the value gap between red, green, and blue. Red receives higher values while green and blue receive reduced values. On the other hand, increasing the lightness pushes the values of all three channels, as a unit, closer to the range limit. For example, increasing the lightness moves the values closer to 255 on an 8-bit scale. This makes the layer appear less saturated and more white. Shadows become brighter while previously bright areas may be pinned to the maximum scale value, such as 255.
- You can also "colorize" the layer by selecting the Colorize check box. *Colorization* desaturates the layer so that it is grayscale, and then adds back the hue chosen through its Colorize Hue wheel. This is similar to the tinting process and is useful for giving a strong color cast to a layer. You can control the saturation and lightness of the colorize result through the Colorize Saturation and Colorize Lightness sliders.

The Tint effect produces a similar result as the Colorize feature of the Hue/Saturation effect. However, it operates by allowing you to replace the blacks and whites with two colors of your choice via Map Black To and Map White To eyedroppers (Figure 8.7). You can mix the tinted result with the original values by setting the Amount To Tint value.

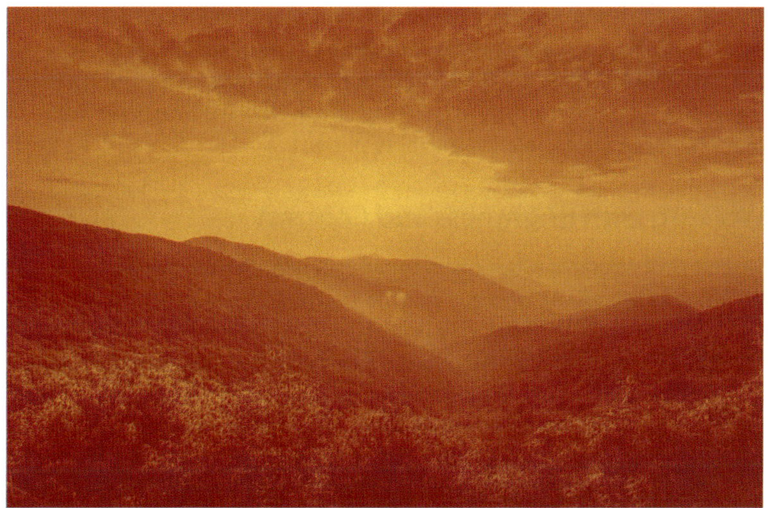

FIG 8.7 The Tint effect is applied to a layer with Map Black To set to dark red and Map White To set to orange.

The Color Link effects also colorizes; however, the colorize color is determined by averaging pixels within a target layer, which you can select through the Source Layer menu. In addition, the CC Toner effect tints a layer based on shadow, midtone, and highlight target colors.

The Color Balance effect allows you to manually adjust the balance between red, green, and blue channels. The effect breaks the color balance into brightness "zones" with Shadow, Midtone, and Highlights slider groups (Figure 8.8). If you raise a slider above 0, the associated color channel receives higher values. The remaining two channels are unaffected. Nevertheless, the resulting hues for the layer change as the overall mixture of red, green, and blue is updated. In a similar way, if you reduce a slider below 0, the associated color channel receives lower values. In addition, the effect provides a Preserve Luminosity check box. Preserve Luminosity maintains the average brightness within the image as the colors are altered; this helps to prevent overexposure if sliders are raised above 0. The Color Balance effect offers an efficient means of matching blacks, matching whites, and changing color casts by altering the channel balance.

fx Color Balance	Reset	About...
Shadow Red Balance	0.0	
Shadow Green Balance	0.0	
Shadow Blue Balance	0.0	
Midtone Red Balance	0.0	
Midtone Green Balance	0.0	
Midtone Blue Balance	0.0	
Highlight Red Balance	0.0	
Highlight Green Balance	0.0	
Highlight Blue Balance	0.0	
	Preserve Luminosity	

FIG 8.8 The Color Balance effect properties with default values.

The Color Balance (HLS) effect operates in a manner similar to the Hue/Saturation effect. A number of effects in After Effects share identical functionality. Although this gives you competing options for adjusting a layer, it also gives you the flexibility of choosing effects whose property sets and user interface options you find the most efficient.

Working with Brightness and Contrast

A number of effects in After Effects are designed to alter the overall brightness/darkness of an image. In addition, they can alter the layer's inherent contrast. The best way to understand what these effects are doing is to examine a histogram. A *histogram*, in terms of digital image manipulation, is a graph that represents the distribution of values. With a histogram, you can identify whether an image is high contrast, low contrast, or fails to include pixels with values in a particular range. For example, the Levels effect includes a built-in histogram. The value scale runs from left to right, where dark values correspond to the graph left and bright values correspond to the graph right. Each vertical line represents the number of pixels in the frame that possess a particular value (Figure 8.9). All pixels are represented, although the small size of the histogram means that the distribution is drawn in a simplified manner. By default, the distribution is shown for all three color channels, with the lines for red, green, and blue overlapping. In addition, white lines are superimposed over the color lines to show the average distribution of all three channels. To more clearly see a single color channel, you can change the channel menu, at the top right, to Red, Green, or Blue. This places the lines for the selected channel in front of the other lines.

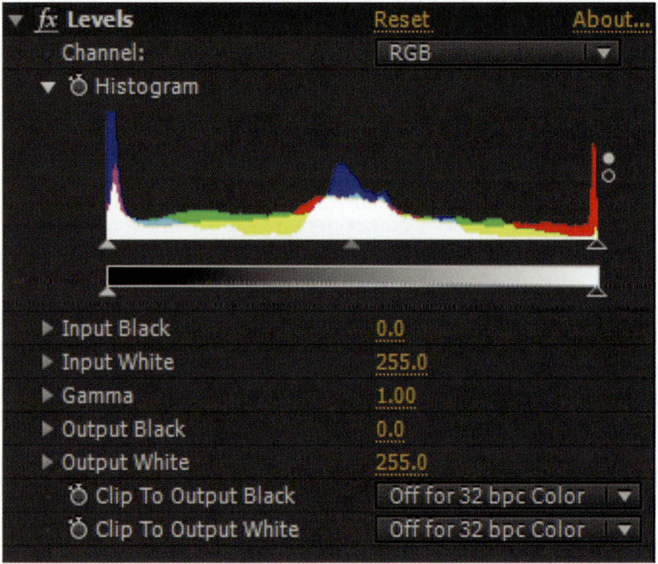

FIG 8.9 The Levels effect histogram, as applied to the ungraded image in Figure 8.6.

When you apply an effect that alters brightness and/or contrast, the distribution of values within the layer is changed. You can think of the change as a push, a stretch, or a compression. For example, if you apply a Brightness & Contrast effect, you can alter the histogram and the layer in the following ways:

Push Towards White Values are pushed to the right of the histogram (Figure 8.10). A compression of the value distribution occurs at the right while the distribution on the left is stretched. The resulting image is brighter with the potential that some values reach the maximum value of the color space, such as 255 (Figure 8.11).

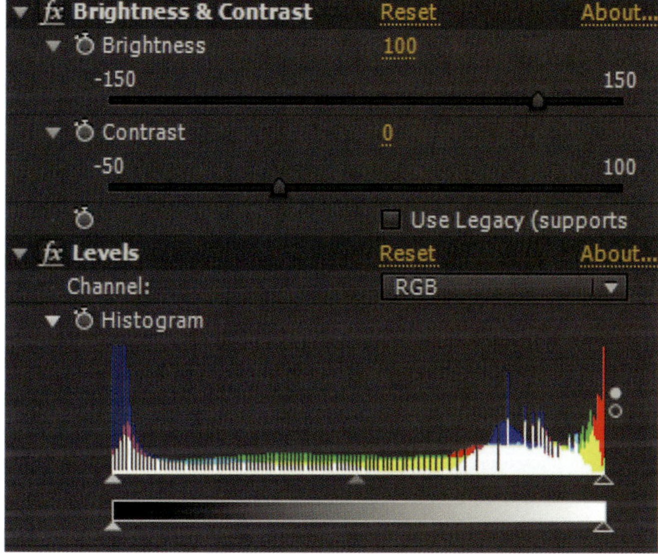

FIG 8.10 Brightness & Contrast and Levels effects are applied. Brightness is set to 150. The histogram reflects the change.

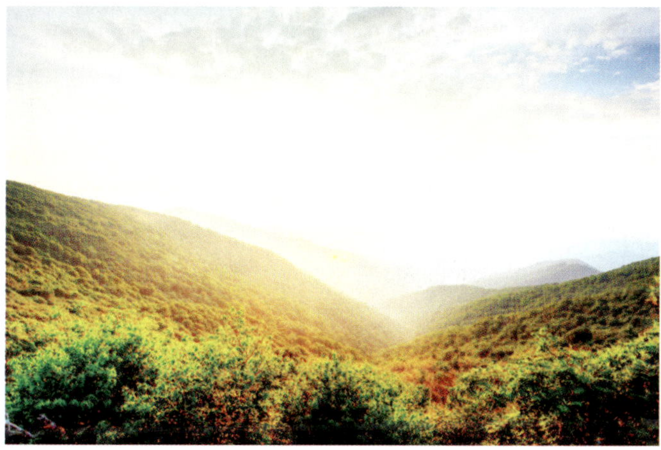

FIG 8.11 The result of the Brightness & Contrast effect.

Push Towards Black Values are pushed to the left of the histogram. A compression of the value distribution occurs at the left while the distribution on the right is stretched. The resulting image is darker with the potential that some values reach the minimum of the color space, which is usually 0. You can achieve this by lowering the Brightness value of the Brightness & Contrast effect below 0.

Stretch Towards Black and White Values are pushed left and right. Value distribution is compressed at the left and right sides and stretched in the center towards both sides. This tends to flatten out the distribution in the center but increase the peaks in the darkest and brightness areas (Figure 8.12). This leads to an image with greater overall contrast (Figure 8.13).

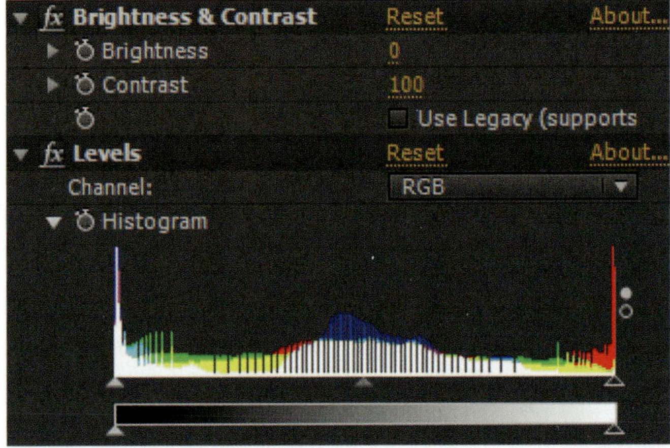

FIG 8.12 Brightness & Contrast and Levels effects are applied. Contrast is set to 100. The histogram reflects the change.

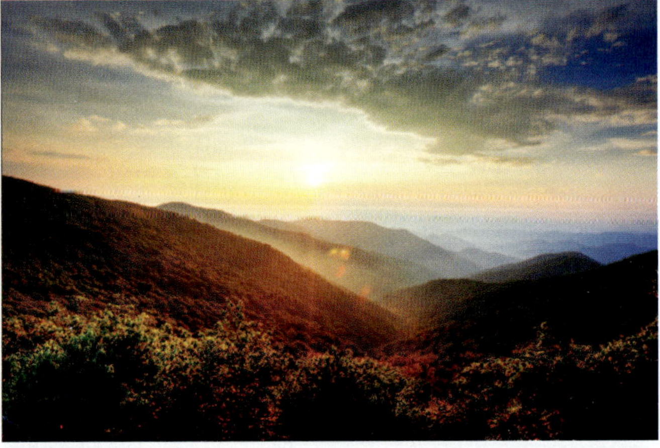

FIG 8.13 The result of the Brightness & Contrast effect.

Compress Towards Midtones Values are pushed towards the center. Value distribution is compressed at the center and stretched at the left and right sides towards the center. This tends to flatten out the distribution on the histogram ends but increases the peaks in the midtone area. This leads to an image with less overall contrast. You can achieve this by lowering the Contrast value of the Brightness & Contrast effect below 0.

You can use any combination of color effects on a layer. In fact, you can apply a Levels effect with default settings to simply view its histogram. However, the order in which you apply effects is important. After Effects applies the topmost effect first and works its way downward. You are free to reorder effects at any time by LMB-dragging the effects name up or down in the Effect Controls panel.

Whenever you apply a color effect in an aggressive manner (with high or low property values), there is the potential for histogram combing. Combing is the stretching of the value distribution in such a way that some values are carried by no pixels and gaps appear in the histogram much like the gaps between comb teeth. Severe combing may lead to degradation, where there are no longer smooth transitions between colors (known as *color banding* or *posterization)*. For example, in Figure 8.14, aggressive darkening leads to color banding in the sky. You can see histogram combing in Figures 8.10 and 8.12 earlier in this section.

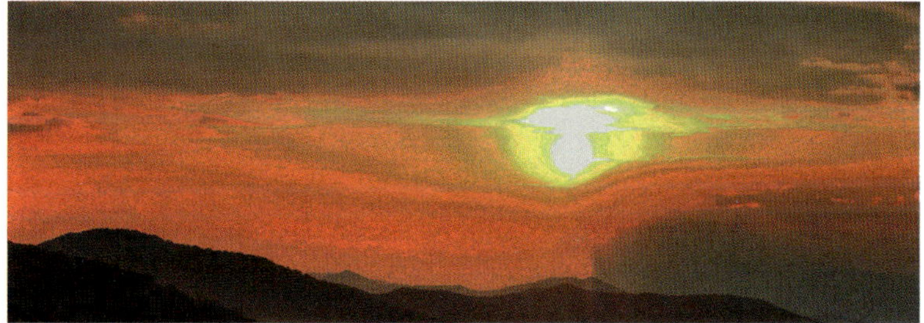

FIG 8.14 Color banding appears in a sky.

You can apply even finer control to brightness and contrast by adding the Curves effect. With the Curves effect, you can interactively insert and move points of a control curve (sometimes called a *response curve*) within a graph. The bottom of the graph represents the darkest available value (0). The top of the graph represents the brightest available value (e.g. 255 in an 8-bit scale). The effect remaps layer input values to new output values based on the shape of the curve. Hence, a default curve remaps 0 to 0, 128 to 128, and 255 to 255 in 8-bit space, producing no change. However, nondefault curve shapes produce predictable changes, as illustrated in Figure 8.15, where an S-shaped curve increases the contrast. An inverted-S-shaped curve reduces contrast. A bowed-up curve increases the overall brightness. A bowed-down curve increases overall darkness.

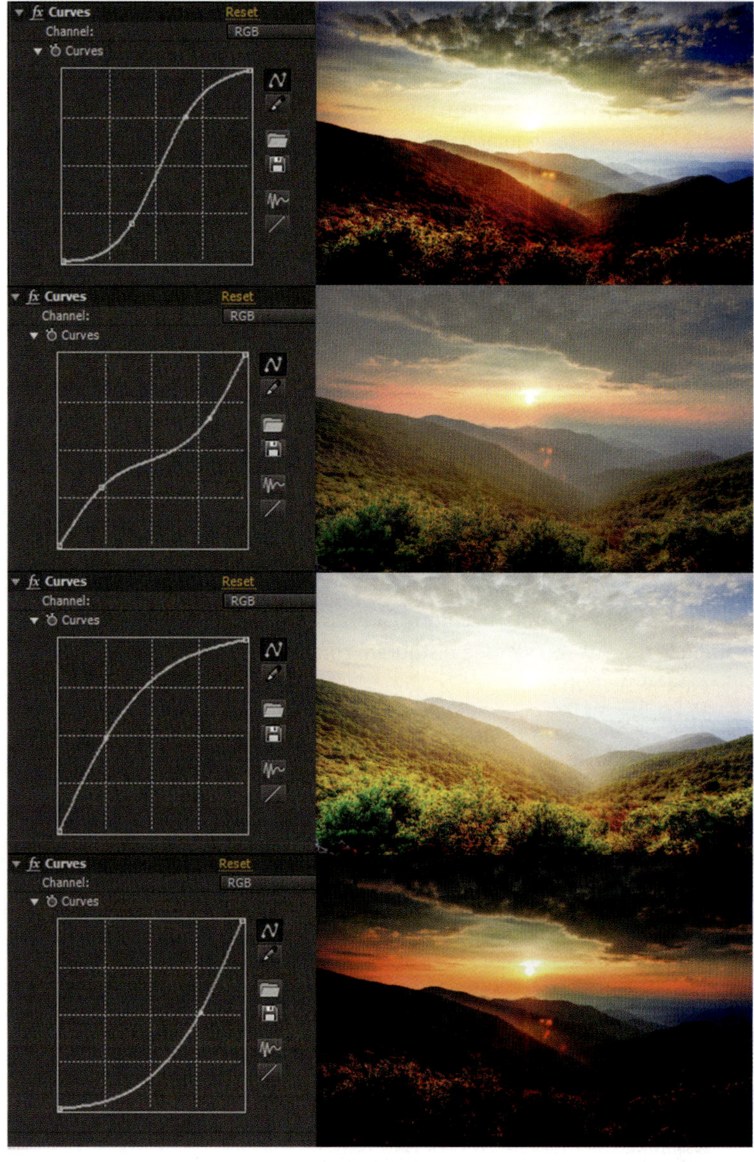

FIG 8.15 Top to bottom: Increased contrast, reduced contrast, increased brightness, and increased darkness, and a product of a custom curve with the Curves effect, as seen in After Effects CC 2013.

To insert a new point, LMB-click the curve. To move a point, LMB-drag it. You can reset the curve by clicking the Reset button at the bottom right of the graph. By default, the effect operates on RGB equally. However, you can alter a single channel by changing the Channel menu, at the top right of the graph, to Red, Green, Blue, or Alpha. The effect can store a unique curve for each channel.

Note that the CC 2014 and CC 2015 Curves effect simultaneously displays the curves for other channels if they are altered in such a way that they don't overlap. The channel curves are colored to match the channel names. The master RGB curve remains white. The alpha curve is dark gray. You can alter any of the curves once they are visible. If they are not visible, change the channel menu to the appropriate channel. The CC 2014 and CC 2015 Curves effect also includes graph size buttons at the top left.

Aside from displaying a histogram, you can also alter the brightness and contrast with the Levels effect. The histogram has three handles, which correspond to a black point, a white point, and a gamma value (Figure 8.16). The handles appear as small triangles directly below the histogram's colored lines. For example, if you move the left handle, it reestablishes the black point. Values to the left of the handle are essentially thrown away and replaced with 0-black. The black point handle actually drives the Input Black property slider. Input Black shows you the value of the new black point.

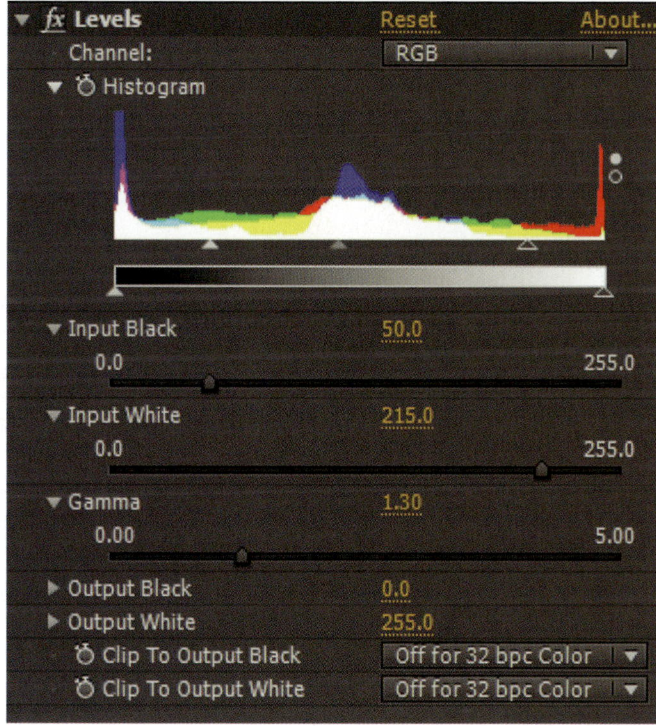

FIG 8.16 A new black point, white point, and gamma value are selected with a Levels effect.

The right histogram handle reestablishes the white point and drives the Input White slider. If you pull this handle to the left, values to the right of the handle are thrown away and replaced with the maximum value in the current color space. This leads to an image where a greater portion is pure white. When you move the black point or white point handle, the gamma handle also moves to stay centered within the new range. (The overall range of values is often referred to as a *tonal range*.) If you manually move the center handle to the right, the image is darkened. If you manually move the center handle to the left, the image is brightened. The center handle remotely drives the Gamma slider. The Gamma value represents the exponent of a power curve that's used to adjust the overall brightness and contrast of an image.

In general, the black point of an image appears as the darkest pixel (pure black) and the white point appears as the brightness pixel (pure white). However, you have the option to choose what is the darkest and brightest value by altering the Output Black and Output White property values of the Levels effect. For example, if you set Output Black to 25 and Output White to 200, the lowest pixel value within a layer is 25 and the highest is 200. This has the effect of making the layer appear faded (Figure 8.17).

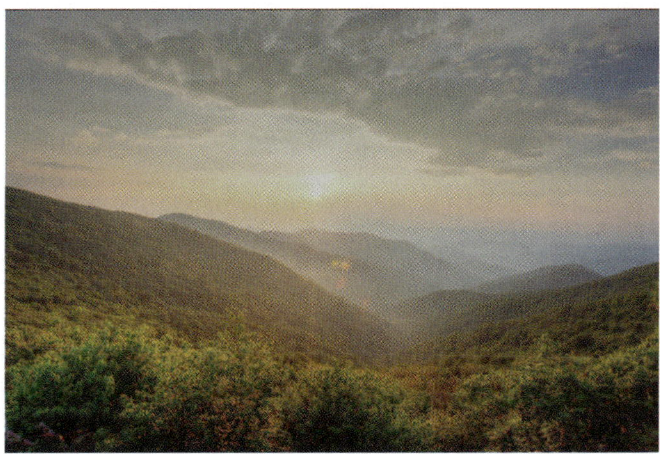

FIG 8.17 A high Output Black value and low Output White value makes the layer appear faded.

Like many effects in After Effects, the Levels effect adjusts itself to the current project bit-depth. For example, if you are working in 16-bit, the slider ranges update to display the correct 16-bit values (once again, After Effects "16-bit" space is actually 15-bit). If you are working in 32-bit, the Levels effect may produce superwhite or superblack (below 0) values. You can force the effect to clip the values to 0 and 1.0 by changing the Clip To Output Black and Clip To Output White menus to On.

After Effects also provides the Levels (Individual Controls) effect. This works in the same fashion as Levels, but splits the properties into red, green, and blue sliders.

Working with Pedestal, Gain, Gamma, and Photo Filters

Several color effects in After Effects use terminology borrowed from the motion picture and photography industries. For example, you can adjust brightness, contrast, black points, and white points with the Gamma/Pedestal/

Gain effect. With this effect, Pedestal sliders control the black point of each channel. Negative values are equivalent to raising the value of the Input Black value of the Levels effect. For example, a –1.0 value for Red Pedestal causes a greater portion of the red channel to carry a 0-black value. This produces a layer that is less red and more blue and green (Figure 8.18). If you raise a Pedestal slider over 0, a greater portion of the channel color is inserted into the layer. You can see the result of the effect in a particular channel by changing the Composition view's Show Channel And Color Management button to the channel name, such as Red. Each channel is displayed as a grayscale image, which represents the brightness/intensity of each channel pixel.

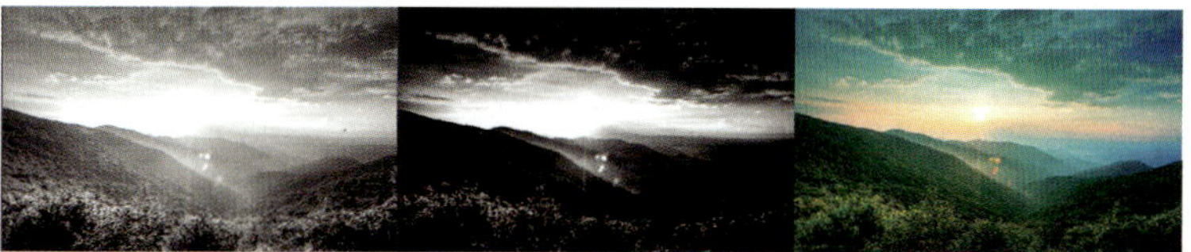

FIG 8.18 Left: Ungraded red channel. Middle: Red channel with Red Pedestal set to –1.0. Right: Result on the RGB view.

The Gamma/Pedestal/Gain effect also provides Gain sliders. These brighten or darken each color channel. The Gamma sliders have a result similar to the Gain sliders. However, the Gamma sliders create a more subtle result whereby values are less likely to be pushed down to 0-black or up to maximum-white.

On the other hand, the Photo Effect filter mimics physical filters placed in front of lenses of real-world cameras. The filters affect the overall color balance of a photo or video sequence by blocking some color wavelengths and exaggerating others. The Filter menu includes a number of presets that emulate specific filters. The virtual thickness of the filter and the intensity of the effect are set by the Density property. For example, setting the Filter to Cooling Filter (82) and the Density to 75 percent shifts white highlights to cyan (Figure 8.19).

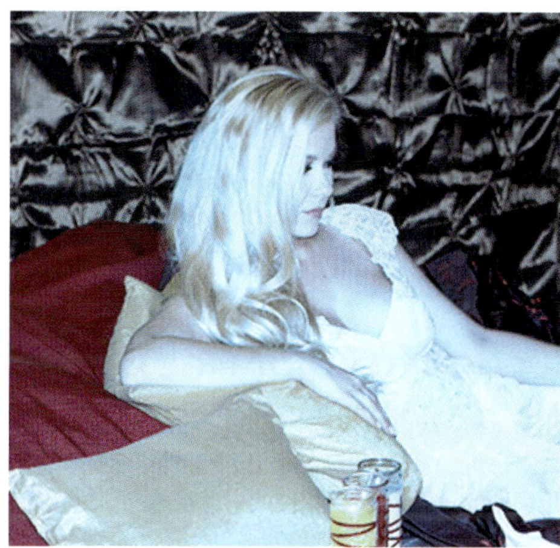

FIG 8.19 The Photo Filter effect "cools" a layer.

You can create your own custom filter by setting the Filter menu to Custom and choosing a color through the Color property. Although the result is similar to the Tint effect, the saturation of the tint is more subtle with the Photo Filter effect.

Working with Stylistic Color Effects

A number of color effects are designed to create surreal or fantastic results. Although these may not be useful for traditional color grading, you can employ them as smaller components of more complex compositions. For example, they may be useful when creating a laser beam, heads-up display, alien vision, or portal effect in a science-fiction-themed shot.

The Colorama effect allows you to remap specific color ranges or substitute specific colors with new colors. This is interactively achieved by manipulating the Input Phase and Output Cycle color wheels (Figure 8.20). In a similar fashion, the Change To Color effect allows you to replace one color with a new one with the From and To properties.

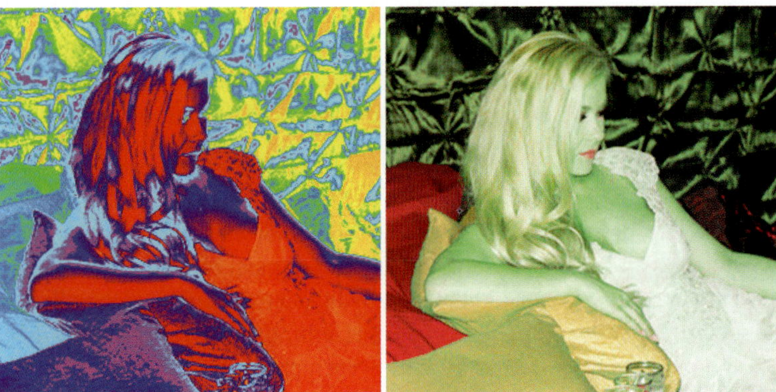

FIG 8.20 Left: The Colorama effect shifts all the hues of a layer. Right: The Change To Color effect replaces one color with another.

The most efficient way to see the potential of stylistic effects is to apply them and experiment with their property values. Other stylistic effects include Black & White (converts layer to grayscale), CC Color Offset (allows you to offset each color channel by adjusting individual hue wheels), Channel Mixer (modifies a color channel by mixing current channels), and Leave Color (desaturates a layer except where there is a chosen color).

An Introduction to Color Finesse 3

The Synthetic Aperture Color Finesse 3 LE plug-in provides an expansive set of color grading tools. You can access the plug-in through the Effect > Synthetic Aperture menu. When you apply the effect, you have the option of working with a simplified interface, which stays in the Effect Controls panel. To choose this, expand the Simplified Interface section. You can also choose the full interface by clicking the button with the same name. The full interface launches in a separate window (Figure 8.21). The window has several unique features, which are discussed briefly in this section.

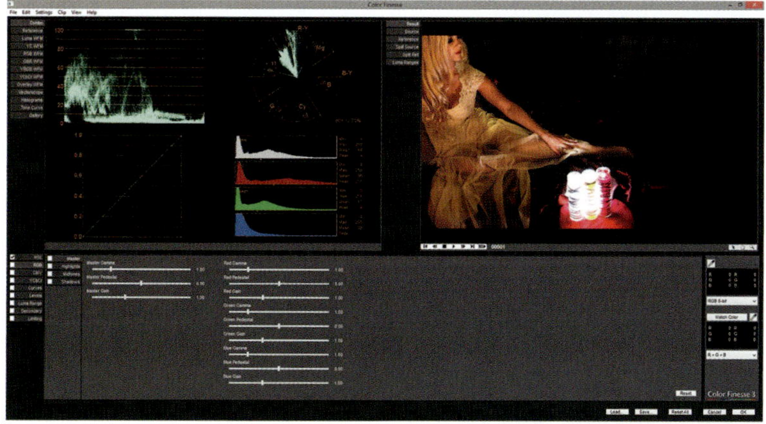

FIG 8.21 The Color Finesse 3 LE full interface window. The Combo readout is displayed at the upper left with a luma waveform and vectorscope at the top of this area.

Color Finesse includes a series of graphic readouts that are patterned after those used in the broadcast television and video production industries. You can access these by clicking the readout names in the top-left column. For example, the vectorscope displays the distribution or color values within the color spectrum of the color space. The vectorscope divides the spectrum into color axes that include red, magenta, blue, cyan, green, and yellow. These colors are indicated with the codes R, Mg, B, Cy, G, and Yl. While hue is indicated around the circumference of the circular readout, chroma (saturation in reference to the difference between the color and white) is indicated from the center point to the outer edge. For example, in Figure 8.22 a green screen plate causes points to cluster along the green axis (for the green screen) and red (for the skin and hair tones).

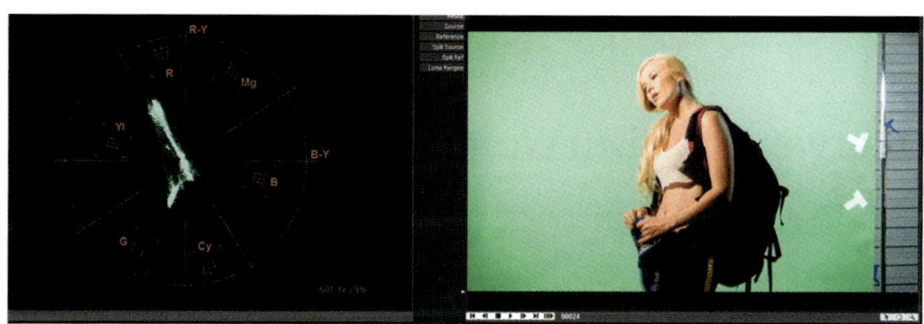

FIG 8.22 A vectorscope view of a green screen plate.

The plug-in also provides several waveform monitors. These are listed as WFM and are designed for several different color channels and color spaces, including standard RGB, luma (luminance only), and YcbCr (color space where luma and chroma are separated). With these waveforms, the pixel intensity distribution is displayed. The vertical scale runs from 0 to 1.0 and indicates the range between 0-black and maximum-white. The left-right direction correlates to the left-right portions of the image. For example, in Figure 8.23 the left and right "wings" correspond to the left and right green screen area of the plate seen in Figure 8.22; the central cluster of points corresponds to the actress in the center of the frame. A waveform offers a means to gauge the general brightness and contrast of an image and how different areas of the frame (as read left to right) correlate to each other. If you choose a waveform that carries multiple channels, like RGB, separate waveforms are displayed next to each other. Comparing channels side by side allows you to gauge color saturation (contrast between color channels) and any color cast. Note that the plug-in also supplies histogram readouts.

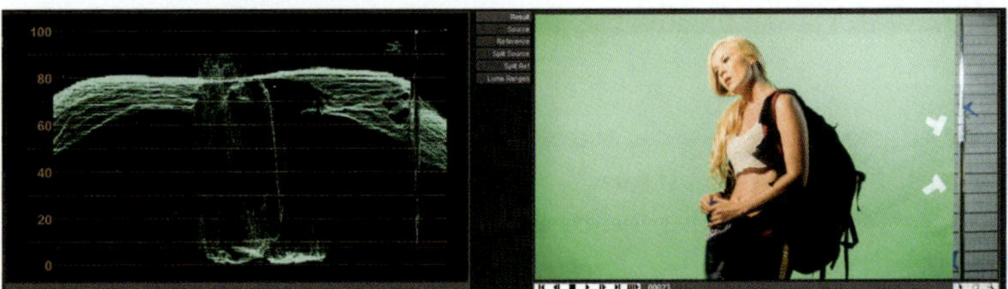

FIG 8.23 A luma waveform view of the same green screen plate.

The lower left section of the Color Finesse window include a battery of sliders that adjust common color components, including brightness, contrast, gamma, pedestal, hue, and saturation. The sliders are divided into master, highlight, midtone, and shadow sections. In addition, you can choose the color space in which to apply the sliders by selecting a space along the program's bottom left column.

You can apply any adjustments by clicking the OK button and thus close the window. You can combine Color Finesse with other color effects.

Overview of HDRI Workflow

After Effects supports High Dynamic Range (HDR) images by offering a 32-bit, floating-point color space via the Depth menu in the File > Project Settings window. (For more information on color space selection, see Chapter 1.) HDR still images or image sequences may be generated in one of several ways:

- A 3D program, such as Autodesk Maya, is set to render with a 32-bit floating-point buffer.
- Multiple photographs of a subject are combined with special HDR software, such as HDR Shop. Multiple photographs are used to properly expose every part of the scene or location.

HDR image formats supported by After Effects include Radiance files (generally ending with .hdr), OpenEXR (which has a 32-bit floating-point variation), and TIFF (which also supports 32-bit floating-point variants). The 32-bit color space varies from 16-bit in After Effects in that only 32-bit carries floating-point architecture. Floating-point architecture allows for arbitrary decimal accuracy, where stored values may be incredibly small, like 0.0000000001, or incredibly large, like 1.5×10^{12}. This offers two main advantages: a high degree of accuracy and a color range much larger than 8-bit or 16-bit can support.

The main disadvantage of a 32-bit image is the inability to see all of the stored values on an 8-bit or 10-bit monitor (which are used universally). When you view a 32-bit image in After Effects, you are not seeing superwhite (above 1.0) or superblack (below 0) values within the view panel. You can only see the values as a numeric printout in the Info panel. When rendering out a composition, only a limited number of formats support the 32-bit color space. More problematically, almost all media destinations (broadcast video, motion picture film, and so on) only operate in 8- or 10-bit. Nevertheless, After Effects supplies several effects to manage and alter HDR images. These are described here.

HDR Compander (Effect > Utility)

This effect compresses or expands the values found within a high-bit-depth image so that the values fit within a lower range. Hence, you can compress the values found within an HDR image sequence so they fall within 0 and 1.0 and can thus be displayed on an 8-bit monitor. For example, in Figure 8.24, an OpenEXR image sequence carries values between 0 and 1.7. Values between 1.0 and 1.7 appear pure white with no variation. With the addition of the HDR Compander effect, the values are brought back within the 0-to-1.0 range. Although the layer appears darker overall, more subtle color transitions appear in the brightest areas around the candles. The Gain property controls the compression. The value carried by the Gain represents the highest HDR value that is compressed into the new 0-to-1.0 range. Gain values below 1.0 expand the range so more values are pushed into superwhite; this may be useful for expanding 8-bit values into a 32-bit space. In addition, a Gamma slider is provided to fine-tune the result. For example, if you raise the Gamma, the shadow areas become brighter without pushing values above 1.0.

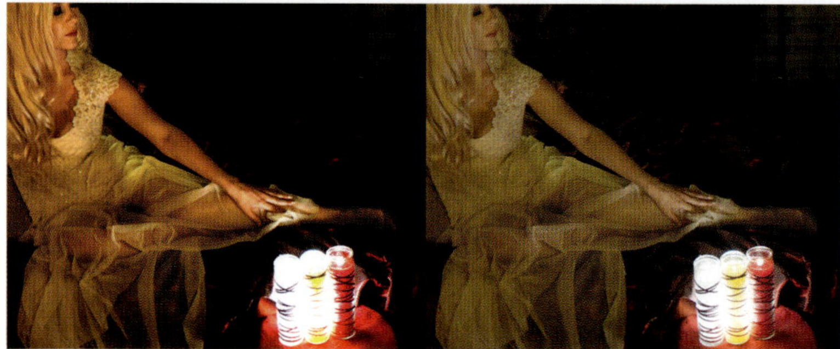

FIG 8.24 Left: Ungraded OpenEXR sequence with values ranging from 0 to 1.7. Right: Result of HDR Compander with Gain set to 2.0 and Gamma set to 1.75. This project is included as *compander.aep* in the *\ProjectFiles\aeFiles\Chapter8* directory.

HDR Highlight Compression (Effect > Utility)

Much like HDR Compander, HDR Highlight Compression compresses superwhite values into the 0-to-1.0 range. However, it only compresses highlights without affecting midtones or shadow areas. Its sole property, Amount, sets the aggressiveness of the compression. If Amount is set to 100 percent, no value in the image will be over 1.0.

Exposure (Effect > Color Correction)

The Exposure effect is designed to adjust the tonal range of HDR images. The Exposure property emulates the F-stop of a real-world camera. An *F-stop* is a number derived by dividing lens focal length by the diameter of the aperture opening. With each increase of F-stop, the amount of light reaching the film or video is halved due to the reduced size of the aperture. Positive Exposure values are multiplied against the current pixel values, giving them higher values and making them brighter. Negative Exposure values reduce the pixel values and make them darker. The Offset property brightens or darkens the shadow and midtone values without affecting the highlights.

Chapter Tutorial: Color Grading Effects

With this tutorial, we'll return to earlier projects and improve them with the addition of color grading. We'll start with a motion-tracking project from Chapter 4:

1. Open *tutorial_4_finished.aep* from the Chapter 4 tutorial directory. This features a corner-pin tracked sign on a wall. The sign's colors are significantly different from the video image sequence (Figure 8.25).

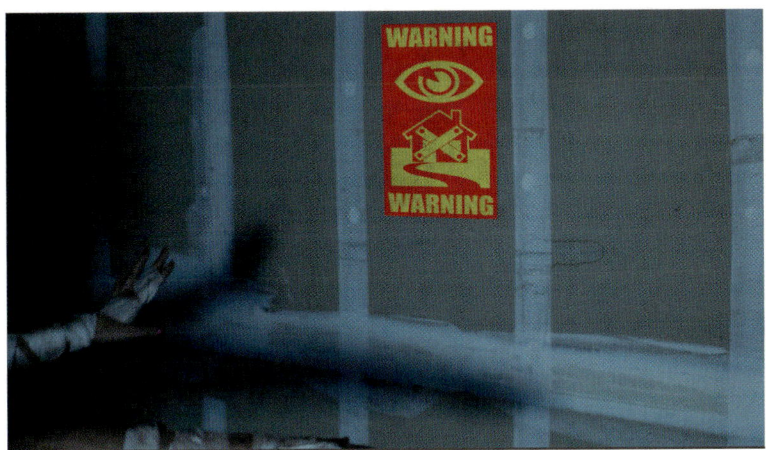

FIG 8.25 The motion-tracked but ungraded sign art.

2. Drag your mouse over the Composition view. Note the value readout in the Info panel at the upper right of the program window. The values should range from 0 to 255. If they do not, go to the panel's menu and choose Auto Color Display or 8Bpc (0–255). (Auto Color Display changes the readout based on the current project bit-depth.)
3. Place your mouse over a portion of the composition that comes the closest to pure white. For example, place your mouse over one of the round nail patches on the wall or over the bandages on the woman's forearms. Note the readout. The readout for a nail patch is roughly 70, 135, 170 in RGB. This shows that the blue channel is at approximately 66 percent (170/255), while green is at 53 percent, and red is at 27 percent. There is almost three times the blue in a "white" area when compared to red. Studying the white point of a layer will help us determine how to color grade the sign art so it fits better with the scene.
4. To properly grade the sign, we need to study its values. Because the sign contains no part that would be considered white, we'll concentrate on the red and yellow areas. Place your mouse over the yellow part of the sign. Here, the red and green channels are almost equal around 130 while the blue channel is a low 30. Place your mouse over the red part of the sign. Here, green and blue are almost equal at 30 while red is around 155. Whereas the white point of the shot is extremely blue, the sign contains little blue.
5. Select the sign layer and choose Effect > Color Correction > Color Balance. The Color Balance effect appears after the Corner Pin effect. Change the Shadow Blue Balance, Midtone Blue Balance, and Highlight Blue Balance to 100. Read the values in the red and blue areas of the sign. The blue component has increased in the yellow, but is essentially the same in the red areas. This shows that the channels are intrinsically linked. To increase

the amount of blue, you have to also adjust the red and green sliders. Experiment by reducing the Red and Green slider values. To determine if the sign's yellow values are correct, you can compare them to the yellow found within the woman's hair. The values are roughly 65, 85, 85 in RGB. To determine if the red values are correct, you can compare them to the red found within the woman's fingernails. The values are roughly 50, 20, 40 in RGB. In this way, you are able to compare "points" for other colors. For example, Figure 8.26 uses the following slider values:

Shadow Red Balance: –40
Shadow Green Balance: –25
Shadow Blue Balance: 100
Midtone Red Balance: –75
Midtone Green Balance: –60
Midtone Blue Balance: 100
Highlight Red Balance: –100
Highlight Green Balance: –25
Highlight Blue Balance: 100

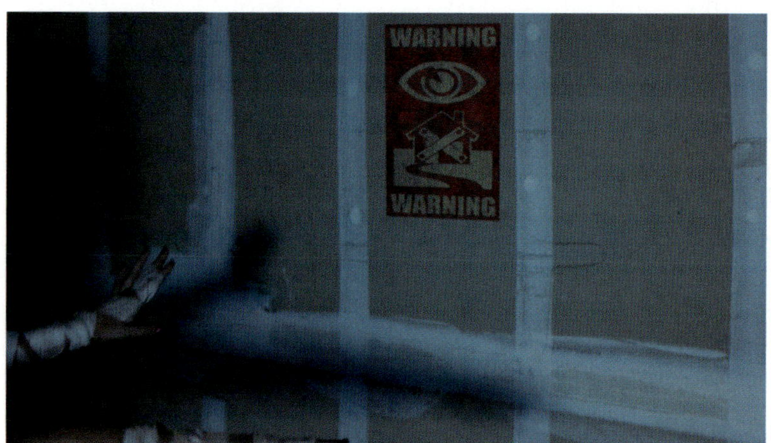

FIG 8.26 The color graded result using the Color Balance, Hue/Saturation, and Fast Blur effects.

6. Although it's important to read red, green, and blue values within the frame as you make adjustments, it's equally important to make aesthetic judgments to determine what settings look the best. Even after the Color Balance effect is adjusted, the sign appears saturated with intensely red areas. You can alter this by adding additional color effects. For example, add the Hue/Saturation effect and reduce the Master Saturation value to –50.
7. As a final touch, you can soften the sign art to better match the softness of the image sequence. With the sign layer selected, choose Effect > Blur & Sharpen > Fast Blur and set Blurriness to 2. Play back the timeline.

The color grading is complete. An example project is saved as *project_4_graded.aep* in the *\ProjectFiles\aeFiles\Chapter8* directory.

You can apply similar color grading techniques to the *color_pin_offset.aep* project in the *\ProjectFiles\aeFiles\Chapter4* directory. However, with this project, the dominant color is purple (intense red and blue). Because the purple color cast of the shot is so intense, you can also use the Tint effect to better integrate the sign. To do so, follow these steps:

1. Open the *color_pin_offset.aep* project. Select the sign layer and choose Effect > Color Correction > Tint. Go to the Effect Controls panel.
2. Use the Map Black To eyedropper to select a dark color from the image sequence. Use the Map White To eyedropper to select a bright color from the image sequence. The sign is tinted purple (Figure 8.27).

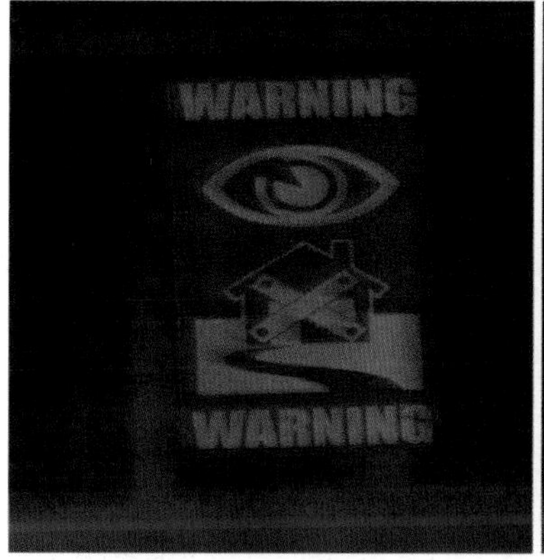

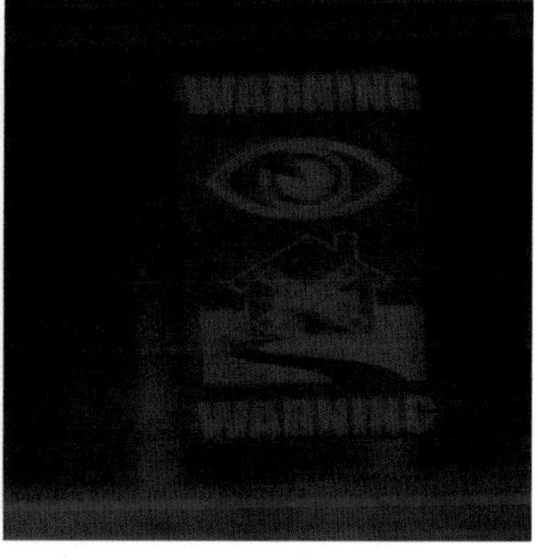

FIG 8.27 Left: Close-up of ungraded sign. Right: Sign graded with the Tint effect and given increased Opacity.

3. If the sign is too difficult to see, raise the sign layer's Opacity (for example, set it back to 100 percent). You can also adjust the selected tint colors by clicking directly on the color swatches and choosing a new color through the color chooser window. The color grading is complete. An example project is saved as *corner_pin_offset_graded.aep* in the *\ProjectFiles\aeFiles\Chapter8* directory.

The Curves effect also offers a convenient means of grading by adjusting the overall brightness and contrast of a layer. For example, you can better integrate the spaceship render demonstrated in Chapter 7. You can follow these steps:

1. Open the *passes_matte.aep* project from the *\ProjectFiles\aeFiles\Chapter7* directory. Go to Comp 2. Note that the spaceship is composed of multiple layers. The reflection is separate from the main shading components.
2. Select the Comp 1 nested layer and choose Effect > Color Correction > Curves. A new Curves effect is added after the original Curves effect.

There is no penalty for adding multiple iterations of an effect to a layer. Raise the leftmost point of the new Curves effect upwards (Figure 8.28). This raises the values of the shadow area of the spaceship. This creates a sense that there is atmospheric haze because no part of the spaceship achieves 0-black. This better matches the hazy background layer.

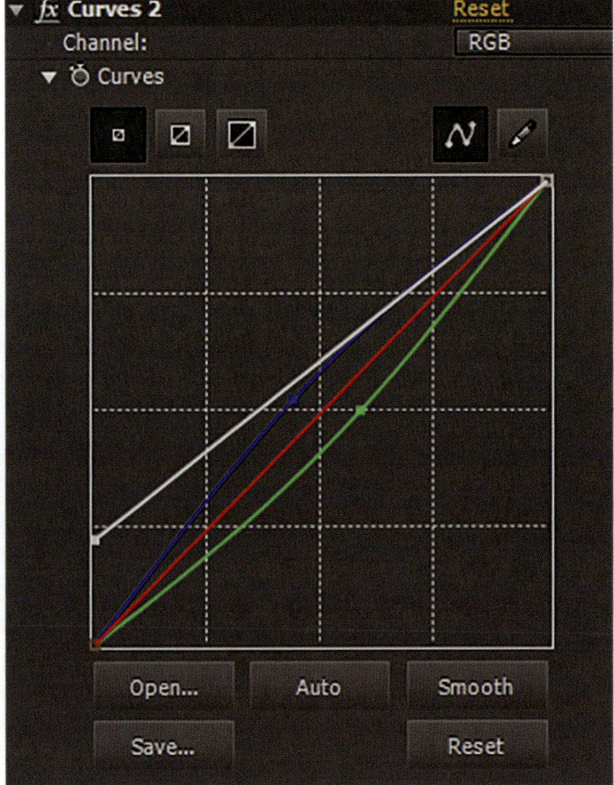

FIG 8.28 The left side of the master RGB curve is lifted up so that the shadow area becomes brighter (as seen in CC 2015). The blue curve is bowed up and the green curve is bowed down to shift the midtone balance toward blue.

3. By default, the Curves effect affects all three color channels. However, you can also adjust individual channels by changing the upper right Channel menu. For example, change the menu to Blue and bow the curve center slightly upwards. Change the menu to Green and bow the curve center slightly downwards. This shifts the midtone balance closer to blue, which better matches the mountains seen in the background (Figure 8.29). The color grading is complete. An example project is saved as *passes_matte_graded.aep* in the *\ProjectFiles\aeFiles\Chapter8* directory.

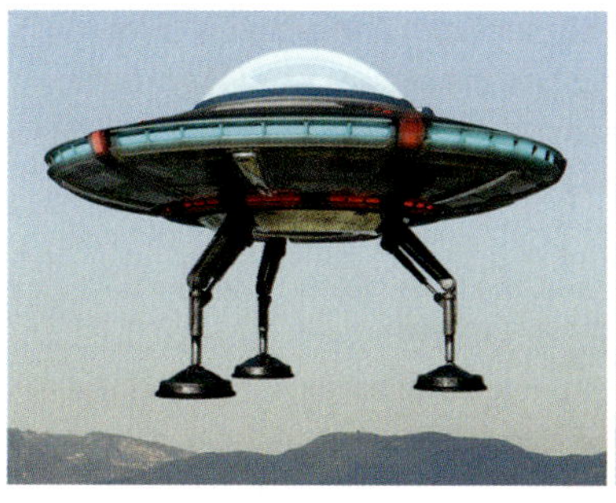
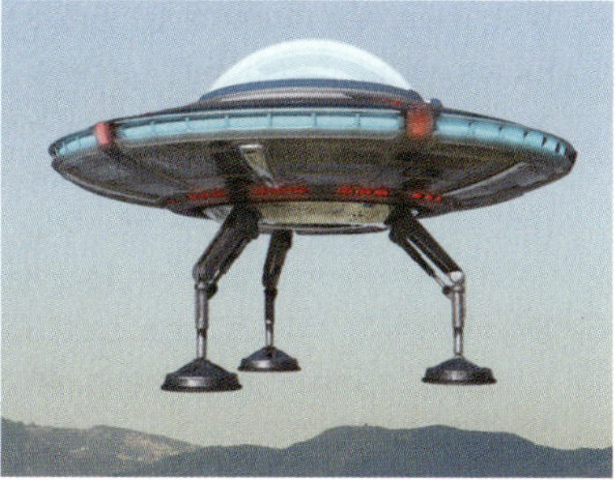

FIG 8.29 Left: Ungraded ship. Right: Ship graded with a Curves effect. The RGB Green and Blue curves are adjusted.

It's not necessary to apply color grading to an entire layer equally. For example, you can limit it to specific areas with masking. For example, we can use this technique to create shadow areas on a green screen shot we worked with in Chapters 2 and 3. You can follow these steps:

1. Open the *tutorial_8_start.aep* project from the *\ProjectFiles\aeFiles\Chapter8* directory. Go to Comp 2. This features a green screen shot of an actress. The green screen is removed in Comp 1. A new 3D render is imported as a new background as part of Comp 2. No color grading is applied at this point.
2. Select the Comp 1 nested layer and choose Edit > Duplicate. Select the new top Comp 1 layer. Using the Pen tool, roughly draw a closed mask that separates the left side of the face and body of the actress (Figure 8.30). Change the Mask Feather to 300.

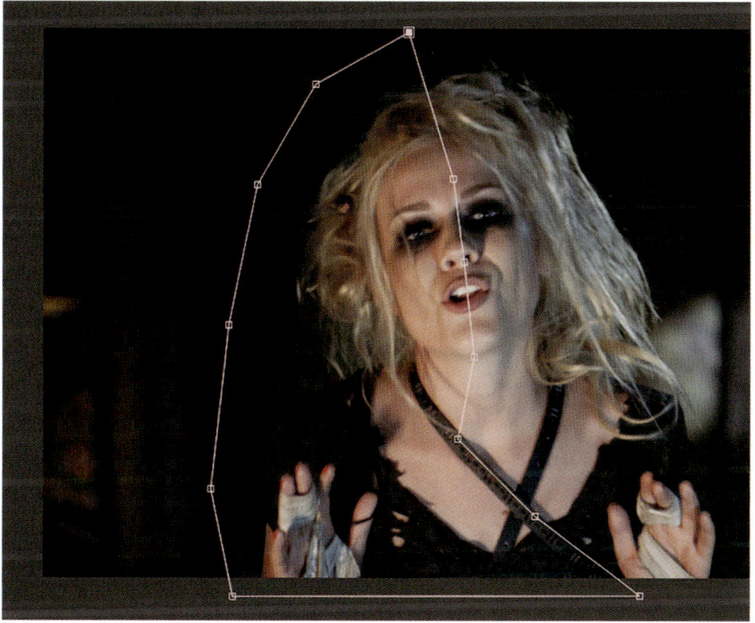

FIG 8.30 A new copy of the green screen layer is masked to separate the left side.

3. With the top layer selected, choose Effect > Color Correction > Color Balance, Effect > Color Correction > Curves, and Effect > Color Correction > Hue/Saturation. Adjust the effects to make the left side darker and more yellowish to match the background render (see Figure 8.1 at the start of this chapter).
4. You are also free to apply color effects to the lower Comp 1 layer to alter the right side of the actress. Color grading different zones of a composition provides a means to creatively "re-light" a shot during the postproduction phase. However, keep in mind that the mask must be animated over time if the subject, like the actress, moves. A graded example of this project is saved as *tutorial_8_finished.aep* in the *\ProjectFiles\aeFiles\Chapter8* directory.

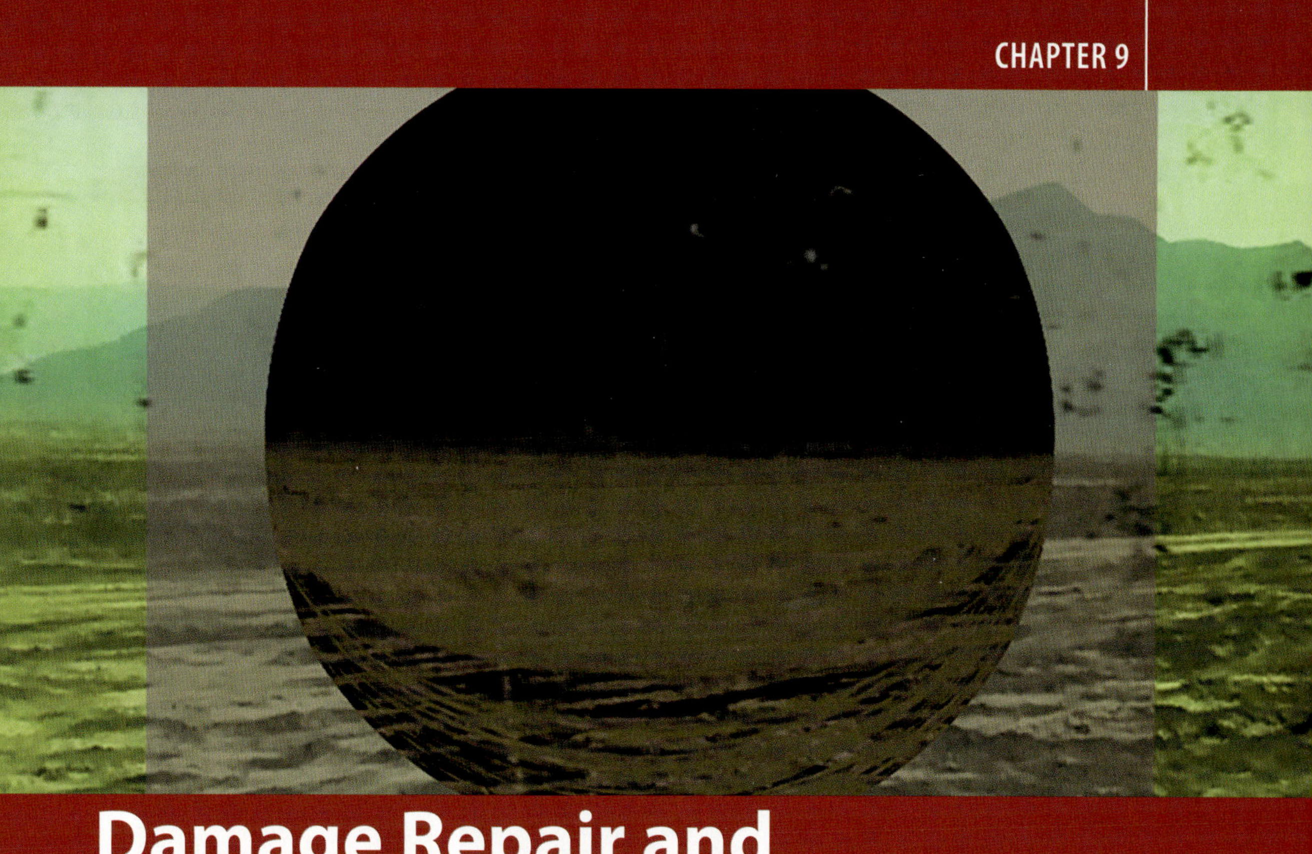

CHAPTER 9

Damage Repair and Distressing

In general, the goal of visual effects compositing is to seamlessly integrate elements such as live-action plates, 3D animation, digital matte paintings, and so on. Part of this task requires the removal or integration of artifacts that naturally occur when motion picture film, analog video, or digital video is captured. Grain and noise are common artifacts that you can remove within After Effects. Conversely, you have the option to *add* noise or grain to elements that lack it, such as 3D renders. Randomly appearing artifacts, which include scratches and dust, require more complex techniques for removal or addition. The After Effects set of paint tools offers a means to remove random artifacts and any unwanted elements through the "paint fix" process (Figure 9.1). Another variation of distress involves the addition of distortion effects.

This chapter includes the following critical information:

- Adding noise, grain, and similar film and video artifacts
- Removing noise and grain
- Repairing and altering footage with paint tools

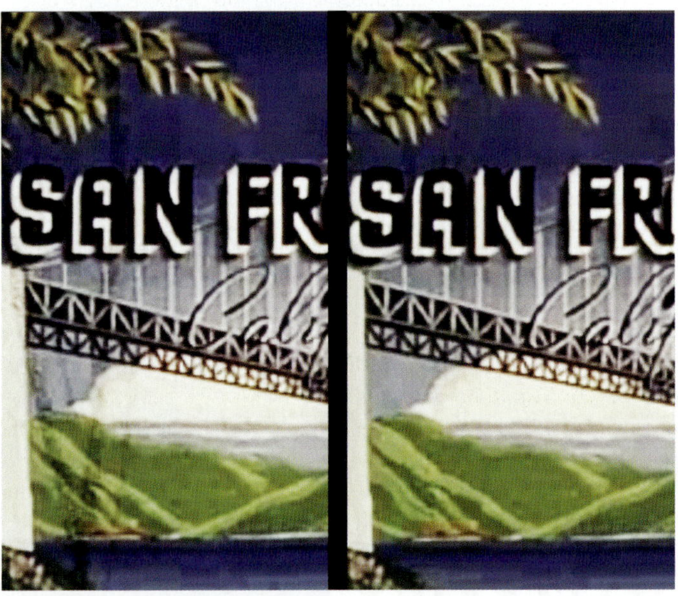

FIG 9.1 Left: Damaged motion picture film footage with two large scratches at the left of frame. Right: Same footage after paint fixes are applied. This process is demonstrated in the "Removing Film Damage" mini-tutorial later in this chapter.

Working with Noise, Grain, and Compression Blocks

Motion picture film captures images with a celluloid or plastic base coated with gelatin containing microscopic, light-sensitive silver halide crystals. The presence of the crystals creates the appearance of *film grain* (Figure 9.2). The grain varies with each frame and therefore appears to be in constant motion. The size, color, and contrast of the grain varies with each specific film stock.

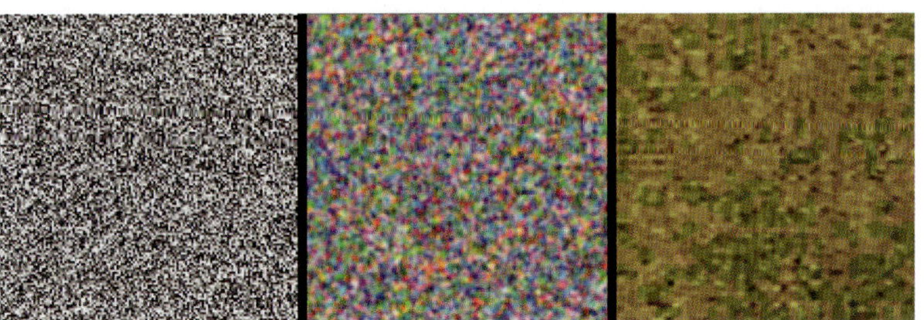

FIG 9.2 Left to right: Close-ups of film grain, video noise, and video compression blocks as they might appear over a gray field.

In comparison, video noise occurs when light photons randomly strike a sensor in a low-light scenario or when random electrical signals are present in a system. Video noise appears as one-pixel, random variations in color or brightness (Figure 9.2). Video static occurs when the only information present is noise (hence, you see static on a television when there is no reception).

Video compression blocks, which appear as irregularly formed rectangular shapes, are created by compression algorithms in order to reduce file size (Figure 9.2). Compression blocks and noise may appear simultaneously in a video sequence. Although professional digital cameras suffer less from noise and compression blocks, all digital video carries these artifacts to some degree.

Noise and Grain Removal

After Effects provides an Effects > Noise & Grain menu. You can use the Remove Grain effect, available in this menu, to remove noise or grain. You can follow these basic steps:

1. When you apply the Remove Grain effect, the result is displayed in a white preview box (Figure 9.3). You can move the preview box to different areas of the frame by LMB-dragging the box center. You can alter the box size by changing the Width and Height values in the Preview Region section. Due to the calculation-intensive grain removal process, it's generally better to fine-tune the effect while previewing a small area.

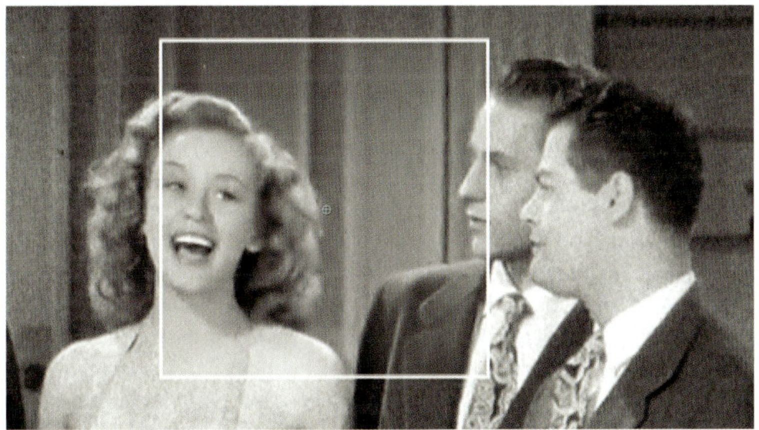

FIG 9.3 Close-up of a grainy motion picture film clip. The Remove Grain effect reduces the grain within its white preview box. The footage is included as *Grainy.##.png* in the *\ProjectFiles\Plates\NoiseGrainScratches\Grainy* directory.

2. Adjust the aggressiveness of the effect by raising or lowering the Noise Reduction property in the Noise Reduction Settings section. The goal is to remove the noise and grain without overly softening the resulting image. To further adjust the result, you can change the Passes value, which sets the number of iterative reduction passes. Lower Passes property values tend to create a blotchier result. You also have the

option to adjust the removal aggressiveness per channel through the Channel Noise Reduction subsection. Color film and video often creates different degrees of noise in the red, green, and blue channels. You can view a color channel at any time by using the Show Channel button menu in the view panel.

3. You can resharpen the result by raising the Amount value in the Unsharp Mask section. The unsharp mask process increases the contrast around edges. The extent of the high-contrast area is set by the Radius property. Use this section with caution. Excessive sharpening may reveal or exaggerate additional artifacts, such as compression blocks, dirt, or other damage.
4. When you are satisfied with the settings, change the Viewing Mode menu from Preview to Final Output. Test the settings at different frames along the timeline.

The clip used in this section is taken from *Soundie: Reg Kehoe and his Marimba Queens*, a short film from the Prelinger Archives, made available via a Creative Commons Public Domain license. For more information, visit www.archive.org/details/prelinger.

There are a number of third-party plug-ins that tackle noise removal. For example, the Neat Video Reduce Noise plug-in offers advanced removal techniques. The following tutorial describes its application.

Neat Video mini-tutorial

To apply Neat Video Reduce Noise, follow these basic steps:

1. Select the layer that contains the noise or grain and choose Effect > Neat Video > Reduce Noise.
2. In the Effect Controls tab, click on the Options link at the top of the Reduce Noise properties section. A separate window opens.
3. The first step to the removal process is the identification of a noise pattern within a region of the frame that includes little variation (e.g. en empty sky or blank wall). The plug-in identifies this area automatically if you click the Auto Profile button at the top left. A blue square appears over the identified region. If the square is less than 128x128 pixels in size, a warning box opens; despite this, you can choose to build a noise profile by clicking the Yes button. The larger the noise pattern region, the greater the success of the plug-in. However, the plug-in often works with small regions.
4. Alternatively, you can LMB-drag a region box in the plug-in window viewer to manually identify a noise pattern region. The box appears yellow (Figure 9.4). To create the noise profile at that point, click the Auto Profile button. With the creation of the profile, the Noise Filter Settings tab becomes available. Switch to that tab.

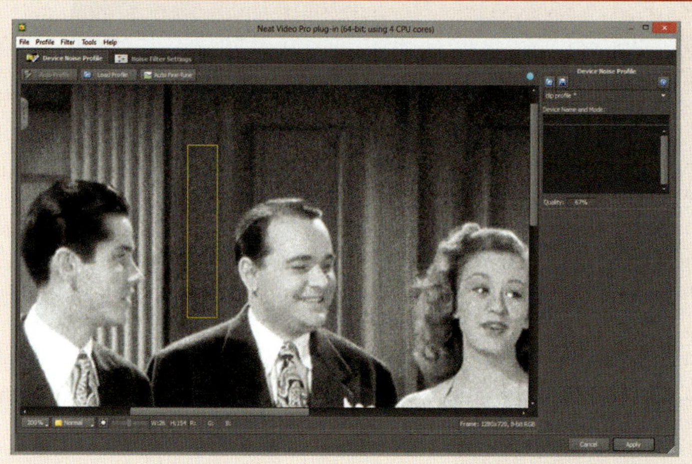

FIG 9.4 The Reduce Noise window with a noise region manually selected by placing the yellow box.

5. The Noise Filter Settings tab allows you to fine-tune the aggressiveness of the noise removal. To adjust the removal based on luminance (brightness), adjust the Luminance slider at the right. To adjust the removal based on color values, adjust the Chrominance slider. The result is visible in the plug-in window viewer. You can resharpen the edges within the frame by adjusting the Amount slider in the Sharpening section. This sharpen varies from the After Effects Remove Grain effect in that it doesn't use an unsharp filter, which tends to create heavy contrast around edge. Nonetheless, high Amount slider values may reveal compression block edges or create diagonal striations.
6. When you're satisfied with the results, click the Apply button at the bottom right. The window closes and the removal is applied to the timeline. For more information on the Neat Video Reduce Noise plug-in, visit www.neatvideo.com.

Adding Grain and Noise

To better match a particular piece of footage, it may be necessary to add noise or grain to a layer. For example, you may choose to add noise to a 3D render to better integrate it with live-action footage. There are two ways to approach this: add generic noise/grain or replicate noise/grain from a different layer.

To add a generic grain to a layer, you can apply the Add Grain effect (in the Effect > Noise & Grain menu). The effect is designed to replicate film grain, which tends to appear larger and more irregular than video noise. However, you can reduce the grain size to make the result more video-like. The effect includes the following properties and property sections:

Viewing Mode This menu allows you to preview a small area and functions in the same way as it does for the Remove Grain effect (Figure 9.5).

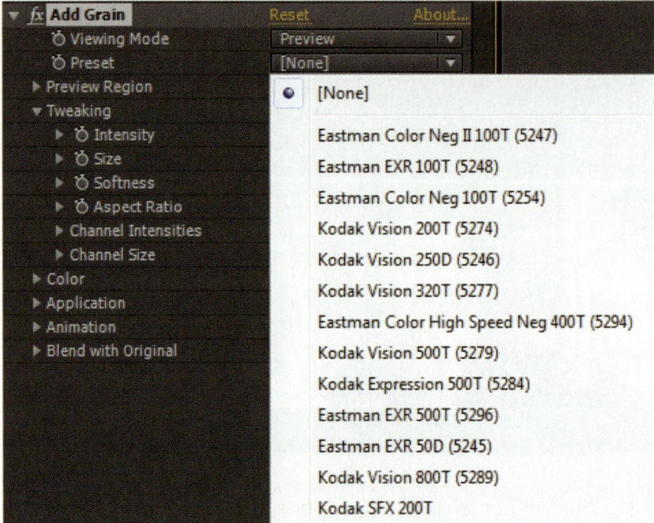

FIG 9.5 The Add Grain effect and its list of available Presets that emulate specific film stocks. Note that the effect shares many properties with the Remove Grain effect.

Preset This menu offers a number of presets that match specific motion picture film stocks. Although this menu is optional, it provides a quick way to create a wide range of looks.

Tweaking and Application These sections set the intensity (brightness), grain size, grain softness, and contrast between the shadows, midtone, and highlight regions.

Color This section allows you to create monochromatic (grayscale) grains or tint them with a single color. Older film and video technologies that produce black-and-white images create monochromatic noise and grain while newer color technologies create color noise and grain.

Animation By default, grain created with the Add Grain effect is pre-animated. You can slow down the rate of the grain change by lowering the Animation Speed property in this section.

In addition, the Noise, Noise Alpha, Noise HLS, and Noise HLS Auto effects create one-pixel-size brightness variations within a layer. These are designed to re-create video noise and video static. With Noise and Noise Alpha, the noise intensity is set by the Amount Of Noise and Amount properties, respectively. Noise Alpha varies from Noise in that it places the variations in the alpha channel, but not the RGB channels. While the Noise effect automatically randomizes the noise pattern, creating static-like animation, you must manually animate the Noise Alpha effect's Random Seed property to create a similar look.

Noise HLS allows you to insert noise into a particular channel of HLS color space. For example, you can insert noise into the S (Saturation) channel to randomly vary the saturation between pixels. Noise HLS Auto automatically varies the noise with each frame. With Noise HLS, you must animate the Noise Phase property to create similar variation over time. Noise HLS and Noise HLS Auto allow you to create film-like grain by switching the Noise menu to Grain and adjusting the Grain Size property. You can also switch the menu to Squared to create a noise distribution that is slightly sparser than the default Uniform noise.

Using Perlin Noise

The Noise & Grain menu provides two effects that are not intended to create a specific noise or grain: Fractal Noise and Turbulent Noise. These effects create a procedural noise pattern based on Perlin noise techniques, which generate a pattern through a random number algorithm (Figure 9.6).

FIG 9.6 Noise pattern created with the Fractal Noise effect when applied to a solid layer.

Noise created by Fractal Noise and Turbulent Noise is not generally used as is, but is combined with other effects. For example, if you apply the Fractal Noise effect to a solid layer, blur the result, and combine it with a lower layer through the Screen blending mode, you can create the illusion of smoke or fog (Figure 9.7).

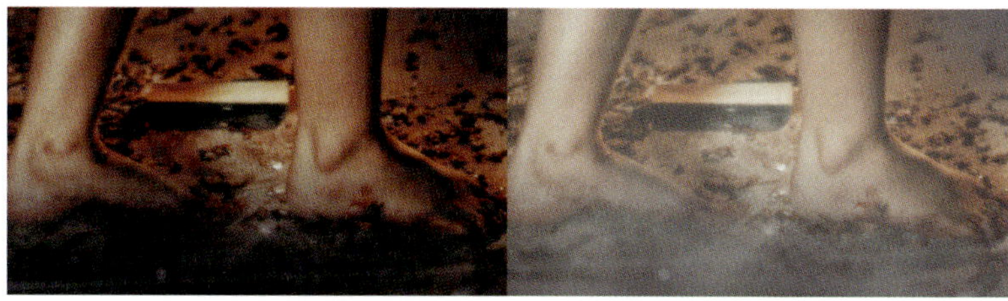

FIG 9.7 Left: Original footage. Right: Fog added by adjusting a Fractal Noise effect. A project file is included as *fractal_fog.aep* in the *\ProjectFiles\aeFiles\Chapter9* tutorial directory.

Fractal Noise and Turbulent Noise effects carry an identical list of properties. By default, Turbulent Noise creates a softer noise pattern. Critical properties for both effects are discussed here:

Scale The Scale property, in the Transform section, affects the size of the noise "grains." Larger Scale values create the illusion that the camera is zooming in to the noise field.

Complexity This slider determines how many different noise patterns are combined to create a more complex pattern. Each pattern that is added is at a different scale, which allows the combination of small and large detail. If Complexity is set to 1.0, the pattern appears smooth. The higher the Complexity value, the more ragged the light and dark edges of the noise grains.

Evolution By default, the noise pattern is static. However, animating the Evolution rotation over time causes the pattern to shift. This creates the illusion that the camera is flying though three-dimensional noise or that different "slices" of a three-dimensional noise are sampled with each frame. If you prefer that the noise simply drifts in one direction, make the noise layer larger than the composition layer and animate its Position X or Position Y over time.

Fractal Type and Noise Type You can create different styles of noise by altering these menus. For example, to create pixelated noise, change the Noise Type menu to Block.

Note that Turbulent Displace, found in the Effect > Distort menu, uses a hidden fractal noise pattern to distort a layer. Hence, it shares many of its attributes with Fractal Noise. The Turbulent Displace effect is discussed in the section "Overview of Distortion Effects" later in this chapter.

Adding Other Film and Video Artifacts

In addition to grain and noise, motion picture film and video suffer from various artifacts discussed in this section. After Effects provides numerous tools and effects which you can use to emulate the artifacts.

Scratches, Dirt, Debris, and Dropout

Motion picture film stock suffers from scratches as positive prints are run through projectors. Alternatively, film negatives may be scratched during processing. Film stocks may also pick up dirt and debris, such as hairs, through extensive handing. Scratches and debris on positive prints appear dark as they block the projector light or interfere with the digital scanning process (left side of Figure 9.8). Scratches and debris that attach itself to a negative appear white as they interfere with processing.

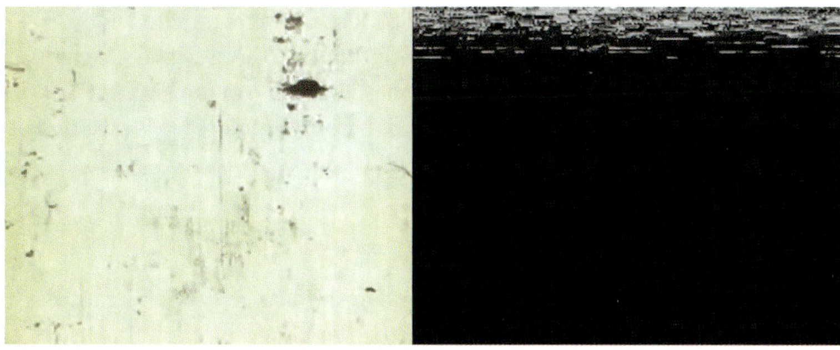

FIG 9.8 Left: Vertical scratches and dirt on a positive film print with an overexposed background. Right: Dropout on analog video, as seen against black.

Although analog videotape doesn't suffer from scratches or display specific pieces of debris, it may be affected by *dropout*. Dropout occurs when magnetic data is missing through damage or wear to the tape. Dropout creates white lines, horizontal distortions, and associated static (right side of Figure 9.8).

An efficient way to create the look of scratches, dirt, debris, and dropout is to blend scanned motion picture footage or captured video footage with a layer that requires the artifacts. For example, in Figure 9.9 motion picture footage of a white, overexposed background is combined with a nondamaged layer. The motion picture footage is placed on top and its layer-blending mode is set to Multiply.

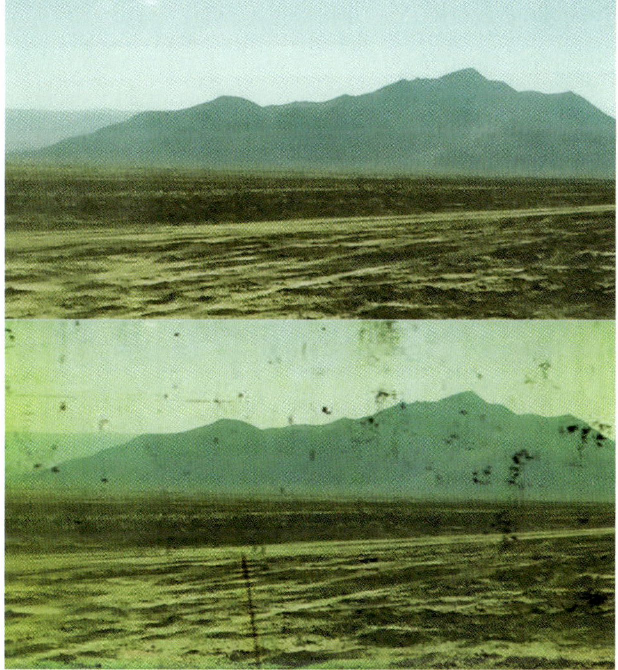

FIG 9.9 Top: Video layer with no damage. Bottom: Dirt and discoloration added with the Multiply blending mode.

Stock footage providers generally offer clips that contain scratched and dirtied film, video static, or blank video with dropout. The scratched footage featured in Figure 9.9 is included as *ScratchesDirt.##.png* in the *\ProjectFiles\Plates\NoiseGrainScracthes\ScratchesDirt* directory. A project file is included as *dirt.aep* in the *\ProjectFiles\aeFiles\Chapter9* tutorial directory.

Film Weave

As motion picture film prints age, they tend to shrink unevenly. This causes the film prints to weave back and forth as the print is fed through the projector. You can re-create this left-right motion by animating the Position X of a layer (Figure 9.10). To avoid seeing empty edges on the frame left and right side, the layer must be scaled larger than the current composition. Although scaling over 100 percent may lead to degradation of the layer, a small-scale increase, such as 102 percent, is generally acceptable. You can also nest a larger-resolution composition into a smaller-resolution composition to create a similar overhang. For more information on nesting, see Chapter 4.

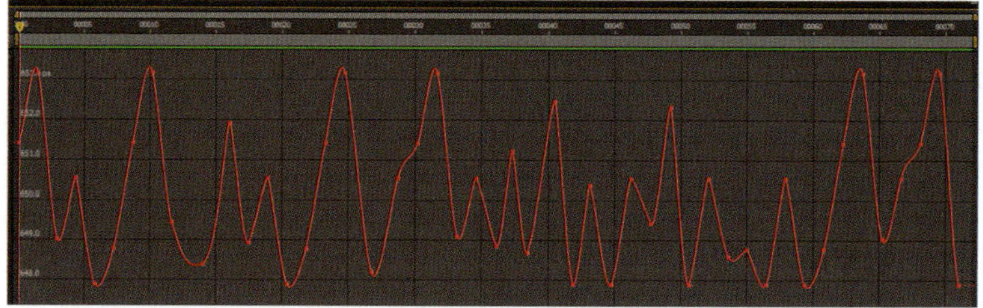

FIG 9.10 Film weave is simulated by creating semirandom left-right motion for a layer. The layer's X Position curve, as seen in the Graph Editor, moves the layer between 0 and 3 pixels with each frame. A sample project file is included as *film_weave.aep* in the *\ProjectFiles\aeFiles\Chapter9* tutorial directory.

Halation, Glow, Glint, and Glare

Halation is the spreading of light around bright areas of an image. This often results from light bouncing off substrates of motion picture film and photographic film stock. In contrast, *glow* occurs when light bounces off participating media in the air, such as fog, haze, smoke, water vapor, and so on (Figure 9.11).

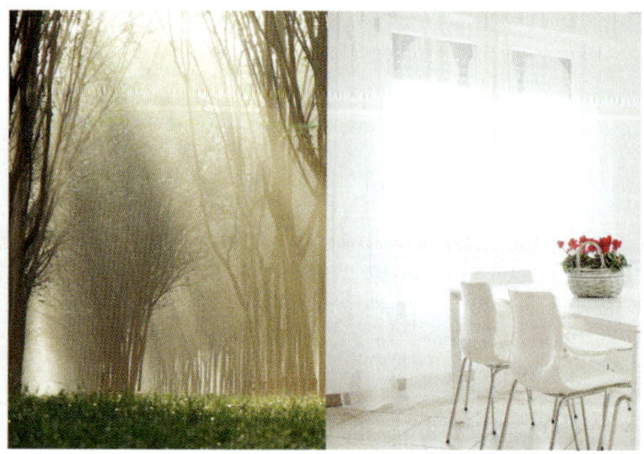

FIG 9.11 Left: Glow created by participating media in the form of haze. Right: Glare from a window erodes the window frame and nearby walls. *Left photo © Ping Phuket/Dollar Photo Club. Right photo © Lulu/Dollar Photo Club.*

Glints and *glares* occur when a bright subject, such as a bright lamp or the reflection of the sun off glass, overexposes the immediate area around the subject (Figure 9.10). Glint varies from glare in that glints come and go in brief flashes. For example, the sun may glint off rippling water.

After Effects provides the Glow effect to create halation, glow, and glare (this is found in the Effect > Stylize menu). To adjust the Glow effect, follow these basic steps:

1. Reduce the Glow Threshold to determine what part of the frame glows (Figure 9.12). Pixels with values above the Glow Threshold are included in the glow.

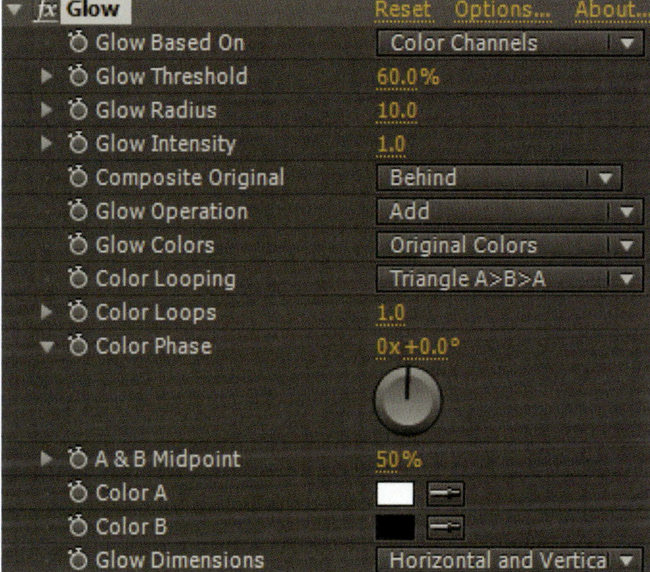

FIG 9.12 Glow effect properties.

2. Adjust the glow brightness by altering Glow Intensity. Alter the softness of the halation and its spread by adjusting the Glow Radius property (Figure 9.13).

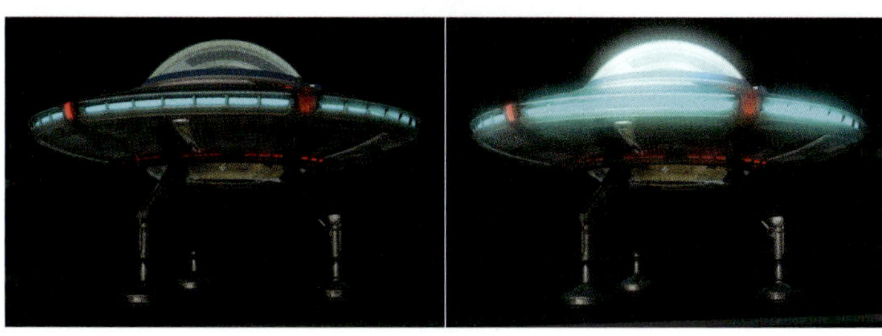

FIG 9.13 Left: Unaltered layer. Right: Halation created with the Glow effect. This project is included as *glow.aep* in the *\ProjectFiles\aeFiles\Chapter9* tutorial directory.

3. By default, the glow colors are based on the original pixels. However, you can select your own colors by switching the Glow Colors menu to A & B Colors and changing the Color A and Color B color swatches.

Note that the glow may extend past the alpha matte edge. Depending on the colors that are used to create the glow, this may create an edge glow that is darker than the colors in lower layers. As an alternative to the Glow effect, you can create your own custom glow with these steps:

1. Duplicate the layer that requires the glow. Select the higher of the two identical layers and apply one or more color effects, such as Brightness & Contrast or Curves, and a blur effect, such as Gaussian Blur or Fast Blur.
2. Use the color effect to make the higher layer significantly brighter. Use the blur effect to blur the higher layer (Figure 9.14).

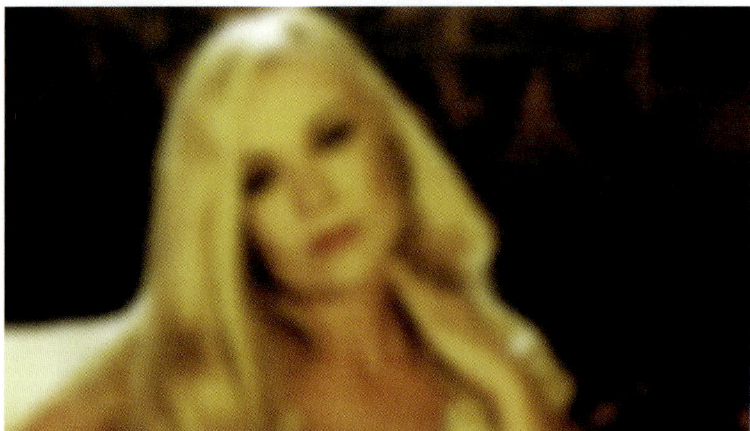

FIG 9.14 A blurred, brightened duplicate of a layer is the first component of a custom glow effect.

3. Switch the higher layer's blending mode to Screen. This allows the bright areas of the layer to show over the original layer. The glow is created (Figure 9.15). If the glow is too intense, reduce the Opacity value of the higher layer.

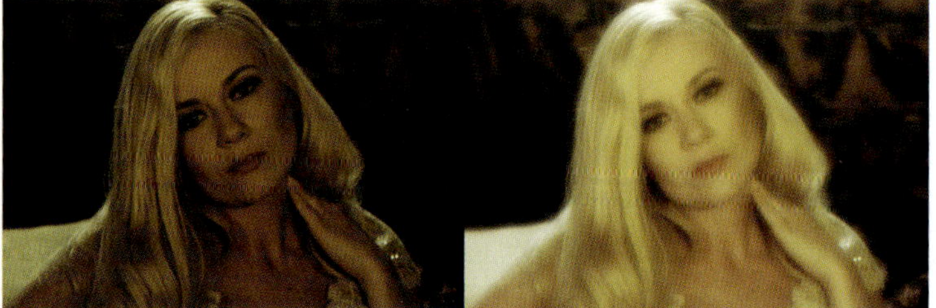

FIG 9.15 Left: An unaltered layer that requires glow. Right: The resulting custom glow after a duplicate layer is blurred, brightened, and combined with the Screen blending mode. This project is included as *glow_custom.aep* in the *\ProjectFiles\aeFiles\Chapter9* tutorial directory.

Lens Flares

When light bounces through the internal mechanism of a lens, it may create a lens flare. Although this phenomenon is related to halation, lens flares often take on specific shapes that relate to the specific lens. For example, common prime lenses, such as 35mm, create the typical chain of hexagonal spots (the hexagonal shape is the shape of the camera aperture). Anamorphic Cinemascope lenses, on the other hand, form horizontal streaks. After Effects provides the Lens Flare effect (Effect > Generate) to create hexagonal- or circular-style flares (Figure 9.16). With this effect, you can choose between three lens types, the flare brightness, and flare origin within the frame. Other plug-ins, such as Video Copilot Optical Flares, Boris FX Lens Flare 3D, and Sapphire LensFlare, offer additional options to create more realistic custom flares.

Color Fading and Shifting

When motion picture film or analog videotapes age, they often degrade. This may cause the original colors to shift. For example, certain motion picture print stocks tend to lose contrast and become more red with age. You can re-create fading and color shifting through color grading techniques, which are detailed in Chapter 8.

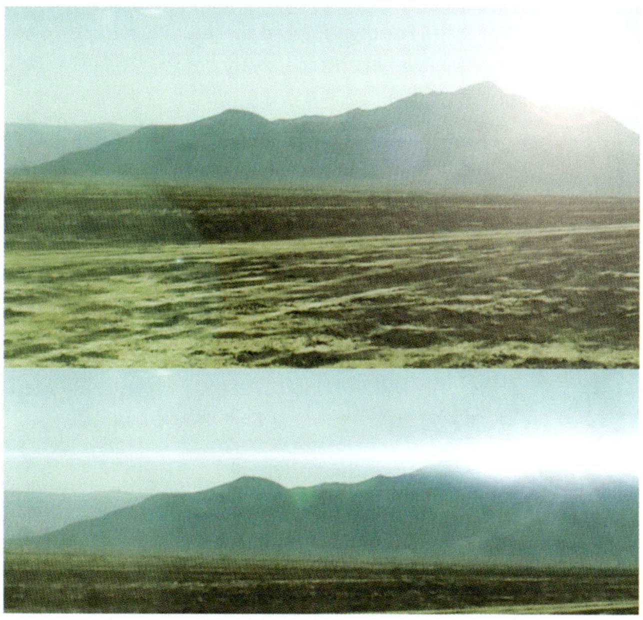

FIG 9.16 Top: Flare created with the After Effects Lens Flare effect. Bottom: Cinemascope-style flare created with Boris FX Lens Flare 3D.

Deprecated Technology

Older forms of motion picture film, analog video, and digital video captured their images through different mechanical, chemical, magnetic, optical, and/or digital processes. As such, each form of film and video capture technology utilized a different color space. For example, the colors in a Technicolor film print appear significantly different from a Kodak Safety film print—even if the same subject with the same lighting was recorded. Along those lines, analog videotape may appear different than 8-bit digital video and both formats may appear dissimilar to 10-bit digital video. Hence, it may be necessary to replicate the color space of a specific capture technology. This becomes a challenge when the technology is no longer used. For an example of this challenge, see the tutorial at the end of the chapter.

A Note on Median Filters

Several effects in After Effects employ median filters and can be used to reduce noise, grain, and small, pixel-sized elements, such as dust, dirt, and short scratches. The effects may also be useful for creating stylized results. For example, the Median effect (in the Effect > Noise & Grain menu), averages pixel values through a convolution filter. The averaged values are halfway between the highest and lowest values within the convolution filter sample area (essentially a small window that slides over the image). This results in a softening of the image, which tends to remove small variations in pixel values. The effect includes a Radius property, which determines the pixel size of the convolution filter. Large property values cause heavy averaging, thus creating a painterly look (Figure 9.17). For the effect to successfully reduce noise or grain without affecting the layer in an excessively detrimental way, the source footage must be high resolution.

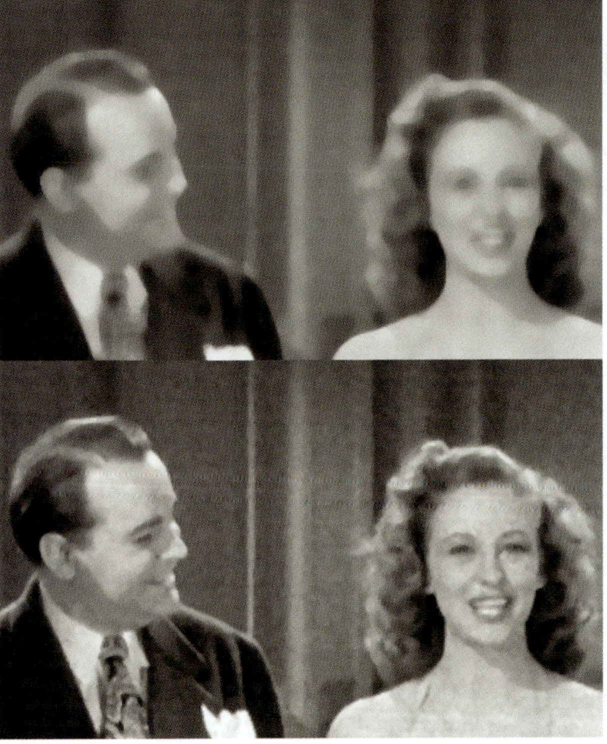

FIG 9.17 Top: Grainy footage with a Medium Radius set to 5. Bottom: Same footage with Radius set to 1.0. This project is included as *median.aep* in the *\ProjectFiles\aeFiles\Chapter9* tutorial directory.

The Dust & Scratches effect (Effect > Noise & Grain) also applies a median filter in an attempt to reduce noise and grain. However, the effect includes a Threshold property, which sets the degree of contrast between sampled pixels required to average an area within the convolution filter window. This sensitivity allows the effect to maintain sharper edges on shapes within the image.

Using Paint Tools

After Effects includes a set of paint tools that allow you to paint strokes on a layer (see Figure 9.20 later in this chapter). Each stroke is based on a specialized spline. You can create solid-colored strokes or clone color values from the current layer or a different layer. You can use the strokes to create motion graphic shapes, such as text, or use the strokes as part of a *paint fix*. Paint fixes remove unwanted elements from an image or otherwise "repair" problematic footage.

Creating a Basic Paint Stroke

To create a paint stroke on a layer, follow these steps:

1. Switch to the Layer view by double-clicking a layer. A stroke must be attached to a particular layer. The Layer view is distinguished from the Composition view in that it carries an embedded timeline and playback controls.
2. Click the Brush tool button in the top program toolbar (Figure 9.18). LMB-drag a stroke in the viewer. Release the mouse button to end the stroke. A colored line is drawn along the stroke. The spline defining the line is hidden initially.

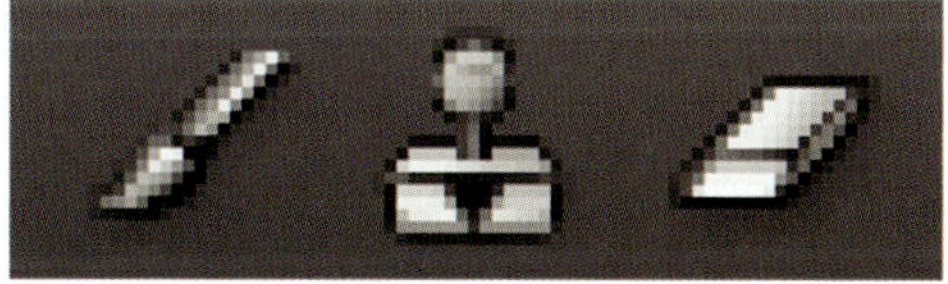

FIG 9.18 The Brush, Clone Stamp, and Eraser tool buttons, found in the top program toolbar.

3. To create another stroke, repeat step 2. Before drawing a stroke, you can alter the stroke's basic properties through the Paint panel at the bottom right of the program window (see Figure 9.21 later in this chapter). If the panel is not visible, choose Window > Paint. The properties include color and opacity. Note that the color of the resulting line is set by the Set Foreground Color swatch (the top left swatch box).

Each stroke you draw is added as Brush *n* to the Effects > Paint subsection of the layer.

Editing a Stroke's Color, Opacity, and Softness

Properties set by the Paint panel appear in the Effects > Paint > Brush *n* > Stroke Options subsection of the layer and may be changed after the stroke is drawn. The properties include Color, Opacity, and Diameter, which sets the line width (Figure 9.19).

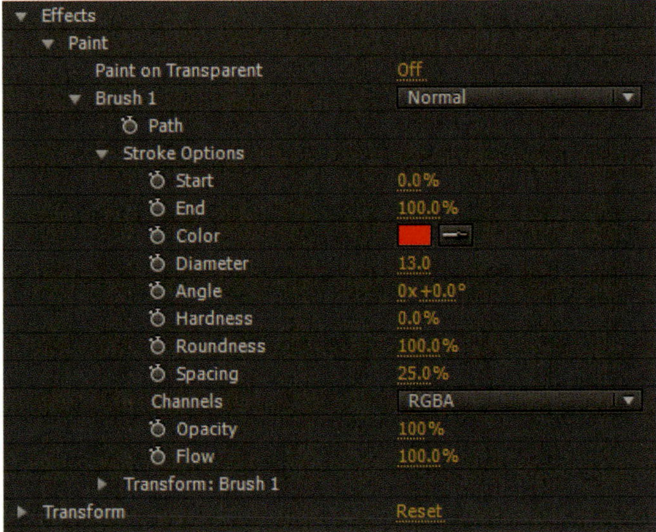

FIG 9.19 The Stroke Options subsection of a Paint tool stroke, as seen in the layer outline.

In addition, you can find these unique properties:

Start and End By default, the colored line runs the entire length of the stroke you interactively draw with the Brush tool. However, you can raise the Start value so that the colored line starts later. Conversely, you can lower the End value so that the line ends sooner. You can animate Start and End over time so that it appears as if the line is drawn as the timeline moves forward. This creates the illusion of handwriting and may be useful for animated motion graphics.

Hardness and Flow Hardness controls the line softness, with higher values making the line hard-edged. Flow sets the opacity of individual shapes used to create the stroke line. Flow values lower than 100 percent cause the line to appear softer—even when Hardness is set to 100 percent.

Spacing, Roundness, and Angle A line created by a stroke is actually a series of overlapping shapes. If you raise the Spacing value, the shapes are spread out over the stroke with larger gaps. When the Roundness property is set to 100 percent, the shapes are circles. When you lower the Roundness, the shapes become more oval-like. If you lower the Roundness and Spacing to 0 percent, the line varies in width in a fashion similar to a line drawn by a calligraphy pen. You can alter the areas of the line that becomes thin and flattened out by adjusting the Angle property.

Blending Mode By default, a stroke created with the Brush or Clone tool is combined with its layer through the Normal blending mode. However, you can change the blending mode menu, beside the Brush *n* name in the layer outline, to any other mode.

Transforming and Erasing a Stroke

Each stroke added to a layer carries an Effect > Brush *n* > Transform subsection. The transform properties are similar to a standard layer and include Anchor Point, Position, Scale, and Rotation. You can animate these properties.

The Anchor Point of a stroke is located at the start of the stroke. However, the stroke itself, which is the specialized spline, is only visible if you select the Brush *n* section name in the layer outline (Figure 9.20). You can interactively move the stroke in the viewer by returning to the Selection tool and LMB-dragging the stroke spline or its Anchor Point. To delete a stroke, select it in the layer outline and press the Delete key. You can add as many strokes as you like to a single layer by returning to the Brush tool.

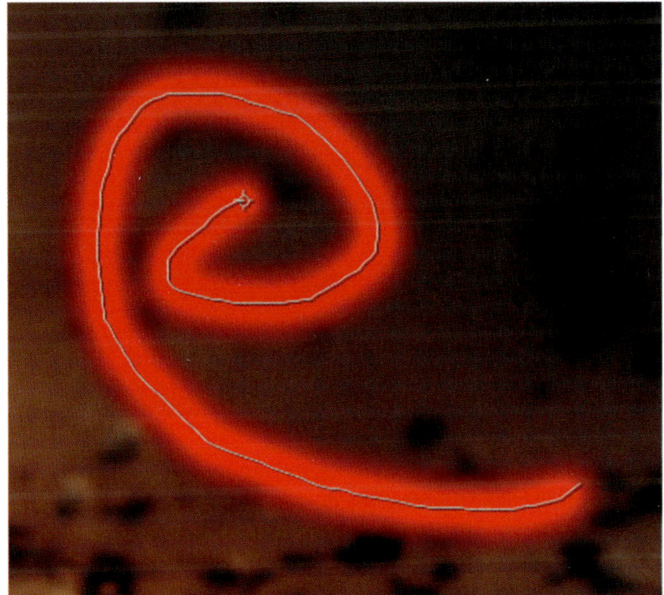

FIG 9.20 A selected stroke reveals its associated spline, which is colored white.

By default, a stroke exists for the entire duration of the timeline. However, you can alter this behavior by changing the Duration menu in the Paint panel before drawing the stroke (Figure 9.21). If you set Duration to Single Frame, the drawn stroke exists on the timeline for one frame. If you set Duration to Custom, you can choose a duration through the frame field directly to the right of the menu. If you set Mode to Write On, the program animates the End property so that the colored line is revealed over time (see the previous section). Returning Duration to Constant ensures that the stroke starts on the frame it was painted and continues to the end of the timeline. You are free to alter the duration of any drawn stroke by LMB-dragging the end of the stroke's duration bar in the timeline panel.

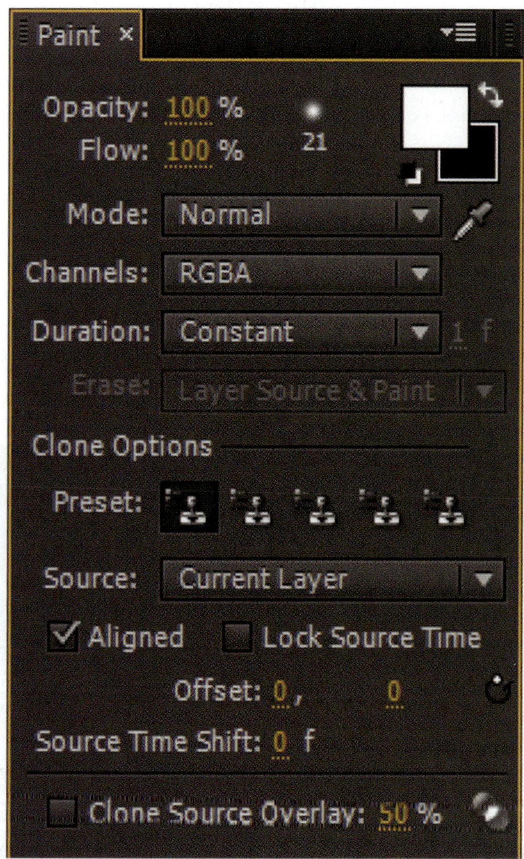

FIG 9.21 The Paint panel.

If you create a stroke with the Eraser tool, the resulting stroke cuts a hole through any other stroke that crosses its path. In addition, the eraser stroke cuts a hole into the current layer. When you switch back to the Composition view, the hole reveals lower layers. Thus, the Eraser tool offers a means to remove parts of a frame that may otherwise be cut out through a masking/

rotoscoping process. An eraser stroke receives an Eraser *n* subsection on the layer and carries the same properties as a stroke created with the Brush tool.

Using the Clone Stamp Tool

The Clone Stamp tool allows you to sample one area of the frame and paint it as a stroke in a different area. This is ideal for making paint fixes and similar repairs to footage. To apply the tool, follow these steps:

1. Switch to the Layer view by double-clicking a layer. A stroke must be attached to a particular layer.
2. Click the Clone Stamp tool in the program toolbar (Figure 9.18 earlier in this chapter). Place the mouse over an area you wish to clone and press the Alt/Opt key. Move the mouse to the area you wish to paint the stroke and LMB-drag to create a stroke. Release the mouse button to end the stroke. Note that the Clone Stamp tool clones any other stroke that may exist on the layer.

A Clone *n* subsection is added to the layer when a Clone Stamp stroke is drawn. The included properties are identical to a Brush tool stroke with the addition of several *Clone* properties. By default, the Clone Source menu is set to the current layer. However, you can switch this menu to a different layer. This may be useful when sampling a clean plate or footage that doesn't include the artifact or element you're trying to paint over. (A *clean plate* is a variation of a shot that removes actors and props in favor of an empty set.) The Clone Position property indicates the XY position where you press the Alt/Opt key to establish the clone source origin for the stroke. Clone Time Shift allows you to offset the frame that's used for the clone source. This is useful when painting over dust, scratches, and other debris that may appear briefly within the frame. For a demonstration of dust removal, see the mini-tutorial at the end of this section.

The Paint panel provides readout options to refine the application of the Clone Stamp tool. The Offset X and Y fields display the distance from the cloned point to the point where you begin the current stroke. The Aligned check box, when selected, offsets each painted stroke so each stroke stays relative to the last point sampled. This allows you to cover a large area without having to resample with each stroke. If Aligned is deselected, each stroke uses the same sampled point and no offsetting occurs. In general, the Aligned option is desirable when creating paint fixes to cover up or remove unwanted elements.

The Preset buttons, on the other hand, memorize the current Clone Stamp settings when a Preset button is clicked. You can switch between any of the Preset buttons at any time. The buttons provide an efficient means to jump between settings when creating extensive paint fixes. In addition, the Paint panel includes a Source menu and Source Time Shift property that allows you to set their namesakes before drawing the stroke. Additional brush options are included in the Brushes panel and are discussed in the following tutorial.

Removing film damage mini-tutorial

The Clone Stamp tool provides a means to interactively remove dust, scratches, and similar damage from footage. For example, as seen in Figure 9.1 at the start of this chapter, a digital transfer of amateur motion picture film reveals such damage. To apply the Clone Brush tool to this footage, follow these steps:

1. Create a new project. Import *Title.##.png* in the *\ProjectFiles\Plates\NoiseGrainScracthes\Title* directory. Interpret the image sequence so that it is read at 24 fps. Place the image sequence into a new composition that is 960x720 resolution, 24 fps, and 32 frames in duration.
2. Play back the timeline and examine individual frames. Many pieces of dust appear for a single frame (Figure 9.22). Scratches appear longer and constantly shift. Double-click the layer so that it opens in the Layer view. Return to frame 1. Play forward, one frame at a time, until you identify a distinct black spot created by dust. For example, on frame 15, a black spot appears in the sky.

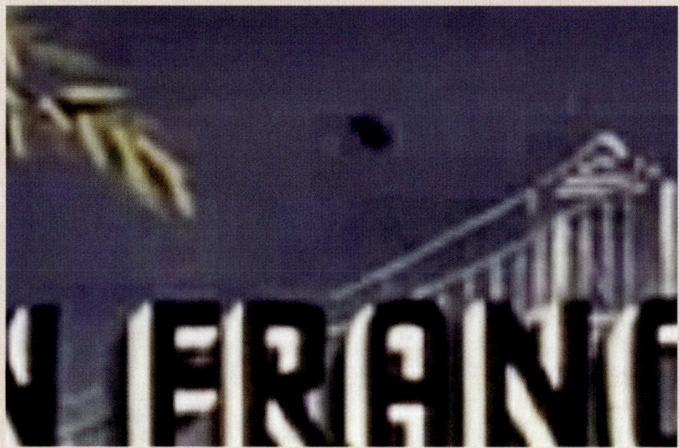

FIG 9.22 A piece of dust appears like a black dot in the sky. Also note the appearance of compression blocks beside the dust and the building. The blocks were created by the digital compression when the film footage was transferred.

3. While the layer is visible in the Layer view, select the Clone Stamp tool from the main toolbar. Adjust the size of the brush by using the Brushes panel (Window > Brushes). You can choose a preset brush from the top of the panel or select a particular Diameter value. If you're using a stylus to paint, you can set stylus-specific traits such as angle and roundness. You can reduce the softness of the brush edge by raising the Hardness value. For this tutorial, make the brush soft-edged and slightly larger than the dust spot.
4. In the Paint panel (Window > Paint), set Duration to Single Frame. In the Layer view, place the mouse to the left of the dust spot (to the right of the tree and over the blue sky). Press Alt/Opt and the left mouse button to sample that area of the frame. LMB-drag over the

dust spot to create a short stroke. The Clone Stamp color, sampled from the sky, covers the spot. Optionally, you can make the stroke long enough to cover up the compression blocks to the left of the spot.

5. Expand the Effects > Paint section of the layer in the layer outline. The stroke is listed as Clone 1. Select the Clone 1 name. The stroke spline is revealed in the viewer (Figure 9.23). Note that the footage bar beside Clone 1 in the timeline has a one-frame duration.

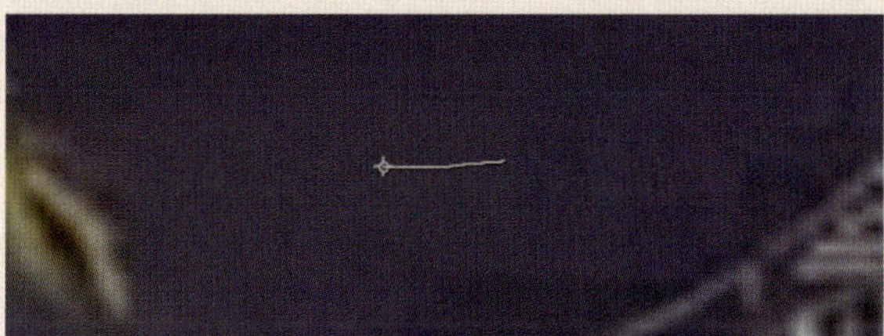

FIG 9.23 A Clone Stamp stroke covers the dust spot for one frame.

6. Step forward one frame at a time and identify a new piece of dust. Repeat steps 3 and 4 to remove the dust. (If the prior Clone stroke is selected in the layer outline, the old stroke is updated with the new one.) Continue this process, repairing as many spots as possible. Some frames include slightly larger patches of dirt. In such a situation, you can create a large brush or, alternatively, paint multiple corrective strokes on the same frame. Some dirt and dust may last two or three frames due to the nature of the film transfer. As such, you are free to LMB-drag the ends of the stroke duration bars to make the strokes last additional frames (Figure 9.24).

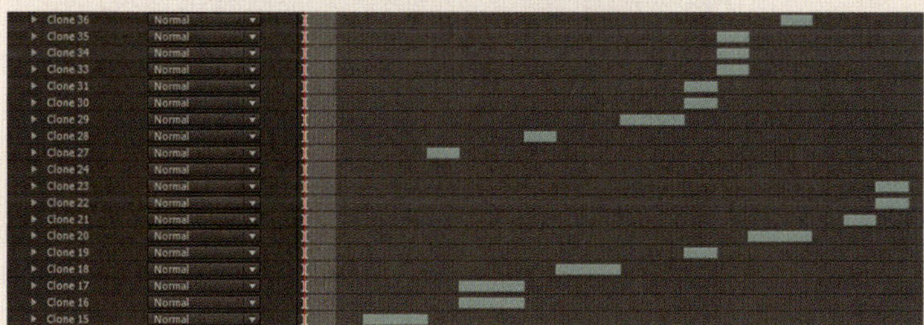

FIG 9.24 Multiple Clone Stamp strokes are painted on a layer. Their durations are adjusted to last one or two frames.

Some areas of the footage are heavily dirtied or stained. For example, frames 20 through 22 reveal dirt spots along the top and bottom left of the footage. There are several approaches you can take to repairing these areas:

- If a problem area is only affected by dirt for a few frames, you can sample pixels from an earlier or later frame on the timeline that might be dirt-free. To do so, change the Source Time Shift property in the Paint panel. For example, if you change the property to –1, the pixels are taken from the previous frame. This allows you to take a sample directly over the dirtied area when Alt/Opt + LMB-clicking. Note that the Source Time

Shift property resets itself to 0 after each stroke is painted. To use this option more efficiently, I recommend Alt/Opt+LMB-clicking to sample the frame, changing the Source Time Shift value, and then LMB-clicking to draw a stroke. To preview the source layer with an offset time, you can raise the Clone Source Overlay value to 100 percent. This displays the source while your mouse hovers over the Layer view. The Clone Source Overlay property is located at the bottom of the Paint panel.

- Alternatively, you can use the Eraser tool to cut out the dirtied area and reveal a lower, clean layer. For example, place another copy of the footage on a lower layer, offset the new, lower layer so that it starts a few frames sooner, and use the Eraser tool to cut holes in the old, upper layer (Figure 9.25). When you return to the Composition view, the lower layer shows through the holes. An example file that uses

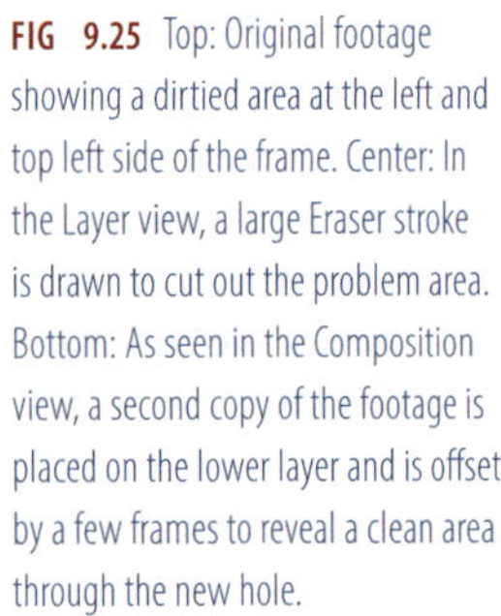

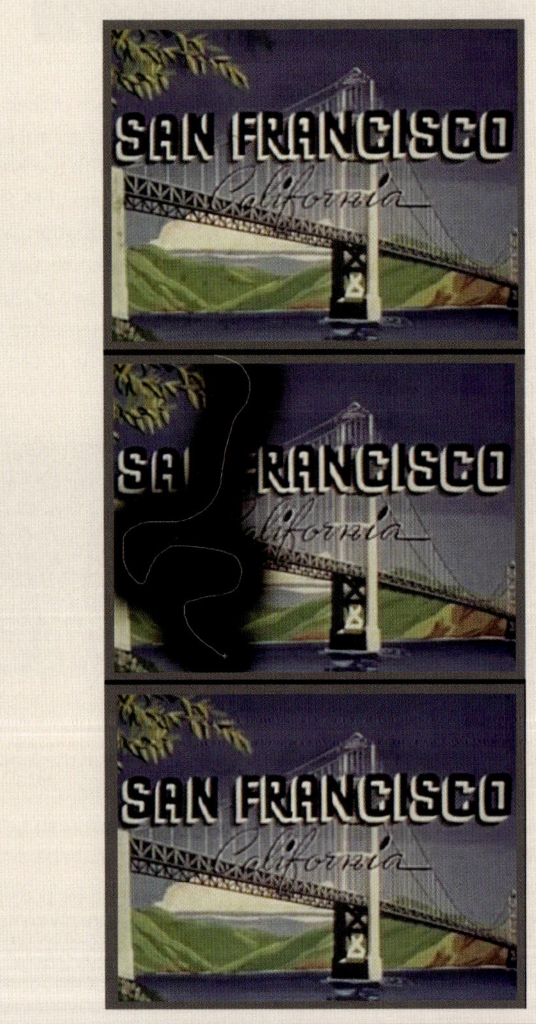

FIG 9.25 Top: Original footage showing a dirtied area at the left and top left side of the frame. Center: In the Layer view, a large Eraser stroke is drawn to cut out the problem area. Bottom: As seen in the Composition view, a second copy of the footage is placed on the lower layer and is offset by a few frames to reveal a clean area through the new hole.

this technique is included as *mini_clone_stamp.aep* in the *\ProjectFiles\aeFiles\Chapter9* tutorial directory.

Note that these two techniques only work if the camera is not moving. Nevertheless, you can apply either of these techniques when removing scratches from a static shot. For an example of this, see Figure 9.1 at the start of this chapter. Keep in mind that the paint fix repairs may never be perfect; however, you can significantly reduce the appearance of dust, dirt, scratches, and other unwanted elements (such as those discussed in the section "Adding Other Film and Video Artifacts" earlier in this chapter).

The film footage in this section is taken from *Amateur film: Summers collection: San Francisco, California, 1941 (Part I)*, which is part of the Prelinger Archives, made available via a Creative Commons Public Domain license. For more information, visit www.archive.org/details/prelinger.

Overview of Distortion Effects

After Effects includes a long list of distortion effects with the Effect > Distort menu designed to alter pixel positions within a layer. Although these effects are not strictly designed to replicate film and video artifacts, they can replicate some unique phenomena captured by film and video cameras. Here are a few examples of their application.

Turbulent Displace

This effect displaces a layer based on the intensity values of a built-in fractal noise pattern. The distortion may be useful for replicating undulating substances or surfaces, such as the swelling of water, the movement of fabric in wind, or the optical distortions to air caused by heat rising off the ground. For example, you can create heat wave distortions by applying the effect to a semi-opaque copy of a layer (Figure 9.26).

The built-in noise of the effect is controlled by properties similar to those carried by the Fractal Noise and Turbulent Noise effects (see the "Using Perlin Noise" section earlier in this chapter). The strength of the displacement is set by the Amount property. The size of the noise "grains" is set by the Size property. By default, the noise and displacement is static. However, you can animate the Evolution property increasing over time to create the undulation.

Optics Compensation

This effect mimics the spherical edge distortions created by some lenses. You can use this effect to match undistorted layers to footage that carries the lens distortion. The Field Of View (FOV) property controls the degree of distortion,

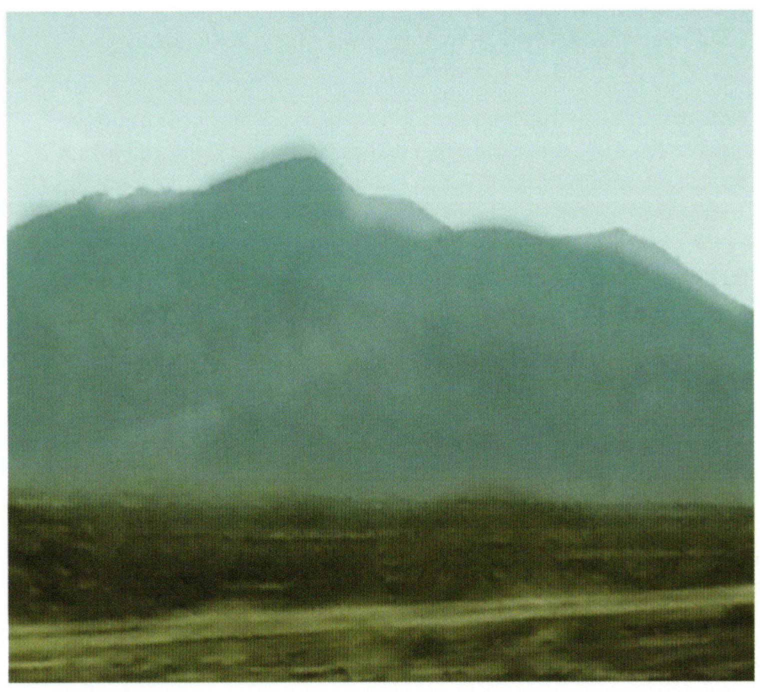

FIG 9.26 Close-up of a heat wave effect created by placing a semi-opaque copy of a layer at the top of the layer outline with the Turbulent Displace and Fast Blur effects. This project is included as *heat_displace.aep* in the *\ProjectFiles\aeFiles\Chapter9* tutorial directory.

with higher values pulling the outer edges inwards. If you select the Reverse Lens Distortion check box, the distortion becomes concave and the edges are pushed outwards (Figure 9.27). You can use the effect with a high Field Of View (FOV) value to stylistically create a "fish eye" lens or "tiny planet" effect. Note that you may need to nest the resulting layer due to the shrinking of the image and the appearance of empty black edges.

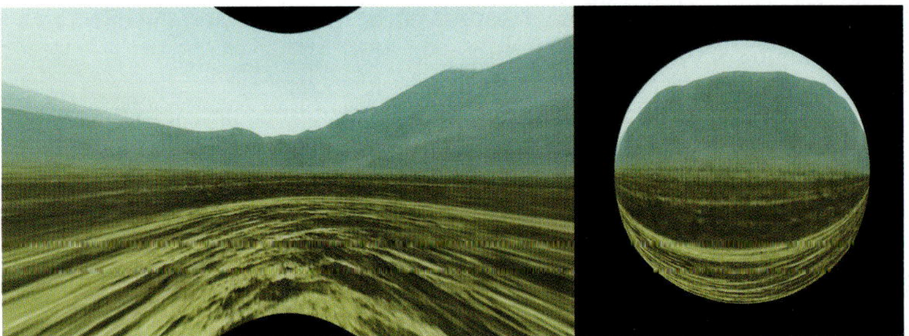

FIG 9.27 A landscape is distorted with the Optics Compensation effect. The Reverse Lens Distortion option causes concave distortion (left), while a high Field Of View (FOV) creates a "fish eye" effect (right). This project is included as *optics_compensation.aep* in the *\ProjectFiles\aeFiles\Chapter9* tutorial directory.

CC Lens

This effect creates a spherical, convex distortion. If the Size and Convergence properties are set to high values, the result is similar to a *light probe map*, a specialized spherical mapping created with High Dynamic Range (HDR) photographs intended for HDR lighting within a 3D program. (For more information on HDR, see Chapter 8.)

Several additional distortion effects provide a means to interactively "push" pixels. Although these are not intended to replicate particular real-world phenomena, they are often useful for common visual effects tasks. These are discussed briefly here.

Mesh Warp and Liquify

The Mesh Warp effect allows you to push pixels around by interactively LMB-dragging a grid overlay in the view panel. The Liquify effect also allows you to push pixels, but provides a wide range of brushes to complete the task. The brush tools are contained within the Effect Controls panel and include Push, Turbulence, Twirl, Pucker, and Bloat. Both of these effects allow you to animate the distortion over time (select the Distortion Mesh check box). Hence, they are suitable for warping an element within a frame. For example, you can use Liquify to bend the fender of a car to simulate the impact of a piece of debris thrown out by an explosion.

Detail Preserving Upscale

This effect provides a more accurate means to upscale (scale a layer over 100 percent). If you switch the Alpha property menu to Detail Preserving and raise the Detail property value, a large Scale value is able to preserve more edge detail than the standard bicubic upscale applied by the layer's Scale transform.

Rolling Shutter Repair

This effect reduces the presence of rolling shutter artifacts (diagonal distortions in moving objects caused by the vertical or horizontal scanning of a frame employed by some digital cameras).

In addition, the Wave Warp effect creates a sine-wave distortion. This is demonstrated in the following tutorial.

Chapter Tutorial: Emulating Low-Quality Video Footage

Sometimes, for stylistic reasons, it's desirable to *intentionally* degrade your work in After Effects. This might be necessary to match new elements to old motion picture or video footage or to make new footage look like it was shot in a different time period or with different equipment. For example, with this tutorial we can take high-quality HD video footage and make it look like it was shot with a standard-definition, black-and-white security camera. Follow these steps:

1. Create a new project. Import the *1_3a_2look.###.png* image sequence from the *\ProjectFiles\Plates\ColorGrading\1_3a_2look* directory. Create a new composition that's 1920x1080, 24 fps, and 48 frames in duration. LMB-drag the image sequence into the new composition.
2. With the new layer selected, add Hue/Saturation, Curves, and Brightness & Contrast effects. With the Hue/Saturation effect, reduce Master Saturation to –100 to convert the sequence to grayscale. With the Curves effect, add one point to the center of the curve and bow the curve center upwards to brighten the midtones and highlights. With the Brightness & Contrast effect, set Brightness to 125 and Contrast to 100. You can combine multiple color correction effects to create more extreme results. With this series of steps, the dynamic range of the image is intentionally reduced with some areas pushed to the maximum value of 255 (Figure 9.28). A limited dynamic range emulates poor-quality video cameras.

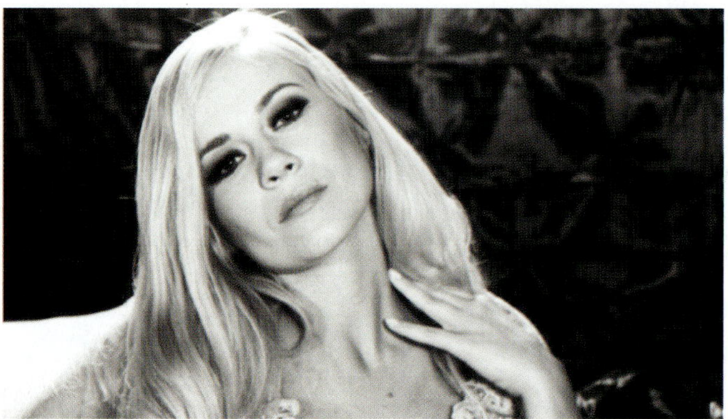

FIG 9.28 HD video footage desaturated and given increased brightness and contrast.

3. Add a Fast Blur effect. Set Blurriness to 3. Additional image softness emulates a low-quality lens or video sensor. With the layer selected, choose Edit > Duplicate. Select the new, upper layer and set the Blurriness of the Fast Blur effect to 30. Set the top layer's blending mode to Screen. Reduce the top layer's Opacity to 75 percent. This series of steps creates a halation-like glow over the old frame, another indication of a low-quality lens.
4. Create a new composition that is 640x480, 24 fps, with a 48-frame duration. 640x480 was the standard resolution of pre-digital, analog standard-definition television. Nest the first composition within the new composition. The first composition overhangs. Reduce the scale of the new layer to 50 percent and position the layer to center the actress (Figure 9.29).

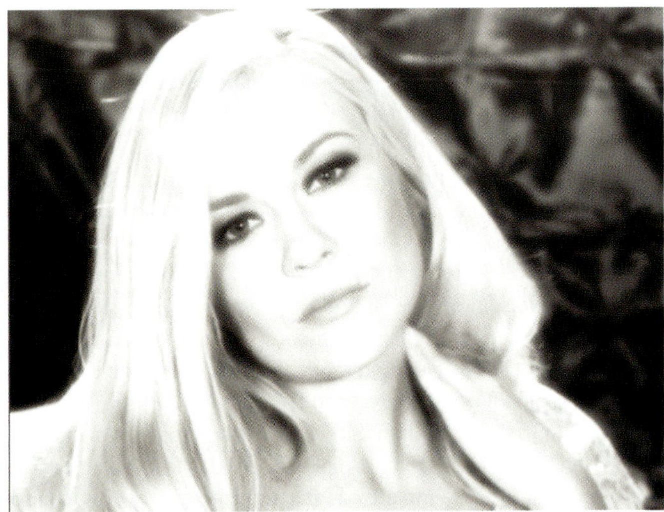

FIG 9.29 The first composition, which has a custom glow added to it, is nested in a second, smaller composition.

5. With the layer selected, choose Effect > Distort > Wave Warp. The effect distorts the layer with a sine-wave pattern. By default, the distortion is vertical, so that it looks like the image is melting. Change the Direction property to 0 degrees. The distortion becomes horizontal. Change Wave Width to 5. This narrows each wave peak and valley. The result is similar to analog video interlacing. Increase the Wave Height. The image is pulled apart to the left and right as if interlaced lines are separated (Figure 9.30).

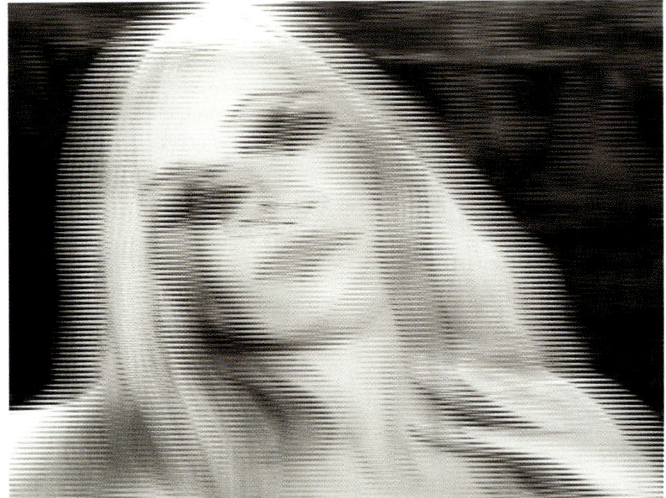

FIG 9.30 The result of the Wave Warp effect with Direction set to 0, Wave Width set to 5, and Wave Height set to 50.

6. Activate the Time icon for Wave Height and randomly animate its values changing over the timeline. Play back and adjust the animation. These steps re-create poor reception or other interference suffered by analog video systems. Add a Fast Blur effect to the layer and set Blurriness to 4. This softens the edges of the sine peaks and valleys.
7. Create a new solid, making it the same size as the composition. Set the solid to a medium gray color. Move the solid to the top of the layer outline. With the solid layer selected, choose Effect > Noise & Grain > Noise. Change the effect's Amount Of Noise property to 100 percent. Deselect the Use Color Noise property. Fine, grayscale noise appears over the solid and is pre-animated so it shifts over time.
8. Change the solid layer's blending mode to Screen. Animate the solid's Opacity, changing it from 5 percent to 50 percent over time. Match the animation to the animation of the Wave Height of the Wave Warp effect. When Wave Height is high, make the solid's Opacity high and vice versa. The result further emulates poor analog reception. Scale the solid layer up to 200 percent. This creates larger noise "grains." Play back. The footage shifts from moderate quality to low quality in a random fashion (Figure 9.31).

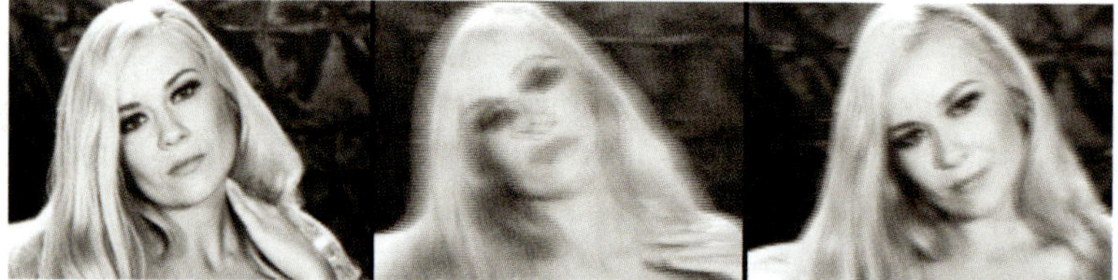

FIG 9.31 A Noise effect adds its namesake to a gray solid layer, which is screened over the footage of the actress. Animation of the Wave Warp effect's Wave Height and the Opacity of the solid layer creates a shifting quality.

A finished version of this project is saved as *low_quality_video.aep* in the *\ProjectFiles\aeFiles\Chapter9* directory.

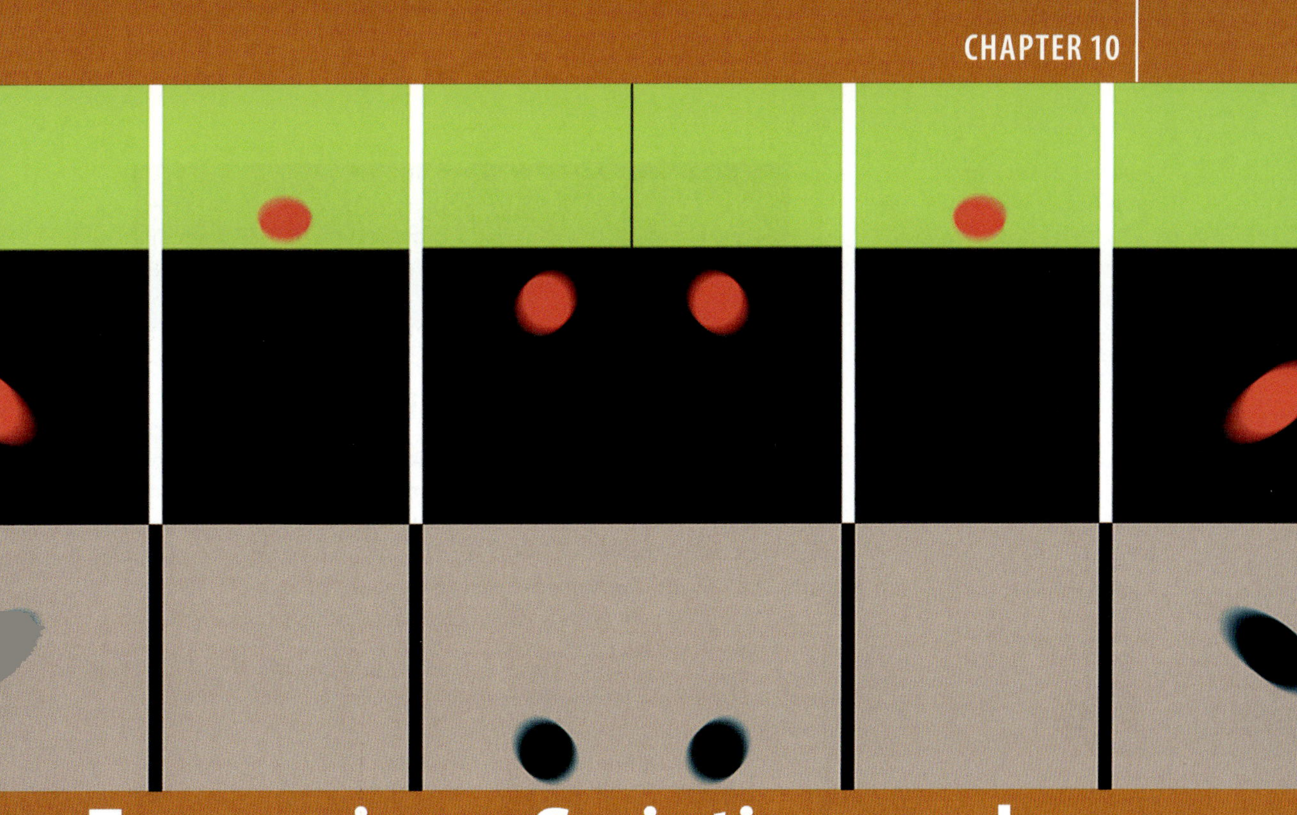

CHAPTER 10

Expressions, Scripting, and Project Management

Visual effects composites can become complex, making them difficult to edit, update, and complete. Fortunately, there are numerous ways to simplify and optimize your workflow in After Effects. For example, expressions allow you to automate property animation and therefore save time when keyframing (Figure 10.1). JavaScript support opens the program to a wide range of scripting tools to make your compositing more efficient. In addition, the program provides many options for adjusting element names, memory management, and interface layout. If you have access to multiple computers with an After Effects installation, you can set up your own After Effects render farm.

This chapter includes the following critical information:

- Creating and editing expressions
- Running JavaScript scripts
- Running an After Effects render farm

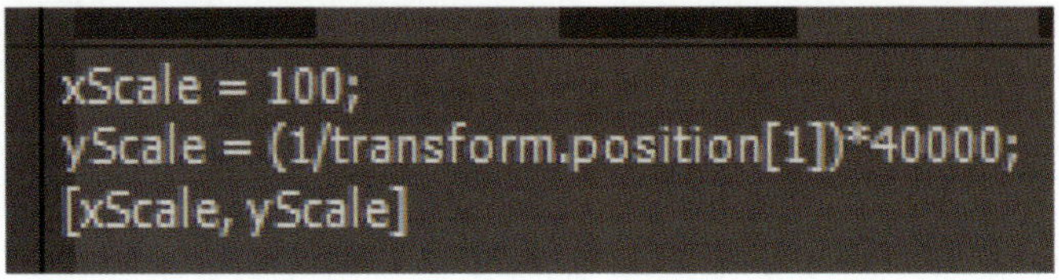

FIG 10.1 An After Effects expression. This is demonstrated in the "Creating an Expression Mini-Tutorial" later in this chapter.

```
xScale = 100;
yScale = (1/transform.position[1])*40000;
[xScale, yScale]
```

Automating with Expressions

Expressions allow you to automate properties within After Effects. That is, you can have the values of one property transferred automatically to another property. The contributing property (which I'll refer to as the *driver*) and the affected property (the *driven*) can exist on the same layer or can be located on two different layers. The properties can be identical (for example, X Position on layer 1 and X Position on layer 2) or dissimilar (Position X on layer 1 and Anchor Point X on Layer 2).

The ability to link properties via expressions prevents or reduces the need for keyframe animation. In addition, you can create complex mathematical equations that relate two properties. This comes in handy when trying to create complex animation that may not be intuitive.

Creating an Expression

To create a simple expression, follow these steps:

1. Identify the two properties you'd like to link through an expression. They can be on the same layer or different layers. Expand the Transform section or sections to reveal the property names in the layer outline.
2. Select the property that is to be driven. Choose Animation > Add Expression from the main menu. An Expression section is added below the property name. A partial expression is added to an expression field in the timeline area to the right of the expression section.
3. Click the Pick Whip button in the new expression section. While continuing to hold down the LMB, drag the Pick Whip rubber band line to the driver property name. A gray box appears around valid property names. Release the mouse button. An expression is created and the expression line is updated (Figure 10.2). To finish the expression, click in an empty area of the timeline.

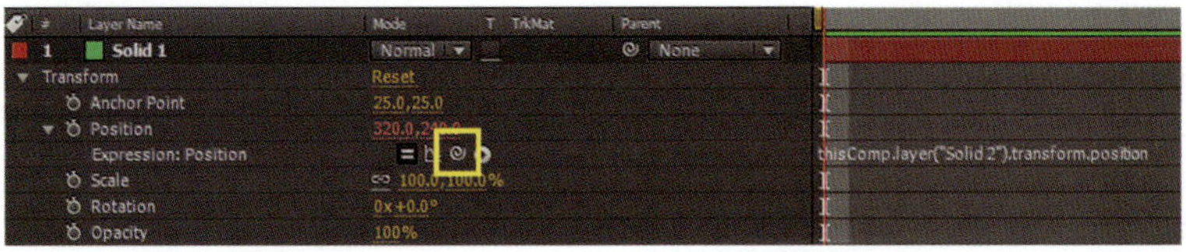

FIG 10.2 An expression is added to the Position property of a solid layer named Solid 1. The Position property of a second solid layer, named Solid 2, serves as the driver. The Pick Whip button is outlined in yellow.

4. As a test, alter the driver property values. The driven property values update automatically to match. These transform changes are visible in the Composition view.

Note that the expressions are sensitive to property channels. For example, the Position property has two channels: X and Y. The Scale property has two channels: X and Y. Opacity, on the other hand, has a single channel, simply named Opacity. When creating an expression, you can connect the following combinations of channels:

- Single-channel to a single-channel
- Two-channel to a two-channel
- Single-channel to one channel of a two-channel property
- One channel of a two-channel property to one channel of a two-channel property

When using the Pick Whip tool, you can make two-channel connections by placing the Pick Whip rubber band line over the property name (such as *Anchor Point* or *Position*). When making a single-channel connection, you can place the line over the property name or the property value field. In order to make a connection to one channel of a two-channel property, place the line over the property value field (such as the X Position field).

When working with a 3D layer, a third channel, Z, is added. As such, you can connect three-channel properties to three-channel properties or single-channel components to each other. Note that you're not limited to transforms but can connect any animatable property as part of an expression, including those included with effects.

To remove an expression, select the property that carries the expression in the layer outline and choose Animation > Remove Expression.

Expression Channel Syntax

When you create an expression, it's represented by a piece of programming code in the expression field. Driver properties are listed in the expression field with the following syntax:

```
composition.layer("layer").class.channel
```

If the driver property exists on the same layer, you can simplify the reference:

```
class.channel
```

You can think of the *class* component as the section within which the property appears. For example, the two-channel Scale property is written as `transform.scale`. If a single channel of Scale is used as a driver, the specific channel is listed. Hence, Scale X is written as `transform.scale[0]`. In this situation, the number within the `[ ]` represents an array position, where `[0]` is the X channel, `[1]` is the Y channel, and `[2]` is the Z channel (if it exists). The Position property is the exception to this rule as its channels are separable with the Separate Dimensions option. As such, X Position is listed as `xPosition`, Y Position is listed as `yPosition`, and so on.

When creating an expression with an effects property, the following format is used:

```
effect("effect name")("property")
```

Writing Expressions

You can manually update a preexisting expression by clicking in the expression field and proceeding to type. To finalize the update, click off the expression in an empty part of the timeline. If the expression becomes invalid due to improper syntax or incorrect layer/property naming, a warning dialog opens and the expression is disabled. You are free to update an expression at any time.

You can also write an expression from scratch and thus avoid using the Pick Whip tool. To do this, select the driven property in the layer outline and choose Animation > Add Expression. The expression field is added with the channel name listed. You can type directly into the field to finish the expression. In this case, you must use an = sign to indicate to what the driven property is equal. You must include the driver property to the right of the = sign. For example, if you want to write an expression that links Position to Anchor Point on a layer, you can write:

```
transform.position = transform.anchorPoint
```

With this syntax, the driven property is always listed on the left. In words, the right-hand property supplies values to the left-hand property. If you are linking properties that exist on two different layers, you must add the layer name:

```
transform.position = thisComp.layer("layer2")
.transform.anchorPoint
```

With this example, `layer2` carries the driver property. `thisComp` refers to the current composition, although you can replace this with a specific composition name with the following syntax:

```
transform.position = comp("Comp 1").
layer("layer2").transform.anchorPoint
```

You can refer to a layer through its index (the layer number listed beside the layer name in the layer outline). For example, you can write `layer(2)` for layer number 2 in the layer outline.

You are not limited to making a one-to-one correlation between properties. You can use mathematical formulas to make the relationship asymmetrical. For example, to make the driven property increase at a rate that is twice as fast as the driver property, include `*2` at the end of the expression line. The `*` symbol represents multiplication. Other math operators include:

- / divide
- + plus
- − minus
- ^ power function

You can invert a resulting expression value (positive to negative or negative to positive) by including `*-1` at the end of the expression line.

You can place the mathematical formulas within parentheses to order the operations. You can also use multiple property names as part of the formula. As a more complex example, two properties are used in the following expression:

```
transform.xPosition = transform.yPosition*
((2/transform.zPosition)-3)
```

This expression carries out the calculation in the following order with innermost parentheses sets taking precedence over outer parentheses sets:

1. 2 / transform.zPosition
2. [Step 1] – 3
3. transform.yPosition * [Step 2]

The expression field supports multiline expressions. Each line must end with a semicolon. You can expand the size of the expression field by LMB-dragging the line directly below the field in the timeline area. Expressions support the use of variables. These may be necessary to pass different values to properties with multiple channels. You can think of variables as temporary "buckets" that carry and pass changing values. A multiline expression that uses variables is demonstrated in the "Creating an Expression Mini-Tutorial" later in this chapter.

Additional Expression Options

When you add an expression to a property, several buttons are added in addition to the Pick Whip tool. For example, you can temporarily turn off an expression by clicking off the Enable Expression switch (Figure 10.3).

You can view the animation curves of the driver property by clicking the Include This Property button and switching to the Graph Editor view in the timeline area. The expression itself is represented by one or more flat-line curves—these are for reference and aren't designed for alteration. However, you can edit the driver property curves.

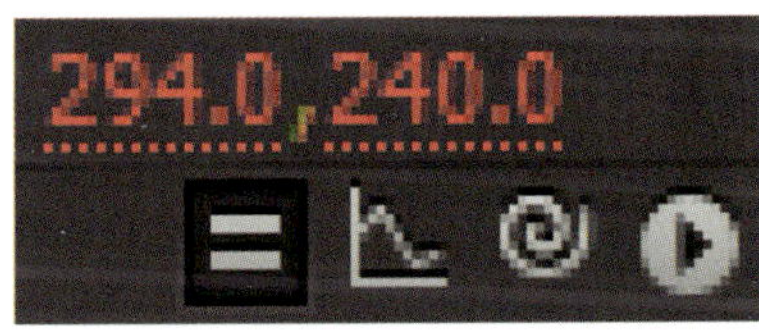

FIG 10.3 Left to right: Enable Expression, Include This Property, Pick Whip, and Function buttons.

You can "freeze" an expression by converting it into keyframes. To do so, select the property that carries the expression, and choose Animation > Keyframe Assistant > Convert Expression To Keyframes. The property receives a keyframe for each frame of the timeline that carry values previously passed to the property via the expression. The Expression switch is automatically toggled to off. Note that an expression trumps keyframes if both a keyframe animation and an active expression exist for a property.

You can incorporate a long list of mathematical functions and internal After Effects functions by RMB-clicking the Function button (Figure 10.2). For example, you can insert a randomly generated value into the expression by following these steps:

1. Prepare to edit the expression by clicking on the expression field in the timeline. A blinking cursor indicates where a new type will appear. If necessary, add a mathematical operator, such as `+`.
2. RMB-click the Function menu, and choose Random Numbers > Random(). The phrase `random()` is added to the expression. Like many functions, `random()` requires a value between the `( )` to become operational. For example, if you place `100` within the parentheses, a random value between 0 and 100 is randomly generated with each frame. This offers a means to create random jiggle, wiggle, rotation, scale fluctuation, and so on.
3. Click off the expression field to update the expression.

After Effects functions provide a means to alter qualities and properties outside standard transforms. For example, you can alter properties of cameras, values of keyframes, resolution of footage, background color of compositions, and so on. For a more thorough examination of the available functions and examples of their use, see the "Expression Language Reference" pages of the online After Effects Help center (helpx.adobe.com/after-effects/topics.html).

Automating Animation with Expressions

At times, keyframe animation can become tedious. Hence, you can use expressions to simplify the animation process.The following tutorial steps you through one such scenario.

Creating an expression mini-tutorial

In this tutorial, we'll add "stretch and squash" animation to a bouncing ball project with the addition of an expression. You can follow these steps:

1. Open the *expression_start.aep* project file included in the *\ProjectFiles\aeFiles\Chapter10* directory. Play back the timeline. This features a

motion graphic animation of a ball bouncing. The ball and ground are constructed from two solid layers. The ball layer has its Position property keyframed (Figure 10.4).

FIG 10.4 A bouncing ball animation is created by animating the Position of a solid layer cut out with a circular mask.

2. Select the Scale property of the Ball layer in the layer outline and choose Animation > Add Expression. The expression is added and the expression field is opened. Click within the field to begin typing. Use the backspace key to remove the initial expression. Type the following:

```
xScale = 100;
yScale = (1/transform.position[1])*40000;
[xScale, yScale]
```

3. Refer to Figure 10.1 at the start of this chapter. To jump to a new line, press the Enter key. If you accidentally leave the expression field, you can return to it at any time by clicking within the field. When the expression is entered correctly and you leave the expression field, the expression is activated. (If an error dialog appears, return to the field and correct the errors; errors may occur through misspelling and similar typing mistakes.) Play back the timeline. The ball stretches when it appears high off the ground. When the ball is close to the ground, it squishes (Figure 10.5).

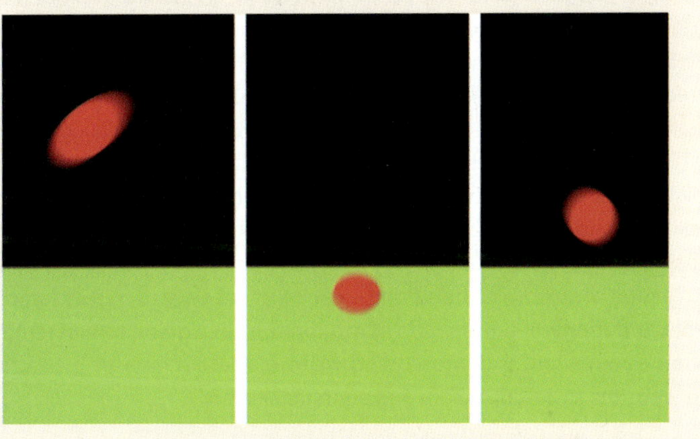

FIG 10.5 Left to right: Frames 1, 5, and 8 after the addition of the expression. The "squash and stretch" animation occurs by relating Scale Y to the Y Position. With this example, motion blur is activated. The Rotation property is also keyframed.

4. Optionally, animate the Rotation value for the ball layer so that the angle of the stretching or squashing matches the motion path and the direction the ball is traveling. Optionally, activate motion blur for the ball layer.

With this expression, the Scale X property is given a static value of 100 percent. The value of 100 is assigned to the variable `xScale`. The Scale Y property, on the other hand, is driven by the ball layer's Y Position. The Y Position is called with an index: `position[1]`. The Y Position value is stored by the `yScale` variable. The `xScale` and `yScale` variable values are passed to the Scale X and Scale Y properties via the last line of the expression. Placing two variables within the `[ ]` is necessary when using a handwritten expression on a double-channel property, such as Scale.

The expression is not a one-to-one relationship. The ball layer's Y Position varies from approximately 180 (in air) to 498 (near ground). In order to reduce the value sizes to make them more suitable for a scaling operation, 1.0 is divided by the Y Position. For example, 1/180 = 0.0055. This also has the effect of making higher Y Position values produce larger numbers while lower Y Position values produce smaller numbers (0, 0 in After Effects screen space is at the upper left of the frame). Hence, 1/498 = 0.002. This causes the ball to become shorter when approaching the virtual ground. In order to make the values somewhere between 0 and 100, the result is multiplied by 40,000. Hence, (1/180)*40,000 = 222.22. You can change the 40,000 to other values to produce a lesser or greater degree of squashing and stretching. A completed version of the project is included as *expression_finished.aep* in the *\ProjectFiles\aeFiles\Chapter10* tutorial directory.

Running JavaScript Scripts

After Effect supports advanced scripting through JavaScript. (A *script* is a sequence of written instructions that is carried out by a program, such as After Effects, instead of the computer processor.) Such scripts are capable of creating complex automation that incorporates program functionality, custom graphic interface components, such as window and dialog boxes, and file importation and exportation. While it is far beyond the scope of this book to cover the intricacies of JavaScript scripting, it's worth covering the installation and running of such scripts. Numerous JavaScript scripts are available to After Effects users. They cover a wide range of tasks, including the creation of custom cameras, the creation of specialized motion graphic effects, and the semi-automation of motion tracking, green screen removal, keyframe animation, and rotoscoping. Many of these scripts are available at such websites as aescripts.com and aenhancers.com.

To run a JavaScript script, choose File > Scripts > Run Script File and choose a JavaScript script. The scripts are text files with the .jsx extension. Some scripts will immediately launch a custom window and await user input. Other scripts will run in the background to achieve a particular task. In general, scripts available outside of After Effects include some type of documentation that explains the scripts' functionality. This might come in the form of pop-up dialogs that appear as the script runs or comments within the script text itself. You can examine the script text by choosing File > Scripts > Open Script Editor and then choosing File > Open through the Editor window. In JavaScript, comments are surrounded by /* */ symbols or appear on lines starting with // (Figure 10.6).

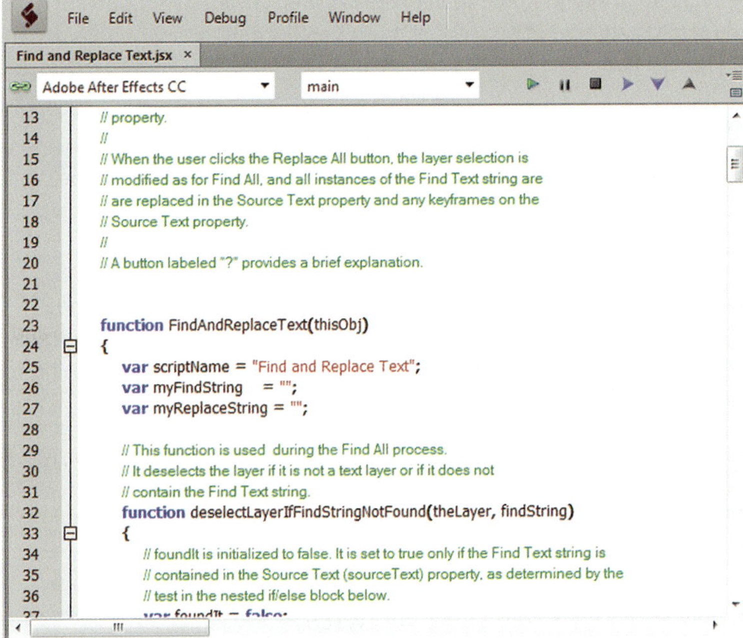

FIG 10.6 A small portion of a script, as seen in the Script Editor. Comments are highlighted in green.

You can install scripts so that After Effects recognizes them automatically. To do so, copy the .jsx file, along with any associated bitmap images (sometimes included for custom graphic interface components or special effects), to the ScriptsUI Panels directory. The directory paths follow:

```
Mac: ~\Applications\Adobe After Effects
version\Scripts\ScriptUI Panels
```

```
Windows: C:\Program Files\Adobe\Adobe After Effects
version\Support Files\Scripts\ScriptUI Panels
```

After Effects lists any scripts located in the ScriptsUI Panels directory at the bottom of the Window menu. As a bonus, After Effects includes its own small set of example scripts as part of the program install. You can access these by choosing File > Scripts > *script name*. These scripts are located in the program's *Scripts*\ directory. If you place your own scripts within this directory, they will be listed in the same menu.

Project Management

Visual effects projects undertaken in After Effects can become confusingly complex due to a large number of layers, effects, and animated properties. Hence, it's often necessary to spend time organizing all the components to make the workflow manageable. These steps include layer renaming, memory management, and customization of the program environment. Optionally, you can spread After Effects render queues across multiple computers as part of a render farm.

Renaming Layers

You can rename layers by RMB-clicking a layer name in the layer outline, choosing Rename, and entering the new name into the field that appears. This is useful for organizing a complex, multilayer composition. Layer names do not affect the layer source names. In fact, you can toggle between the layer name and the source name by clicking the top of the name column in the layer outline. You are also free to rename a composition at any time by selecting the composition tab in the timeline or composition name in the Project panel and choosing Composition > Composition Settings.

Managing Memory

When you play back the timeline, After Effects writes out temporary files to a disc cache. With a large or complex project, a significant amount of space can be used and the operating system efficiency may be affected. Hence, it sometimes is beneficial to purge the cache. You can do this by choosing Edit > Purge > All Memory & Disc Cache. The location of the disc cache is set by the Media & Disc Cache section of the Preferences window (found through the Edit menu). You can also set the disc cache size, in gigabytes, here. You can set the usage of system RAM memory through the Memory page of the Preferences window.

If a project is utilizing an unacceptably large portion of RAM memory or is rapidly filling the disc cache, consider the following steps to make the project more efficient.

Using Reduced Quality

While testing and adjusting a project, view the composition with reduced quality. Set the Resolution/Down Sample Factor Pop Up menu (Figure 10.7) to Half, Third, or Quarter. Each of these settings skips pixels. Thereby, calculations involving layer blending and effects application are more efficient and smaller temporary image files are written to the disc cache.

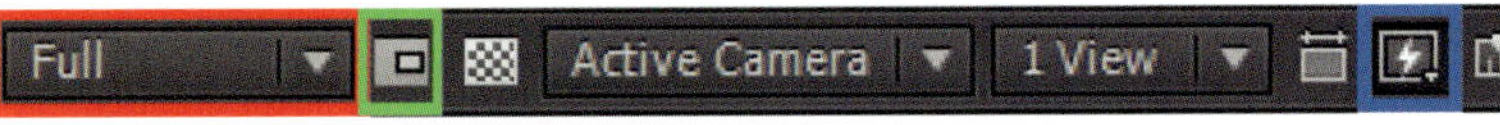

FIG 10.7 The Resolution/ Down Sample Factor Pop Up menu (red), Region Of Interest button (green), and Fast Previews menu (blue), as seen at the bottom of the Composition view panel.

Fast Preview

When you transform a layer or alter effect properties, every pixel within the frame is updated. With complex compositions, there can be a lag between the update of the property values and the display of the image in the view. You can reduce this lag by switching the Fast Previews menu (Figure 10.7) from Off (Final Quality) to Fast Preview. With this setting, only 1/4 of the pixels are displayed *while* the property values are changing. This is particularly useful when interactively transforming the layer or moving an effect slider back and forth in real time. You can also set the menu to Wireframe. With this setting, only a wireframe bounding box is displayed for each layer. This is useful for quickly positioning, rotating, or scaling a layer. If you are using the Ray-Traced 3D renderer, you can set the Fast Previews menu to Draft, which reduces the number of rays traced to the minimum of 1.0, or Adaptive Resolution, which adaptively reduces the pixels based on current memory demands. For more information on the Ray-Traced 3D renderer, see Chapter 5.

Testing Regions

By default, the Composition view shows the entire frame. However, you can preview smaller areas and therefore reduce calculation times by clicking the Region Of Interest button (Figure 10.7) and drawing a region box in the view. Areas outside the box are ignored until the region is disabled by clicking the Region Of Interest button off.

Pre-Rendering

Render a portion of the project to disc and re-import it as an image sequence. For example, render Comp 1 and re-import it. All the layers and effects used for Comp 1 are thereby flattened into a single, new layer. This reduces memory usage as Comp 1 becomes an imported series of images and no processor time is used to combine the old Comp 1 layers or apply a series of effects. After Effects provides a means to do this by including Composition > Pre-Render. Pre-Render loads the current composition into the render queue. At the same time, Pre-Render automatically sets the Post-Render Action menu, in the Output Module Settings window, to Import & Replace Usage. This causes the program to replace the prior contents of the composition with the newly rendered sequence. Before undertaking this process, save a copy of the project that contains the original composition with all the intact layers and effect settings.

Reducing Resolution

If your intended output resolution is smaller than your source footage, reduce the footage resolution before working with it. For example, if the source footage is 1920x1080, yet your output resolution only need be 1280x720, reduce the footage to 1280x720. You can create a temporary After Effects project to reduce the footage resolution. With this example, you can create a 1280x720 composition, drop the 1920x1080 footage into the composition with a Scale of 67 percent, and render the composition through the render queue.

Customizing the Program Environment and Keyboard Shortcuts

You can rearrange panels at any time. (Panels are listed in the Window menu and appear with named tabs within the various program frames.) To move a panel to a new location, LMB-drag the panel's named tab into a different frame. When you do so, a ghosted box appears within the new frame. Release the mouse button to drop the panel into the new frame. You can also undock a panel so that it floats free. To do so, RMB-click the window tab name and choose Undock Panel.

You can save the current program workspace, with its current panel and frame arrangements, by choosing Window > Workspace > New Workspace. Name the workspace in the New Workspace window. The workspace is then listed in the Window > Workspace menu. You can switch to a different workspace at any time by choosing Window > Workspace > *workspace name*. You can return to the factory workspace by choosing Window > Workspace > Reset "Standard". The program provides additional workspaces designed for particular tasks in the same menu (e.g. Animation, Motion Tracking).

After Effects includes a large number of keyboard shortcuts. These are stored in a text file, which you can review or alter. To locate this file, choose Edit > Preferences > General. Click the Reveal Preferences In Explorer (Windows) or Reveal Preferences In Finder (Mac OS X) button. An external directory window opens, revealing the en_US Shortcuts.txt or similar language-specific text file. You can alter this file in a text-editing program. The keyboard shortcuts follow the syntax `"`*`operation`*`" = "(`*`key combination`*`)"`. For example, the shortcut for creating a new project is `"New" = "(Ctrl + Alt + N)"`.

Using Built-In Render Farm Support

After Effects comes with built-in render farm support. A *render farm* is a collection of computers that are able to split a render queue. For example, computer 1 might render frames 1 to 50 while computer 2 renders frames 51 to 100. Render farms reduce overall render times and are commonly used by animation, visual effects, and motion graphic studios. To utilize this support, you must have the following:

- Two or more computers with the same valid version of After Effects and any required plug-ins installed
- A network drive that stores shared project files that is accessible by all the render farm computers

If these components are available, you can follow these basic steps to set up an After Effects project that is ready to render on a multicomputer render farm:

1. On the shared network drive, create a directory named *_WatchFolder*. You can locate this directory anywhere on the drive.
2. Open the After Effects project that you would like to place on the render farm. Add the project to the render queue by selecting the appropriate composition and choosing Composition > Add To Render Queue. In the Render Queue tab, click *Best Settings*. In the Render Settings window, select Skip Existing Files in the Options section. Close the window.
3. Set the options within the Output Module (e.g. file type, audio). Choose a file name and location through Output To. Choose a location on the network drive so that all machines on the render farm render to a shared directory (this prevents the farm computers from rendering identical frames).
4. Save the project to the *_WatchFolder* on the network drive.
5. Choose File > Dependencies > Collect Files. In the Collect Files window, set the Collect Source Files menu to None (Project only). Select the Enable 'Watch Folder' Render check box (Figure 10.8). Set the Maximum Number Of Machines to the number of farm computers you'd like to use. Click the Collect button to close the window.

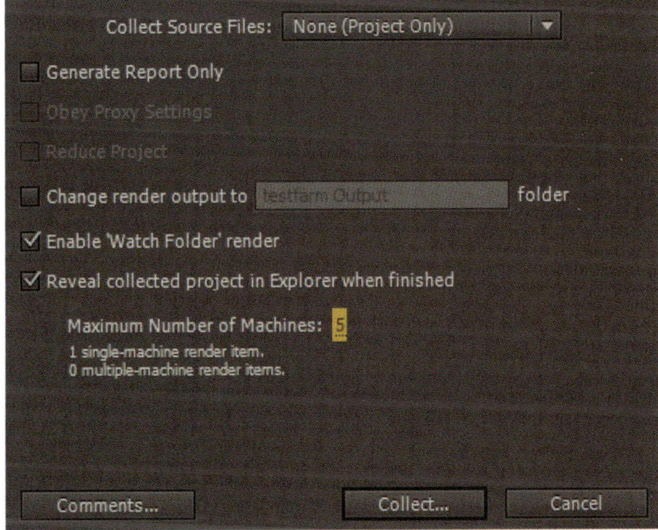

FIG 10.8 The Collect Files window.

6. Go to each render farm computer, launch After Effects, and choose File > Watch Folder. A file browser window opens. Navigate to the _*WatchFolder* directory on the network drive and click the Choose button. The Watch Folder window opens and After Effects actively scans the selected directory (Figure 10.9). When a farm computer detects an After Effects project file, it opens the file and begins to render the render queue. To cancel the watch for a particular farm computer, click the Cancel button in the Watch Folder window for that computer. (At the time of this writing, File > Watch Folder was disabled for After Effects CC 2015; however, CC 2014 is able to render CC 2015 Watch Folder projects.)

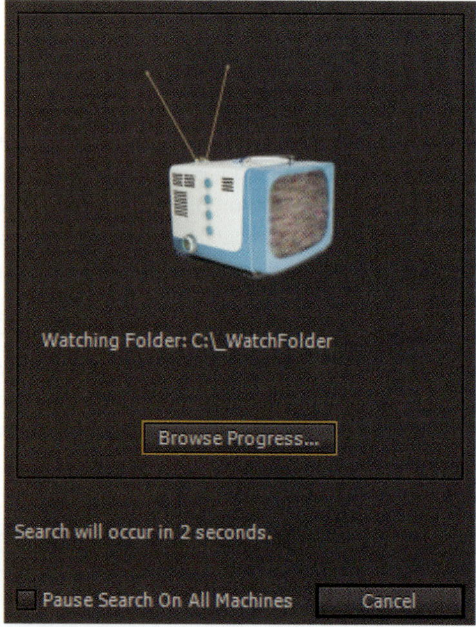

FIG 10.9 The Watch Folder window between _*WatchFolder* directory scans.

Book Wrap-Up

After Effects is a deep program with a seemingly inexhaustible number of menus, options, and effects. Hence, I've intentionally concentrated on those components within the program that have proven to be the most useful with my own visual effects experience (which spans close to three decades). That said, there is no single way to tackle a particular visual effects task. In fact, the more you composite, the more flexible you'll become and the more likely you'll develop your own techniques—and there's the beauty of the art form. Whatever the path, have fun and thank you for reading this book!

Index

L

M

N

O

P

Q

R